Gesualdo

Frontispiece   *The altarpiece of Santa Maria delle Grazie, Gesualdo. For a description and discussion of this painting, see pages 31-35.*

Gesualdo
The Man and His Music

GLENN WATKINS

Preface by
IGOR STRAVINSKY

The University of North Carolina Press, Chapel Hill
Oxford University Press, London

Copyright © 1973 by Glenn Watkins
All rights reserved
Manufactured in the United States of America
First published in Great Britain by Oxford University Press
ISBN 0–8078–1201–3
Library of Congress Catalog Card Number 72–78154
First printing, February 1974
Second printing, May 1976

Library of Congress Cataloging in Publication Data

Watkins, Glenn Elson, 1927–
    Gesualdo, the man and his music.

    Bibliography: p.
    1. Gesualdo, Carlo, principe di Venosa, 1560 (ca.)–
1613.
ML410.G29W4   784'.092'4 [B]   72–78154
ISBN 0–8078–1201–3

Preface

Gesualdo di Venosa: New Perspectives

by IGOR STRAVINSKY

Musicians may yet save Gesualdo from musicologists, but certainly the latter have had the best of it until now. Even now he is academically unrespectable, still the crank of chromaticism, still rarely sung.

Two new publications, Professor Watkins's monograph and the CBS recording of the sixth book of madrigals, should help to scotch the prejudice of the scholars. Professor Watkins provides the composer with surrounding scenery not previously in view, and in which he does not fade but stands out more vividly, if in different colours, than before. The recording, on the other hand, corrects the view of the music as a case of samples, simply by providing it with its own context; the largely tendentious interest in Gesualdo had deprived him even of his own 'normalcy'. Together the two publications fill in the lacunae to the extent that apart from the continuing search for the lost book of six-voice madrigals, the major goals are reduced to two: the recovery of performance style (a by-no-means-impossible quest) and the recording of the complete music.

Seeking Gesualdo's origins in the Neapolitan school, Professor Watkins exposes Pomponio Nenna in the role of principal model. At least six of Gesualdo's texts, including *Ancide sol la morte*, *Mercè grido*, *Tu·segui*, and *Deh, coprite*, were set by Nenna first. Apart from this coincidence, if that is what it was, Gesualdo appears to have helped himself to elements of Nenna's chromatic style and to have pocketed harmonic progressions verbatim. In fact, Gesualdo's imitations are so sedulous in some instances as to appear to us like plain light-fingering. Perhaps that was how they were thought of at the time, too, but the ingenuous opinions of a powerful prince's not-so-fellow musicians are unlikely to have been committed to paper. And, anyway, apart from a missing credit line in history, no monstrous injustice has been done. Nenna never received the touch of Zephyr. He is as devoid of musical interest, compared to Gesualdo, as Holinshed is of poetic interest, compared with the Shakespeare based on him.

It has been known since at least 1934 (Pannain: *Istituzione e Monumenti*) that Gesualdo's sacred music (what was then known of it) shared a style formed by Nenna, Macque, Trabaci, and others. But *ante* Watkins almost nothing was known of Neapolitan influences on the secular music. Its radical chromatic tendency was linked to Wert, Rore, Luzzaschi, and other madrigalists of the Ferrara court, though judging from the little I know of these composers, Luzzaschi alone comes close enough to have been warrantably put forward as a stepping stone. Now, with Professor Watkins's discovery of the Nenna examples—as with the discovery of the Oldowan Fossil Cranium, the decipherment of Linear B, and any other discovery involving contingent systems of classification—the entire history of the subject must be revised or scrapped. As discovery breeds discovery, too, Professor Watkins's should provoke explorations through the whole of sixteenth-century Neapolitan music. For a beginning, one would like to know more of some of the shadowy figures in Gesualdo's own circle: Luigi Tansillo of Venosa, for example, and Giovanni Leonardo Primavera, whose seventh book is dedicated to the Prince. And what of the madrigal style of the '*infelice*' Troiano, who was not merely shadowy but umbrageous, being the first of the composer-murderers who were to enliven the peninsular musical scene down to and through Alessandro Stradella, and whose fraternity was soon to include Gesualdo himself? Can any particular of Gesualdo's settings of the word '*uccide*' be traced to him?

For the rest, Professor Watkins surveys all of the forms, sacred and secular, as the composer inherited and bequeathed them. He ably anatomizes the complete music, too, and not only the music, but also the texts, for the musico-dramatic gesturing of the secular pieces depends on devices of oxymora, sexual symbolisms ('I expire', 'I die'[1]), and other conventional insipidities. Further and finally, Professor Watkins newly maps the composer among the peaks of Mannerism, and concludes this first sensible study of him with a fully documented history of the misunderstandings of his music down to *c.* 1970.

★ ★ ★

As aforesaid, the most novel perspectives extending from the CBS account of Book Six are of the composer himself. Before the appearance of this

---

[1] 'Drowning' is a veil of the same sort in the Elizabethan madrigal—the seafaring English—and it may be one, too, for example, in Bennet's:
'O when, O when begin you
To swell so high that I may drown me in you?'

admirably crammed grammy-award contender ('I am dubbed,' says Shakespeare's Philip the Bastard), our musical bees had been extracting the composer's headier harmonic pollen as if he had cultivated only a single kind of flower. But the complete book shows him to be a composer of always strongly characterized and expertly made 'normal' music whose special inventiveness lies in such other areas as rhythm and the intensifying of vocal colour by means of unusual combinations in extremes of range. (I wonder whether some of these 'normal' pieces are not more gratifying to sing than the chromatic ecstasies of *Moro lasso*, in which the demands of the ensemble must all but extinguish the performer's individuality?) Finally, Book Six, which represents the apogee of the radical chromaticism of the era, also reveals the composer as anomalously conservative-minded, at least by the lights of those contemporary aesthetes and *précieux* for whom monody had gained the inside track and contrapuntally voiced harmony of Gesualdo's brand was disappearing from the course.

Whether Book Six was the most propitious choice with which to inaugurate a new Gesualdo series is hard to say, but the larger physical requirements of the other music may have borne on the decision: Books Three and Four include six-voice madrigals; Book Five varies more widely in tessitura; the sacred music uses five-, six-, and seven-part choirs. In any case, the stringencies of Gesualdo's madrigal form, in no matter which volume, may deter all except the doughtiest listener. Extraordinary absorptive powers are needed to digest a succession of twenty-three complete statements, each of great compactness—for if Gesualdo does not expand, neither does he dilate, and if his form is small, it is at the same time never elliptical. Another obstacle for modern listeners, if merely an implicit one, is in the limited possibilities of harmonic extension through key relationships. To a certain extent this is offset by novelties of sequence and juxtaposition, but the music will seem inexplicably static to some nevertheless, and as little satisfying to dumpling-lovers as a dinner of twenty-three canapés of caviar.

Nor are Gesualdo's most overt means of keeping awareness of formal limitations at bay invariably the most successful. In fact, the most completely satisfying madrigals tend to avoid contrast for its own sake (Pope: 'The lights and shades, whose well-accorded strife'), and either confine themselves to a single mood or follow the free run of the composer's death wish, in which he certainly knew his way around, musically speaking. Monotony threatens, in any event, only when, pretending that matters are looking up, he pays too many courtesy calls on the happy ending. Finally it must be said that, as Gesualdo's mode of expression is dramatic, highly intimate, and very much in earnest, he weights the traditional madrigal of poised sentiments and conceits, of amorous delicacies and indelicacies, with a heavy load. But this is in-theory criticism. In practice, which is to say, while listening, no unoccupied faculty remains with which to question the balances and proportions of 'form' and 'content'.

The extraordinary unity of character and style in Book Six—it would be impossible to exchange any madrigal with an example from the earlier books —opens the suspicion that the composer himself may have been responsible for the selection and ordering of the pieces. For one thing, the ingenious grouping in several kinds of pairs would seem to have been arranged by an 'inside' hand. Thus the first two, and the first and last, the numbers four and five, eleven and twelve, thirteen and fourteen, eighteen and nineteen, are paired by 'key'. Pairing is likewise effected by tempo and mood; by the incidence of *ballo* metres (nos. 22 and 23) and pastoral modes (*Al mio gioir* and *Tu segui*); and by similarities in initial canonic departures (*Ardo per te* and *Ardita Zanzaretta*), final cadences (nos. 11 and 12), 'instrumentation' (the two-tenor madrigals, nos. 18 and 19). Changes of tempo are managed by doubling or halving the unit of beat—the practice of the time—but rhythmic irregularity is introduced in about half of the madrigals by the use of metres of unequal length. An example occurs on the first page, in the partly-in-six, partly-in-four *Se la mia morte brami*, where the effect is strikingly similar to the effect of Wilbye's enlargement of the metre to drag the musical pace at the words 'whereon man acts his weary Pilgrimmage.'[2] The rhythmic inventions throughout Book Six are a match for the harmonic ones, in fact, and in such instances as the virtually metreless beginning of *Quel 'no,'* and the lashing syncopations with the word 'tormenti' in *Candido e verde fiore*, they are as 'revolutionary.'

★ ★ ★

The chief obstacle to the recovery of performance style is pecuniary. In a few hours' leave of absence from a bread-winning routine of taping television commercials and disposing of seasonal oratorios, even the most excellent singers cannot achieve the blends, the exactness of intonation, the diction and articulation that the Prince's singers would have had to master by edict and as a result of living with the music the year round. (And probably under threat of flagellation, too, though the composer, a votary of *le vice anglais*, seems to have preferred *that* in reverse—Marsyas flaying Apollo, so to speak.) In short, the world is in need of permanent madrigal consorts, and of Martha

[2] The 'Ay me' in Wilbye's *Weep, Weep, Mine Eyes* is so like a Gesualdo 'oimè,' incidentally, as to suggest direct connection.

Baird Rockefeller Grants to sustain them. Only then can the styles be reborn, not only of the Prince of Venosa, but also of Marenzio and Monteverdi, Wilbye and Weelkes.[3]

In the case of the *Musica Riservata* style, edifying descriptions by ear-witnesses abound. Thus, Cerone reports that 'The madrigalist does not sing in a full voice, but artistically, in a *falsetto* voice or *sotto voce*'; to which I would add that pitch clarity in the denser harmonic coagulations can be attained in no other way, certainly not with woolly *vibrati*. Zarlino (whose theoretical writings influenced Nicolas Poussin[4]) affirms that 'the madrigal singer must perform his part just as the composer has written it'—i.e. without embellishments, and *a cappella*; the *concertato* madrigal introduced in Monteverdi's fifth book was without issue in Gesualdo. Padre Martini further informs us that 'madrigals are to be sung softly' and that 'bold dissonances were permitted in madrigals because perfect intonation was easier to achieve by a few singers than by the crowd of singers in church music'. Finally, Mazzochi's reference to Gesualdo might be taken to infer that our composer employed *crescendo* (and the regraduation), as well as other dynamic shadings (*sfumato*) himself. The grounds for this illation are simply that Mazzochi had invented a system of notating dynamics, and that what he praises in Gesualdo is his exactness in notation. But the question is fodder for a thesis, and that is where I must leave it.

★ ★ ★

My own attentions to Gesualdo between twelve and ten years ago led to a number of ramblings, musical and otherwise. Twice I visited the seat of the composer's family name, an unpicturesquely squalid town, the more so after Acerra and the other architecturally attractive villages of the Campania. On the first occasion, a listless day in July 1956, I had come to Naples by boat—my last such expedition, I resolved, the debarking ordeal alone taking longer than a transatlantic flight, not to mention (if I may be pardoned the apophasis) the simultaneous marathon concerts by competing brass bands, the continuous pelting by paper streamers, and the orgies of weeping by separating and reuniting Neapolitans. I remember that on the way to Gesualdo we visited the Conservatory of San Pietro a Maiella, and the fish stalls near the Porta Capuana; and at Montevirgine, watched the procession

---

[3] Cf. Gesualdo's *Beltà poi* and Weelkes's *Cease Sorrows Now*, at the words 'I'll sing my faint farewell'.

[4] As late as the eighteenth century, the architect Vittone was illustrating his exposition of the Renaissance ideal of proportion with analogies derived from music theory.

of a parthenogenetic cult, a parade of flower-garlanded automobiles led by boys carrying religious banners and running like lampadephores.

Gesualdo's castle was the residence then of some hens, a heifer, and a browsing goat, as well as of a human population numbering, in that still Pill-less, anti-Malthusian decade, a great many *bambini*. None of these inhabitants had heard of the Prince of Venosa and his deeds, of course, and in order to explain our wish to peek at the premises, some of his lurid history had to be imparted to at least some of the tenants. A result of my own attempts to do so was that I soon became the object of very alarmed looks, the audience having confounded the composers in the story (blame my poverty-stricken Italian) and mistaken *me* as the murderer of *my* first wife.

The castle is measly. Apart from the lion rampant emblazoned in the *sottoportico* and the well-known inscriptions on the courtyard wall, there was little evidence of occupancy at any time by an armigerous prince. The interior appeared to be furnished from the Apennine equivalent of Wool- worth's, but as it was greatly in need of a dispersion of aerosol, I did not see much of it. In short, it was difficult to imagine the high state of musical culture that once flourished on this forlorn hill, the singers, the instru- mentalists, the church choristers, and, not least, the great, if emotionally disequilibrated, composer whose last madrigal books were first printed here.

The portrait of the composer in the Capuchin church was dirty then but undamaged, whereas on my return three years later the picture had been cleaned but the lower left corner of it, just above the composer's head, was torn. (You can't have everything.) We were met there by a Padre Cipriano who said he was gathering materials for a biography of the composer, and that the most interesting of the documents so far turned up for inclusion were some verses by Gesualdo's ill-fated wife. I did not doubt this opinion; in fact if the lady's writings describe her amorous experiences in any detail, Padre Cipriano's book, if he ever wrote it, could become the first musico- logical tome to be published by Grove Press. The Padre served some thimblesful of the local liqueur, but while we were swallowing this furniture polish, complained of the American occupation of the town in 1944. His story has been repeated in kind a great many times since then and through- out the world, of course, but in the case of the Sack of Gesualdo, my sympathies were entirely with the G.I.s.

I visited other sites associated with the composer after that, but not expressly, not on his trail. I was in the Este Library at Modena, and in Ferrara several times, but on behalf of the Schifanoia frescoes and the Etruscan Museum, and incidentally to drink Lambrusco. I even went to Mesola once, on an excursion to Pomposa Abbey and Comacchio, the latter loud with the clack of wooden shoes then, but now stranded in the ooze of the newly drained delta; other visitors be warned that Mesola, the Xanadu of the Estes, celebrated in a madrigal by Tasso and Wert, is now a very dreary town hall. As for Venosa, Horatian Venusiae, the city of the composer's principality, I have been no closer to it than Brindisi, perhaps not even that close, technically, as I did not leave the Greek ship—so overcrowded that tents were pitched on its main deck—which had called in its harbour, and on which I was bound for Venice.

The purpose of my next trip to Naples, in October 1959, was to conduct a programme of my music in the Teatro San Carlo.[5] Neither Gesualdo the place nor Gesualdo the musician had any part in my itinerary. (Deliberate sightseeing was limited to Sperlonga, a pool shivering with eels in a grotto that surged like a sea shell.) But I *did* go to Gesualdo again finally, and, back in Naples, sought out the composer's tomb. It lies in the pavement of the Gesù Nuovo (whose *diamanti* façade is the most equable of pigeon roosts— a facet for each bird—whatever the pecking order), in the vicinity of some very grand mausolea. 'Carolus Gesualdus', the epitaph begins, but it is entirely devoted to genealogy, failing to mention any contributions to music, or even that the interred was a musician at all. But then, very little attention has been paid to the music for four hundred years. And, come to think of it, that burial plaque is still in excellent condition. Perhaps, after all, 'The Gilded Monuments of Princes *Shall* Outlive . . .' their powerful madrigals.

I.S.

Hollywood, 7 March 1968

[5] Named for the composer's maternal uncle. The composer's paternal uncle was Cardinal of Santa Cecilia in Rome, and a witness to the notorious trial of the Prince of Mantua's potency, popularly known as the Congress of Venice. See *The Prince's Person* by Roger Peyrefitte.

Table of Contents

Plates

à 2 v.:

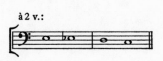

Introduction

While neither the life nor the music of Gesualdo have been totally neglected in critical writings of the past, there is no doubt that the former has been the object of more detailed treatment. Even so, the two principal biographical studies have considered conspicuously discrete aspects of Gesualdo's life. The work by Cecil Gray (1926) is especially informative about the period prior to his appearance as a published composer, that is before his second marriage in 1594, but is largely innocent of the details that follow. Vatielli's monograph of 1940 sought to remedy this deficiency, but, valuable as it is, it fails to place the additional details in the context of Gesualdo's entire career.[1]

These first studies have provided an indispensable foundation upon which to build. I have, however, re-examined virtually all the primary documents and while doing so found other relevant materials in the Italian archives. These included not only the invaluable chronicles of Equicola, Merenda, Da Monte, and Spaccini, but also the letters of Gesualdo, his second wife Leonora, her half-brother Cardinal Alessandro, Alfonso Fontanelli, and Ridolfo Arlotti, as well as legal documents such as Gesualdo's second wedding contract and his last will and testament. Some of this material had been treated before, other portions not at all, and none of it in a context where it could disclose its largest meaning. For the most part I have allowed these documents to speak for themselves, quoting generously from the most important ones, since seemingly unimportant details may frequently prove informative and revealing. Additional biographical discoveries may well be made at some future date, but it is doubtful if they will substantially alter the picture which emerges from the sources utilized here.

In view of the abundant and fascinating details concerning Gesualdo's earlier years, it is disappointing that information relating to his maturity is so spotty. Yet I have tried to avoid too easy judgements about the complex nature of the composer, and have parried the temptation to plump out his life story with speculation and conjecture for those years which are leanest in terms of supporting documentary evidence. For a coherent account of

[1] Alberto Consiglio's *Gesualdo ovvero Assassinio a cinque voci. Storia tragici italiana del secolo xvi* (Napoli, 1967) is an historical novel and traces only those events relating to Gesualdo's first marriage.

the composer's development as a musician we must ultimately look to the music itself.

A discussion of Gesualdo's music presents special difficulties. The central problem, however, is not the same now as when Kroyer, Keiner, or Heseltine wrote earlier in this century. Then too little material was available for a truly considered judgement. Now we are increasingly able to see Gesualdo's music in the stylistic context of his time. A recitation of the details of his compositional technique *in vacuo* is no longer sufficient, just as it is no longer possible to characterize the music as so personal in idiom as to be irrelevant to musical events which preceded or followed it. The suggestion that Gesualdo's tortuous experiments were in the history of music merely a highly fascinating by-path, which ended up a blind alley, can no longer be considered a prudent evaluation of the composer's position.

The opportunities for re-assessment have been compounded by developments in art and literary criticism. The acceptance of Mannerism as a recognizable style in the decades following the High Renaissance has led in recent years to a total re-consideration of that period. But while the art historian may once again be in the lead in fashioning an aesthetic canopy, his codification of the concept of Mannerism is still sufficiently partial that the music historian may be able to supplement current judgements of the limits of the term as well as its larger meanings. I should like to emphasize, however, that this book does not pretend to provide a comprehensive appraisal of musical Mannerism, any more than it claims to be a history of the late Italian madrigal or a chronicle of musical life at the courts of Ferrara and Naples. Hopefully it may one day prove helpful to the construction of all of them.

The reasons for the separation of music and biography in this volume should be apparent: the biographical material, though it has a bearing on the music, is of such proportion and independent interest that it demands separate treatment. At the same time frequent cross-references between the two sections help to provide the requisite coherence.

It is a pleasure to express my gratitude to all who have helped in the production of this volume: especially the librarians and staffs of the Library of Congress, the British Museum, the Library of Christ Church College, Oxford, the Archivio di Stato and the Biblioteca Estense in Modena, the Biblioteca Civica in Ferrara, the Biblioteca di Conservatorio di San Pietro à Majella in Naples, the Civico Museo Bibliografico Musicale in Bologna, and the Biblioteca Musicale di Santa Cecilia in Rome. To Giancarlo Bertoni, who was a devoted assistant and friend in retracing some of my steps in the Modenese archives, and to my colleague, Prof. Richard Crawford, who read a large portion of an early version of the manuscript and made numerous valuable suggestions, I owe a special debt. In addition I am grateful for the initial encouragement of numerous friends to write this book, as well as that given by the administration of the University of Michigan School of Music during its preparation. Grants from the University of North Carolina Research Council, the University of Michigan Horace H. Rackham Fund, as well as the American Council of Learned Societies gave the impetus necessary to bring the project to its completion.

The complete works of Gesualdo, edited by Wilhelm Weismann and myself, are published by Ugrino Verlag of Hamburg. All examples of Gesualdo's music in this book are drawn from this edition.

The photographs for the illustrations were made by Columbia Records Inc. and loaned to me for reproduction in this book. I am most grateful to the company for its kindness.

Finally I should like to comment upon the preface which graces this book. My first contact with Stravinsky was prompted by the release of the first of a series of Columbia records devoted to the works of Gesualdo. Two responses for Holy Week were contained therein, and as I was preparing an edition of Gesualdo's sacred works at the time and noted inaccuracies in the scorings which had been utilized for the recording, I wrote to Mr. Craft through Columbia Records. I shortly received a reply from Japan, acknowledging not only the errors but an interest in seeing my completed volume when it was published. At the same time I was about to prepare the volume of incomplete motets in 6 & 7 voices, and Stravinsky, who had already provided his own completion of one of them, offered photostats of the volume for my use in this project. In the process of scoring these motets I discovered canonic indications which reduced the number of missing parts in two of them. I sent copies of my transcriptions to him in Venice in September 1959, suggesting that he extend his original contribution to a set of three by completing the missing single part in the two canonic motets, *Da pacem* and *Assumpta est Maria*. He did so and returned the music to me within the month. The following March (1960), I received word that he had composed his *Monumentum pro Gesualdo*, and in June I was invited to come to California for concerts and a recording session which would include this new work.

During the following period I finished my contributions to the complete edition of Gesualdo and began work on the present book with a trip to the archives of northern Italy in the late summer of 1962. By the time I next visited the Stravinskys in Hollywood in August of 1965, an early version of the manuscript had been completed, and I took it with me. During this visit I discussed the work with Stravinsky and left it behind when I departed.

I remember his particular interest in the section devoted to posthumous critical reaction to Gesualdo's music; the remarks of Fétis, who was unknown to him, he found particularly fascinating.

Continuing interest in the progress of the work was a source of encouragement to me throughout its preparation. The early offer to provide a preface to the book when it was ready for publication was ultimately realized by Mr. Craft in consultation with Stravinsky in March 1968. Mr. Craft's five complete LP records devoted to the music of Gesualdo, Stravinsky's two sets of Gesualdo compositions, and their personal pilgrimages to Gesualdo territory provide only partial evidence of a connoisseurship which is further disclosed in this perceptive appreciation of a master who fascinated both of them.

PART ONE

The Man

CHAPTER ONE

༒

The Early Years: 1560-1590

Family Origins and Connections

THE village of Gesualdo sits lonely and isolated in the foothills one hundred kilometres east of Naples. It is not an unpleasant country and the view which the castle commands is impressive. This is no accident, for the castle was built in its present position as early as the middle of the seventh century in order to serve as a fortress. The town of Gesualdo thus had its beginnings, and it received its name when a Cavaliere Gesualdo,[1] in the service of the Duke of Benevento, was assigned control of the castle estate. The town did not achieve autonomous status, however, until the eleventh century at which time a prior Lombard dynasty became extinct and was replaced by one of Norman lineage. A series of Norman Lords, Barons, and Princes of Gesualdo then ruled uninterruptedly from 1059 to 1636.[2]

Through a series of good marriages the family in time acquired titles and property in a seemingly endless stream, so that the head of the family became Lord and Count many times over—of the lands of Gesualdo, Frequento (Frigento), Acquaputrida (Mirabella), Paterno (Paternapoli), Cantomango, San Barabato, Boneto, Luceria, Caggiano, and S. Lupolo. The title of Prince of Venosa, however, came quite late. Luigi Gesualdo, Carlo's grandfather, married Isabella Ferrillo, daughter of Alfonso, second Count of Muro. She brought him a considerable dowry including the Lordship of Venosa.[3] They had seven children, three girls and four boys. The two

---

[1] Cf. Lellis, *Discorsi delle Famiglie nobili del Regno di Napoli* (1663), II, pp. 2–3, for a colourful account of this figure and Cecil Gray and Philip Heseltine, *Carlo Gesualdo* (London, 1926), pp. 3–5, for a synopsis. An updated version of the biographical portion of the latter is in Gray, *Contingencies* (London, 1947).

[2] Gesualdo's ancestry is amply recounted in the seventeenth-century histories of the Italian nobility. Ammirato, Summonte, Aldimari, and Lellis give the most important notices. Arturo Famiglietti's *Gesualdo nella sua storia* (Cosenza, 1968) considers the town, its most important events and personalities, from earliest times to the present.

[3] This she obtained from Gonsalvi di Cordova in 1513. When Alfonso, her father, died, he left to Isabella the land of Montefredove which then passed into the Gesualdo

eldest sons were Fabrizio, Carlo's father, and Alfonso who was made Cardinal
by Pope Pius IV in 1561 and Archbishop of Naples in 1596. One of the girls,
Donna Sveva, married Don Carlo d'Avalos, Principe di Montesarchio, son of
Alfonso,[4] Marquis of Vasto. Donna Sveva's marriage is especially notable
for the connection which it established between the houses of Gesualdo and
d'Avalos, families whose destinies were later to become so entwined.[5]

To mark the occasion of Fabrizio Gesualdo's marriage to Girolama
Borromeo, sister of Carlo Borromeo and niece of Pope Pius IV, his father
Luigi Gesualdo was granted the title of Prince of Venosa by King Philip of
Spain. (The elevation of Don Carlo's uncle Alfonso to the rank of Cardinal
in 1561 was also undoubtedly due to this connection.) The marriage of a
Gesualdo to a Borromeo and the resultant connection with the Papacy was
to have considerable import for the family over the next half century.

Birth and Youth

Luigi Gesualdo, first Prince of Venosa, died on 17 May 1584 and Fabrizio
inherited his possessions in the same year. He had by Girolama Borromeo
four children: Luigi, Carlo, Isabella, and Eleanora. Luigi died at the age of
twenty, leaving Don Carlo as the only surviving male heir. While it is
almost certain that Carlo was born in the period 1560-2, no evidence for a
specific date of birth has survived.[6]

If we are to believe the historian Ammirato, Don Carlo's father was not
only interested in *belles lettres* but also greatly appreciative of music and
perhaps a composer himself.[7] We do know that Fabrizio maintained a group
of musicians in his house.[8] He could not of course afford to collect and
support a retinue of artists to compare with the famous courts of northern

---

family. From then on Luigi was noted for his wealth and his connections. See Ricca,
Nobiltà, I, p. 120.

[4] Alfonso d'Avalos will be remembered as the poet of the madrigal *Il bianco e dolce cigno*
immortalized by Arcadelt, as well as the equally renowned *Anchor che col partire*
set by Rore and others.

[5] The other children were Giulio, who died in infancy; Carlo, who assumed the title
of Signor di Palo and married Lauro Caracciolo, sister of the Marchese di Casadalbero;
Costanza, wife of Ferdinando Orsini, Duke of Gravina; and Maria, wife of Nicolantonio
Caracciolo, Marquis of Vico.

[6] Modestino, p. 48, hazards a guess regarding Carlo's birthdate: 'Assuming the natural
order of things, and assuming that his brother who died was born in 1561, [Carlo]
opened his eyes to the light of this world in 1562.'

[7] Ammirato, Parte Seconda, p. 13. Cf. the present volume, p. 7, fn. 15.

[8] Cf. preface by E. Dagnino to *Madrigali di Pomponio Nenna*, Istituto italiano per la
Storia della Musica, Monumenti II, vol. 1, pp. v–xii.

Italy, but some surprisingly fine artists are to be found among his registers.

Carlo must thus have been exposed to music and the arts from boyhood, though there is no evidence of any particularly early effort at composition comparable, for example, to Monteverdi, who had actually published by the age of fifteen. Gesualdo's teacher is generally considered to have been Pomponio Nenna (1555?–1617), but in light of the similarity of their age a teacher-pupil relationship has been questioned.[9]

One director of his musical training may have been the Netherlander Giovanni Macque who preceded Nenna to Gesualdo in the service of Don Carlo's father during 1588–9, and from 1590 on worked not far away at the Annunziata in Naples. By the time of Macque's arrival Gesualdo was a man approaching thirty, but his first attempts at composition may not have begun much earlier than this.

In addition to Nenna and Macque, other musicians associated with the *casa Gesualdo* are known: Scipione Stella, composer; Fabrizio Filomarino, composer and a skilled lutenist about whom we hear more in the correspondence of the Ferrarese nobleman Fontanelli; Scipione Dentice, who published at least five books of madrigals; Rocco Rodio, a composer and theorist of some reputation; Giovanni Leonardo Primavera Giovanni dell'Arpa, Leonardo Muzio Effrem, Scipione Cerreto, Giustiniano Forcella, Domenico Montella, and Bartolomeo Roi.[10] As a member of this group Scipione Cerreto understandably expressed his admiration for Don Carlo in his *Della prattica Musica, vocale et strumentale* of 1601:

> This Prince not only took delight in music, but also kept for his
> pleasure and entertainment at his court and at his expense many
> excellent composers, players, and singers; so that I often think that
> if this nobleman had lived at the time of the ancient Greeks, who
> considered ignorant one who knew nothing of music, regardless of
> his accomplishments in other branches of learning (as witness the story
> of the philosopher Themistocles who was greatly embarrassed and
> disgraced for not being able, at a banquet, to play upon some instru-
> ment) surely they would have raised up unto his memory a statue,
> not of marble, but of gold.[11]

Torquato Tasso (1544–95), the foremost poet of his age, who moved from one court to another in a continuing state of paranoia, spent con-

---

[9] Influence of one composer upon the other is of course another matter, particularly during the period 1596–9, when both frequented Gesualdo. See further page 213 ff.

[10] D. Romano Micheli, *Musica vaga et artificiosa* (1615), Preface.

[11] Cerreto, op. cit., p. 154.

siderable time in Naples in the late 1580s and early 1590s.[12] Tasso met Gesualdo on the first of these visits, and their close friendship, which is documented by personal correspondence, resulted in a joint production of madrigals as well as poems written not only about Gesualdo himself, but about both wives, including stanzas on the death of the first and his marriage to the second. In fact we shall see how Tasso reflects in his lyrics most of the most important moments in Gesualdo's life from 1588 to the poet's death in 1595.

The First Marriage and Tragedy

The year 1585 was a signal year in Carlo's life. His elder brother had just died, making him heir to the family titles and suggesting the importance of an early marriage. Within the year Carlo's father arranged a betrothal with Donna Maria d'Avalos, the daughter of Fabrizio's sister Donna Sveva, and hence Don Carlo's first cousin. It is said that she was a person of great gifts and remarkable beauty. A likeness of Donna Maria survives in a picture of the Carafa family in the church of San Domenico Maggiore in Naples, but it hardly conveys the magic and charm that must have been hers. She was already twice a widow though she had scarcely passed the age of twenty-five. In fact, as the period of mourning for her second husband had not yet elapsed, it was necessary for the family to obtain a Papal dispensation for her marriage to Don Carlo.[13]

The two fortunate gentlemen who preceded the Prince of Venosa into wedlock with Donna Maria d'Avalos were: (1) Federigo Carafa, Marchese di San Lucido, who married her in 1575 when she could have been no more than fifteen. There were two children: Don Ferrante, who died a few months after his birth; and a daughter who later married Marc Antonio Carafa. Federigo died after three years, perhaps from an excess of connubial bliss according to one chronicler,[14] though another described him as 'admired by the whole of nobility as an angel from Heaven'. (2) Alfonso Gioeni, a Sicilian, son of Giovanni Gioeni, Marchese di Giulianova. This marriage took place

---

[12] For extremely interesting details of these visits, see Modestino, *Della dimora di T. Tasso in Napoli, 1588, 1592, 1594* (Napoli, 1863).

[13] The second marriage ended in the death of the husband in 1586 (Modestino, p. 48) and not divorce as Gray & Heseltine, p. 12, would have it. The Papal dispensation was thus not for a divorce, but for an abridgement of the period of mourning, allowing her to marry Don Carlo forthwith.

[14] Gray & Heseltine, p. 12, give the following Italian as authority, but I have been unable to locate its source: 'forse per aver troppo reiterare con quella i congiugiamenti carnali.'

in 1580. Donna Maria had thus 'given sufficient signs of fecundity'[15] to suggest that the new marriage would prove fruitful.

The wedding of Don Carlo and Donna Maria took place in 1586 in the church of San Domenico Maggiore in Naples. It was followed by nuptial celebrations of royal magnificence which continued for several days in the Palazzo San Severo, next to the church. This residence, which belonged to Giovanni Francesco of Sangro, Duke of Torre Maggiore and Prince of S. Severo, was frequently used by the Prince at this time.

At some time during the next four years a son, Don Emmanuele, was born.

The year 1590 brought a tragedy which was to mark the remaining years of the Prince's life. The story has been repeatedly told. It has been variously recounted in the chronicles, popularized, vulgarized, made the subject of endless poems, and later even fashioned into a novella. We have a myriad details, but a considerable amount of sorting out is required to get at the truth, and even then a few enigmas remain. Two sources in particular enable us to establish the basic facts of the case. The first of these has come down to us in a number of manuscript copies, varying slightly in detail from copy to copy.[16] Referred to as the Corona MS, it is one of the most colourful of the *chroniques scandaleuses* of the period. Gesualdo's story is the most elaborate of the tales contained therein.[17]

How much ruin lust has brought to the world is evident for the pages of writers are filled with it, and there is no doubt whatsoever that it

[15] Ammirato, Seconda Parte, 13: 'Tolse dunque Carlo per havergli à procrear figliuoli Maria d'Avalos sua cugina carnale nata di D. Carlo & di Sveva sua zia, la quale havuto due altri mariti prima, *havea dato segni sufficienti di fecondità*; ma stata con esso lui alcun tempo, e non generatone figliuoli, con infelice disavventura l'an. innanzi à questo passò della vita presente, è Carlo intendentissimo della Musica, si come al padre son sempre piaciuti gli studi delle buone lettere, e in tale stato, come si è potuto vedere si tova a'di nostri la casa Gesualdo.'

[16] Thirty-six copies in various versions are to be found in manuscripts dating from the seventeenth to the nineteenth centuries, fifteen in the Biblioteca Nazionale di Napoli alone. Donald Krumel of the Newberry Library in Chicago has informed me of a copy of the Corona MS recently acquired by them and has kindly put it at my disposal. It does not differ materially from the Borzelli source mentioned in fn. 17.

[17] The first study of this manuscript was made by Borzelli in 'Notizia dei mss. Corona, ed il Successo: Di Donna Maria d'Avalos principessa di Venosa e di Don Fabrizio Carafa duca d'Andria', in *Rassegna scientifica, letteraria e politica*, anno II, nn. 5–6 (Pararia, 1891). A second more complete study appeared as a separate monograph under the title *Successi tragici et amorosi di Silvio et Ascanio Corona* (Naples, 1908). The manuscript version used for this study is to be found in the Biblioteca Brancaccia in Naples. The document was first translated into English by Cecil Gray. However he based his translation on a copy less complete than that presented by Borzelli, whose text is used here as the basis for a new translation.

brings along with it all sorts of evils and discords, and weakens the body and does harm to all virtues and goodness of the soul. It is lust for which men debase themselves in order to submit the body and soul to the inconstant will and unbridled desire of an unbalanced and vain woman; for we see a man, at a mere nod from her, place himself in danger of losing his soul, honour, and life, and often struck by the just anger of God serve as a wretched spectacle to a whole people, as we shall hear in the present story.

To Don Carlos d'Avalos, Prince of Montesarchio and to Donna Severina Gesualdo, first families of greatness and nobility in the city and kingdom of Naples, there was born, among others, Donna Maria, who, having reached the age of fifteen and being no less celebrated for her name than famous for her beauty, was married to Federigo Carafa, Marchese of San Lucido.[18] They sired two children, a male named Ferrante who died a few months after his birth and a daughter who, brought up in a noble manner, and whose parents being dead, married Marcantonio Carafa. The Marchese of San Lucido having engendered these two children, as has been said, passed from this to a better world, Donna Maria remaining a widow. The year of mourning having scarcely passed, she was again married by her parents, with the dispensation of the Pope, to D. Carlo Gesualdo, Prince of Venosa, her cousin.[19] The marriage was celebrated with royal magnificence in the house of this Prince, situated near the church of San Domenico, in which house there were festivities for several days. This marriage for the space of three or four years was a happy one, whence, living more like lovers [than husband and wife], there was born as the fruit of their conjugal love a son named D. Emmanuele, who in the course of time succeeded Don Carlo, his father, in the principality.[20] But the enemy of human nature not being able to endure the sight of such great love and such conformity of tastes in two married people, implanted in the bosom of Donna Maria unchaste and libidinous desires, and an unbridled appetite to enjoy the beauties of a certain cavaliere. He was Don Fabrizio Carafa, Duke of Andria, perhaps the most handsome and graceful cavaliere in the city, vigorous and flourishing and

[18] Tommaso Costo, in a letter to the Cardinal of Santa Severina, 3 April 1575, reports the marriage of Federigo Carafa and Donna Maria d'Avalos, the event of which Pellegrino of Capua sings a poem. Cf. Borzelli, *Successi*, p. 193, fn. 1. Federigo's premature death is announced by Costo on 3 November 1578.

[19] Costo, *Lettere*, Bk. I, pp. 27–29, also includes information relating to Donna Maria's second marriage which is completely ignored in the present account.

[20] This is not correct. Don Emmanuele died a few months before his father.

1(a)   *The countryside at Gesualdo with the castle in the distance.*

(b)   *The castle courtyard.*

not yet thirty years of age, so delicate and yet so irascible in his manner that at one moment you would have esteemed him an Adonis for his beauty and at another a Mars for his fury. He was joined in marriage to Donna Maria Carafa, daughter of Don Luigi, Prince of Stigliano, by whom he fathered five children,[21] including Don Luigi, a monk of Monte Cassino, and Don Vincenzo, who was General of the Jesuit Fathers, both of whom died with the title of sanctity.

The lovers' uniformity of minds, the occasions presented by dances during festivities, the equal desire of both to enjoy the beauty of the other through their gazes were all so much fuel which burnt in their breasts. The first messages of their desires were their glances which with the tongue of the heart of love betrayed the fire which burnt in each other's breast. From glances of love they proceeded to written messages, given to and received by faithful messengers, in which they invited each other to battle on the fields of love. This Archer, although blind, was most adept at bringing the lovers together, and knew well how to find an appropriate place for their meeting.

They met alone for the first time in the garden of Don Garzia of Toledo, in the town of Chiaia, in the pavilion whereof the Duke did lie concealed, awaiting his mistress and beloved, who, on the pretext of diversion and entertainment, started off with a simple retinue of a faithful maid named Laura Scala and some gentlemen of hers. While she was going about in the garden, pretending that she was afflicted with a pain in her body, she betook herself from the group of those waiting on her, entering, guided by the wife of the gardener who had been well paid by the Duke, into the house where he was hiding. Seeing her approach, he came without wasting time, and taking her in his arms, kissed her a thousand times—as she did him—and with the greatest ardour they were moved to enjoy together the ultimate amorous delight.

This was not the last time that they were together in their pleasure, but many, many times for months on end such usance continued in the said house of Don Garzia as well as in other secret places according as their wit and fortune provided the opportunity. Many times in the very bedroom of the Princess, with the maid as a sentinel, did they dally amorously together, and as evil, amorous meetings became

21 Gray's description of Donna Maria as 'a lady not only of great beauty but also of supreme goodness' is not present in Borzelli. Gray also mentions four children as issuing from the second marriage; Borzelli's source states 'con la quale aveva generato cinque [5] figli', and presents the additional information which closes the paragraph.

habitual, it was no longer possible to keep their love secret, especially from him who with most jealous eyes gazed on the proceedings and actions, although private, of Donna Maria. Their sins were first disclosed and then punished in their body—and perhaps would have been similarly punished even in their souls, if at the extreme moment God out of his mercy had not enjoined them to make an act of true contrition and thereby made the whole population a laughing stock.[22]

The first who noticed their mutual love was Don Giulio Gesualdo, blood uncle of the Prince, who being fiercely enamoured of Donna Maria's beauty, and not heeding the fact that she was the wife of his nephew, had left no stone unturned in order to effect his intent. But he had not only been rebuffed by her, but sharply reproved for his mad love, even to the point of her threatening him that, should he persist in such thought and device, she would inform her husband that he was a plotter against her honesty. For which reason, realizing that neither through gifts nor prayers nor through tears had he been able to make her pliant to his will, and believing truly that she was a chaste Penelope, poor Don Giulio resigned himself and ceased to importune her. But when whispers came to his ears of her loves and pleasures with the Duke, and having perceived them by more than one indication with his own eyes, so great was the anger which assailed him on seeing that she was another's whore, that, without losing a moment's time, he went to report the matter to the Prince. At such grievous news Don Carlo remained more dead than alive. But in order not to be too prone to belief on the basis of the reports of others, he determined that that which had come to his ears should be evident, too, to his eyes.

In the meantime, the lovers having been informed that their crimes were already known, the Duke put an end to their pleasures; but Donna Maria not being able to bear such respite urged him to reinstate the interrupted delights. The Duke, however, explained to her how he knew that their love had been revealed, and pointed out the danger to their honour and their life as well, unless they abstained from their amorous excesses.

To these salutary reasonings the Princess replied to the Duke that if his heart was capable of fear, he had better become a lackey, since

[22] The sense of this is rather difficult to understand and Gray omits it. It probably refers to the philosophy of the church which allows for atonement of even the greatest sin if forgiveness is sought. The body may be punished (i.e. they were murdered), but the soul may be saved through confession. Thus the populace in pointing a guilty finger ultimately is the one who looks foolish. See p. 25 for an explicit notice by Spaccini of Donna Maria's behaviour in her final moments.

nature had made an error in creating a cavalier with the heart of a woman, and had erred in making her—a woman—with the heart of a cavalier. It was not worthy of him to show such plebeian virtue, for, if he was capable of harbouring fear, then should he chase from his breast any love of her and nevermore appear before her.

At this angry reply, which touched him to the very quick, the Duke went hastily to his beloved and unhappy lady, and said to her: 'Fair Lady, you wish that I should die? Then let me die. For love of you, this soul of mine will be happy to leave its body, a victim of such beauty. I have the strength to meet my death, but not the fortitude to suffer yours. For if I die, you will not continue alive, and this is the fear which makes a coward of me. I have no heart for this. If you have no eyes to foresee this calamity, give me assurance that the Duke of Andria alone will be the victim of your husband, and I shall show you whether I can bear the thrust of a sword. You are cruel, not to me, who have found you greatly merciful. But cruel you are to your own beauty which, still fresh, you risk allowing to rot in the tomb.'

To this the Princess replied: 'My Lord Duke, more deadly to me is a moment when you are away from me than a thousand deaths that might result from my crime. If I die with you, I shall never be far from you; but if you leave me, I shall die alone far from all my heart holds dear, which is you. Resolve, then, either to show yourself disloyal by going away, or to show yourself faithful by never abandoning me. As for the reasons which you have expressed, you should have given consideration to them before, and not now when the arrow has sped to its mark. I have the courage necessary to suffer the wound of cold steel but not your zeal in going away. You should not have loved me, nor I you, if such fears were to present themselves. In short, I so wish and so command, and to my wish let there be no opposition unless you would lose me forever.'

To the above-mentioned speech the Duke, bowing humbly, replied: 'Lady, since you want to die, I shall die with you. Such is your wish; so be it.' And he left, pursuing still his accustomed pleasures.

The Prince, now alert and attentive to every action, having with great speed had all the locks of all the doors of the palace removed and put out of working order so that the Princess should not suspect anything, spread the news one day that he was going to go hunting, as it was his custom to do, and that he would not return that evening but, rather, the following day. The day when he was to go hunting having arrived, and accompanied by many kinsmen and friends who were aware of the ruse, all dressed as hunters, he mounted his horse pretending to go to a place called Astruni, eighty-two miles from Naples.

In the meantime he left orders with several of his most trusted servants that during the night they should leave all the necessary doors open, that they should pretend that the doors were shut, and that they should watch and see if the Duke were to come. The Prince then left and went to hide himself in the home of a relative of his until it was time to leave.

The Duke, having been informed that the Prince had gone a-hunting and that he would not return that evening, betook himself at four hours of the night to his accustomed pleasures. Having been received by Donna Maria with her wonted affection, both, having disrobed, got into bed where several times they gave each other solace, and overcome by fatigue from such supreme pleasure both soul and body drifted into sleep.

Toward midnight the Prince returned to the palace accompanied by a troop of armed cavalieri who were relatives of his. Having entered the house, he betook himself with dispatch to the bedroom of the Princess in front of which was stationed a careful sentinel, Laura Scala, her faithful maid, who was half asleep on a bed. The maid, hearing the noise made by these people, was on the point of shouting, but her life being threatened by the Prince, she withdrew more dead than alive, and the Prince, breaking down the door of the bedroom with a blow of his foot, and entering therein ablaze with anger with his companions, found his wife lying naked in bed in the arms of the Duke. (In the meantime, all having gone into the bedroom, the good maid seized the opportune moment and took to her heels, nor was anything more heard of her.)

At such a sight one can well imagine how dumbfounded the poor Prince was, who, nevertheless, shaking himself loose from the stunned state which such a scene had precipitated in him, slew the sleepy lovers with many dagger thrusts before they could catch their breath.

This happened on the night which followed the day of 16 October, 1590. The bodies were dragged outside the room and left on the stairs, the Prince ordering the servants not to move them from that place; and having made a placard which explained the cause of the slaughter which they affixed to the door of the palace, he went with some of his relatives to his state of Venosa.

The bodies of the wretched lovers remained exposed all the following morning in the middle of the stairs, and the entire city ran thither to view such a spectacle. The Princess's wounds were all in her belly and especially in those parts which most ought to be kept honest; and the Duke gave evidence of having been even more grievously wounded than she.

It is said that while the said cadavers were lying on the said staircase a monk of San Domenico, a terziario,[23] used the said Donna Maria even though she was dead.[24]

The body of the Duke was taken away to be buried that same evening and the body of the Princess the following day. Such was the end of their unchaste love.

We are informed[25] that on the night of the tragedy it was revealed to Maria Carafa, the Duke's wife, in her devotions before a painting of the Holy Virgin,[26] that her husband was soon to meet his death, and at the same time the grace of repentance for his sins was received through the intervention of the Holy Mother. It is related that 'she got up from her prayers and told her intimates what had happened that night, and on the following morning when she repeated her story, it was interpreted as the effects of a fatuous vision. But no more than five or six hours had passed before the news of the disgraceful murder came to them.'

We learn elsewhere of the Duchess Maria's silent sufferings prior to the tragedy,[27] as well as her ultimate retreat to a Dominican convent. As, however, the latter event occurred eighteen years to the month after her husband's demise, it cannot plausibly be suggested that her sorrow drove her to a nunnery, as some have proposed. Apparently the cloistered life

[23] terziario: 'belonging to the third class of Franciscan monks and not living a cloistered life' (A. Hoare, *A Short Italian Dictionary*).

[24] Gray omits the details of this paragraph. Vatielli, as will be seen, also omits a few of the more unsavoury details described by Spaccini.

[25] In an eighteenth-century manuscript by Giovanni Pastore, *Memorie storiche della città di Andria*. See Borzelli, *Successi Tragici*, pp. 195–6.

[26] The painting is still preserved in the ducal palace at Andria.

[27] Aldimari, *Historia genealogica della Famiglia Carafa* (1691), Bk. III, p. 385: 'The Duke of Andria being in love with one of the first ladies of the city, as noble as she was licentious, and having enjoyed the unsavoury fruits of her love, slowly began to see his wife, the Duchess Maria, for what she really was, and to go so far as to insult and mistreat her. The Duke, not profiting in the least from warnings for his safety by his friends who tried to dissuade him from this fated adventure, was found one night with his love by the husband and was wretchedly slain together with the adultress on the 17th (sic) of October 1590. The Duchess Maria, being left without her husband, and being only twenty-five years old, decided to become a religious and a celibate, and therefore entered the convent of Sapienza at Naples, of the Dominican Order, on the 21st of November, 1608, with the name of Sister Maria Maddalena.'

came naturally to her, as we are told that she was inordinately religious and given to the austerities of the devotional life. It was even said that after she retired to the convent, she had to be given a private cell because of the inflamed condition of her soul, which was such that her shouts and sighs disturbed the other inhabitants.[28] But her agonies were not long endured, for 'having lived there in the exercises of Christian virtue she rendered her soul to God on the 29th of December, 1615, at the age of 49'.[29]

Another report of the tragedy itself is the chronicle of the Venetian ambassador to Naples at this time.[30] Though brief, it is, with the exception of the inquest itself, closest in time to the event to come down to us. Under the heading 'Napoli, 19 (*sic*) October 1590', we read:

> Don Carlo Gesualdo, son of the Prince of Venosa and nephew of the Most Illustrious Cardinal, on Tuesday at the sixth hour of night with intent mounted the stairs in company of his companions to the room of Donna Maria d'Avalos, his wife and blood cousin, considered the most beautiful lady in Naples. He first killed Signor Fabrizio Carafa, Duke of Andria, who was with her, and afterwards killed the lady herself, in this manner avenging the injury which he had received. These three princely families (Gesualdo, d'Avalos, Carafa) were intimately connected with and related to almost all the other noble families of the kingdom, and everyone seems stunned by the horror of this event. The Illustrious Lord Viceroy himself was greatly dismayed at the news, for he loved and esteemed the Duke highly as a man who both by nature and through application was possessor of all the most noble and worthy qualities which appertain to a noble prince and valorous gentleman. Various ministers of justice, together with officials of the Courts have been to the palace, and after making various inquiries commanded that all persons connected with the case should be sequestered and guarded in their own houses; but up to the present nothing more has been heard of the matter.

Fortunately a full record of the investigation has been preserved in the report of the proceedings of the Grand Court of the Vicaria.[31] Three

[28] Gray & Heseltine, p. 40, apparently unaware of the lapse of time involved, sees this as a consequence of the Duke's maltreatment of her.

[29] Adlimari, loc. cit.

[30] Printed in Mutinelli, *Storia arcana e aneddotica d'Italia raccontata dai Veneti Ambasciatori* (1855–8), vol. II, p. 162; translation of the concluding part as in Gray & Heseltine, p. 19.

[31] These proceedings were at one time contained in MSS I.D.73 (third volume), X.C.32, and I.D.35 of the Biblioteca Nazionale in Naples. It was first printed in its entirety by Modestino in 1863 in his study of Tasso, pp. 52–66.

testimonies are recorded therein: (1) that of the examining officials, taken some days after the tragedy as a form of inquest; (2) the testimony of a maid-servant of Donna Maria, a Silvia Albana; and (3) the testimony of Pietro Malitiale, also called Bardotti, a personal servant of Don Carlo. It is logical that where discrepancies occur between this testimony and the Corona MS or other sources preference should be given to this document.

Informatione presa dalla Gran Corte della Vicaria. Die 27 octobris, 1590, in quo habitat Don Carolus Gesualdus.

(Evidence taken by the Grand Court of the Vicaria on 27 October 1590, in the house of Don Carlo Gesualdo.)

It having come to the attention of the Grand Court of the Vicaria that in the house of the most illustrious Don Carlo Gesualdo in the square of San Domenico Maggiore, the illustrious Signora Donna Maria d'Avalos, wife of said Don Carlo, and the illustrious Don Fabrizio Carafa, the late Duke of Andria, had been killed: the most illustrious gentlemen Don Giovan Tommaso Salamanca, Fulvio di Costanzo, Royal Counsellors and Criminal Judges of the Grand Court, the Magnificent Prosecuting Attorney of the Grand Court, and I, the undersigned Master of the said Grand Court have come together to confer in the house of the said Don Carlo. In the upper apartment of the said house, in the last room of same, all of the above-mentioned gentlemen entered, and within the room there was found dead, stretched out on the floor, the most illustrious Don Fabrizio Carafa, Duke of Andria, who seen by the said gentlemen and by me, Giovan Domenico Micene, was recognized to be Don Fabrizio Carafa, Duke of Andria. His only clothing was a woman's nightdress with fringes at the bottom, with ruffs of black silk, and one sleeve all red with blood; and the said Duke of Andria was covered with blood and pierced with many wounds, thus: an arquebusade on his left arm which went straight through his elbow, and even went through his breast, the sleeve of the above-mentioned shirt being scorched; signs of diverse wounds made by pointed steel weapons on the breast, arms, on the head and on the face; and another arquebus wound in his temples and over his eye where there was a great flow of blood. And in the same room there was a gilt couch with curtains of green cloth, and within the said bed was found dead the above-mentioned Donna Maria d'Avalos who was in her nightshirt all bathed with blood. On being seen by the said gentlemen and by me, the above-mentioned Master of the Court, she was recognized as being Donna Maria d'Avalos, who had been slain and whose throat had been cut; also a wound on the head on the side of her right temple, a stab on the face and a number of dagger thrusts on her hand and right arm, and on her breast and side there was evidence of two other wounds inflicted by weapons; and on the same bed was found a man's shirt with lettuce-shaped ruffs, and on a chair of crimson velvet nearby there was found an iron gauntlet, a burnished iron glove; also in the same room a pair of trousers in various shades of green and a coat of yellow cloth, and a pair of green silk hose; a pair of white cloth drawers and a pair of cloth slippers—all of which clothing was without holes, nor had they been pierced by sharp weapons nor stained with blood. In the quarter of the lady's apartment the door was found to be smashed at the bottom and could not be shut with the handle in view of the fact that the keyhole was so gouged out that it could not be shut, nor could one secure the door nor the lock of said door. It was damaged in such a way that the key could not have gone in and therefore said door could not be shut.

And having entered in the said room where there was a small door opening on to the spiral staircase which goes down into Don Carlo's apartment, a bolt lock was found thereon . . .; and upon these said gentlemen arriving in said apartment, Pietro Bardotti, who was in charge of the linen and clothing of said Don Carlo Gesualdo, gave a key to the said signori saying that when he went into the room where he found the Duke and Donna Maria d'Avalos slain, he also found the present key on a chair next to the bed. This he gave to the said signori, which he declared to be a pass key, which opens the door of the large room of the apartment of the above-mentioned house. And I, the undersigned Domenico Micene, being present and having taken the said key, through the order of the above-mentioned signori and having gone to examine the lock of the door of the said room, there was found in it another regular key for that lock; and having tried and measured the said key, given me by the said Pietro, it was found to open the lock of the door of the said room just as the regular one does. And at the same time by order of the said signori two coffins were sent for, which were brought into the same room, where the Reverend Father Don Carlo Mastrillo, a Jesuit, came along with two other Jesuits. And when they had washed the body of the said Duke of Andria, one could see clearly that he had the above-mentioned wounds: i.e., an arquebusade on his right arm which went through his elbow and side, with two shots, and an arquebusade on the eye on the side of the temples, which went from one side to the other, and a bit of the brain had oozed out; and also he had many wounds on his head, face, neck, chest, stomach, kidneys, arms, hands and shoulders—wounds made by sharp sword thrusts, quite deep, many of them passing through the body from one side to the other. The body was found immediately upon entering through the door of the said room, three paces distant from the bed where lay the said Donna Maria d'Avalos. And under his body on the floor there were holes which seemed to have been made by swords which had passed through the body, penetrating deeply into the floor. The body having been washed and dressed with a pair of black silk hose and collar of black velvet, the Reverend Father Don Carlo Mastrillo, who had come to receive the body on behalf of the wife of the said Duke, the Countess of Ruo his grandmother, and the Prior of Hungary [Vincenzo Carafa] his uncle—had him taken away. And having placed the body inside a coffin by order of the said most illustrious signori, it was given to the above-mentioned Jesuits who put it in a coach and took it with them; and the above-mentioned clothing, which had been found on the chair within the said room belonging to the said Duke, together with the glove, gauntlet and pass key, were consigned to me, the above-mentioned Domenico Micene, in order that I might hold them in safe-keeping.

And then there came the illustrious Marchioness di Vico, aged aunt of the said Donna Maria d'Avalos, in order to have her dressed; and as soon as she was dressed by the women servants, she was placed in another coffin, all of which along with the body was given to the illustrious Signora Duchessa of Traietto, an old woman, according to the wish and request of the illustrious Donna Sveva Gesualdo, mother of the said Donna Maria, and she was taken to the church of San Domenico.

And it is moreover reported that the said Judges together with the said Lawyer, having descended into the mezzanine room where it is said that Don Carlo slept, found in one of the rooms three halberds, one of which had a crooked point, and all three were covered and stained with blood; and there was found in said room a round shield of iron, large and with a fringe of black silk around it, a large gilded silver knife, and a sword similarly gilded, and two wax torches which had been lit and which had also been left behind in said house.

In witness whereof

By order of the above-mentioned illustrious gentlemen, I Dominico Micene, Master of the Grand Court, have written the above account with my own hand.

Evidence examined and taken by me, Master Giovanni Sanchez, with the assistance of Master Mutio Surgenti, fiscal advocate, by order of the Excellent Masters, concerning the death of the illustrious gentleman Don Fabrizio Carafa, Duke of Andria, and of the Lady Maria d'Avalos. The 28th October, 1590, in the house of the illustrious Duke of Torremaggiore, lately inhabited by Don Carlo Gesualdo and Don Maria d'Avalos.

Silvia Albana, aged twenty, being, as she said, woman servant of the late Donna Maria d'Avalos and in charge of the wardrobe of the said Lady and of all that which concerned her person, having served her for six years, bore witness on oath:

To the question as to what she knew of the death of said Donna Maria d'Avalos, and who had killed her and how, she said that the truth as she knew it was as follows: That on Tuesday evening the 26th of the present month, which was a week ago, after having supped, when it was four hours of the night, Signora Donna Maria went to bed, which said witness, together with Laura Scala who is also a woman servant of said Lady, prepared for sleeping. They undressed her and left her lying in bed, whereupon Laura went to sleep, as usual, in the room near which the above-mentioned Lady was reposing, and the witness set about cleaning and preparing the clothes for the following morning, Wednesday. Then did the said Lady Donna Maria call witness to her and when she had entered her room, the Lady asked her to give her some clothing with which to dress. Said witness asking her why she wished to dress, Donna Maria replied to her that she had heard the Duke of Andria whistle, and that she wanted to go to the window, just as the witness had seen the said Lady do many times; and on a number of occasions, when there was moonlight, she had seen that it was the Duke of Andria in the street; and she had recognized him by the light of the moon because she had many times seen him by day and knew him very well, and she heard him speak to the said Lady.

In the meantime, Donna Maria ordered the witness to act as a guard should she hear anyone about the house, and the said Lady having ordered that some clothing be brought to her, witness brought her a little gray skirt and a shawl for her head; and the said Lady, having dressed, went to the open window, and went out on the balcony, first ordering said witness that she should be on guard should she hear anyone about the house or in the courtyard. And witness did as she was directed. And at the time that Donna Maria opened the window she heard the clock strike five hours of the night, and a half hour later —which made it five and a half hours of the night—the said Donna Maria called the witness, and she saw that she closed the window and told the witness to undress her. Thus she took off her petticoat and saw that said Donna Maria lay down in bed, and then ordered that she should bring a night shirt saying that the one she had on was wet with perspiration; and she brought it to her, and it had a little collar worked with black silk and a pair of cuffs of the same colour, and she ordered her to leave it on the bed—which night shirt then the witness had seen the Duke of Andria wearing when in the morning she discovered him in the very room where said Lady Donna Maria slept, dead on the floor, covered with blood and with many wounds. And when said Lady Donna Maria had told her to leave said night shirt, which the witness had brought her, on the bed, she ordered her to light a candle for her and leave it on the chair. Thus did the witness light a short, thick wax candle in a silver candlestick and placed it on the chair. And witness wishing to leave in order to go to sleep, Lady Donna Maria said to her: 'Shut the door without turning the handle and do not come in unless I call you.' The witness did so and went back into her room; and as the said Signora Donna Maria had told her not to enter unless called, she did not wish to undress. Thus all dressed she placed herself on the bed, and reading a book she fell asleep.

While sleeping, she suddenly heard open the door of the room where she was, which is by a spiral staircase which leads to the mezzanine where Don Carlo Gesualdo lived. Awakening with that noise and thinking she must have dreamed it, she saw, just as a lamp in the room wherein she was was dying out, three men enter whom the witness did not recognize. And scarcely had she seen them, out of the fear engendered in her, than they opened the door of the room wherein the said Lady Donna Maria was sleeping. And she saw that one of them, who was the last of the three, was carrying a halberd, but could not see whether the others bore arms. Immediately upon the above-said men entering the room, the witness heard two shots, and almost at the same moment the words, 'There he is!' Scarcely had she heard these words than she saw Don Carlo Gesualdo, husband of Signora Donna Maria, enter into the room by the staircase. And after the said Don Carlo, came Pietro Bardotti with two lighted torches in his hands. And said Don Carlo was carrying a halberd, though she did not notice whether he bore other arms, and he said to the witness:

'Ah, traitress, I shall kill you. You shall not escape me now!' And ordering the said Pietro Bardotti not to allow her to leave, he entered into the room of Signora Donna Maria, but before entering he told Pietro Bardotti to fix one of the two torches he was carrying under the portiere which was at the door. Pietro so did, and at this moment the witness fled into the room where the boy child was, and staying there awhile she heard speak in the room the said Don Carlo, saying: 'Where are they?' And the nurse begged that for the love of God he should not hurt the child. Whereupon Don Carlo, ordering Pietro Bardotti to close the door of the closet where the Lady kept her jewels, left. Then witness hearing no noise in the room, came out from under the bed and saw with torch in his hand the above-mentioned Pietro Bardotti, who said to her: 'Fear not for Don Carlo has departed.' And on witness asking what had happened, Bardotti replied: 'Both of them are dead!'

And the witness did not have the courage to go into the room until morning when the other servants came and it was already daybreak. Then did they all enter into the room and saw Donna Maria d'Avalos dead with her throat slit and with many wounds on her own bed, on which lay a man's shirt, and on a chair near the bed a pair of green man's trousers with green silk stockings, and a pair of slippers with a white doublet; and near the door was a dead body with many wounds covered with blood; and coming near she recognized that it was the Duke of Andria. And this is what the witness knows adding that the Duke was wearing the Lady's night shirt.

Upon being questioned if she noticed whether or not the clothing which was on the chair was soiled and to whom they belonged, witness answered that the clothes which she saw were not soiled or spotted, and that she judged them to have been the Duke of Andria's, although she could not say for certain. Upon being interrogated as to what time it might have been when the three men came who, as mentioned above, entered by the staircase followed by Don Carlo, witness replied that when she got out from under the bed the clock struck seven.

On being asked if she knew where Don Carlo Gesualdo was and who had gone with him, she replied that she did not know because ever since the morning of their departure when we came here with Don Giovanni and the other Lords Justiciary and the Fiscal Lord Advocate, she had been shut up in the women's apartment where she was watched by a guard and had spoken to no one.

On being questioned as to what happened to the body of Donna

Maria she said that on Wednesday morning the Marchioness of Vico had come and had had said body dressed, and that witness had helped do this; and thus dressed the body was placed in a coffin, and she heard that it was taken to the church of San Domenico. And this was all she knew. On being asked: 'Whence did the said Duke gain entrance?' she replied, 'I do not know.'

Silvia Albana bore witness as above.

On the same day, in the same place, Pietro Malitiale, alias Bardotti, about forty years of age, said that he was in the service of Don Carlo Gesualdo as valet, and that he has served him and his house for twenty-eight years. The witness, having been sworn in, was questioned concerning the occurrence and his knowledge thereof, firstly, what had happened to Don Carlo and how long was it since he saw him last? He answered that he did not know his present whereabouts and that he had not seen him since the Tuesday evening of the week before; and that on the Wednesday morning when he left the house on horse it was around seven hours of the night, but said witness did not see him leave. Being asked why said Don Carlo left at night and with whom, he replied: Gentlemen, I shall tell you the truth. On said Tuesday, which was the 26th of the present month, which is a week ago today, the said Don Carlo supped at the third hour of the night in his mezzanine room, in bed and undressed, as he was accustomed to doing every evening. He was served at supper by present witness along with Pietro de Vicario, a waiter, Alessandro Abruzzese, and a young priest who is a musician. As soon as he had supped, all the above-mentioned—Pietro de Vicario and the others—left, and said witness remained in order to lock the door. After he had secured the door, Don Carlo lay down to sleep, and witness helped to cover him up. After undressing, witness himself fell asleep. Thus sleeping he heard Don Carlo call him at around six hours of the night asking for a drink of water. The witness went to the well to draw same, and when he had descended to the courtyard, he saw that the street door was open at that hour; and having taken up the water, he saw that Don Carlo was dressed with his coat and trousers on; and he told witness that he should give him his long cloak to put on. When witness asked where he wanted to go at such an hour, as it was six hours of the night, he replied that he wanted to go hunting. When said witness said to him that it was not the time to go hunting, Don Carlo replied, 'You will see the kind of hunting I am going to do!' And he finished dressing himself, and told witness to light two torches; when these had been lighted the said Don Carlo took from under the bed a sword and gave it to the witness to carry under his arm, also a dirk and a dagger together with a small arquebus. As soon as he had taken the arms, he went to the staircase which goes up to the apartment of Donna Maria d'Avalos, and as he was going up Don Carlo said to the witness, 'I am going to slay the Duke of Andria and that whore, Donna Maria.' And as he was going up, witness saw three men, each of whom was carrying a halberd and a small arquebus; and these armed men on the arrival of the witness, threw open the door at the top of the stairs which led to Donna Maria's room.

As soon as the three men had entered the said room of Donna Maria, Don Carlo said, 'Kill that scoundrel along with this harlot! Shall a Gesualdo be made a cuckold?' And then witness heard the sound of firearms but heard no voices because the witness had stayed outside the room. Remaining thus awhile, the three men came out, and he recognized one to be Pietro de Vicario, a servant, another as Ascanio Lama, and a third as a servant whose name was Francesco; and they descended by the same staircase by which they had come up armed. Then Don Carlo came out, his hands covered with blood, but he turned back and re-entered the room of the said Donna Maria, saying, 'I do not believe they are dead!'

Witness then entered with a torch and saw a dead body near the door. The said Don Carlo went up to the bed of Donna Maria and inflicted still a few more wounds upon her saying, 'I do not believe she is dead.' And he ordered the witness not to let the women cry out, and the said Don Carlo descended the staircase by which he had come; and witness heard a great noise of horses below, and in the morning he saw that the said Don Carlo was no longer there, nor were his servants, nor any members of the court of Don Carlo. And this is what the witness knows.

Signum crucis.[32]

Little was seen of Gesualdo for a considerable period. He went immediately following the tragic events to the Viceroy, Don Giovanni Zunia, Count of Miranda, seeking advice as to his best course of action. Returning to his residence in Gesualdo, it was been recounted that he

[32] The above translation is by the author. Only minor deviations in substance from Gray will be noted, but the wording, here somewhat more literal, is naturally considerably changed. See Modestino, op. cit., pp. 52–66, for the original Italian.

razed the forest surrounding it in a manner recalling Macbeth. While there is no evidence which confirms his actions during this period, his removal to Gesualdo would have been a likely action. Sufficiently distant from Naples, his country castle would have provided a good place to lie in hiding at least temporarily.

The news of the tragic event spread at once, and Gesualdo, despite the provocation for his acts, was generally viewed as the guilty party and a heartless assassin. Some appeared outraged because he had used accomplices in carrying out the act. This is curious in view of contemporary practice, and also of the clear evidence that the Prince was not only involved in the slaughter but personally took part in his wife's murder. Indeed, it is not unlikely that, as the Prince had a double murder on his hands, he brought servants along specifically to take care of the Duke of Andria, so that he might devote his full attention to Donna Maria. In the testimony of the Princess's maid servant we learn that three men preceded the Prince into her apartment and were heard to say 'There he is!' Forthwith Don Carlo entered and said, 'Traitress, I shall kill you. This time you shall not escape me.' This suggests that Gesualdo's helpers, while entering first, disposed of the Duke of Andria and left the Princess to Don Carlo. In the record of Gesualdo's man-servant, Bardotti, the Prince is described as having emerged from the bedchamber, 'his hands covered with blood'. Even then he re-entered the room to inflict several additional dagger thrusts, all the while muttering 'I do not believe she is dead.'

Literary Reflections on the Murder

There is a sizeable body of contemporary literature concerned with the tragic events of October 1590. Pierre de Bourdeilles (c. 1540–1614), Seigneur de Brantôme, in his *Vies des Dames Galantes*, alludes to the popular sentiment mentioned above:

A very different fate befell Donna Maria d'Avalos in the Kingdom of Naples not long ago. She was one of the fairest princesses in the land, wife of the Prince of Venosa, and became enamoured of the Count of Andriano, himself the handsomest of princes. They were surprised by her husband (by a stratagem which I would detail, but that account thereof would take too long) who found them abed together, and had them both done to death forthwith by hired men. And on the morrow the passers-by found those two beautiful bodies stretched together on the ground before the street door, cold and stiff, for all the world to see, whereat many paused to weep over them and pity their sad condition.

There were some among the relatives of the dead Lady who took deep offence at this business, although in accordance with the laws of that country; saying that she had been done to death by knaves and servants whose hands were unworthy to shed such fair and noble blood, and that her husband should rather have given the stroke with his own hand, and on this score alone they would have had vengeance on him either by law or otherwise; but naught came of it.

That, by your leave, is a foolish and extravagant consideration, whereof I beg the judgment of our great lawyers and jurisconsults; whether 'tis more monstrous to kill by your own hand the wife you have loved, or by that of a rogue or a slave? There are many arguments for this and that opinion, which I will forbear to mention, fearing lest they should seem too light and inconsiderable besides those of such great Persons.

I have heard it said that the Viceroy, who was uncle to the lady, warned her and her lover when he heard of the stratagem afoot; but such was to be their destiny, and the conclusion of their sweet loves. This lady was daughter of Don Carlo d'Avalos, second brother of the Marquis di Pescayra, who would himself have been dead a long while past if such fortune had befallen any one of his amours.[33]

Other opinions ranged from one extreme to the other, some declaring the murdered ones to be as worthy of pity as the murderers.[34] There is, however, only one other contemporary testimony that concerns itself with any of the actual details of the murder, and that is the chronicle of Spaccini.[35] The entry in question, under the date 21 September 1613, is inspired by

[33] Pp. 20–21 of the privately published English version (1924).

[34] A case in point is the historian Ammirato (Pt. II, 174) who, speaking of Fabrizio Carafa, exclaims: 'Others have written of this unhappy youth; it is enough for me to say that his excesses in loving and being loved were the cause of his death; a death wept for by many, by all piteously felt, and only by a few not completely forgiven'. Letti, *La doppia impieccata*, and Lupis, *Disinganni del Mondo*, thus argue the question. Even Gray & Heseltine, pp. 63–74, devote a chapter to 'Carlo Gesualdo considered as a Murderer'. Cf. especially Borzelli, *Successi*, p. 203. Other manuscripts residing in the Biblioteca Nazionale di Napoli which treat the Gesualdi or the Prince of Venosa specifically in relation to these matters include: (a) *Peripetie del mondo raccolte da N. Bucca*, MS X.A.32, 'Del Principe di Venosa'; (b) *Disgratiato fine di alcune Case Napolitane di Autore Incerto, raccolte da N. Bucca*, MS X.C.20, under 'Il Principe di Venosa fini senza eredi'; and (c) *Rovina Marra, Duca della Guardia nel anno di Cristo 1633*, MS X.A.A.8, under 'Principe di Venosa, Gesualdo.'

[35] *Cronaca Modenese di Gio. Batt. Spaccini (1588–1636)*, a cura di Emilio Paolo Vicini (Modena, 1911 and 1919). Serie delle Cronache, Tomo XVI e XVII, of *Monumenti di Storia Patria delle Provencie Modenesi*. Original manuscript in the Archivio storico del Comune di Modena housed in the Biblioteca Estense.

news of Gesualdo's death. The opening shows Spaccini's tongue as one well fashioned for gossip. It begins:

There is news of the death of the Prince of Venosa, husband of Princess D. [Leonora] da Este, sister of His Excellency; who, to tell the story of his youth very briefly, took for a wife the most noble D. [Maria] d'Avalos, which made for very bad company. The lady who got married only to enjoy a husband, being unappreciated, provided herself with a cavaliere who could make her happier than her husband. But since he realized what was going on, he had made a false lock, made of wood but disguised to look like iron, which was installed in the door of his wife's room. Then he pretended to go to the country. In the meantime the Lady ordered the lover to come the following night. They retired and finally tired of the act of love; in the meantime Prince Gesualdo came incognito to the castle. He took armed men with him to the room of his wife and knocked down the door. The Duke of Andria had already got up, and Gesualdo, having with him two guns, upon entering shot the lovers. The Duke's bravery and courage availed him not in the face of the armed company, who killed him on the spot. The Prince went to the bed with a 'stilo' and began to molest his wife, who asked pardon for the sins she had committed; and she asked for time to confess. But all was in vain, and pulling the sheets over her head, she expired reciting the *Salve Regina*. And for this reason he retired to Gesualdo, and never returned to Naples, attending to music, being extremely excellent in this regard.[36]

The account continues with descriptions of his later life, to which we shall return.

[36] Spaccini, p. 41: 'È nuova della morte del principe di Venosa marito della Principessa D. (Leonora) da Este sorella di S.A.: qual per raccontar brevemente la sua vita in gioventù prese moglie D. (Maria d'Avalos) nobilissima, il che vi faceva malissima compagnia: la dama che s'era maritata per godere il marito, sendone sprezzata, si provviste di Cavaliere che la contentasse meglio del marito, ma accortosene fece alla camera della moglie fare una chiavadura di legno finta di ferro, poi finse d'andare in campagna; la dama tra tanto diede ordine all'amante venesse la seguente notte, e ritiratosi e stanchi dell'atto venereo; tra tanto il Principe Gesualdi venuto incognito, in casa, armato gente alla stanza della moglie andò, facendo gittar a terra l'uscio, il Cavalier di già s'era levato et haveva con lui due pistole, nell'entrare le sparò agli amanti, benchè non gli facesse nulla, per esser prodo et valente, con l'arme in mano, nell'istesso tempo l'amazzorono; il Principe andò al letto con uno stilo e cominciò a tempestare la moglie, qual vi domandava perdono del comesso fallo, e vi desse tanto tempo si potesse confessare, ma tutto fu indarno; ma ritiratosi il lenzuolo in testa, recitando la *Salve Regina* spirò. Il che per questo si ritirò a Gesualdo, nè mai più ritornò a Napoli, attendendo alla musica, sendo riuscito eccelentissimo.'

Other documents dealing with the tragedy also belong to the realm of literature,[37] and tell us less about factual details than the emotions engendered amongst the populace of Naples.

Toward the end of 1590 we have a letter from Don Vicenzo Caracciolo to Torquato Tasso. In this letter he brings news of the death of Donna Maria and Don Fabrizio. Caracciolo asks Tasso for his thoughts on this event in a composition of some kind, in view of the fact that all the Neapolitan poets had done as much. Tasso answers him thus:

> The lateness of the consolation of the letters from Your Excellency cannot be criticized because your courtesy continues, and I hope for the future that they will continue. Nonetheless, it pains me that they were given to me Saturday evening, after the courier had already left, so that I was unable to send back by the same means the two sonnets which I now send you on the subject of which all Naples sings and weeps. Among so many, my trifles will go less noticed; I was never so little inclined to play the poet at greater length.[38]

Rome, 11 November 1590.

Both Don Carlo and Donna Maria were well known to the poet, and the difficulty Tasso must have had in sorting out his emotions in this affair can be imagined.[39] Undoubtedly he did not wish to give offence to the Prince of Venosa, whom he praised many times in his poetry after this date as well as before.[40] And yet 'all Naples sings and weeps'. He could hardly do less than offer a sonnet or two.

In Morte di due Nobilissimi Amanti

Piangete, o Grazie, e voi piangete, o Amori,
Feri trofei di morte, e fere spogli
Di bella coppia, cui n'invidia e toglie,
E negre pompe e tenebrosi orrori.

---

[37] The short story by Anatole France entitled 'Histoire de Donna Maria d'Avalos et de Don Fabricio Duc d'Andria' (in *Le Puits de Sainte Claire*) embellishes the events. By the judgement of its author Don Carlo was not a very pleasant character: 'He was a Lord very much feared for his jealous and violent character. His enemies reproved him for his deceptive qualities and his cruelty. They called him a mastiff made up of fox and wolf and twice a stinking beast.'

[38] Modestino, p. 42. Cf. also Tasso's *Lettere*, vol. V, n. 1287.

[39] An earlier sonnet by Tasso in praise of Maria d'Avalos is 'Questa del puro ciel felice immago', *Opere*, ed. Rosini (1822), V, 23.

[40] Other poems to Gesualdo by Tasso include, besides the enormous wedding ode on the event of his second marriage, the sonnets 'Alta prole di regi eletta in terra' and 'Carlo, il vostro leon c'ha nero il vello' (an allusion to the heraldic device of the Gesualdo family, a black lion with five red lilies upon a silver field), as well as a canzone 'Muse, tu che dal cielo il nome prendi'.

Piangete, o Ninfe, e in lei versate i fiori,
Pinti d'antichi lai l'umide foglie;
E tutte voi, che le pietose doglie
Stillate a prova, e i lacrimosi odori.

Piangete, Erato e Clio, l'orribil caso'
E sparga in flebil suono amaro pianto,
In vece d'acque dolci, omai Parnaso.

Piangi, Napoli mesta, in bruno manto,
Di beltà, di virtù l'oscuro caso;
E in lutto l'armonia rivolga il canto.[41]

On the Death of Two Most Noble Lovers

Weep, O Graces, and you too bewail, O Loves, the cruel trophies of death and the cruel spoils of the beautiful couple whom death enviously takes from us, both the funeral pomps and the shadowy horrors.

Weep, O Nymphs, and strew blossoms on this couple, their moist leaves painted with old lamentations; and all you who vie with each other in distilling the piteous anguish and the scent of tears.

Weep, Erato and Clio, for this horrible event, and scatter, with mournful sound [your] bitter complaint, henceforth, instead of sweet water, [O] Parnassus.

Weep, sad Naples, clothed in mourning, for the dark fate of beauty and of virtue, and may the song address its harmony to grief.

Sullo Stesso Argomento

Alme leggiadre a maraviglia e belle,
    Che soffriste morendo aspro martirio,
    Se morte, amor, fortuna, il ciel v'uniro,
    Nulla piu vi divide e piu vi svelle;

Ma quai raggi congiunti o pur facelle,
    D'immortale splendor nel terzo giro
    Gia fiammeggiate, e del gentil desiro
    Son piu lucenti le serene stelle.

Anzi è di vostra colpa il Cielo adorno,
    Se pure è colpa in due cortesi amanti,
    Fatto piu bello all'amoroso scorno!

---

[41] Tasso, *opere*, ed. B. Maier (1963), II, 233.

Chi biasma il vostro error nei tristi pianti,
Incolpi il sol che ne condusse il giorno
Ch'in tal guisa fallir le stelle erranti.[42]

On the same subject

O souls, marvellously lovely and beautiful, who suffered in dying bitter torment, whether it was death, or love, or fortune, or heaven that united you, nothing divides or uproots you any more.

But like rays conjoined, or even torches of immortal splendour in the third circle, you already flame, and the serene stars shine more brightly because of your gentle desire.

Nay, Heaven is even adorned by your sin (if ever there is sin between two courteous lovers), it is made more lovely by your amorous disgrace!

Whoever blames you for straying among the sad sighs [of love] let him accuse the sun which brought forth the day when the wandering stars so erred.

Besides these two sonnets, Tasso wrote at least two more which are clearly on the same subject.[43] In addition, an almost endless succession of lyrics and rhymes proceeded from Neapolitan pens of the time. Some were by poets of some distinction, such as Ascanio Pignatelli, Horatio Comite,[44] and especially Giambattista Marino.[45] Many are anonymous and of little literary worth.[46]

As examples of some of the more interesting ones, the following two anonymous contributions may be cited.

[42] Ibid., p. 232.

[43] They are 'Poichè d'un cor due amiche' and 'Ferro in ferir pietoso', Ibid., pp. 232–3. Tasso's poems on the topic are treated extensively by R. Giazotto in 'Poesia del Tasso in Morte di Maria Gesualdo', in *La Rassegna Musicale*, XVIII (1948), p. 15. This has appeared since in a collection of essays, *Musurgia Nova* (1959), under the title 'Pianto e poesia del Tasso in morte di Maria Gesualdo', pp. 157–67.

[44] Modestino, pp. 74–5, cites these works complete. Gray & Heseltine, p. 39, contains a sonnet by Teodore Scipione.

[45] Cf. Borzelli, *Il Cavalier Giovan Battista Marino* (Napoli, 1898), pp. 8–9, for Marino's two sonnets on the subject, as well as Mirollo, *The Poet of the Marvelous, Giambattista Marino* (New York, 1963), p. 9, fn. 7. Gesualdo sets one of Marino's lyrics, 'O chiome erranti, o chiome', in his volume of six-voice madrigals of 1626.

[46] A host of these poems are to be found in the MS XIII.G.49 of the Biblioteca Nazionale of Naples. Many are difficult to read, and the verses take every form imaginable. In addition to the Naples manuscript and the works of Tasso there are occasional poems dealing with the subject in the seventeenth-century MS Vaticano Ottobioniano 3090 and MS 1552 of the University of Bologna. A rather more elevated example than most is a beautiful elegy 'La Morete di Chiari Amanti' by Camillo Pellegrino, the elder; cf. Borzelli, *I Capitoli ed un poemetto di Camillo Pellegrino Il Vecchio* (Naples, 1895).

Il sepolcro di Maria parla al pellegrino
Sembrami, o peregrin, udir chi sia
    Colei che sotto il sasso mio si serra,
    sappi ch'è la bellissima Maria
    D'Avalos chiara in ciel non solo in terra.

Ebbe tre sposi illustri e morte ria
    le diede il terzo e qui giace sottera.
    Esempio a'ciechi amanti or basti questo,
    che già si sa per tutto il mondo il resto.

The Tomb of Maria speaks to a pilgrim
It seems to me that I hear who she is, o wanderer, who under my stone
is sealed. Know that she is the most beautiful Maria d'Avalos re-
splendent not only on earth but in heaven.

She had three illustrious husbands; the third one gave her death.
And here she lies under the earth. Let this suffice as an example to
blind lovers. The rest is already known by all the world.

Dialogo d'un Viatore e D. Maria d'Avalos
V. Sei diva e dormi, o pur sei donna e morta?
M. Morta sono e son donna. V. Or dimme, come
      moristi? M. Uccisa giacqui ed il mio nome
      è Maria, nel morir ben poco accorta.
      Per amor spenta fui, che spesso porta
      a tal fin chi lo segue. V. E qual cognome
      è il tuo? M. D'Avalo aˡˈer che mille some
      d'onori e di trofei seco rapporta.
V. E da cui t'accendesti? M. Del più vago
      e valoroso cavalier che mai
      fosse dal Tebro, Idaspe, Battro e Tago.
V. Narra come colui nomosse. M. Ahi, Ahi
      ch'un'altra volta il fio a morte pago,
      rimembrando il suo nome e crescer fai
                    li miei tormenti e guai.
V. Dimmel se il sempiterno alto giudicio
      diminuisca il fiero tuo supplicio.
                    Il nome fu Fabricio
      che come fabbro il cor tal mi percosse,
      che mai dal suo voler più non si mosse.

V.   Di qual famiglia ei fosse
dammi noticia. M. Di Carraffi illustri
nobili e antiqui di mill'anni e lustri
                          nè mai pictori industri
o passati o moderni col pennello
potrien giovan di lui pinger più bello.
                          Fu di beltà modello,
d'Andria era duca e a me si fe'suggetto
ed io gli diedị albergo nel mio petto,
                          ed ivi tanto stretto
l'ebbi, che non curai che l'empia sorte
per tal ragion ne conducesse a morte.

V.   E come l'ore corte
fatte vi fur? M. Quando credeam secreti
goder d'amor li frutti dolci e lieti
                          ne i più sonni quieti
fummo interrotti ed io ed egli ucciso
giacqui, e lo spirto fu da noi diviso;
                          ma il mio vago Narciso
di novo Marte a l'improvviso assalto
destossi e fuor del letto usci d'un salto
                          e con il cor di smalto
e con la spada in man tanto sostenne,
che gloriosamente a morir venne.
                          Questo (ahi lassa!) mi avvenne
per troppo amar ed io ne son contenta,
che, s'alta colpa l'alma mia tormenta,
                          io vo' ch' il mondo senta
che per il mio Fabricio infamia e interno
reputò gloria e paradiso eterno.

Dialogue of a Passerby and D. Maria d'Avalos

P. Are you a goddess and asleep; or are you a woman and dead?
M. Dead I am and a woman. P. Now tell me how you died. M.
Murdered I lay and my name is Maria; of death was I little wary.
Through love was I extinguished, which often brings to such an end
whoever follows it. P. And what is your surname? M. D'Avalos the
proud which a thousand abundances of honours and of trophies carries
with it. P. And by whom were you inflamed? M. By the most comely
and most valorous knight who ever was from Tiber, Hydaspes, Bactrus,

and Tagus. P. Say what his name was. M. Ah, Ah! I suffer the pains of death anew remembering his name, and you cause my torments and woes to be augmented. P. Tell me his name and may the high eternal justice diminish your harsh punishment. M. The name was Fabrizio who like a smithy so did shape my heart that never more departed from his will. P. Tell me of what family he was. M. Of the illustrious Carafa, noble and ancient by a thousand years and lustra. Never could skilful painters, whether past or modern, with a brush be able to paint a youth more handsome. He was a model of beauty. Of Andria was he Duke and he made himself subject to me. I gave him lodging in my breast, and there so close I held him that I thought not that impious fate should lead us both to death. P. And how were the hours (of this life) made short to you? M. When we thought we in secret were enjoying the sweet and happy fruits of love, in the most quiet sleep were we interrupted, and I and he lay slain. And the spirit was from us divided, but my lovely Narciso at the sudden assault of this second Mars awoke, and with one jump from the bed did leap, and with his heart of stone and sword in hand endured so long that gloriously he came to die. This, alas, befell me because of having too much loved. And I am content with it. For if great sin torments my soul I wish the world to know that for my Fabrizio's sake I hold infamy and hell to be glory and eternal paradise.

A Painting at S. Maria delle Grazie

While Don Carlo's activities between the murder of his first wife and his second marriage in 1594 are for the most part left unrecorded, it can reasonably be assumed that he spent a considerable time at his castle in Gesualdo. During this period he undertook to build a Capuchin monastery, with a chapel entitled S. Maria delle Grazie. At the entrance to the cloister of the Capuchins the following inscription tells us that the project was brought to its completion in 1592.

> Dominos Carolus Gesualdus
> Compsae Comes III. Venusii Princeps III.
> Hos templum Virgini Matri dicatum
> Aedesque religionis domicilium
> Pietatis incitamentum
> Posteris a fundamentis erexit.
> A.D. MDXCII

We may guess that Gesualdo turned more and more to thoughts concerning his soul in the weeks and months following the horrible tragedy, and ultimately hit upon the idea of building the monastery as an act of atonement.

Of greater interest than the buildings themselves is a painting which hangs in the church of S. Maria delle Grazie to this day. The picture contains the only known portrait of the Prince himself, and is of interest for this reason alone. But beyond this the subject of the painting and the personages involved suggest one of the most mysterious aspects of Gesualdo's whole personal story. The quality of the painting is not particularly remarkable, and the artist's identity is not known. Modestino suggests Silvestro Bruno, whose works we know Gesualdo valued, having his paintings in several rooms of his palace. Others attribute it to Girolamo Imparato. In any case the style and composition of the painting are typical of *maniera* painting *c.* 1590. The large number of saints and figures piled upon the surface of the painting, the intricate and literal iconography, the elegant hands and gestures, all characterize the late phase of Mannerism.

At the top of the picture in the centre the Redeemer sits in judgement. The Prince appears in the lower left-hand corner in a kneeling position dressed in the Spanish fashion, while Saint Carlo Borromeo, Archbishop of Milan and his maternal uncle, 'attired in his Cardinal's robes, places his right arm protectively on his erring nephew's shoulder, with his face turned towards the Divine Redeemer in the act of presenting him'.[47]

The remainder of the picture is made up of a host of saintly figures, all identified by name on the canvas.[48] On the left-hand side of the picture, from top to bottom, are the Blessed Virgin Mary, St. Francis, and the Magdalene with her traditional jar of perfume, followed by Carlo Borromeo and Gesualdo himself. On the right side of the picture in the same order are to be found the Archangel Michael, St. Domenic, St. Catherine of Siena, and one other figure wearing the black habit of a Franciscan nun, who is not clearly identifiable. Modestino and Catone[49] have suggested that she is the sister of Carlo Borromeo, who after becoming a nun took the name of Sister Corona, thus explaining the crown which she wears in the picture.[50]

---

[47] Gray & Heseltine, p. 42.

[48] This is in harmony with Borromeo's own injunction (*Instructiones*, bk. i, ch. 17) for clarity in painting and the representation of figures. Blunt (*Artistic Theory*, p. 111) paraphrases it thus: 'Angels must have wings; saints must have haloes and their particular attributes, or if they are really obscure, it may even be necessary to write their names below them to avoid confusion.'

[49] Catone, *Memorie Gesualdine* (1840).

[50] It is tempting to identify this figure as the wife of the deceased Duke of Andria,

All of the figures in the picture make the same gesture. They fix their eyes on the Redeemer while pointing to the sinner, Don Carlo. The only exception is the Magdalene, who looks at Gesualdo with both arms out-stretched toward the person of Our Lord, acting as intercessor in the most personalized manner of any of the figures in the picture. The raised right hand of Christ would appear to indicate that Gesualdo's sins are absolved.

More puzzling and provocative, however, is the remaining portion of the picture. For toward the bottom of the painting we see that the canvas is engulfed in the flames of Purgatory, together with roasting likenesses of five adult figures. Two of these are being lifted out of the fires of damnation by angels: one, a woman, is to be seen toward the centre of the picture with a helping hand dipping down from above; the other, a man, is being saved by an angel who has a secure grip around his waist. Already out of the flames, but apparently rising from them, is the figure of a child with wings and with both hands pointing upward at right angles, possibly in a posture of innocence.

Is it any wonder that a personal story has been read into this portion of the picture? What a pity that the artist did not identify these figures as he did in the upper part. It is only natural to conjecture that the two adult figures in the process of being saved represent the slain lovers Donna Maria and the Duke of Andria. What could be more appropriate in a picture which clearly depicts the Prince in an act of imploring forgiveness for his sins than to confess the action for which forgiveness was being sought?

More difficult to explain is the figure of the child. Tradition in the village of Gesualdo holds that there was more to the tragic events of October 1590 than was revealed in the official inquest. It is contended that Donna Maria had given birth, in addition to the first son Don Emmanuele, to a child who would have been only a few months old at this time. Later writers have suggested that this is not improbable, since Silvia Albana in her state-ment testified that when Don Carlo came into the apartment in order to kill the adulterers, the wet-nurse had said 'for the love of God do not kill the child.' The statement, however, is not conclusive that a new infant had been born, since Emmanuele could not have been more than two or three years old, and would also surely qualify as a child about whose welfare a servant

---

whom we have noted became a nun, thus providing a kind of symmetry in the picture by placing the two wronged parties at similar positions in the picture, both in a kneeling position. This, however, would seem to be clearly impossible when it is remembered that she took her vows only on 21 November 1608, while the picture was painted much earlier. In any case she entered a Dominican Order, not Franciscan, with the name of Sister Maria Maddalena.

might be concerned. The tradition contends, moreover, that Gesualdo believed that he recognized in the presumed child certain features of the Duke of Andria. His mind having been thus poisoned, he soon reached a state of mental frenzy, had the infant 'put in a cradle in the large hall of his castle, and suspended it with cords of silk hanging down from two nails which were hammered into the arch. He then ordered that the crib be subjected to wild undulations, until through the violence of the motion, not being able to draw breath, the child rendered up its soul to God.'[51]

In spite of the widespread circulation of this tale, one thing is certain: no documents survive, official or unofficial, which record the birth of a second son to Donna Maria. The story of the *bimbocidio* has been a problem for heated conjecture in most writings on Gesualdo. Modestino was reluctant to succumb to the horrible tale:

> We would have considered this tradition to be a fable, being unable to conceive of such cruelty towards a creature innocent of harming others, were it not for a monument built by Don Carlo and alluding to this cannibalistic deed and thereby in a sense bearing witness to it. We can suppose that his soul, after such ferocious acts, must have suffered an extraordinary degree of perturbation, and that remorse must have dwelt in his heart like a worm in a corpse.[52]

Vatielli, who wrote a monograph on that portion of Gesualdo's life which is connected with the Este court, openly rejects the possibility of such a monstrous crime. In an attempt to support his conjecture, he suggests that the picture in the monastery at Gesualdo is merely a *Sacra Conversazione*, and that the over-size figure of a child is probably Don Alfonsino, born of Leonora d'Este and Gesualdo, who died at the age of five or six.[53]

In attempting to analyse this fascinating picture, however, several points may be kept in mind. Firstly, the picture has little in common with the typical *Sacra Conversazione* and indisputably adds elements of the Last

---

[51] Modestino, pp. 83–84, contains the earliest mention of the story which I have found, and he can do no more than attribute it to tradition. The passage from MS X.A.A.8, Biblioteca Nazionale di Napoli: Don Ferrante della Marra (Duca della Guardia nell'anno 1623) *Rovine di case Napolitane del suo tempo*, quoted in Borzelli, p. 217 and Gray & Heseltine, p. 49, only confuses the issue. I have read a description of this gruesome event in a record book at S. Maria delle Grazie, but it is in a modern hand. I was informed by a brother of the convent that it was merely a copy of an older and original document formerly residing in SS. Rosario, another church in Gesualdo which was begun in 1578. This account, whatever its authenticity or age, may well have been Modestino's source of information.

[52] Modestino, op. cit., p. 84.

[53] *Il Principe di Venosa e Leonora d'Este* (Milan, 1941), pp. 69–70.

Judgement.[54] Secondly, the Renaissance artist was frequently less than accurate in detailing the exact age of children, and a general confusion of proportion from infant age through five or six years is common. The unusual size and central position of the child in relation to the other figures in the picture is striking, but it is in the tradition of Renaissance classicism from the time of Masaccio and Michelangelo on, that is, the infant Hercules type.[55] With the basic theme and intent of the picture so unarguably established, it would make little sense to introduce into it either of Gesualdo's two officially documented children. The first child Emmanuele, whom he had by Maria d'Avalos, clearly does not qualify because he did not die in infancy. He grew to maturity, married, and in fact had a child of his own, though he preceded his father to the grave by a few months. Neither does the second child, Alfonsino, whom he had by his second marriage to Leonora d'Este, who died in 1600. The monastery chapel is known to have been completed eight years before, in the year 1592, within two years of the date of the murders. The shape of the canvas clearly demonstrates that it was commissioned to fit an arched niche at the altar of the chapel, and it is most likely that the niche was designed to receive this very picture.[56] It is improbable that the picture would have been painted after Gesualdo's second marriage in 1594. We may infer that the painting was commissioned for the new chapel (the subject was obviously not the product of an artist's fantasy but expressly dictated by Gesualdo himself), and completed some time between 1590 and 1594. The presence of a child of his second marriage in the picture thus seems clearly precluded.

It should finally be stressed, however, that the introduction of a third unrecorded child is not actually demanded. Is it not possible that the winged *putto* of the S. Maria delle Grazie painting is none other than Amor? Could it not be Cupid, whose invincibility had always been a central characteristic, attending on the salvation of the two lovers?

The end of the affair

Except for the rash of poems from Neapolitan pens and the legend of the

---

[54] The author is grateful to Prof. Frances Huemer for help in reading this picture. He alone, however, is responsible for the conclusions presented.

[55] Unfortunately an altar-table hides the lower portion of the picture as it is reproduced in both Gray and Vatielli. The complete picture is thus printed here for the first time. Cf. frontispiece.

[56] When the author visited the chapel in September 1962 and again in February 1970 the painting had been removed from its original position and was hanging on a side wall. Its intended and original position can be determined by the partially obstructed photo of it which appears in Gray & Heseltine facing page 40.

infanticide, which apparently was circulated only verbally, the murders soon passed into history. It can be guessed that the parties involved did their best not to fan the blaze. After the initial inquest no more was heard officially. A public proceeding would have been too clamorous and would have linked together the names of the most noble Neapolitan families: Gesualdo, Carafa, d'Avalos. In addition Alfonso Gesualdo, paternal uncle of Don Carlo, had ambitions in the church; he was already Dean of the College of Cardinals, and in only a few years was to be made Archbishop of Naples. Evidently everyone wished to suppress the scandal as quickly as possible. Gesualdo in his own interest, and to everyone else's satisfaction, had removed himself from the scene.

CHAPTER TWO

❦

Ferrara: 1594-1596

I T would be a mistake to accept the dramatic events of Gesualdo's life
before 1590 as his 'story'. Not a single composition of his had been
published before that time, and although it can be safely assumed, as we
shall see later, that he had written all the madrigals of the first two books
before his second marriage in 1594, their conservative style shows that the
most important influences lay ahead. Of these few were to be more decisive
than his association with Ferrara, to which he journeyed to take a new wife.

The Situation at Ferrara

The Este court at Ferrara had been for decades one of the most brilliant of
all Europe, and its sponsorship of the arts was legendary. The names of the
musicians alone who had seen service in this illustrious house would have
been sufficient to establish its reputation: Obrecht, Josquin, Isaac,
Willaert, Rore, Brumel, Vicentino, Isnardi, Luzzaschi, Marenzio, and Lassus.
Such names as Rore, Vicentino, and Luzzaschi are evidence of a decidedly
progressive taste, and this was true in other fields as well.[1] The presence at
Ferrara during the course of the century of Ariosto, Guarini, and Tasso,
the three great Italian literary figures of the period, meant that the Este court
stood unrivalled in the field of literature during the Cinquecento. In addition
to musicians and poets, the Estes assembled writers, philosophers, painters,
and artists of every kind.

At the time of Gesualdo's arrival at Ferrara, the incumbent ruler was
Duke Alfonso II. Alfonso had to face a curious and difficult situation. By an
agreement made years earlier it had been determined that the fief of Ferrara
would revert to the Papacy if the Duke failed to produce an heir. The situation at Ferrara had become increasingly less rosy as the first two marriages

---

[1] For a discussion of music and musicians at the Este court during the Renaissance, see
Solerti, *Ferrara e la corte Estense*, pp. 115–28, 'Musica e canto', and particularly New-
comb, *The Musica Secreta of Ferrara in the 1580's*, unpublished Ph.D. dissertation
(Princeton University, 1970).

of Alfonso II passed without producing issue. At forty-five and twice a widower, he searched for a third wife and selected Margherita Gonzaga, the daughter of the Duke of Mantua, then only sixteen years of age. As it was to turn out, this union, too, proved unfruitful.[2] In 1591 Alfonso determined that a personal confrontation with the Pope would allow him to plead his cause effectively. He had hoped to suggest that, lacking an heir, the rule of the Estes be allowed to continue through his nephew, Cesare d'Este, Gesualdo's brother-in-law-to-be and cousin to the Grand Duke of Tuscany. There was, however, another branch of the House of Este, that of the Marchese di S. Martino, which was related to the Sfondrato, the family of Pope Gregory. Alfonso was informed that should he choose to pass the dukedom to Filippo d'Este, the Marchese di S. Martino, instead of Cesare d'Este, he could easily obtain from the Holy See the new investiture necessary to insure the Este succession. Not being particularly fond of Don Cesare, the Duke agreed to this arrangement.

Alfonso arrived in Rome to present his case on 10 August complete with a retinue of 700 men and 400 horses. Everything appeared to be going smoothly and the issue seemed all but settled, when on 19 August Pope Gregory was confronted with a bull of Pius V, interestingly enough only recently renewed by Gregory himself, which expressly forbade any alienation of the fiefs of the Church.

Clearly the implications of the bull would have to be studied, and toward this end the Pope appointed a congregation of thirteen cardinals, which included as one of its principal members Cardinal Alfonso Gesualdo, Don Carlo's paternal uncle. It soon became apparent, however, that the sentiment of the congregation ran against the investiture hoped for by Duke Alfonso. The Pope was greatly disturbed by the conflict which had arisen, but, though plagued increasingly with illness during the negotiations, refused to suspend the proceedings.

Duke Alfonso now began to make it known that he was willing to increase his tribute substantially. Bolstered by such promises, the Pope felt it appropriate to put the question to the congregation of cardinals once more: 'whether the bull of Pius V applied to a Papal disposition of a fief that had not already fallen vacant, supposing that an obvious advantage to the Church resulted therefrom.'[3] Opinion was divided, and Cardinal Gesualdo was one

---

[2] Some families, it might be added, were not willing to leave so much to chance. A contemporary example of the extreme lengths to which noble houses were known to have gone is seen in the figure of Vincenzo Gonzaga of the ruling house of Mantua— the house which provided Duke Alfonso with his last wife. Cf. M. Bellonci, *I segreti dei Gonzaga* (Firenze, 1947); also Boulting, *Tasso*, pp. 252–3.

[3] Pastor, *The History of the Popes*, XXII, p. 382.

of the figures most prominently against any such disposition. Little did he realize how such a stand might ultimately affect his own house in generations to come.

In spite of the generally unfavourable reaction, Gregory XIV, at a consistory held on 13 September 1591, declared that the bull of Pius V did not affect the current question facing Ferrara, and without further ado had a consistorial decree drawn up to such an effect. However, opposition continued on the part of the cardinals, who resented the fact that their opinions had been shunted aside through the Papal issue of a *motu proprio* which did not require their subscription. Soon, after further bitter exchanges on the matter, the Pope's health took a sudden turn for the worse. He summoned the cardinals to his deathbed, addressing 'a touching discourse to them in Italian. . . . During these words no eye remained dry. Cardinals Gesualdo, Altemps, Pelevé, Radziwill and Aldobrandini were especially moved.'[4] Gesualdo, as Dean of the Sacred College of Cardinals, led the others in replying to the Papal advices, assuring the dying Pontiff of their eternal loyalties. Strangely, however, on the same day, 4 October, a Papal constitution was published confirming the fact that the Papal bull of Pope Pius V did indeed apply to the present question of Ferrara, and served as a guarantee against the alienation of church property in all cases.

This, as it turned out, was the end of the matter. But Alfonso still had six more years to live, and it can be guessed that, having seen the inner workings of the Curia, he resolved not to abandon his attempts to secure succession, for he knew that 'the death of a pope, the change of an alliance, a fortunate marriage, or a substantial grant of money always offered an ultimate escape.'[5] The Dean of the College of Cardinals, Alfonso Gesualdo, had been one of the major stumbling blocks in this last attempt to revise the ruling regarding Ferrara. Why not put out feelers as to the possibility of a marriage between this cardinal's nephew, Don Carlo Gesualdo, recently made available as a prospective husband through the death of his first wife, and a cousin of the Duke's, Eleonora d'Este?[6] The fact that Don Carlo now held the title of Prince of Venosa as a result of his father's death in 1591 further enhanced his qualifications. The stage was set for the execution of such a contract.

The obvious objection to Gesualdo's acceptability in our minds today, namely his reputation as a murderer, was far less a handicap to him than we

[4] Ibid., pp. 384–5.

[5] John Walker, *Bellini and Titian at Ferrara*, p. 75.

[6] Eleanora was the sister of Don Cesare who had earlier been denied the Este succession by Rome.

might imagine. The Duke himself was known to have indulged in such activities, having killed, amongst others, a cavalier engaged in an illicit affair with his sister. And the Duke's unemotional attitude regarding murder may be seen in a letter by him to his envoy about the poet Tasso, who was already in the throes of madness and suffering from delusions of hostility on the part of Alfonso:

> With regard to Tasso, concerning whom you wrote, it is our will that you should tell him frankly that we are willing to receive him if he is minded to return. But first he should be made sensible that he is full of melancholy whims, and that those suspicions of malice and persecution are pure delusion. This he ought to be aware of from one out of many evidences. For he has a strange notion that we wish to put him to death, though we have always been gracious to him and made much of him; and he ought to know that if such had been our design nothing would have been easier than to effect it.[7]

Gesualdo's record in this respect could be considered to reveal, if anything, only a minor blemish.

The Second Marriage

Little more than a year after Alfonso's return from Rome negotiations relating to a marriage between Don Carlo Gesualdo and Donna Leonora d'Este were under way. While the first transactions of which we are aware were initiated by Cardinal Alfonso Gesualdo, Carlo's uncle, and Teofilo Forni, there is good reason to believe that Alfonso II may have encouraged such an approach to the Ferrara court. There are indications that the proceedings are moving smoothly in a letter of 2 October 1592 from Cardinal Alfonso to the Bishop of Modena, whom he asks to aid Forni in his overtures.[8]

The marriage contract was signed on 20 March 1593.[9] Don Cesare d'Este, Leonora's brother, therein promises the hand of his sister in marriage, her father Alfonso having died on 1 November 1587. The rites of matrimony of the Catholic church are prescribed, and Don Cesare pledges to the future

---

[7] Boulting, *Tasso*, p. 221.

[8] Santi, 'La storia della *Secchia rapita*', in *Memorie della Regia Accademia di Scienze*, Ser. III, vol. IX, p. 319, fn. 2. Vatielli, *Il Principe di Venosa e Leonora d'Este*, p. 17, gives the name Siliprindi for the Bishop; Santi gives Silingardi.

[9] Preserved in Archivio di Stato, Modena, b. 376, fasc. 58/2011: 'Contratto di matrimonio di Eleanora col Principe di Venosa in data 1593: copia semp., con unita lettera di Cesara di lei fratello.'

2(a) *Don Carlo. A detail of the painting in the chapel of Santa Maria delle Grazie, Gesualdo.*

(b) *Donna Maria. A detail of the painting of the Carafa family in the church of San Domenico Maggiore, Naples.*

(c) *The Palazzo di San Severo, Naples, where the murder took place.*

spouse a dowry of 50,000 scudi. As for the Prince of Venosa, he pledges to sustain and care for his wife in his house and to make a donation to the first born of 350,000 ducats in the monies of the King of Naples.[10] He also promises to furnish his wife with an annual allowance of 600 ducats in the coin of the realm.

In a letter to the Duchessa di Ferrara dated 28 April 1593, the Prince presents himself as Leonora's prospective husband:

> Since through the grace of God and through the favour of the Duke's Highness my marriage with Donna Eleonora, my Lady, has been so kindly and graciously arranged, wherefore I am become now a servant bound with double bonds to all of this most Serene House, I have judged it my duty to present myself as such, and to do reverence to Your Highness with the present letter until such time as it be permitted me to do it in person. I beseech you that you deign to give me that place in your country which the devotion and reverence with which I am prepared to serve and revere forever merit, in order that the knowledge that this particular request also has been granted may make even happier in my mind the conclusion of this most honourable family union. And I cordially kiss the hands of Your Highness praying God that he concede perfect happiness to you.[11]
>
> Venosa, 28 April 1593
> The most affectionate servant
> of Your Highness who kisses
> your hands,
> The Prince of Venosa

While it seems logical to assume that Gesualdo was not averse to the idea of making a liaison with the Estes, in the light of his recent experiences the idea of marriage *per se* undoubtedly held less attraction for him. Nevertheless, Carlo's solicitation of help in these matters from his uncle, Cardinal

---

[10] Equicola, *Genealogia delli Signori prencipi in Ferrara*, Biblioteca Communale Ariostea, Ferrara, MS Cl. II, n. 349: 'A di 20. di marzo Don Carlo Gesualdo Prencipe di Venosa promesse pigliar per sposa la Sna. Donna Leonora che fu figlia del Sr. Don Alfonso da Este con dotte de v:di M/50 et promesse assignare v:di M/350 al primogenito nascete investendoli in tanti bene stabili nel Regno di Napoli.'

Da Monte, *Storia di Ferrara dalle origini al 1643*, 3 vols., Libro Secondo: *Delle cose di Ferrara al tempo dei Duchi*, Biblioteca Estense, Modena, MSS Q.4, 6–8 (*olim* VIII.H.1–3) and W.6, 17–19 (*olim* VIII.A.17–19); vol. II, p. 219 reads: 'A di 20 marzo (1593) D. Leonora da Este, sorella di Don Cesare, fu promessa per moglie a D. Carlo Gesualdo principe di Venosa con dote di scudi cinquentamilla.'

[11] Original Italian in Vatielli, p. 18. This letter is one of a large number of letters of Gesualdo to be found in the Archivio di Stato, Modena. Most are in the hand of a secretary and consist of the routine expressions of politeness and courtesy demanded of the nobility.

Alfonso, discloses that he was interested in making the best impression possible. In view of Duke Alfonso's plight in relation to an unrelenting Rome, however, it ultimately resolves to a question of who was chasing whom. In any event Duke Alfonso's willingness to conclude the marriage for political reasons suggests that final negotiations were easily arranged.

We have very little information regarding Donna Leonora before her marriage to Gesualdo, and Don Carlo probably was equally ignorant of her before his trip to Ferrara for the ceremony. It is unlikely that they had ever met in person, but it is not difficult to understand Gesualdo's enthusiasm for concluding an alliance with the House of Este. Its brilliance in matters which most concerned the Prince, the arts, was well known. What composer would not have been excited at the prospect of establishing connections at a court where he could exchange ideas with the best professionals of the day, not only in Ferrara but in nearby Mantua and Venice. Naples by comparison, its own activity and greater proximity to Rome notwithstanding, must have seemed to Gesualdo somewhat remote from the centre of progressive musical activity. He was undoubtedly willing to take his chances with a new bride.

Leonora, his bride-to-be, was the daughter of Don Alfonso, Marchese di Montecchio, uncle of Duke Alfonso II and brother of Duke Alfonso I.[12] Alfonso, Leonora's father, married Giulia della Rovere, daughter of Francesco Maria, Duke of Urbino, in 1549. Three children issued from this marriage: Alfonsino, who married Marfisa d'Este; Cesare, who married Virginia de Medici; and Leonora herself. The generally reliable Ferrarese chronicler, Merenda, records that 'On the night of 23 November 1561, a little girl was born to the most Illustrious Signor Don Alfonso d'Este, uncle of our Duke, who was named Leonora.'[13] Thus she and Gesualdo were virtually identical in age.[14]

Upon the death of his first wife Alfonso took a young widow, Violante Segni,[15] as mistress, and by her had two illegitimate offspring, Ippolita and Alessandro, who was later made a Cardinal by Pope Clement VIII. In 1583 Alfonso legalized his union with Violante by marrying her. He died four

12 The multiple use of the name Alfonso among such close relatives has been the cause of misunderstanding with some writers.

13 Merenda, *Memorie istoriche di Ferrara*, Biblioteca Estense MS H.3.3. (*olim* IX.D.2), p. 152: 'L'anno 1561 il di 23 di novembre la notte deguente nacque una zitella all'Ill. sig. Don Alfonso d'Este, zio del nostro sig. Duca, qual fu chiamata Leonora.'

14 There has been some dispute as to Donna Leonora's age. Litta, *Famiglie celebri italiane* (1819), and other writers have listed her birthdate as 1551, but there seems to be no contemporary evidence for this. Cf. also *Archivio segreto Estense*, Sezione 'Casa e Stato', Inventario (1953).

15 Signa is sometimes given.

years later on 1 November 1587, Violante not until 1609. Of her brothers Leonora was to become particularly fond of Cesare, who after Duke Alfonso II's death became Duke of Modena, and Alessandro, who in later years of crisis was virtually Leonora's only consolation.

There are a few contemporary descriptions of Leonora, but for the most part they are composed of the usual generalities and do not allow us to draw a clear picture of her. Annibale Romei in his *Discorsi* refers to 'this most gracious maiden, as one who is beyond measure inclined towards virtue and desirous of learning',[16] and we find another highly laudatory description of the Princess written by Ridolfo Arlotti from Modena to Baldassare in October 1608: 'The Princess of Venosa is the Princess of Venosa, and let that be enough; since to be the Princess is to be endowed with every virtue, excellence, and glory; which, if I were to try to describe their greatness and number, it would be like trying to measure the waters of the ocean or count its grains of sand.'[17]

In February 1594 Don Carlo Gesualdo, Prince of Venosa, set out for Ferrara to attend his second marriage. The diarist Guarini[18] relates that the cortege was quite grand and comprised 300 pieces of luggage carried by twenty-four mules. We know also that Gesualdo was accompanied by two musicians from his camerata: Fabrizio Filomarino, lutenist, and Scipione Stella, composer and instrumentalist. The latter had been an organist for a period of ten years at the Annunziata in Naples prior to joining Gesualdo's Court in 1593. In Ferrara he was to be responsible for editing Gesualdo's first two books of madrigals and in 1595 brought out a book of his own motets. Most important of all the personages in his retinue was Count Alfonso Fontanelli, who had been sent by the Duke to escort Gesualdo personally on the final portion of the journey, as well as to keep the Duke posted as to the progress of their travels and probable time of arrival. Fontanelli had been an Este diplomat for years and was also a man of letters and a composer of some distinction. Craft sums up his qualifications well: 'He had been sent as the Duke's equerry to accompany Gesualdo and report

---

[16] The entire *Discorsi* is to be found reprinted in Solerti, *Ferrara e la corte Estense*; see p. 180. fn. 1.

[17] Letter found in Biblioteca Estense, MS G.1.6. (*olim* IX.F.17), pp. 8v–9r: 'La Sig. Principessa di Venosa è la Sig. Principessa di Venosa, e ciò basti, poscia che in conseguenza ne viene che in lei tutte le virtù, tutte le gratie, tutti i meriti, e tutte le glorie s'accogliano, della quali s'io m'affatticassi, per descrivere la grandezza e il numero, sarebbe un affaticarmi per misurar l'acqua e contar le arene del mare.'

[18] Cf. Vatielli, p. 19. Guarini, *Diario di tutte le cose accadute nella nobilissima città di Ferrara*, vol. 1, Biblioteca Estense MS H.2.16 (*olim* VIII.B.8), pp. 267–8, 273, also comments upon the marriage festivities, but largely duplicates the events chronicled in Merenda and Equicola.

on him. He was well qualified to do this. As a nobleman he could meet the Prince on a near social level, as a diplomat he could be trusted to manage him, and as a lettered man his description of the awesome quarry would be lively if perhaps inexact. More important than any of these, from our point of view, he would be able to appraise Gesualdo's music according to the lights of the Ferrara court.'[19]

Fontanelli did not accompany Gesualdo the entire distance from Gesualdo to Ferrara but only from Argenta on, hardly more than a day's journey from Ferrara. Two of Fontanelli's communications to the Duke on 15 February from Argenta express his fear that Gesualdo might be coming by a different route than had been advised.[20] Dispatches of 15–17 February confirm that everything is in a state of suspense pending Gesualdo's arrival. Finally a letter of the 18th signals the Prince's appearance.[21] Ambagious as well as somewhat prolix it is nevertheless extremely informative, and undoubtedly satisfied the Duke's initial curiosity about the prospective new member of the family.

> I met the Prince at the ferry, who arrived in a coach accompanied only
> by Don Cesare Caracciolo, the Count of Saponara following in a litter.
> Here, having offered him an open barge as a defence against the sun

---

[19] Robert Craft, 'A Journey with Gesualdo.' Columbia Record ML 5341/MS 6048.

[20] 'My fear that he might go by way of Bologna may appear unfounded to you, but I heard that Cardinal Gesualdo wrote to the Bishop of Modena to get in touch with the Prince before he arrives in Ferrara. It seemed that this meeting might well take place in Bologna. . . .'

[21] Thirteen of Fontanelli's letters have been preserved in the Archivio di Stato, Modena, which give us details not only for the end of the trip to Ferrara but also for the journey back to Gesualdo in May–June, a stay with Gesualdo in the South through the summer, and his return to the Este court in the Fall. The most important parts of these are incorporated into the following discussion. The complete list of letters is as follows: 15 February 1594, Argenta; 15 February, Argenta; 17 February, Argenta; 18 February, Argenta; 19 February, Argenta; 21 May, Venice; 23 May, Venice; 14 June, Gesualdo; 25 June, Gesualdo; 9 September, Naples; 16 September, Naples; 23 September, Naples; 9 October, Gesualdo. All except the two letters from Venice are located in *Dispacci da Napoli*, Busta no. 11 (# 2769/65); these two are in *Dispacci da Venezia*, Busta no. 88 (# 3345/72). After the final draft of this book was completed Anthony Newcomb's 'Carlo Gesualdo and a Musical Correspondence of 1594' appeared in *MQ* (October 1968), pp. 409–36. This article encouraged me to reconsider several points in my own transcriptions of these letters, all of which had originally been undertaken in conjunction with an archivist at the Archivio di Stato in Modena. Newcomb considers only those letters which deal specifically with music, but his treatment is especially thorough and inspires confidence. In several instances I was happy to discover that he corroborated exceptions which I had independently taken to Vatielli's transcriptions. The Italian text of the complete Fontanelli correspondence appears in Nino Pirrotta's "Gesualdo, Ferrara e Venezia" in *Studi sul teatro veneto fra Rinascimento ed età barocca* (Firenze, 1971), pp. 305–19.

while travelling along the Po, His Excellency was pleased to come into the boat with the above-mentioned two gentlemen as far as Argenta; tomorrow we will travel the same way as far as Gaibana which, according to many reports, we can reach. On leaving the boat he decided to get into a carriage since he wanted to escape the mud so as not to have to change his clothes. He has it in mind to beseech Your Highness most warmly that tomorrow evening you will permit him to see Signora Donna Leonora. In this he shows himself extremely Neapolitan. He thinks of arriving at twenty-three o'clock, but I doubt this because he does not stir from his bed until extremely late. With respect to this I shall not send another courier. . . . Suffice it to say that we will come by boat as far as Gaibana, and then we shall go in the direction of the road which Orazio reports to be good for this purpose.

The Prince, although at first view he does not have the presence of the personage he is, becomes little by little more agreeable, and for my part I am sufficiently satisfied of his appearance. I have not been able to see his figure since he wears an overcoat as long as a nightgown; but I think that tomorrow he will be more gaily dressed. He talks a great deal and gives no sign, except in his portrait, of being a melancholy man. He discourses on hunting and music and declares himself an authority on both of them. Of hunting he did not enlarge very much since he did not find much reaction from me, but about music he spoke at such length that I have not heard so much in a whole year. He makes open profession of it and shows his works in score to everybody in order to induce them to marvel at his art.[22] He has with him two sets of music books in five parts, all his own works, but he says that he only has four people who can sing for which reason he will be forced to take the fifth part himself, although it seems that he is confident that Rinaldo will enter into the singing and do well.[23]

He says that he has abandoned his first style and has set himself to the imitation of Luzzasco, a man whom he greatly admires and

[22] Cf. Newcomb, op. cit., p. 413, who suggested the sense of this sentence. It is an interesting point in that it indicates that Gesualdo carried two versions of his madrigal books with him, one primarily intended for performance use, the other for study purposes. This is especially intriguing in light of the score edition which was ultimately prepared and published of all of Gesualdo's madrigals. Could it be that Molinaro, the editor of this 1613 edition, was privy to Gesualdo's own scores and that the irregular barrings there reflect Gesualdo's personal taste? Cf. the discussion on pp. 177–8 of this book.

[23] Probably Rinaldo dall'Arpa.

praises, although he says that not all of Luzzasco's madrigals are equally well written, as he claims to wish to point out to Luzzasco himself. This evening after supper he sent for a cembalo so that I could hear Scipione Stella[24] and so that he could play on it himself along with the guitar, of which he has a very high regard. But in all Argenta we could not find a cembalo for which reason, so as not to pass an evening without music, he played the lute for an hour and a half. Here perhaps Your Highness would not be displeased if I were to give my opinion, but I would prefer, with your leave, to suspend my judgement until more refined ears have given theirs. It is obvious that his art is infinite, but it is full of attitudes, and moves in an extraordinary way. However, everything is a matter of taste. This Prince then has himself served in a very grand way and with some little Spanish ceremonies, for example, having the lighted torch brought in before the cup, covering his plate while he drinks, and similar things.

So much and no more shall I say for the time being to Your Highness, reserving to relate in person the most important discourses made to me by His Excellency. The Count of Saponara is a person of handsome figure, appears to have been a great *torneador a piedi*, and is highly esteemed by the Prince. I do not believe that the Count is interested in any considerations other than those which pertain to the Prince, nor has he any pretensions at all with respect to his title. Signor Don Cesare Caracciolo is a young lad also esteemed by the Prince, but not on an equal to the Count. Stella[24] is a young man who, says the Prince, intends to compose music other than motets and is a most valiant person.[25]

Argenta   Your most faithful and devoted
18 February 1594   servant,
                                                       Alfonso Fontanelli

Fontanelli was a good reporter, and in this letter he provides us with the most intimate glimpse of the Prince that has come down to us. Although at first he appears to be nothing special to look at, he 'becomes little by little more agreeable.' From what we learn of the Prince's appearance in the only portrait we possess, he was not a particularly handsome man. If

[24] Vatielli, op. cit., p. 22, transcribes 'S. Palla' in both places. The original letter, however, clearly reads 'Scipione Stella' in the first instance; in the second 'lo Stella' is especially convincing in view of his forthcoming motet collection of 1595.

[25] This translation follows that made by Aldous Huxley for Columbia Record ML 5341. A number of minor alterations, however, have been made in accordance with the original in the Archivio di Stato, Modena.

we would believe the picture, Gesualdo was a person of sallow complexion, inordinately long fingers (appropriate to a virtuoso on the lute), small mouth, and a tall, narrow face. These physical features are however reminiscent of the mysteriously elongated shapes of Mannerist painting from Parmigianino to El Greco, and may be attributable more to an artistic style than to any genuine representation of the Prince.

'I have not been able to see his figure because he wears an overcoat as long as a nightgown,' says Fontanelli, and neither do we see the figure, because of the kneeling posture, in the painting. 'He talks a great deal.' We need hardly wonder that Gesualdo, having been more or less out of circulation for the last few years, was more than willing to talk with a gentleman of culture; but this does not entirely explain his loquaciousness. He was probably equally anxious to display his considerable musical knowledge. The anticipation of meeting Luzzaschi, whom he admired, in Ferrara also must have inspired Gesualdo to speak of him at length to Fontanelli, to ask questions about him, and to reveal his own inclinations as a composer. His willingness to discuss hunting is understandable in view of his love for the *caccia* and the fine breed of horses which he raised. Fontanelli was to learn more of this when he returned to Gesualdo with the Prince a few months later.

We are not sure of Fontanelli's personal sentiments about Gesualdo's music. 'It is full of attitudes, and moves in an extraordinary way.' This is safe enough; it cautions to be on the lookout for something not run-of-the-mill, and yet does not commit the observer to a critical evaluation. As to the discussion of music, Fontanelli apparently listened in disbelief. He had not heard so much talk on music, even in Ferrara, in a year! Moreover, Gesualdo's penchant for music was so strong that he could not think of spending an evening without it, indicating its paramount position in the Prince's life.[26]

Another letter written the same day reads:

It is 4:30 p.m. and the Prince is not yet dressed, but I think that by 5 p.m. we shall be in the boat, which we shall not leave before Gaibana, as I have written you, and there they intend to get into a coach. The Count of Saponara said to me that if someone wishes to meet the Prince, he should do so with a coach. But as he said this in passing, I pretended

---

[26] This is borne out in a letter of Emilio de' Cavalieri dated 19 December 1593, when Gesualdo was passing through Rome: 'The Prince of Venosa, who would like to do nothing but sing and play music, today forced me to visit with him and kept me for seven hours. After this, I believe I shall hear no music for two months.' Cf. Newcomb op. cit., p: 411, fn. 3.

not to understand in order not to introduce anything that might displease Your Highness.

I wrote at length tonight with the intention of not writing again, but if the messenger had had an accident, it would not have been right that Your Highness be without news. I doubt that we shall get to Ferrara without torches, but I cannot be sure.

Marriage Festivities and Court Life

Gesualdo and his party arrived in Gaibana six miles south of Ferrara on the afternoon of the 19th of February. Here he was met by the nobility of the city and a horse guard sent ahead by Duke Alfonso. Arriving at the gates of the city Gesualdo and his train were received royally by the Duke 'con grandissimo honore' and escorted to the castle.

Ferrara was probably unlike anything Gesualdo had ever seen. Montaigne, who had visited it in 1580, was ecstatic not only about the splendour of the palaces but also and especially the broad, well-planned streets, and the abundant parks. Tasso described Ferrara as 'one of the noblest cities in Italy and adorned with many noble families and rich with many ornaments, and perhaps as much through art as through nature.'[27] Perhaps the ultimate adornments were the gardens and the sumptuous suburban villas such as Belvedere, Castellina, and Mesola, where great feasts were frequently celebrated, and where *concerti, rappresentazioni,* and *balli* in honour of illustrious guests and princes were held. Ferrara's growth during the sixteenth century had been carefully planned. This was due in large measure to the influence and genius of one Biagio Rossetti, called by some the first city planner, a noted architect who lived in Ferrara in the earlier part of the century, and whose vision is just today again being taken into account.[28]

Gesualdo's entrance into the city inaugurated a series of festivities in connection with the forthcoming wedding. Duke Alfonso had made elaborate preparations for this, one of the last large-scale celebrations before the Duchy of Ferrara passed into memory. The wedding formed a fitting climax to a succession of such festivities sponsored by the Este court over the centuries. The events of these days are chronicled in detail in two sources. Equicola, whom we have met before, provides the shorter account.[29]

[27] *I dialoghi di T. Tasso,* vol. II, a cura di C. Guasti (Firenze, 1858–9).

[28] See Bruno Zeri, *Biagio Rossetti* (Torino, 1960). Not to be confused with a Veronese composer of the same name who lived to the middle of the sixteenth century.

[29] MS Cl. II, n. 349, in the Biblioteca Civica, Ferrara. Original Italian text, with minor omissions, quoted in Torri, 'Nei parentali (1614–1914) di Felice Anerio e di Carlo Gesualdo, Principe di Venosa,' in *Rivista musicale italiana,* XXI (1914), p. 505. Same parts as included in Torri translated in Gray, *Contingencies,* pp. 189–90. On p. 502

The Prince of Venosa, Carlo Gesualdo by name, arrived in Ferrara on 19 February 1595, in order to wed the most illustrious Donna Leonora d'Este, and took up residence at the Court with a retinue of about one hundred and fifty persons. The wedding took place on the 21st of the 2nd month, in the presence of the Este family only, in the chamber of our Most Serene Duchess with the Most Reverend Bishop of Ferrara officiating.[30]

On the 20th His Serene Highness the Duke gave a banquet for a hundred noble gentlewomen together with a few noble gentlemen. There were twenty-three courses, and ten small tables were laid out together with a large one for the Duke and the most eminent ladies, to whom were added the bride and bridegroom. After the banquet the Duke arranged a display of jousting, in open field above the great hall where ball-games were played, in which twenty-one knights on horseback and another thirty-one on foot took part, with magnificent crested helmets and rare feats of skill.

On the night of the 21st His Highness had a ballet performed in the great hall, with beautiful music, by twelve noble gentlewomen, and six of these ladies were dressed in costumes which, though made of pasteboard, had the appearance of brightly burnished metal.

On the 22nd the Lord Don Cesare d'Este gave a sumptuous banquet at which were present the Duke and Duchess, the bride and the bridegroom, and the principal nobility of the city. The table was arranged in the form of a T.

A more elaborate and complete account is recorded by Merenda:[31]

---

of the Torri article, a picture, supposedly of Don Carlo Gesualdo, is reproduced. This painting, an oil portrait by T. Manzini dated 1875 and now hanging in the R. Conservatorio di musica in Naples, was used by Columbia Records (ML 5234) as an album cover for a disc devoted to his works. Its date and the fact that it bears no resemblance to the portrait of S. Maria delle grazie in Gesualdo make it of dubious value.

[30] Da Monte, *Storia di Ferrara*, Biblioteca Estense MS Q.4.6–8 (*olim* VIII.H. 1–3) II, pp. 219–20, also confirms the date and place of the wedding: 'A di 21 febraro Don Carlo Gesualdo sposo D. Leonora d'Este nella camera della Duchessa colli intervento di Mons. Fontana vescovo di Ferrara e di tutta la case Estense.'

[31] Merenda, *Memorie istoriche di Ferrara*, Biblioteca Estense MS H.3.3. (*olim* IX.D.2). 'L'anno 1594, volendo Sua Altezza honorare le nozze della signora Donna Leonora d'Est figliola del quondam signore Don Alfonso d'Est zio del nostro Serenissimo, le quali nozze furono concluse l'anno 1593, con il Prencipe di Venosa Napolitano di Casa Gesualdi: cominciò à fabricare nella sala grande sopra la cantina (adi 26 di Genaro) facendo in detta Sala far alzar palchi per ogni banda intorno à detta sala. e questi palchi erano di legname.

In the year 1594, His Highness wishing to honour the forthcoming marriage of Donna Leonora d'Este, daughter of the late Sig. Don Alfonso d'Este, uncle of our most esteemed Duke—a marriage which had been contracted in 1593 with the Prince of Venosa, Neapolitan of the House of Gesualdo—they started to build in the big hall above the cantina on the 26th of January a series of stands constructed on each side of the hall, and these were made out of wood. At the same time they had laid a pavement of stones over and corresponding in cut to the other pavement of said hall which is made out of large squares. And over the said pavement he had put a quantity of sand from one side to the other in order that the horses which had to run on it would not hurt themselves.

Sunday night, which was the 20th of February, a ball took place until 11 p.m., when they went to the Hall of the Giants for dinner where there was a table about twelve feet long at which the Princes, and the gentlemen of the House of Este ate, and in said hall there were ten round tables with ten seats, each filled with ladies.

While they were eating the *combatenti* were preparing to fight in open field in the hall. As soon as the Princes and cavaliers had finished eating, they retired to the big hall; and at the end of the hall toward San Domenico there were three cavaliers, masters of the joust. One was His Most Illustrious Highness Don Cesare d'Este, the others Sig. Ippolito Bentivoglio, Marchese di Gualt'ero, and Sig. Giulio di Tiene, Marchese di Scandiano. At the other end of the hall were all the *combatenti*. All the ladies sat with our Serenissima [the Duchess] and the

---

Fece fare parimente in detta Sala una selciata di pietre acconcie in taglio sopra l'altra selciata di detta Sala la quale è di quadri grandi, e sopra la detta selciata vi fece porre quantita di sabbia da un capo all'altro di detta Sala acciò li cavalli che vi dovevano correre sopra non si facessero male correndo.

La domenica sera poi che fù il vigesimo giorno di febraro vi ballò sino alle cinque hore di notte poi vi andò nella sala de Giganti à cena dove era una tavola longa circa piedi dodici alla qual tavola mangiarno Li Prencipi e Signori della Casa d'Est, et in detta sala eravi dieci tavolini tondi con dieci poste per ciascheduno tutti pieni di Gentildonne.

Mentre che si cenava li signori combatenti si preparavano al Combattere à campo aperto nella sala sudetta.

Cenato poi ch'hebbero Li Prencipi e signori si ritirorono nella sala grande, e dal capo della sala verso San Domenico stavano li tre cavalieri mantenitori della giostra. L'uno era l'Illustrissimo signore Don Cesare d'Est: et il signore Ippolito Bentivogli marchese di Gualtiero: l'altro il signore Giulio d'Ateneo Marchese di Scandiano.

Dall' altro capo stavano tutti li combatenti. Dipoi tutte le dame erano con la nostra Serenissima, e la signora sposa insieme, quale tutte erano sopra li palchi detti di sopra con molto altro popolo.

lady bride in the stands together with many other people.

They began to fight like this: each cavalier broke two *picche* on foot against the *mantenitore* [the master of the joust]; then they came forward fencing, dealing one another a considerable number of blows. After that they mounted their horses and broke a lance running toward one another.

When they had finished all of these acts of gallantry, they retired, one part on one side, another part on the other, hammering one another as they did so with a *piceda,* which they broke in fighting. The tournament finished in this way. Then there followed a ball with the ladies and gentlemen dancing together. And then the festivities were finished, and it was day, and they all retired, sleeping until 1 p.m.

The Prince at this hour sent for the Most Reverend Bishop of Ferrara, and without pomp and ceremony Sig. Donna Leonora d'Este and Sig. Don Carlo Gesualdo, Prince of Venosa, were married.

The ceremony took place in the *capelletta* of the Duchess of Ferrara in her rooms.

On this day, towards evening and after dinner, they started the preparations for the ballets in the same hall where the party had taken place in the evening. Before this they had dismantled the floor made of superimposed paving-stones leaving the squared floor underneath in perfect condition.

At sundown they began to gather in the said room, and when they were assembled they began to dance, and they danced until midnight.

Si cominciò à combattere in questo modo: Ogni cavaliere rompeva due picche à piedi contro il Mantenitore, e poi venivano al stocco, e vi davano molti colpi: di poi montavano à cavallo, e rompevano una lancia à rincontro l'uno dell' altro.

Finito poi tutti li cavallieri di far queste prodezze si ritirorno parte da una banda, e parte dall'altra cominciando à martellarsi adosso con una piceda, e rotta la piceda alli stocchi, e con questo si finì il torneo, e poi ballorno un ballo con le dame, e signori, e poi fù finita la festa ch'era giorno, e v'andorono tutti à riposare sino alle hore dicinone.

Il signore Duca à quest'hora sudetta mandò à chiamare il Reverendissimo di Ferrara, e senza pompa e cerimonie si sposò la signora Donna Leonora d'Est col signore Don Carlo Gesualdi prencipe di Venosa.

Il contrato si diede nella *Capelletta* della Serenissima di Ferrara alle sue stanze.

Il giorno doppo desinare verso la sera si comminciò à prepararsi per fare li baletti nella stessa sala dove era stata fatta la festa la sera; avanti di che era di gia stata disfatta la selciata fatta di pietre poste in taglio come è detto di sopra e nitata, e polita benissimo, restando pollitissima la sua prima selciata di quadri.

Alle 24 hore poi si cominciorno à ridurre in detta sala; e ridotti cominciorno à ballare, e ballorno sino alle sei hore della notte. Parti poi lo sposo e la sposa con bella comitiva di gentilhuomini e gentildonne et andorono à cenare à casa della sposa.

Then the bride and bridegroom, together with the gentlemen and ladies, went to eat at the bride's house.

On the 22nd of February, the day of the Carnival, they played a fine game of quintain in the square, where all these gentlemen were present. And when it was finished, all the court and the cavalieri who played went to the bride's house for dinner where a wonderful party took place with much magnificent display.

The bridegroom never returned to stay in the castle where he first lived, for when he and his retinue came to Ferrara, they lodged with the Duke until his marriage. He came to Ferrara on the 19th of February.

The first Sunday of Lent the Duke ordered all the nobility to parade in *La Giovecca*, and through the city.

On the third of March, Thursday, they went to hear the music of the nuns of San Silvestro; the following day they also went to hear the nuns of San Vito, both truly worthy of being heard.

The following Sunday in the evening they went to *La Giovecca* in the house of the dalla Pena family to hear a pastorale, which was composed by a man from Ferrara of the Bellay family.

On Monday after lunch they went to Belriguardo and remained there until Thursday. On Sunday, the 13th of March, the *concerto grande* performed in the hall of the new rooms, all the gentlemen being present.

The Prince of Venosa by now was with his bride in the house of the Most Illustrious Don Cesare d'Este in the Palazzo di Diamanti, and this Most Excellent Don Cesare was the brother of the bride. His household

---

Alli 22 di febraro il di' di Carnevale fù fatta una bellissima quintanata in piazza dove erano presenti tutti quelli signori, e finita che fù tutta la Corte, e Cavalieri giostranti andorono à Casa della sposa à cena dove si fece una bellissima festa; et un' apparato bellissimo.

Il sposo poi non ritornò più ad allogiare in castello dove prima era allogiato; perche quando venne à Ferrara lui e tutta la sua famiglia fù allogiato dal signor Duca sino à tanto che sposò la sposa: e fù alli 19 di febraro che venne à Ferrara.

La prima Domenica di quaresima il signor Duca ordinò che tutta la nobiltà si vedesse per La Giovecca, e per la Città.

Alli 3 di Marzo in giorno di giovedi andorno à sentire la musica delle Suore di San Silvestro: il giorno seguente andorno parimente a sentire la musica delle Suore di San Vito l'una e l'altra veramente degna d'essere udita.

La domenica seguente la sera andorno ad una pastorale recitata su la giovecca in casa di quelli dalla Pena composta da un cittadino ferrarese delli Bellay.

Il Lunedi doppo pranso andorno a Belriguardo e vi stetero sino al giovedì, e la Domenica che fù alli 13 di Marzo si fece il concerto grande nella sala delle Camere nuove presenti tutti questi signori.

stayed in the house of Forni next to the Chiesa degli Angeli, but the expenses were paid by the Prince, who from time to time would go out and about the city with the Duke and other times to the country with the same Duke.

The Musical Scene: Madrigal Books 1 and 2 published

Of particular interest in the above account is the reference to the guests' attendance at a concert given by the nuns of San Silvestro and of San Vito. We learn from one of the most colourful descriptions of Ferrarese court life of the time, Bottrigari's *Il Desiderio*,[32] that musical performances by the sisters of San Vito were especially renowned. Visiting monarchs (e.g. Marguerite of Austria) and even a Pope (Clement VIII) had taken the time to hear them when they were in Ferrara. Artusi likewise praises them at the beginning of his *Delle imperfettioni della moderna musica*. It is noteworthy that the nuns, who were adept not only at singing but also at the playing of instruments, manipulating the cornetti and trombones with amazing skill, were self-coached. The questioner in *Il Desiderio*, hearing of their marvellous attainment, conjectures that the nuns' proficiency was newly acquired as a result of the instruction of Fiorino, the maestro di musica, or Luzzaschi. He is immediately put down.

> What do you mean, a new thing? It is not at all new. If I were to speak of tens and twenties of years I would not be mistaken. Because of this, in great part, can one understand how the great perfection of their concordance comes about. Neither Fiorino nor Luzzasco, though both are held in great honour by them, nor any other musician or living man, has had any part either in their work or in advising them; and so it is all the more marvellous, even stupendous, to everyone who delights in music.[33]

Bottrigari gives us an especially vivid description of the role of music at the time of Alfonso II, and indicates something of the extent of its importance:

Il Prencipe poi di Venosa si stava dalla sua sposa in casa dell'Illustrissimo Signore Don Cesare d'Est nel Palazzo di Diamanti e quest'Eccellentissimo Signore Don Cesare era fratello di detta sposa, e la sua famiglia stava nella casa delli Forni dalla Chiesa degli Angeli a spese però del signore Prencipe il quale alle volte andava fuori di casa per la città col signore Duca; et alcune altre volte in Campagna col medesimo signore Duca.'

[32] Hercole Bottrigari, *Il Desiderio ovvero de' Concerti di varii strumenti Musicali* (Venice, 1594); facsimile edition by Kathi Meyer (Berlin, 1924); English trans. by Carol MacClintock. American Institute of Musicology, *MSD*, 9 (1962), pp. 58–61.

[33] Bottrigari, *Il Desiderio*, trans. MacClintock, p. 59.

His Highness has two large, decorated rooms, designated as music
rooms, since they are restricted to the use of the musicians ordinarily
serving under a stipend of the Duke. There are many of them, both
Italians and Oltramontani; those of good voice and of beautiful and
gracious manner in singing as well as those of the highest excellence
in playing the cornetti, tromboni, dolzaine, piffarotti, as well as others
accomplished on the viole and ribecchini, and still others proficient on
lute, guitar, harp, and clavicembalo; of which instruments there are the
greatest number and variety, both used and unused, always kept near
at hand. . . . The musicians may repair to these rooms as they wish
and please, together or separately, and practise there both playing and
singing. There are also, besides the musical compositions in manuscript, many, many books of printed music by the best men of this
profession, kept in scrupulous order each in its appointed place. And
the instruments are all always in order and tuned, and capable of being
taken up and played at a moment's notice. And they are so kept by
maestri who know how to tune as well as manufacture them most
excellently, and these men are consequently held in the permanent
employ of the Duke for this purpose.[34]

An inventory of instruments in the Palazzo dei Diamanti, residence of
Duke Cesare d'Este at this time, made on 18 December 1600 preparatory
to having them moved to his new residence in Modena, reveals a truly
staggering array of musical instruments of every conceivable nature.[35]
Surprisingly there is no mention of the famous archicembalo that Vicentino
had built at Ferrara some years earlier, an instrument of several keyboards
and microtonal divisions of the octave. We know of its existence, however,
amongst others from the account of Bottrigari, who states that the great
number of strings in this instrument made it very difficult to tune as well
as to play. He adds that, because of its difficulty, most skilful players seldom
cared to meddle with it, although Luzzaschi knew and understood it and
was able to play upon it with amazing skill.[36]

Also in Ferrara were the famous singing ladies, who through their personal

---

[34] Translated by the author. See also MacClintock, *Il Desiderio*, pp. 50, 52.

[35] Cf. L. Valdrighi, 'Cappelle, concerte e musiche di casa d'Este dal secolo 15 al 18',
in *Atti e Memorie delle RR. Deputazioni di storia patria per le provincie Modenesi e Parmensi*
(Modena, 1884), Ser. III, vol. II, parte II, pp. 473–4. Newcomb's *The 'Musica Secreta'
of Ferrara in the 1580's* (Ph.D. dissertation, Princeton University, 1970), which was
completed too late to be taken into account here, also contains many valuable lists
and inventories.

[36] See Bottrigari, op. cit., trans. MacClintock, pp. 50–2, for a detailed description of the
problems involved in playing this instrument.

musical inspiration as well as their vocal virtuosity furthered the cause of the new solo style. Two basic periods for their activities have been established, one before 1580, the other after, the turn toward greater virtuosity being associated with the second period. At the pinnacle of their renown (1583–9) there were four sopranos in the *concerto delle dame*, and the *tre dame* commonly 'mentioned in connection with concerts at Ferrara (Laura Peperara, Lucrezia Bendidio, Tarquinia Molza) probably never sang together.'[37] Lucrezia Bendidio belonged to the earlier period, as we see in a letter from Canigiani dated 14 August 1571, regarding a performance before two visiting Austrian princes:

> In the evening there were private festivities at the court where the princes danced *alla tedesca* and *all'italiana*; and finally came a concert of music of around sixty voices and instruments, Luzzasco playing the gravicembalo in the background. Signora Lucrezia and Signora Isabella Bendidio sang, each alone and then the two together, so exquisitely and so smoothly that I do not believe that it would be possible to hear better.[38]

Tarquinia Molza belonged to the later period, but had already left Ferrara by the time of Gesualdo's arrival there.[39] That the *concerto di donne* was still active during his Ferrarese sojourn, however, is clearly established. Alfonso II maintained an unremitting interest in music to the end, functioning as a veritable taskmaster to Luzzaschi and the other musicians in matters of preparation for a performance. It is known that he not infrequently attended rehearsals, and established a demanding and unrelenting schedule for such activities. Merenda describes in fascinating detail the concert life at about the time of Gesualdo's second visit:

> The Most Serene Lady Margherita Gonzaga, wife of our noble Duke Alfonso II, Duke of Ferrara, coming to Ferrara had in her service a lady called Laura Peperara, a Mantuan, young and unmarried; and she

---

[37]-Cf. Anthony Newcomb's review of Luzzaschi, *Madrigali per cantare e sonare a uno, due e tre soprani* (1601), a cura di Adriano Cavicchi, in *JAMS* XXI, 2 (1968), pp. 222–3.

[38] Solerti, *Ferrara e la corte estense*, p. cxxxiv.

[39] At one point she made a bid for Tasso's affections, to no avail. She later found her artist man in the figure of Giaches Wert, composer at the neighbouring court of Mantua, whose visits to Ferrara for a time reached a fever peak. Tarquinia, a widow, had become maid of honour to Alfonso's third duchess, but 'banished herself at a look from the Duke in 1589, when her relations with Wert became court scandal.' (Boulting, *Tasso and His Times*, p. 198).

had also another lady who sang, who was called Livia da Arco, also unmarried. The Duke had at that time assigned to the said Madame a certain signora Anna Guarina, who sang and played the lute; and Signora Laura played the harp and Signora Livia also began to play the viola. The maestri were Signor Fiorino, maestro di capella of His Highness, and Signor Luzzasco, organist of the Duke, and thus His Highness began to have them practise every day together in their singing, in such a way that as of this time in Italy, or perhaps even outside it, there is no *concerto di donne* [ensemble of ladies] better than this. And every day during summer-time, they begin to sing after dinner at 7 o'clock and continue until 9—the organist at the harpsichord, Signor Fiorino with the large lute, Signora Livia with a viola, Signora Guarina with a lute, and Signora Laura with the harp. And the Duke and Duchess are always present. They sing from a book of music for a basso and two other voices, all singers of the Duke. In the winter time they begin at half past six and continue until after half past eight, and when princes come he takes them to the Duchess's quarters to listen to the *concerto*. His Highness has married all three of these ladies to some of the principal gentlemen of the city, and has given them rooms at the court for convenience in rendering their service; and these three ladies go about continuously in the carriage with Her Serene Highness, the Duchess. This *concerto* continues until this very day of September 1596.[40]

Can there be any doubt of Gesualdo's genuine delight with such a rich musical environment? Imagine his pleasure then when he, at this very time, makes his début as a published composer. For Gesualdo's first books of madrigals were issued by the ducal press of Vittorio Baldini in 1594. We learn from the preface that the book which was now entitled *Libro Secondo* had appeared in print once before, though under the pseudonym Gioseppe Pilonij.[41] As the Prince's rightful name had not been attached to it, however,

---

[40] Merenda, *Storia di Ferrara*, Biblioteca Estense, MS VII.C.I, p. 144v. See also Solerti, op. cit., p. cxxxvi for Italian text, and Bottrigari, op. cit. pp. 52–62, for additional descriptions.

[41] 'Vedendo io di quanto amiratione sia l'opera di vostra Eccellenza Illustriss. al mondo, data in luce sotto il nome di Gioseppe Pilonij, & essendo la stampa (come suole) in alcuni errori trascorsa, io per l'ardente desiderio, & obligo, che tengo di servirla, come devotiss. Servitore, che le sonno, hò preso cura di rivederla minutamente, & con diligenza corretta, di nuovo ristamparla nella medesima stampa, nella quale pur hora hò stampate l'altro libro de suoi divini Madrigali. Prego in tanto l'Eccel. vostra à formi gratia di accogliere con lieta fronte l'animo mio il quale con gli altri conoscendo di quanto preggio fosse il parto suo, non hò potuto patire, che alcuno accidente le levi la bellezza, che per natura egli havea tratto dal fecondo intelletto di

he could hardly have taken public pride in its appearance. Scipione Stella,[42] a member of Gesualdo's Neapolitan academy who accompanied the Prince on his journey to Ferrara, served as editor of these two volumes. It will be remembered from Fontanelli's letter of 18 February 1594 that Gesualdo had brought along with him 'two different books of music in five parts, all his own work.' Hence, the music was readily at hand in Ferrara for such publication to be undertaken. Perhaps Gesualdo had already hoped that his madrigals might be published in Ferrara, and had brought them for that purpose.

An obsequious preface to the first volume dated 10 May 1594 is directed to the composer. The protestation that the edition was made without the Prince's knowledge or permission should probably not be taken seriously.

> The ardent desire and ready willingness which I have to serve Your Excellency has made me bold to gather and have printed these madrigals (a precious sample and product of Your Excellency) without asking your permisson. I realize that, being in your service, it was not meet that I should so much presume; but your benevolence assures me that you will pardon me, and I beg you to do so assuring Your Excellency that this has not been a result of presumption but of the inner devotion of my spirit and of the reverence with which I regard you and with which I kiss your hands, wishing for you from our Lord God continuous prosperity.[43]

Tasso and Gesualdo

As part of the nuptial celebrations there appeared from the press of Vittorio Baldini in the same year two books of epithalamia in honour of the married couple. Among the poets of the *Rimi diversi*, which includes a variety of

---

vostra Eccel. Illustriss. alla quale con ogni riverenza mi dono, e consacro. Di Ferrara il di 2 Giugno 1594.
      Di Vostra Eccel. Illustrissima
          Affettionatiss. Servatore
           Scipione Stella'

[42] A volume of Stella's motets was also printed in Ferrara in 1595. See pp. 253–4.
[43] 'L'ardente desiderio et pronta volontà che tengo di servire all'Eccell. V. m'ha dato ardire di raccogliere et dare alla stampa questi Madrigali (precioso saggio et parto dell'Eccel. Sua) senza domandargliene licentia; conosco ch'a me che sto alli suoi servigi, non era conveniente di pigliar tanta confidenza; ma la sua benignità mi assicura che sia per iscusarmi et ne la supplico assicurando l'Eccellenza Vostra che ciò non è proceduto da presentione, ma dall'interna devotione dell'animo mio et dalla riverenza con che l'osservo con la quale vengo a baciarle le mani desiderandole dal Signor Iddio continua prosperità.'

odes, sonnets, and madrigals, are Gio. Maria Guicciardi, Annibal Gritio, Orlando Pescetti, Lucillo Martinenghi, Adriano Grande, Bartolomeo Tortelletti, Claudio Paci, Bartolomeo Burchellati, Giulio Morigi, and Antonio Beffa Negrini. The second collection is a book of Latin verses, *Diversorum poemata*, largely by the same group of authors.[44]

It will be noted that Tasso is nowhere to be found in either of these collections. He had at one time planned to join Gesualdo on his journey to Ferrara for the wedding celebrations, but the Duke reportedly refused to receive him because he had directed his recently re-published *Gerusalemme* to another Signore, suppressing not only the original dedication to Alfonso but also deleting many references to him in the text. This undoubtedly explains Tasso's absence from the two volumes. Tasso's enormous ode of eighteen ottave stanzas on the occasion of this marriage, *Lascia, o figlio d'Urani, il bel Parnaso*, survives independently, however, to attest to his admiration for the Prince.[45] The opening three stanzas read thus:

> Lascia, o figlio d'Urania, il bel Parnaso,
>   E'l doppio colle di quel verde monte,
>   E i seggi ombrosi e foschi, e da Pegaso
>   Aperto col piè duro, il chiaro fonte:
>   E'n riva al Po discendi anzi l'Occaso,
>   Cinto di rose la serena fronte,
>   Con quella face, onde la notte illustri,
>   E col giogo, ch'imponi all'alme illustri.
> Nella città, c'ha più onorate palme,
>   Che'l sacrato Elicona ombrosi allori,
>   Mille famose in guerra, e care salme,
>   Ond'ella il ferro del suo nome indori,
>   Vedrai due pellegrine, e nobil'alme,
>   Degne di gloria, e d'immortali onori,
>   E per volar dagl'Iperborei agl'Indi,
>   Maggior virtù non vedi o quinci, o quindi.
> Per questo giogo, a cui si lieta inchina
>   La nobil coppia de' duo' casti amanti,
>   Nova prole all'Italia il Ciel destina,
>   Qual già domar solea mostri e giganti:
>   Per cui questa del mondo alta regina
>   Di porre il duro giogo ancor si vanti

[44] Only a single copy of both volumes exists, and this, in its original nuptial binding of white leather with gilt edges, is preserved in the Biblioteca Civica in Ferrara.

[45] *Rime di Torquato Tasso* (Pisa, 1821), iv, pp. 180–4.

All'Asia doma, all'Affrica rubella,
Onde i suoi vincitori ancor appella.

(Leave, O son of Urania, lovely Parnassus, and the double hill of that green mountain, and the dark and shady seats, and the clear fountain sprung by Pegasus with his hard hoof; and to the bank of the Po descend before sunset, your tranquil brow by roses girt, holding that torch with which you illuminate the night, and with the yoke which you place on noble souls.

In the city, which has more honoured palms than sacred Helicon shady laurels, a thousand beloved dead, famous in war, wherewith she gilds the iron[46] of her name,[47] you will see two lovely and noble souls worthy of glory and immortal honours, and were one to fly from the Hyperboreans to the Indies, no greater virtue could you see here or there.

Through this yoke, to which so happy bend the noble couple, the two chaste lovers, Heaven destines new progeny to Italy, such as were wont to subdue monsters and giants; through whom this lofty queen of the world still may boast of placing the hard yoke on mastered Asia, on rebellious Africa, and so still calls upon her champions.)

Tasso, once again in difficult straits with the Este court, apparently saw in Gesualdo a likely candidate to help his cause along. This is made especially clear in two letters written at this time. The first is to Gesualdo, dated 22 June 1594.

Since I rejoiced with Your Excellency on the occasion of your marriage, and with a few stanzas demonstrated to the best of my ability my devotion and respects, I have come to Naples with the intention of purging myself, and have already commenced the treatment. May it please God that it will benefit me sufficiently to enable me to survive until the return of Your Excellency. In the meanwhile, if you are in any way able to help me or do me any favour, know that it is well merited on account of my great affection and esteem. In expectation of your gracious favours and those of your uncle, the Cardinal, I kiss your hand.[48]

During his later years Tasso's feeling about his post at the Ferrara court vacillated between two extremes; during his stays at Ferrara he was anxious to leave, and during his absences he was anxious to return.[49] He could never

[46] ferro.   [47] Ferrara.
[48] See Tasso, *Lettere*, n. 1497, for original; trans. after Gray & Heseltine, pp. 57–8.
[49] Cf. letter cited on p. 60.

quite bring himself to break completely with the Este court, and the Duke had ample reason for retaining his services. His association with a poet who, though tinged with madness, had written the most important epic of his time, the *Gerusalemme liberata,* inspired him to an extraordinary degree of patience in dealing with the disquieted genius. A regular process of communications to Alfonso on Tasso's behalf is recorded, written from almost every quarter imaginable, secular and ecclesiastical, and when Gesualdo's ties with Ferrara became cemented through his marriage to Leonora, it is only natural that he, too, became a target of his persuasions.

Gesualdo arrived in Naples shortly after the above letter from Tasso and spent the next several months there. About the time of Gesualdo's planned return to Ferrara in December 1594, Tasso wrote the Duke once more, and with what proved to be his dying breath implored him to listen to the Prince.[50]

> If the past could return, there is nothing I would rather choose than always to have served your highness, or at least not to have lost your favour by misfortune. But since it is impossible to correct the past, which is long, in what remains to me of the future, which is very short, I will take more care to avoid your highness's displeasure than that of anybody else. This has been my resolution for many years, however obstructed or badly executed. I beg you anew to have compassion on me, and I pray God with the most devout heart to grant me this pardon, and that of your serene highness. Deign to consider what I have written to the Prince of Venosa and what I have said several times to your ambassador, and may God send you long life and happiness. Rome, 10th of December, 1594.

By Tasso's own word he had not long to live. He had left Naples to go to Rome in November, where, shortly after having written this last letter to the Duke, he died in a monastery overlooking the city.

The Return to Gesualdo

Merenda announces the Prince's departure from Ferrara in a brief entry:[51]

> He left Ferrara on 15 May and went to see the Duke of Mesola who had gone there just for pleasure. He remained with His Highness until

[50] Wilde, *Conjectures and Researches concerning the Love, Madness, and Imprisonment of Torquato Tasso,* vol. 2, p. 270. Original in *Lettere,* v, no. 1519.

[51] Equicola states: 'A di 15. Maggio l'Illsmo. Sr. Don Carlo Gesualdo parti di Ferrara per andare alla patria.'

two days before Ascension Day. From here he then went to Venice where he stayed for several days. There he was supplied with ships to go back to his domain.

The journey to Gesualdo is recorded by Fontanelli who was once again assigned by the Duke to accompany the Prince. Evidence on every hand confirms that Gesualdo left for the South without his new wife. As he was to return to Ferrara in December for a sojourn of two years, his journey alone does not seem out of the ordinary. It would have been natural enough, however, had the Prince desired to take his new spouse with him to introduce her to Neapolitan society. Vatielli suggests that this was done, but nowhere in the Fontanelli correspondence from May to October is there any mention of the Princess in his letters to the Duke.[52] If for this reason alone, her presence on this journey seems precluded.

Fontanelli's first letter, dated 21 May 1594, is from Venice:

The Prince was forced to stop all day Wednesday in Chioggia due to the terrible wind, which obstructed passage through the port. He arrived here on Ascension Day around 6 p.m. where he found the ceremony of the Marriage of the Sea (*Sposalizio del mare*) was postponed for the same reason that obstructed the trip.

Now he is here, and the free time he has from his study of music, he expects to spend enjoying and admiring the city which he likes so well. He goes around the city incognito and has already refused a visit from the Legate (which is the way they refer to the Nunzio here), and he received the visit of the Patriarch only with displeasure even though he had an express commission from Cardinal Gesualdo to send his compliments.

This notwithstanding the gentlemen of the city this morning gave him some refreshments with the intent of doing it every day, from what we have understood, and perhaps to stock the galley, which they have already granted him, when he leaves. I do not know if the Prince has been completely satisfied by this demonstration, but from what Ariosti will relate to you, you will be able to determine for yourself.

The Prince never stops exalting the things of Ferrara (*le cose di Ferrara*),[53] and particularly this morning about the music-making

[52] The reference in the letter of 23 May from Venice, indicating that Gesualdo and his family were served at dinner, is hardly conclusive.

[53] This phrase was misread by Vatielli, op. cit., p. 38, as *arie di Firenze*. On the basis of this misreading he developed a thesis of Gesualdo's knowledge and admiration of the activities at Florence at this time. While it is not impossible that this is true, this particular letter does not suggest the point, and indeed nowhere else in the Prince's

of the Ladies of Ferrara he spoke enthusiastically to a gentleman
from Naples who ate with him. That he expresses himself energetically
and effectively Your Highness knows full well. It may well be that
the situation concerning this Florentine[54] who sings and plays
the archlute will transpire as Your Highness imagined, but if I
had no order reminding me that Your Highness did not entirely
like the idea, I would go no further than [to say] that perhaps the
place could be filled by another person. The Prince says that he
wants to leave within two days, but I do not think that he will.[55]

Fontanelli's doubt proved correct. Gesualdo remained in Venice for
several weeks, and it is logical to assume that during this period Gesualdo
entered into discussion and perhaps even contracts with the Venetian printer
Gardano, who was to print many of his madrigals in years to come. Of equal
interest for him must have been the music at San Marco. When we remember
that Giovanni Gabrieli had succeeded Claudio Merulo there as first organist
ten years before (1584) and was to remain there until his death (1612), it is
reasonable to wonder if a meeting between the two composers took place. A
letter of 23 May by Fontanelli indicates that it probably did.

The Prince was then visited in the name of His Most Serene Highness
[the Doge] of the Most Serene Republic by two 'Savii' from the main-
land who honoured him by the pretended title. He was persuaded that
they were 'Savii grandi' (an honour already conferred upon Paolo
Giordano Orsino), but we did not care to disillusion him in order to
enjoy his favour. This demonstration induced him to resolve to visit
the Doge, and he intended to do so today. But as a visit to the dock-
yard had been scheduled and as His Excellency was not quick to stir
from his room, things were delayed to the point that the visit was
deferred to another day. His Serenity will use the title of Excellency
in addressing the Prince, and if, in the judgement of the most serious
senators, this seems excessive, afterwards they will attribute such
inappropriate behaviour to the old age of the Doge, which for some

---

correspondence is there any similar reference. Vatielli's error is understandable. The
difficulty of the script is considerable throughout these letters, and in addition
Ferrara is abbreviated at the crucial point as 'Ferr.ᵃ'. He similarly misread 'Cav.'
as 'Cardinale' instead of 'Cavaliere' in the same passage. Newcomb, 'Carlo Gesualdo
and a musical correspondence', p. 419, essentially corroborates this point.

54 Newcomb, op. cit., p. 421, suggests that the Florentine in question may be Francesco
Rasi.
55 This and the following letter of 23 May are located in *Dispacci da Venezia*, Busta no. 88
(3345/72), Archivio di Stato, Modena.

months now has excused the occasional *lapsus linguae* when he has addressed people in a manner either deficient or excessive. All in all this could be considered a plot devised by those who desire the satisfaction of the Prince (who knows nothing of these doings), but they know that if this were discussed in council difficulties would arise. Be that as it may, it would appear that the name of Cardinal Gesualdo is highly regarded here, but I do not think one can say loved, because of his interests elsewhere.

This morning, instead of the meal usually served at the shipyard to gentlemen of high rank who visit it, they served a very formal dinner to His Excellency and all his family, a courtesy extended towards the Duke of Nivers and to such others as were deemed worthy of being accorded this honour. However these gentlemen were surprised that the Prince, without having seen everything before eating and all having been readied for him to see, nevertheless hastened to leave, showing less curiosity than the reputation of the place and possibly his own taste justified. The surprise was even greater because it was still fresh in the memory how the above mentioned Duke of Nivers came very early in the morning, desired to come back after lunch and stayed until night. But it does not seem surprising to me that a soldier prince should enjoy such things more than a Neapolitan gentleman. . . .[56]

On Monday the Prince was invited to dine by the Patriarch, and there was music. But in Venice they sing badly, and His Excellency has a taste difficult to satisfy, as Your Highness knows. Thus he could not restrain himself from withdrawing from the room, summoning the director and cembalist and reproving them in such a manner that I felt sorry for them. He has not yet been able to see Giovanni Gabrieli, organist of San Marco, but he is laying so many snares for him that ultimately he, too, will fall into the nets and, having made an appearance, will no doubt leave with displeasure. Father Costanzo Porta was here and was invited at once, but he was just about to leave for Padua. Fortunately for him. Meanwhile, the Prince has been composing continually, and, just now having constructed two new madrigals, he says that he plans to come to Ferrara with such thick bulwarks [*belloardi d'opere*] (these were the terms he used) that he will be able to defend himself against Luzzaschi, who is the one enemy he fears; the others he pokes fun at.

Many times I have been present during the act of composition and

---

[56] The next few paragraphs, by Fontanelli's admission, are a digression concerning the Duke of Nivers.

could, if I wished, relate many particulars to the good, and few things to the contrary. But to me neither the one nor the other appears necessary, and in this matter it seems sufficient to straddle the question.[57]

On 14 June Fontanelli again addresses the Duke:

We left Venice at 2 o'clock, but we stayed one day and one full night in the port awaiting the right weather for sailing. After having passed the Gulf and having arrived in Istria, we did not leave the coast of Dalmatia. Once having arrived in Augusta, however, we proceeded into the Gulf, and on the day before Corpus Christi we landed in Barletta. Here the Prince stopped all day and until quite late the following one, in order to escape the tremendous heat of Puglia. Then we travelled all night and at two p.m., we arrived in Venosa, the Prince being met by several well-dressed and well-horsed gentlemen. Here we stayed all that day, and the next day we turned toward Caposelle, passing through many towns of the Prince, and particularly through Calitro, where at that time there was a breed of horses which was led to the place where we were passing by so that I could see it. I was really impressed, not so much for the beauty of the mares and colts, which is incomparable, as for the quality of the stallions, which are the handsomest that the eye could behold, and particularly admired their hocks and their marvellous gait.

We stayed that evening at Caposelle, which is a place favoured by nature in its most beautiful waters. The following day we came to Gesualdo, a pleasant place (and not very much visited), pretty to the eye as much as one could wish with truly gentle and healthy air. One could see from here many other properties of the Prince, who, from what I can see, has a very big state and very devoted servants. Here, besides his several tastes and passion for music, the Prince takes great pleasure every day in discussing local matters, and continues to speak of Your Highness with veneration and affection. Within four to six days, I will go, God willing, to Naples, which is not more than 50 miles from here. I am writing a great deal to Don Cesare because I was asked to do so, but having nothing else to say to Your Highness, I close.

It is not known precisely when Gesualdo undertook to renovate and redecorate the castle at Gesualdo, but it might well have been at this time.

[57] The paragraph ends with a sentence which is illegible: 'La partita consisterà nell'-acc.^to (?) . . . del tempo.'

The renovation, which is attested to by the inscription atop the central courtyard wall, would have had to have taken place after 1591, when Don Carlo's father, Fabrizio, died, since Carlo's name is inscribed along with the titles Prince of Venosa and Count of Consa. It is equally plausible that it was undertaken some time between October 1592 and February 1594, that is to say between the first contacts regarding a possible marriage contract and the date of the wedding. That Leonora did not accompany her husband on this trip may indicate that Don Carlo undertook the journey primarily to discharge matters of a business nature. Once more, on 25 June 1594, we learn from Fontanelli:

> Since I have not yet gone to Naples, I do not have very much to say to Your Highness. However, I shall not lose the opportunity of the present dispatch. The Prince is still here and finds pleasure in hunting, getting up very early in the morning, arousing the admiration of everybody, and in music. He has already composed five or six most artful madrigals, a motet, an aria, and has brought to a good point a dialogue for three sopranos, made, I believe, for the Ladies [of Ferrara]. At the same time he attends with much diligence to certain duties, public as well as domestic, showing the wish to get them over quickly and quietly and be free of them as soon as possible.

The information that Venosa set immediately to work upon his return to Gesualdo is of especial interest because of the compositions that are listed: five or six most artful madrigals (naturally); a motet (we can account for this); an aria, and a dialogue for three sopranos. As the term 'aria' was sometimes used in the late sixteenth century as an equivalent for canzonetta, it is probable that this is one of Gesualdo's two such designated pieces. The dialogue for three sopranos, on the other hand, cannot so readily be accounted for as there are no surviving examples answering to such a description from his pen. Such a piece suggests a desire to try his hand at a new style, as a result of his experiences at Ferrara. We know that through his earlier discussions with Cavalieri, as well as with Corsi later in the year, he had been and would be exposed to a considerable amount of talk concerning the first Florentine experiments at monody. In addition the presence of Francesco Rasi, singer and player of the chitarrone, in Gesualdo's employ emphasizes that he could hardly have been innocent of developments of the period. Rasi, active at both Florence and Mantua, participated in many performances of Peri and Cavalieri during the late 1590s.[58] An even

---

[58] See C. Palisca, 'Musical Asides in the Diplomatic Correspondence of Emilio de'Cavalieri' in *MQ* XLIX (1963), p. 339; Newcomb, op. cit. pp. 421–2.

more direct influence was probably Luzzaschi, who had written repeatedly for the *concerto di donne,* and who must have shown some of his products to Gesualdo. It is unlikely that he would not have frequently seen and heard Luzzaschi's madrigals for three sopranos and continuo which although not printed until 1601 were undoubtedly written much earlier, being left unprinted in order to preserve them solely for Este consumption.[59] If Gesualdo's dialogue was for three sopranos in the manner of Luzzaschi, it is particularly to be regretted that the work has not survived, considering his other sorties into unfamiliar musical territory such as the instrumental gagliarda or the canzon francese—the latter being in some ways the most extraordinary piece he ever wrote. Even if it was only an unaccompanied piece, with a high degree of melodic virtuosity in the upper three parts, it would still be a welcome addition.[60]

Four more letters from Fontanelli's pen survive from September and October of 1594: apparently they did not get off for Ferrara as quickly as they had hoped. Yet Fontanelli's letters offer continuing hints of Gesualdo's personality and abilities as well as of the proficiency of the members of his academy.

> I think it is my duty to let Your Highness know that I have left Gesualdo and come to Naples, where I arrived the day before yesterday. I had a chance to see the greater part of the nobility at Chiaia at a certain church service. I receive great favours and honours, not so much from the dependents of the Prince of Venosa as from other gentlemen and cavalieri who show me the greatest consideration due to the fact that I belong to the court of Your Highness.

Stating that a delay of a few more days will allow him the opportunity to give a more intimate report concerning the nobility, he continues.

> And I will write about music, too, Sig. Ettore Gesualdo having already given orders for me to be taken to hear the most important [musicians]. In the meantime, I have discovered that the fame of your Ladies is quite great down here, and that the name of Luzzasco has such a reputation that everyone who wishes to claim distinction declares him-

[59] Cf. Kinkeldey, 'Luzzasco Luzzaschi Solo-Madrigale,' in *Sämmelbände d.I.M.G.,* IX, 4. Alessandro Striggio writing in 1584 from Ferrara to Firenze sends a piece entitled 'Dialogo a 2 soprani dimunuiti et fugati per il concerto' to which was added an intabulation for the lute, promising on his return to Florence to write songs 'in imitation of those at Ferrara.' See Vatielli, op. cit., p. 39.

[60] Newcomb's suggestion, op. cit., p. 427, that the six-voice madrigal *Donna se m'ancidete* (Bk. III) would qualify as the work in question is tempting in light of its chronology and especially the employment of three sopranos. It can be less convincingly viewed as a dialogue, however.

self to be his imitator. It is true that he is universally most celebrated.

Naples   Your most devoted and faithful servant,

9 September 1594   Alfonso Fontanelli

★ ★ ★

. . . I have heard quite a bit of music here. I like what Mr. Fabritio Filamarino does on the lute (and I say this to Your Highness and to no one else) better than the Prince of Venosa. It is true that his hand is not so good or strong, but perhaps a gentler hand is sweeter to my ears. Don Antonino, who is the first bass in Naples, and who was formerly in Your Highness's service, has a really beautiful voice, and he fuses the notes in the low voice smoothly. The low range of his voice is in no way inferior to the high and middle part, all having the same quality, which is a beautiful thing. His voice is no longer so ornate, however, as Melchiore's.[61] Sig. Ettore Gesualdo sings like a cavaliere and plays the viola wonderfully. But I confess to have found no miracles at all in Naples. And Your Highness might well believe this, as they go crazy over the Prince's Florentine [Rasi?] who is here with me. He is heard by everyone with so much pleasure that whenever he appears the coaches of the ladies and cavalieri compete to go there to hear him. I remain astonished at this. This morning I saw the riding school of the King, and yesterday I was invited for lunch by a few young cavalieri; I saw also some dancing according to the customs here and a tournament on foot. . . .

I forgot to tell you that Luzzasco has such a reputation here that even though I ask to hear new works, everybody wants his things to be sung, as he is called Maestro. And Fabritio Filamarino particularly says that he would not die happy if he were not to be allowed to work under the discipline of Luzzasco for six months at least.

Naples   Your most devoted and faithful servant,

16 September 1594   Alfonso Fontanelli

★ ★ ★

Tonight Fabritio Filamarino, after having played the lute really divinely in my opinion, came with me in the coach, and after having said to me again what I have already written to Your Highness about

---

[61] Probably the Roman basso Melchiorre Palantrotti who is mentioned by Peri as having performed Plutone in his *Euridice*. Cf. Newcomb, op. cit., p. 432, fn. 35.

his wish to be with Luzzasco, he mentioned his wish to live in the court of Your Highness with the title of servant, with only the thought of serving you in things of music. He knows how much you take pleasure in this virtue, and in what esteem those associated with you are held in the world. He would not have said a single word, doubting his worthiness of such a grace, but he did not want his ardent wish to enjoy at least six months with Sig. Luzzaschi to be unknown to you.

It is my duty to let Your Highness know it, and no one else. I heard Giovanni Leonardo dell'Arpa who is an old man, so kind that wherever I go he follows me. Today at Ettore Gesualdo's there was a congress of musicians where a great number of noble people came to listen. This Giovanni de Leonardo has a hand which one can tell must have been admirable at one time, and particularly in the art of damping the strings. But his improvisation (*fantasia*) is somewhat old-fashioned. Count Luigi Montecuccoli will say something to Your Highness with reference to my return.

Naples   Your devoted and faithful servant,
23 September 1594   Alfonso Fontanelli
P.S. The Archbishop, being particularly kind to me, will allow me to hear the Nun who is so famous.[62]

★   ★   ★

Fontanelli's next letter is from Gesualdo, whither the prince had been recalled by certain business matters. After announcing his intention to wait as long as necessary in order to accompany the Prince of Venosa back to Ferrara, he once again turns to musical matters.

Meanwhile we spend the time continuously in music, Sig. Ettore Gesualdo and Sig. Fabritio Filamarino, who came with me from Naples, and other virtuosi of this profession having arrived there as though to make an offering to the temple of this Apollo. Sig. Ettore will come to Ferrara, and he is just now ready to leave for Naples to put himself under your orders. He is a most worthy gentleman. As to music, he sings his part by the book in as pleasing a manner as a gentleman can. He has rather a good tenor voice. He also sings the soprano part, but the voice is not so pure in this range, even though graceful. He plays the basso di viola exquisitely, however, and he touches the strings with much grace and a certain mystery. He plays the *chitarra* also very beautifully. He has been, moreover, a wonderful

[62] Apparently Ferrara held no monopoly on nuns who were virtuoso musicians.

torneatore a piedi and a *corritor di lancia a cavallo*, but now is so sick that I do not think he is able to do either. . . .

Sig. Fabritio Filamarino in playing the lute and guitar is in my opinion what I first wrote, and the more I hear him the more I am satisfied with him. He will not come to Ferrara, even though he has been invited by the Prince, because of certain considerations, but he does not show himself averse to one day being able to come there, as Your Highness will hear.

Here I vow to Your Highness and recommend myself humbly to your protection with the understanding of not writing you any more except from Rome.

Gesualdo   Your devoted and faithful servant,
9 October 1594   Alfonso Fontanelli

★   ★   ★

Evidently there were further delays, because Gesualdo did not arrive in Ferrara until December. Fontanelli's willingness to wait throughout the period on the slightest pretext indicates that he remained behind in order to accompany him. If Ettore Gesualdo did not change his plans, he, too, was a member of the party. As Ettore edited the Prince's third and fourth books of madrigals, which were to be published in Ferrara in the coming months, the likelihood of his presence on this journey is underscored. Fabritio Filamarino, for all his hesitancy, ultimately succumbed to the invitation and appears to have stayed in Ferrara until early 1596.[63]

The party had apparently counted on arriving in Ferrara by Christmas, but on 17 December they were overtaken by a furious storm of snow and ice and forced to stop at Florence.[64] On 21 December Gesualdo wrote to Duke Alfonso that his arrival would probably be delayed until the first of the year. It is tempting to speculate how the time may have been spent in Florence, and who was involved. Evidence of personal contact with Jacomo Corsi and presumably other Florentines is contained in a communiqué from the Este ambassador to the Medici court of 24 December 1594.[65] Gesualdo's discussion over the better part of a week with Corsi, principal personality of the Florentine camerata after Bardi's departure from Rome in 1592, indicates unequivocally that Gesualdo was well informed of current musical developments. If he chose to eschew the new style of accompanied solo song (and

[63] Cf. Newcomb, loc. cit., who points to letters by Filamarino in the Modena Archivio di Stato which corroborate this point.
[64] Vatielli, p. 41; Newcomb, p. 435.
[65] Newcomb, op. cit., pp. 422–3.

of this we cannot be absolutely certain), it was only after meeting figures closely associated with the new aesthetic. A progressive figure in so many respects, he undoubtedly found himself frequently obliged to defend his choice of the increasingly old-fashioned madrigal. Given his loquacious bent, that Gesualdo held his own in such circumstances may well be imagined.

The party's departure for Ferrara before the turn of the New Year is corroborated in a notice by Equicola to the effect that 'In the same month, December of 1594, Sig. Don Carlo Gesualdo, Prince of Venosa, came to live in Ferrara in the palace of Sig. Marco de Pio, taking lodging on the Via delli Angeli, which he had leased, and there he conducted Sra. Donna Leonora Estense his wife, and all her household.'[66]

Residence in Ferrara

The Prince and Princess stayed in Ferrara for about two years, and apparently they remained throughout this period in the palace of Marco Pio.[67] The stay in Ferrara was one of the most productive periods in Gesualdo's life. His third and fourth books of madrigals were composed there and published in the years 1595 and 1596 respectively. It is also not unlikely that he wrote more motets of the kind that he had composed in Gesualdo before returning to Ferrara. Though neither of the two books of *Sacrae Cantiones* appeared until 1603, there is no reason to insist that they were composed all at once or immediately prior to their publication. We may recall, in fact, from Fontanelli's correspondence that Gesualdo had already composed some motets by June 1594.[68]

During this period he must have enjoyed associations not only with the best Ferrarese musicians but also with those of nearby Mantua and Venice, having already established personal contact in both cities, as well as Florence and Padua. It is unfortunate that not a word about any of this is recorded,

[66] Da Monte, *Storia*, registers a similar account: 'Del mese Decembre dell anno medismo (1594) venne ad abitare a Ferrara D. Carlo Gesualdo nel Palazzo dei Pij, al'incontro del Monastero di Santa Catarina Martire; e vi condusse D. Eleonora sua moglie, e tutta la famiglia.' Guarini, *Diario di tutte le cose*, Bibl. Estense MS H.2.16 (*olim* VIII.B.8), vol. 1, mentions under the more specific date of 29 December 1594, 'Il Principe di Venosa fu di ritorna ad affitto in cinque anni il Palazzo di Marco Pio all'via degli Angeli.'

[67] Pio was to die a tragic death soon after, but not before a bitter animosity developed between him and Leonora's half-brother, Cardinal Alessandro, who is credited with his murder.

[68] The unlikely possibility that the fifth and sixth books were also completed at this time is discussed on pp. 165–8.

for we might learn something more about Gesualdo's view of the new solo style, or even discover allusions to further compositions by him in this style. It is difficult to believe that he avoided such productions completely. We could perhaps understand Gabrieli at San Marco, for example, resisting any attempt to write in a wide range of forms. But in view of the significant theatrical tradition at Ferrara, it seems curious that Gesualdo should not have written pieces suitable for use there: arias, intermezzi, instrumental works of various kinds—or in the manner of Luzzaschi's accompanied madrigals for one, two, or three solo voices—if for no other reason than to show the north Italians something of the talents which could spring from Naples. It seems improbable that he cultivated the madrigal so single-mindedly that he would not be diverted from time to time, particularly with the various performing media readily available, and highly polished performances guaranteed by the virtuosi at hand. It is likely also that much of this music, if it was written, was laid aside after its performance, as being occasional in nature, and that the quantity of such pieces was insufficient to gather them together for publication (as witness the gagliarda and the canzon francese). Had there been a number of them, however, their dissimilar nature would in no way have prevented them from being published together, for mixed collections by a single composer, such as Horatio Vecchi's miscellaneous collection of 1590,[69] were not unknown. In 1597 Vecchi's *L'Amfiparnaso* was published, having been performed at Modena three years before. His return in 1596 to Modena, whither the Este court moved on the death of Duke Alfonso II, insured a natural alliance. In this connection it is hardly necessary to point to the dedication to Gesualdo's brother-in-law, Alessandro d'Este, in order to suggest that the two composers were undoubtedly acquainted with one another.

Amongst Gesualdo's other acquaintances we know that Fontanelli was a composer of considerable skill. In Einstein's view he epitomized the Ferrarese madrigal. In addition Fontanelli himself says that he turned on occasion to the writing of accompanied madrigals in the style of certain of Luzzaschi's later productions. In 1590 he wrote to Ridolfo Arlotti:

> In Mesola and in other places I have less time to attend to the composition of music than in Ferrara. For all that you should have by Christmas a madrigaletto composed in the guise of an aria, so written

---

[69] *Selva di varia ricreatione di Horatio Vecchi, nella quale si contengono vari soggetti a 2, a 3, a 4, a 5, a 6, a 7, a 8, a 9, et a 10 voci, cioè Madrigali, Capricci, Balli, Arie, Justiniane, Canzonette, Fantasie, Serenate, Dialoghi, un Lotto amoroso, con una Battaglia à diece nel fine, et accomodatovi la intavolatura di Liuto àlle Arie, ai Balli, et alle Canzonette* (Venice, Gardano, 1590, 1595).

that only the soprano must be heard as a vocal part, the other parts played on the clavier or other instrument. I do not compose this kind of song willingly, since if I do not take care in its preparation it appears to me a waste of work, and if I do it seems a waste of time.[70]

And again, on 5 April of the same year, he protests: 'I send you the Aria on the most recent words which I have at hand. This is a kind of music I do not compose willingly.'[71] This suggests that, willing or not, many composers of the day were writing pieces in the new style, even those not normally associated with it; and that Fontanelli, like others, may have considered such compositions easier to write than polyphonic works and hence less worthy of his time and trouble. We can only guess at the contacts which Gesualdo may have made during this two-year period: meetings, perchance, with Wert, Vecchi, Caccini, and Monteverdi; definitely with G. Gabrieli, Luzzaschi, Fontanelli, Corsi, and others. In any event, the evidence of rich musical associations and even potential influences is reasonably clear.

[70] Vatielli, pp. 51–2.   [71] Vatielli, p. 52.

CHAPTER THREE

❧❀❧

The Last Years: 1597-1613

Domestic Crisis

IT cannot be precisely determined when Don Carlo left for Gesualdo after his extended sojourn in Ferrara.[1] There are reports that Gesualdo's conduct had not always been beyond reproach while still at Ferrara, and that certain of his amorous adventures were so overt as to disgust the Court and Ferrarese society.[2] Talk of maltreatment of his new wife, a recurring complaint later, also begins to enjoy some circulation. Whatever the reason for the Prince's decision to leave for Gesualdo, we know that again Leonora did not accompany him. During the period 1594-6, however, she had given birth to a baby boy, Alfonsino, and it could easily be argued that she preferred to avoid the rigours of an arduous journey with a new infant.

By February 1597 Gesualdo begins to write rather insistently to the Duke that he wishes his wife to return home. It may be that by now Neapolitan tongues had begun to wag. The marriage had occurred three years before, and it seems probable that the Princess had yet to be introduced to society there. Both Duke Alfonso II and Don Cesare exhort Gesualdo to come himself to fetch his wife and child, but he replies that he is in bad health and that his physicians have advised him not to undertake the hardships of such a voyage which could only aggravate his asthmatic condition.

By October Leonora had still not returned home, and on the ninth of that month the Duke died. With him the glory of Ferrara slipped away, for he had died without heir. His death ended his efforts to win a reversal of the Papal decision of 1591. Gesualdo's uncle, Cardinal Gesualdo, had only recently (1596) been elevated to the rank of Archbishop of Naples, and had the Ferrara question been raised anew, he might have put the weight of his office behind such a request. It is known that the Duke had tried continuously even in his last months to increase his influence with the church

---

[1] Guarini, cf. Chapt. 2, fn. 66, states that his residence lasted for five years, but this is clearly erroneous.

[2] Santi, 'La Storia della Secchia rapita', in *Memorie della Regia Accademia di Scienze*, Ser. III, vols. VI and IX (Modena, 1906, 1909). See also Vatielli, p. 42.

by securing the promotion of Leonora's half-brother Alessandro to the rank of Cardinal. This, however, had been repeatedly turned down.

Don Carlo, still in bad health and unable to come in person, sent his condolences by the Neapolitan Marcello Filomarino. As the curtain came down on the court at Ferrara its attractiveness waned, and on the first of September two gentlemen sent by the Prince of Venosa, the Count of Saponara and Fabrizio Sanseverino, arrived in Ferrara in order to accompany the Princess and Alfonsino together with Count Alfonso Fontanelli back to Gesualdo.[3]

In a letter of 8 September 1597 to Don Cesare d'Este, Leonora's brother, Gesualdo announces the safe arrival of his wife:

> The arrival of the Signora Principessa, my wife, in good health, has not only tempered my great sorrow, which I· had owing to her long delay after I had known of her departure from Ferrara, but also has brought joy to me as Your Highness can easily imagine from the great affection which I have for her.
>
> It has been a pleasure again to see on this occasion Sig. Count Alfonso Fontanelli sent by Your Highness . . . and I believe that by now Marcello Filomarino must have arrived, sent by me to bring condolences to Your Highness due to the loss of the Duke, my Master.[4]

Don Carlo's expression of sentiment, as conventional as it was effusive, undoubtedly fooled no one. The three-year-old marriage was already well tarnished, and the 'great affection' which he held for her had not been regularly demonstrated for some time. He was, however, probably happy to have the Princess in Gesualdo at last, if only for appearance's sake.

Between this time and Gesualdo's death, the Estes received several hundred letters from the Prince, and about six hundred from the Princess.[5] The latter disclose from time to time unusually valuable information, but those of the Prince are surprisingly barren.[6]

Of her four brothers, two were particularly close to Leonora in these years. One was Cesare, newly Duke of Modena whither the ducal seat was transferred when the duchy of Ferrara was reclaimed by the Papacy on Alfonso II's death. Leonora's visits to the north were henceforth not to

---

[3] Vatielli, p. 43.　　　[4] Ibid, p. 61.

[5] Preserved in the Archivio di Stato in Modena.

[6] More than one Gesualdine has been intrigued by the thought of disclosures from the sizable correspondence only to be ultimately disappointed. Vatielli, p. 61, sounded fair warning: 'In running through many of his letters to the Estes and to other of his relatives, there is to be noted a warmth of expression, of affection, and of constant attachment to his wife, an anxiety for her health, and the heartbreak of her being

Ferrara but to Modena. The other was her half-brother Alessandro, for whom Alfonso had tried to obtain a cardinalate. The elevation ultimately came, but only after Alfonso's death, and it has been suggested that Alessandro's promotion came as a result of Pope Clement VIII's desire to alleviate the House of Este's grievance at the forfeiture of Ferrara. A letter from Alessandro dated 3 March 1599, which brings news of his promotion, concludes thus:

> In relation to our seeing each other again, let us not lose hope, dear sister; for as long as we have life, everything is possible. Therefore at the right time, I shall deny neither myself nor you this exchange of happiness. In the meantime see to it that I hear news of the state of your health and your prosperity on many occasions, that it may comfort me; so that if I cannot extinguish, at least I shall be able to temper the most ardent desire I have to embrace Your Excellency.
> . . . And I kiss you and our dear little Don Alfonsino. . . .[7]

An endless procession of letters confirm that Leonora came to lean more and more heavily upon Alessandro for personal and spiritual strength in these years of domestic crisis. An unnaturally deep attachment between the two was suggested even at that time, as we shall see later. We know that Cardinal Alessandro was not unsusceptible to the beauties of the fair sex, for when already a priest he was attracted to the young sister of Marco Pio, whose palace the Gesualdos had leased during their residence at Ferrara. She was seduced by the Cardinal, and went forthwith to a convent, assuming the name of Sister Camilla.[8]

---

away. These sentiments are in open contrast with his bad conduct toward the Princess, with the maltreatment which he inflicted upon her, of which there is irrefutable testimony and proof. In truth these letters have an official character, and almost all are in the hand of his secretary: letters, hence, of convenience, ceremony, of propriety, as the style and use of the time required, of obsequious phrases of respect; in substance not sincere and even hypocritical—in order to hide from his relatives his true sentiments towards the princess and to have them believe other than what was the case.' The author is indebted to Mrs. Ruth Adams whose translations of several of these letters she early made available for study. Later the author with the assistance of Prof. Vincent Scanio undertook an intensive and independent examination of hundreds of these letters. Unfortunately, this decisively confirmed Vatielli's description in that they yielded very little of any interest.

[7] *Lettere di Alessandro d'Este*, Bibl. Estense, MS F.6.6. (*olim* MS 11.*21); also found in *Lettere del Priore Arlotti*, Bibl. Estense, MS W.5.6. (*olim* MS 11.*26), ff. 72v–73r, and MS G.1.6. (*olim* IX.F.17) headed, 'Alla Sra. Prencipe[ssa] di Venosa per il Carle d'Este.' Cf. Santi, p. 321 for original Italian.

[8] Vatielli, p. 62, fn. 24. Alessandro may also have been the murderer of Marco Pio, but whether or not this had any connection with an amorous affair with his sister is not certain.

But to return to Don Carlo's abuses of Leonora. It is said that he 'began to display bad treatment toward his wife, arriving at the point of despising her, being very rude to her, beating her, and making her give up all desire to live. And all this to say nothing of the humiliation and other offences to her dignity, staying without any regard for her with two other women.'[9] Cardinal Alessandro, who had received the news of these excesses, proposed in a letter to Don Cesare of 27 February 1600 'to take her away from there.' He likewise suggested that the Pope be petitioned for permission to initiate proceedings for a divorce. Leonora, however, would not give her consent at this time, 'still having some affection for the Prince.' It is understandable that while there was a child, divorce may have seemed an extreme step. In order, however, to restrain Gesualdo in his maltreatment of the Princess, the two brothers threatened to appeal to Cardinal Alfonso, Archbishop of Naples and Gesualdo's paternal uncle. Leonora opposed this also. Cardinal Alessandro wrote from Rome to his brother Cesare on 4 November 1600, 'Our sister does not wish any word about her bad treatment to be spoken to Cardinal Gesualdo, and she has written to me about this.'[10]

At times we gather from the correspondents that, fervent as their letters are, they cannot tell all; that certain matters, undoubtedly relating to the domestic crisis, had best be discussed only in person. One letter from the Cardinal to the Princess reads in part:

> I assure you at the same time that I anxiously await news from Your Highness concerning the state of your health, news which could buoy my soul, which is not only depressed but tired from the weight of the most heavy cares, past and present. I have actually quite a lot to write about that concerns us deeply, but it would be better to speak about these things in person, which perhaps will be possible for us at some other time. I will say only this much then while we are here in Modena, where we enjoy the quiet life—a way of life which is so precious that I find it difficult to express. . . . Kiss the hand of the Prince in my name, and embrace for me a thousand times little Don Alfonso, your and my dearest joy.[11]

9 Santi, p. 322.
10 Ibid.: 'Non piace alla Sig. Principessa nostra sorella che de'suoi accidenti si muova parola al sig. card. Gesualdo, e me l'ha scritto alla libera.'
11 Biblioteca Estense, MS W.5.6. (*olim* MS 11. 26), a letter in Arlotti's hand to the Principessa di Venosa for Cardinale d'Este, 75v–76r.: 'L'assicuro insieme c'hormai vivo antioso, non che desideroso d'intendere di V.A. del suo stato, et della saluti sua, novelle che sollevino alquanto l'animo mio abbattuto non già, ma stanco dal peso delle gravissime cure passate, et presente. Di noi et delle cose nostre havrei molto da scrivere; ma sarebbe meglio il parlarne. Il che forse ci sara concesso anco una volta.

In October of this same year, 1600, Alfonsino, the only child of Carlo and Leonora, died. Gesualdo expressed a grief whose sincerity we cannot doubt in a letter to Don Cesare dated 22 October.[12]

It has pleased the Divine Majesty to call unto himself my Don Alfonsino, after an illness of seventeen days of fever and fluxes, and, indeed, I could not in this world experience a greater torment. My sorrow, however, is somewhat mitigated when I think that, surely, he now must enjoy the extreme glory of heaven.

It will be remembered that this is the child some believe represented in the picture in the Cappuchin monastery in Gesualdo. Don Carlo still had a living son, Don Emmanuele, born of his first wife, who was at this time in the service of Leonora's brother, Cardinal Alessandro.

To express the condolences of the Este court on the death of Alfonsino, Don Cesare sent to Gesualdo one of his courtiers, Lucillo Gentiloni. A few months later Alessandro, too, determined to go to Gesualdo in the guise of making a personal presentation of his condolences, but also certainly with the intention of determining for himself the marital situation between Leonora and Don Carlo. The visit took place during the first part of May 1601.[13]

On 16 May Leonora wrote to Cesare: 'The Cardinal, our brother, was here to favour me with a mere five-day visit, bringing much consolation and happiness as Your Highness can well imagine. But I was soon deprived of this source of happiness.'[14] A more detailed account of the journey and visit is disclosed in a letter of Ridolfo Arlotti, who accompanied Cardinal Alessandro on this voyage, to Donna Ippolita, Princess of Mirandola and sister of Leonora.[15] After describing the rigours of the journey from Rome, including a storm at sea and a successful avoidance by Cardinal Alessandro of a seemingly inevitable confrontation with Archbishop Alfonso Gesualdo in Naples, he speaks of their arrival in Gesualdo:

The Princess of Venosa . . . and the Prince, in order not to deprive him

---

Diro questo solo in tanto che siamo a Modena dove si gode una certa quieta ch'io non so esprimerla. . . . Bacia mio nome le mani al Sig. Principe, et abbracci mille volti per me Donn'Alfonsino sua et mia carissima gioia.'

[12] Vatielli, p. 62.

[13] Spaccini, XVII, p. 187, in his entry for the tenth of that month states, 'Today Cardinal d'Este left for Naples and Venosa in order to visit the Prince of Venosa, his brother-in-law, and the next day was followed by Cardinal Montalto together with many friends.'

[14] Cf. Santi, pp. 322–3.

[15] *Lettere di Ridolfo Arlotti*, Bibl. Estense, MS. W.5.6. (*olim* MS 11.*26), reprinted in Santi, p. 323.

of his pleasure, put on a clever show of dissimulation in such wise that the one greeted him at the head and the other in the middle of the staircase. The greetings were both sweet and bitter, as can be imagined, especially between sister and brother, who at the first meeting greeted each other more with tears than with words, opening the hidden affections of their hearts. He stayed there five days and the entertainment was, for the most part, music by Isabella and her daughter, both of whom if they seemed sirens in Ferrara appeared to be angels in Gesualdo. All went into ecstasy with the exception of Mr. Livio Zabarella who was not in the least moved, reacting almost as though he had listened to Magagno and Begotto sing their silly pavanes.

But Mr. Baldassare Paolucci who knows the customs of that country and observes them, pretended that he wanted to stab himself and hurl himself from the window. Count Massimiliano Montecuccoli, grieving over the fact that he had been overcome in harmony by two women, vowed that he would break the drum. The Cardinal, the Princess and the Prince always dined together and alone, and the supply of food was so great and its exquisiteness was such that neither Lucullus nor Mark Anthony nor Cleopatra nor Fagnano could have conceived of improving on it.

For all the feigned social behaviour of the principals, and whatever the success of Cardinal Alessandro's mission, his visit undoubtedly helped to increase the affection between brother and sister. A few weeks later the Princess writes to the Cardinal,

> In the unhappiness of the loneliness in which Your Excellency left me upon your departure, I have been comforting myself by writing to you often as I have done up to the present. But adverse fortune contests my comforts by denying me all but one reply from you . . . I have taken pen in hand again, and I greet you with that affection which you have always and always will be able to perceive in me, which is from the heart and most reverential and ardent.[16]

The correspondence between Leonora and Alessandro, which soon reached a fever peak, is the principal evidence used by Santi[17] in his incestuous interpretation of passages in Tassoni's contemporary *Secchia rapita*, an epic poem still well known to the Modenese today. Santi professes to see in an episode between Principe Manfredi and the Contessa di Caserta (10th canto)

---

[16] *Lettere di diversi*, Biblioteca Estense, MS F.6.6. (*olim* MS 11,*21). Cf. Santi, p. 323.
[17] Santi, pp. 317–28.

parallels of relationship and action with the Cardinal and Leonora. He contends that the poem, which was written in 1613, would dare to have involved these illustrious personages in such a tale only now that the Prince himself was dead. However, notwithstanding Alessandro's doubtful moral character, Vatielli remains convinced that it is all a matter of the 'petty maligning of the chroniclers and the fantasy of the poets.'[18] The letters are indeed impassioned, but nothing conclusive can be determined, since the circumstances would in any case have inspired the two to share confidences and to solicit emotional comfort.

The Cardinal's attempts to persuade Leonora to come to Modena by his description of the quiet life there were ultimately successful, and as early as November 1601 she made known to him her desire to visit Modena for a stay of at least four to six months. On the 17th of that month Alessandro wrote to Duke Cesare: 'We shall have to have her invited with skill and secrecy by the Duchess or by Your Highness, giving the impression that the expenses will be paid by yourself in order to obtain the consent of her husband. She would like to come next April.'[19]

Don Carlo was, however, opposed to the visit. As time passed Leonora's sufferings, not only psychological but physical, multiplied. Her letters between 1604 and 1609 provide a virtual doctor's chart of her condition, and there is no doubt that on a number of occasions her relatives were gravely concerned.[20]

When in April 1607 Don Cesare asked that his sister should come to Modena to recuperate in its salubrious air, Gesualdo countered with references to the difficulties involved and his own continuing illness. No doubt, as brother and sister suspected, Gesualdo feared that Leonora could be more explicit in person than by letter about her maltreatment. On the other hand, a legitimate desire to have her in Gesualdo for the forthcoming marriage of his son Don Emmanuele to Donna Maria Polissena of Furstenberg could have been at least partially responsible for his opposition to her journey. This wedding took place on 22 October 1607. Leonora remained for the event but left immediately for Modena: Gesualdo had agreed that the Princess could assist at the celebration there of his nephew Alfonso's marriage with Isabella di Savoia in the spring of 1608. It is noteworthy that Don Carlo himself showed no interest in making the journey with her. In fact, we have no record of any travelling by the Prince from the time of his return to Gesualdo in 1596 until his death. It is likely that he confined himself almost

[18] Vatielli, p. 64.
[19] Santi, p. 324.
[20] Archivio di Stato, Modena, MS Nap.-Sic., busta 9, 1252/41.

exclusively to Gesualdo and Naples, and tended to become increasingly a recluse.

He had only permitted Leonora to go to Modena, however, until the marriage celebrations had been concluded, and thereafter he began to insist repeatedly that she should return to him. Leonora would gladly have remained longer had it not been for what she deemed to be her marital duty and also perhaps the fear that her absence had given rise to unpleasant rumours, all of which led her to concede that she would 'return home a willing martyr; to suffer Purgatory in this life, so that she might enjoy Paradise in the next'.[21]

On 20 October 1608 Cardinal Alessandro wrote from Modena to Angelo Raselli, his *maestro di casa* in Rome, that the Princess of Venosa would leave shortly for Gesualdo by way of Tivoli.[22] On 22 October she departed, accompanied by Count Paolo Manfredi, Governor of Sassuolo, a little town on the hills near Modena.

But a short time after her arrival in Gesualdo she once again fell gravely ill. Nor did things improve the following year. Spaccini wrote on 4 August 1609:

The major-domo Prondolo has left for Venosa. It seems that the Princess does not get along well with her husband, as she never did, and it would not be at all surprising if she were to return. Besides her stepson [Emmanuele] has married, and God only knows how they get along together. She could have stayed in Modena when she was there, but she was afraid that tongues would wag, just as the Duchess of Urbino caused them to do.[23] If the Princess does return, she will give them something to talk about more even than the Duchess.[24]

However, a letter from the Prince himself dated 10 September 1609 reluctantly agreed to send her back to Modena for a period of six months in hopes that she might recover her health. She arrived there on the evening of November 7th, and this time remained not six months but almost a year. Because of the long delay in her return to Gesualdo, rumours of a divorce began to circulate.[25] In a *Cronaca* conserved in the Archivio del Collegio di S. Carlo in Modena, under the date 7 November 1609, we read, 'The Princess

[21] *Lettere di Ridolfo Arlotti a Baldassare Paolucci*, Biblioteca Estense, MS G.1.6. (*olim* MS IX.F.17, not XI.F.17 as Santi cites it): 'ritornarsene, martire volantaria in Regno, a patire il Purgatorio in questa vita, per godere il Paradiso nell'altra.'
[22] Santi, p. 325.
[23] The Duchess of Urbino was the sister of Duke Alfonso II, who brought an end to the most notorious of her affairs by having her lover killed. Cf. p. 40.
[24] Cf. Vatielli, p. 66.
[25] See Litta, *Famiglie celebri italiane*, Parte III, Tavola XV.

of Venosa has undertaken a divorce with her husband with the consent of Pope Paul V on the grounds of excesses and prodigalities,' and, it continues, 'languishing because of the extravagances of her husband, she finally arrived at such a state that she determined upon a divorce, and the Pope conceded it.'[26] It may well be that she agreed to allow her brothers to petition the Pope. It may also be true that he actually granted permission. But Leonora determined not to go through with such a drastic action, and she finally yielded to the continued urgings of the Prince to Duke Cesare to give 'his kind permission that she return here to console me,' and left for Gesualdo on 10 October 1610. Don Carlo sent his cousin Cesare Gesualdo to Modena 'in order to accompany and serve her on this voyage.'[27]

In the autumn of 1612 the Prince and Princess received a visit from their nephew, Prince Luigi d'Este, returning at that time from a voyage to France and England, but otherwise we know nothing of events between Leonora's final return and the death of Don Carlo in September 1613.

In his last years Gesualdo must have occupied himself increasingly with music, for the *Responsoria* for Holy Week as well as the fifth and six volumes of madrigals all appeared in 1611. In view of his other duties as lord and prince of a large estate, he must have led a busy if not particularly social life. For the musician it is disappointing, to say the least, that most of the information which we possess concerning the last fifteen years of his life relate almost exclusively to his domestic trials.

Gesualdo's Death

There are several letters in Leonora's hand, written in the days immediately following his death on 8 September 1613, among which is the following to her brother:[28]

> Most Serene Prince, My Master and Brother,
> Whosoever loseth his dear consort, remains naturally most disconsolate and most afflicted. This has just happened to me now that I am without the company of my dear Prince, who died on the eighth late in the evening, and went to enjoy the heavenly realm, leaving this earthly state. From this loss Your Highness can imagine my feelings which could not

[26] Santi, p. 325, fn. 1.   [27] Several letters along the route record her trip back: two from Rimini on 28 October; two from Tivoli on 10 November; and finally one written to the Duke upon her arrival back in Gesualdo on 19 November 1610, after a stop in Rome.

[28] See Vatielli, p. 68, for Italian text. Archivio di Stato, Modena, MS Nap.-Sic., busta 11 (1253), contains several letters from Leonora relating to Don Carlo's death. While a number are legible, the longest, which is to Duke Cesare and in her own hand, is unfortunately badly damaged and virtually unreadable except for the opening sentence which announces the subject.

be more sorrowful and bitter, which I will do my best to mitigate with the hope of finding the same place which I have always had in the favour of Your Highness. Meanwhile I am sending you a copy of the last will and testament so that you can judge which part I am entitled to, and I am yours most faithfully.

Gesualdo   Your humble and devoted
13 September 1613   sister
                                                                Leonora d'Este

To the end Leonora plays the princess, maintaining the correct form even to a brother who knew everything. While she may not have been joyous at her consort's passing, it cannot be doubted that she must have felt a final sense of relief. One modern writer has suggested that Gesualdo's death was the result of foul play,[29] but there is no evidence which points to this. It is difficult to believe that Leonora for all her long suffering would have been moved to such extremes, especially when we recall that she could not even bring herself to the much less drastic remedy of divorce. The only other candidate for this fantasy murder would be his daughter-in-law, Donna Polisena, wife of his son Don Emmanuele who died only shortly before his father. We know that she was stubbornly to contest Don Carlo's will. Perhaps if we are willing to cast her as a character of extreme temperament and Borgian inclinations, we might attribute to her both the murder of her husband and father-in-law, with the intention of forcing the Princess Leonora, as she did, to withdraw many of her claims with regard to the estate. Interestingly enough, father and son did indeed die within a month of each other.

So much for untenable theories of Don Carlo's demise. We may more usefully turn our attention to medical considerations. We have already noted that Gesualdo suffered certain ailments, which he frequently gave as an excuse not to travel. He was almost certainly violently asthmatic, himself describing the symptoms in several letters. But beyond this well attested ailment, there is evidence of other physical irregularities which might ultimately have taken their toll. A letter of the Genoese Michele Giustiniani,[30] addressed to Giulio Giustiniani, procurator of S. Marco, and dated 10 October 1674, reads:

Most Illustrious and Excellent Highness,
This room of Gesualdo, where I find myself in order to settle the business of an Abbey of mine which is not going well, gives me the

[29] Gray & Heseltine, p. 43.
[30] Included in *Lettere memorabili* (Rome, 1675); Italian text given in Vatielli, p. 67.

opportunity to remind Your Excellency of my respect and at the same time to inform you that in this place on the 3rd of September, 1613, the death of Don Carlo Gesualdo, Prince of Venosa, Neapolitan cavalier, most excellent musician as his printed works show, and player of the arch-lute, took place—a death hastened by a strange illness, which made it soothing for him to be given blows on the temples and other parts of the body by putting over those parts a small bundle of rags.

A strange recompense, indeed, that as the Prince had elicited admiration and gladness from the listener with the melody and sweetness of his music and its sound, so he received relief and quietness in his internal pain from the heavy beatings.

Owing to the pitiful death of this cavalier, which happened a few days before [sic] that of Don Emmanuele, his only son, the estate of Venosa passed to Prince Luduvisio by means of Donna Elizabetta Gesualdo, his wife and Gesualdo's niece.

This is fundamentally the same information as in the chronicle *Rovine di Case Napolitane del suo tempo* by Don Ferrante della Marra of 1632:

The third misfortune was that through the agency of God, he was assailed and afflicted by a vast horde of demons which gave him no peace for many days on end unless ten or twelve young men, whom he kept specially for the purpose, were to beat him violently three times a day, during which operation he was wont to smile joyfully. And in this state did he die miserably at Gesualdo, but not until he had lived to witness, for his fourth affliction, the death of his only son Don Emmanuele, who hated his father and had longed for his death, and, what was worse, this son died without leaving any children save only two daughters whom he had by Donna Polisena of Fustemberg [sic], a German princess.[31]

Masochism is clearly implicit in both accounts, but the function that the action was intended to perform is perhaps more accurately and dispassionately related in Thomas Campanella's *Medicinalium juxta propria principia* of 1635, where under the heading of 'Monstrosa cura' we read:

The Prince of Venosa, one of the best musicians of his age, was unable to go to the stool, without having been previously flogged by a valet kept expressly for the purpose.[32]

[31] Trans. in Gray & Heseltine, pp. 49–50.
[32] Campanella, op. cit., p. 111: 'Princeps Venusia musica clarissimus nostro tempore cacare non poterat; nisi verberatus à servo ad id adscito.' Trans. after Gray & Heseltine, p. 51.

There is one additional source of 'medical' evidence, and it is the closest to the scene in point of time. It is our friend Spaccini, whom Vatielli accused of having a bad tongue. His remarks come at the end of a lengthy entry for 21 September 1613, recording the news of Gesualdo's death barely two weeks before. The passage concludes:

And for this reason he retired to Gesualdo, and never returned to Naples, attending to music, being extremely excellent in this regard. In the meantime he had a very beautiful concubine who attracted him in such a way that he had no eyes for the Princess Leonora. Yet when the Princess was far away, he would die of passion to see her, and then when she returned, he would not pay much attention to her. He could never sleep unless someone stayed with him, embracing him in order to keep his back warm. And for this purpose he had a certain Castelvietro of Modena, who was very dear to him, who continuously slept with him when the Princess was away.[33]

Burial and Will

Gesualdo was buried according to the stipulation of his will in the church of the Gesù Nuovo at Naples. The inscription on the tablet over his tomb records that the Gesù Nuovo was the victim of a severe earthquake in the year 1688 during which the sepulchre of Gesualdo disappeared. The facts of its restoration in the year 1705 are recorded in an elaborate tablet below the one cited above. It is executed in a beautiful, full-colour mosaic with the Gesualdo coat-of-arms of a black lion and five red lilies topped by a crown.

The will, which was made on 3 September 1613, five days before the Prince's death, is a thirty-six-page document.[34] Unduly prolix, and replete with the legal language of the day, it nevertheless contains a number of items of general interest. Section two of the postscript to the main body of the will, for example, records Gesualdo's wish to leave a sum of 40 ducats a month to a Don Antonio Gesualdo, his natural son. We are in no position to know who the mother was, but the information that there was an illegitimate son whom he recognized confirms the allegations of Spaccini and others.

He beseeches the Holy Father through his infinite mercy and

---

[33] See Santi, p. 326, for Italian text.
[34] Archivio di Stato, Modena, *Archivio Segreto Estense*, busta 19 (376-16) 376, fasc. 2011/3. *Inventario*, Sezione 'Casa e Stato,' (Rome, 1953), p. 169: 'Testamento di suo marito Carlo Gesualdi principe di Venosa, 1613 Septembre 9 (sic); tre copi semp.—p. 3 cart.'

through the precious blood which was shed on the wood of the cross, that he deign to forgive my sins, and take my soul up into the place of salvation, asking in this the help of the most glorious Virgin Mary, Holy Mother, and the glorious apostles S. Peter, S. Paul, S. Michele, S. Domenico, S. Carlo, S. Maria Madalene, S. Caterina di Siena, and S. Francis,[35] all of whom I pray may deign to intercede for me; and all of this in spite of my infinite wickedness, and sins committed against his divine precepts, that through his grace my soul may be gathered unto eternal life.

He names as universal heir a child yet to be born of Donna Polissena Furstemberg, his daughter-in-law, who was left pregnant at the death of her husband, Don Emmanuele—provided the child is a son. To Donna Polissena herself and to Donna Isabella Gesualdo, his niece, he leaves a sum of 100,000 ducats each. Should Donna Polissena's child be a girl, Donna Isabella, his niece, becomes his universal heir, and the new-born girl is then assigned the sum of 100,000 ducats as a dowry.

Large sections of the will are concerned with the administration of the estate, its various properties and personalities. A few items, however, are of special interest: Section 19 calls for the construction of a chapel in the Gesù Nuovo in Naples where he is to be buried, specifying that certain adornments should be executed, that it should be called the chapel of Madonna Santissima, and that it should be undertaken by his heirs with a view to completion within five years and at a cost of 30,000 ducats; Section 22 stipulates that his wife, the Princess, shall receive a sum of 250,000 ducats, and also (Section 24) an annual allowance of 4,000 ducats to be taken from the best incomes of the estate so long as she remains a widow and continues to live in one of three places, the castle at Gesualdo, the castle at Taurasi (Tauran), or in Naples 'nella masseria nostra di San Antonio.' To Donna Polissena (Section 25) he assures, besides the monies guaranteed in Section 1, a similar annual income of 4,000 ducats a year, and freedom from attempts by anyone to make claim against the belongings of her late husband, Don Emmanuele.

He specifically requests that the castle at Gesualdo be kept always in good order and repair (Section 38), and that water continue to be carried to the castle. In the postscript, he directs that 500 masses be celebrated at the privileged altar of the Capella di S. Gregorio in Rome, and that another 500 masses be celebrated—these to be distributed in other

[35] Compare this group of figures with those represented in the altar painting of S. Maria delle Grazie.

churches at the direction of the Princess Leonora; but particularly that there should be celebrated as soon as possible in the church of San Marciano di Fuento 1,000 masses at the discretion of the fathers there, for which suitable alms are to be left. He also calls for the completion of the church of SS. Rosario in Gesualdo. S. Maria delle Grazie had already been completed in 1592, but the construction of SS. Rosario, commenced as early as 1578, had languished. This, too, was to be undertaken under the guidance of Donna Leonora, and for this undertaking he stipulates a sum of 10,000 ducats.

In section 4 of the postscript he requires the construction of the major altar of SS. Rosario di Gesualdo to be appropriately completed, and says that for its preservation and upkeep he will provide 50 ducats a year *in perpetuum* with the stipulation that the fathers of this church are obliged to celebrate at this very altar one mass per day *in perpetuo* for the soul of the maker of this will, that is Gesualdo himself.

He also calls for the erection of a church in honour of his uncle San Carlo Borromeo (Section 5), the site for which is to be determined by his wife the Princess, and his aunt the Duchess; here six masses a day are to be said for his saintly uncle. He does not stipulate the amount of money to be spent for this project, and it probably remained more of a wish than a realistic hope on his part. To begin a church is one thing, to complete it another. We are reminded in this connection of the efforts of Gesualdo's paternal uncle Cardinal Alfonso, Archbishop of Naples, who was responsible for the building of the famous Sant'Andrea della Valle in Rome. This church, today remembered by opera lovers as Tosca's church, was considered in its day to be a rival of the more famous Gesù in Rome. Initially inspired by the spirit and money of Archbishop Gesualdo, it ultimately languished, while Alfonso turned his attention to Naples 'where a new apse was built for San Gennaro, the Monte di Pietà was constructed, and new parish churches in the suburbs were created in part at Gesualdo's personal expense.'[36] Don Carlo's idea of stipulating that a church be built at his expense in honour of his uncle, who had already been made a Saint in 1610, was, however, a laudable enough request if the money could be found, and showed his good intentions in his hour of death to those who might come to judge him.

He finally ends his testament with a request for perpetual alms to be given to the friars of S. Maria delle Grazie di Gesualdo in the nature of

---

[36] Howard Hibbard, 'The Early History of Sant'Andrea della Valle,' *Art Bulletin*, December 1961, Vol. XLII, No. 4, pp. 289–318. Cf. also Ferdinando Ughello, *Italia sacra sive de episcopis italiae* . . ., VI, Venice, 1720, p. 167, CIII; and Daniello Maria Zigarelli, *Biografie dei vescovi e arcivescovi della chiesa di Napoli*, 1861, pp. 148 ff.

bread, meat, and wine ('et perpetuamente si dia loro l'elemosina di pane e carne et vino'), and likewise, failing this, to pay four times the amount to the church of SS. Rosario (Section 8).

With Don Carlo's death all Leonora's troubles were not over. She remained, true to the injunction of the will, in the castle of Gesualdo for another two years. This period was spent largely in trying to clear up the estate and perhaps attending to the larger requests as outlined in Gesualdo's final testament. Clearly there was enough in it to require a lifetime of attention if a person were to be completely conscientious in carrying out every detail of the document. To help her in administering the estate her brother Don Cesare, the Duke of Modena, sent for her assistance in these matters a Modenese notary, Geminiano Ronchi. It is said that she had to cope with various underhand dealings of Donna Polissena, who was understandably irate at being excluded from the principal benefices of the will due to the birth of a baby girl. Donna Polissena allegedly tried to have the will annulled.

While she did not succeed in this, 'her complaints and continual intrigues persuaded Leonora to renounce her legal right to reside in the Neapolitan area, and by the end of 1615, accompanied by the Marchese Ernesto Bevilacqua, she returned once and for all to Modena.'[37]

Don Ferrante della Marra, in his chronicle of the misfortunes that accrued to the house of Gesualdo, includes two final items. He writes:

And although he had arranged that the elder of these [daughters of Donna Polissena] should marry within the family, his house suffered two more misfortunes. Firstly, against his express dispositions the young Princess of Venosa was married, by order of the King, to Prince Nicolino Ludoviso, nephew of the Pope, Gregory XV; and she now lives at Bologna, having caused the loss to her family of the principality of Venosa, and also the state of Gesualdo which had been in the family for little less than six hundred years.

The second of these two other misfortunes—and to my thinking, greater than all the others—was that after the death of Don Emmanuele, the Princess Polissena went to live with her aunt, the second wife of the Prince of Caserta, Andrea Matteo Acquaviva; and having lived thus for many years did acquire an evil reputation, for not only was she all this time concubine to the said Prince, but secretly had several children by him.

Thus did it please God to destroy, both in possession and in honour, a princely house which was descended from ancient Norman kings.[38]

We have only a few additional references to the later years of Leonora. Two relate to her return to Modena in January 1615. On the twelfth of that month Spaccini states:

This morning they have taken 30 pieces of artillery and 50 small mortars to the Gates of Bologna. At 11 p.m. the Serenissima Infante [Virginia de Medici, Duke Cesare's wife] came out to receive the Princess of Venosa, sister of the Cardinal and a widow. Even the Duke, the Cardinal, and the Princes went to meet her together with cavalry and several coaches, and they made extravagant greetings since there were a lot of people in the streets to see her.[39]

Later that same month on 28 January 1615, Spaccini writes: 'The fathers of S. Domenico placed a balustrade in front of the organ in the church so that she [the Princess of Venosa] can hear the divine offices.'[40] This is all we hear of her for fifteen years. She must have increasingly been drawn to the church during this time, for in Spaccini's final mention of her in May 1631 he draws a rather touching picture.

The Princess of Venosa, after many anxieties and seeing the workings of this faulty world and how frail and infirm they are, announced that she wants to retire to the nuns of S. Eufemia, although I think that the Duke does not like it very much. She has taken a house in the neighbourhood of the convent in order to be able to go there when she wants to.[41]

Her final will and testament, dated 28 November 1637, tells us that her last years were spent in the contemplative life.[42] News of her death in that year is also confirmed by Vedriani under events for the year 1637:

The Princess of Venosa, who had retired many years before, died in Modena alone with two women in the convent of S. Eufemia. Buying the house of Count Bianchi next to the convent, she finished her life

---

38 Trans. after Gray & Heseltine, pp. 50–51.
39 Santi, p. 326, fn. 2.
40 Ibid., p. 327.
41 Loc. cit., fn. 1.
42 Preserved in the Archivio di Stato, Modena. *Archivio Segreto Estense, Inventario* (Rome, 1953), 169: 'Suo testamento publicato in data 1637 Novembre 28: rog. originale, con unite le copie aut. di quattro codicilli datati 1633, 1635 e 1637—fasc. 4 cart.'

in continuous prayers, alms, and holy works, leaving to the nuns the said house which is now used as an infirmary.[43]

Thus she died at the age of 76, and was laid to rest in the church of S. Domenico, many miles distant from her husband, little suspecting that because of him her immortality had been assured.

[43] Vedriani, *Historia dell'antichissima città di Modena*, Pt. II, 667.

Conclusion

⌒∿⌒

PATRONAGE was a paramount factor in the production of art music in the sixteenth century. The nobility, whether in the courts or the church, flamboyantly adapted the purely functional aspects of entertainment and worship to the prospect of personal aggrandizement. In Gesualdo, however, the noble is not merely patron but creator. The Prince has become Artist. Nothing could more clearly dramatize one of the meanings of *musica reservata*, namely music of and for an élite.

The melancholy temperament traditionally associated with the Mannerist artist, particularly in painting and literature, is here found in full flower. Gesualdo's alternating capacity for acts of violence or the life of a recluse suggests parallels in the life of Pontormo, Rosso, Michelangelo, and Tasso. Temperamentally he is as much an artist as a prince. His concern for his own immortality is commensurate not only with his rank but also with his regard for the importance of his creations.

Gesualdo lived through the initial aftermath of the Counter-Reformation, but his faith in his church was unshaken, and he forged new weapons for it in his sacred music, which harmonized with the new zeal of the church fathers and their awakening desire to appeal to man's emotional nature. He not only wrote for the church, he built for it. He commissioned his portrait in the context of an altar painting when he could have afforded to have it painted in an independent context a dozen times over. In his will he not only called for the completion of a second church which in his lifetime had only been begun, but proposed the erection of a third in honour of his saintly uncle, Carlo Borromeo.

He suffered the uncertainty, and frequently very probably the anguish, of the creative personality, while at the same time holding a title that released him from the need to prove himself personally. That his lot as an artist was made in some ways more difficult because of the responsibilities of his station, or that it brought as many liabilities as assets, can hardly be questioned. Initially, at least, it must have been difficult for him to be taken seriously by his artistic peers; nor, indeed, has his social equivalent appeared on the musical scene in such a prominent manner since his time.

The vagaries of his private life contrast with his steady maturation as a composer. While his life may have been bounded by psychic ambivalences, a sense of guilt, or an uneasiness in personal relationships, his work was infused by an amazingly secure sense of direction. If the materials were cast in a most refined, even precarious balance, a steady hand and heart ruled supreme when it was most important that they so do. He was the agent through which the late phase of musical Mannerism received its quintessential expression. For this it was appropriate, if not inevitable, that the Prince and Artist should join hands, that patron and creator become one. At the same time there are signs of a not totally comfortable alliance. There is no need to wonder why no more Gesualdos were forthcoming.

PART TWO

The Music

CHAPTER FOUR

❧❧❧

The Question of Mannerism

THE music of Gesualdo may be viewed as leading from the central
movement of the Renaissance, while standing somewhat apart from
it; and moving toward, but stopping short of, the Baroque. As
such, it is characteristic of the spirit which prevailed between the High
Renaissance and the Early Baroque. The richer the time the greater the
variety of possible interpretations, and the century from 1520 to 1620 is
sufficiently rich to have inspired an abundant and diverse literature. Yet
for all its chronological breadth, which to a degree guarantees some over-
lapping, this period increasingly emerges as one which possesses a clearly
perceivable orientation and an identifiable stylistic character—that of an
Age of Mannerism.

Both music historian and art historian have begun to question whether
the label 'Renaissance' should assume the entire descriptive burden of the
period from 1400 to 1600. In music there have been occasional attempts to
postpone the beginnings of the Renaissance until the age of Ockeghem in
order to produce a more manageable historical block. But art historians are
inclined to label the period 1475–1520 the High Renaissance, and the most
representative artists of this time suggest a striking aesthetic parallel with
their musical contemporaries, such as Obrecht, Josquin, and Isaac. To delay
the beginnings of the Renaissance until the mid-fifteenth century blends
the High Renaissance and Early Renaissance too closely to do justice to
either. The lack of a clear distinction in the field of music between the terms
High Renaissance and Late Renaissance has led to additional confusion,[1]
and the increasing substitution of Mannerism for the Late Renaissance has
only served to compound the problem.

Since the term 'High Renaissance' carries with it the tone of a qualitative

---

[1] Reese, for example, in the opening page of his admirable book on the Renaissance
remarks: 'The author prefers the term "Late" to "High", since the latter may suggest
an unwarranted implication that the music of the fifteenth century is inferior to that
of the sixteenth,' implying a chronological identity between the two terms.

judgement, music historians have been reluctant to adopt it. Their wariness may, however, be unnecessary, for the idea of a zenith of attainment is not our confection but a fundamental Renaissance notion. The Renaissance musician-theorist for the first time began to view his art in terms of a pattern of progress toward an ideal of perfection. He largely viewed antiquity as the last great period of artistic endeavour, and consequently saw the long stretch of time between the ancients and his own period as a great infertile valley. Numerous reasons for this stance could be offered, not least his colossal ignorance of the music written in the intervening years. But for whatever reason, the doctrine of progress began to hold an ever stronger attraction for him as the value of his own productions increased in his mind.

The Crisis of the 'Ars Perfecta'

By the time of Glareanus' *Dodecachordon* (1547) the concept of the achievement of an *ars perfecta* was sufficiently established to be stated in print. The fifteenth century had seen not only the rejuvenation of the art of music, but the achievement of an ideal in the figure of Josquin des Prez. The same phenomenon occurred in the visual arts where Raphael and others had similarly provided mankind with a model for perfection and grace and had defined the classic style. Once established, however, the figures who represented it best posed a dilemma. If theirs was an *ars perfecta*, what course of action was open to the artist who followed? One could either continue to imitate these models or react against them. Neither possibility could have seemed especially attractive. Imitation, even of so exalted a model, is no more than that; yet to react against perfection automatically implied a decline. As Gombrich has said, 'It lies in the nature of this conception of the gradual unfolding of an ideal that it must come to a stop once perfection is reached.'[2]

Glareanus stated unequivocally that in the works of Josquin he had found the perfect art 'to which nothing can be added, after which nothing but decline is to be expected.'[3] In light of this conclusion the only recourse was for each generation to nominate its own candidate for a place at the summit. So it was that Hermann Finck in his *Pratica musica* of 1556 hailed Nicolas Gombert as a worthy heir to Josquin's throne, as Zarlino similarly acclaimed

---

[2] E. H. Gombrich, 'Introduction: The Historiographic Background,' in *The Renaissance and Mannerism*, Acts of the Twentieth International Congress of the History of Art
[3] (Princeton, 1963), II, p. 165.
   Glareanus, *Dodecachordon* (1547), p. 241: ars perfecta, 'cui ut nihil addi potest, ita nihil ei quam senium tandem expectandum.'

Willaert in his treatise of 1558. In the idea of a 'worthy successor' Finck and Zarlino may have imagined that they had momentarily delayed a crisis, but a sequence of such manouevres was ultimately destined to create a credibility gap.[4]

In reality Glareanus, Finck, and Zarlino could hardly have believed that nothing had transpired in the world of music by the 1550s to challenge the idea of a classic style defined at its moment of apex thirty years before. The smooth-flowing, polyphonic ideal of the Netherlands composers had not only served as a norm in the North, but through the travels of the composers had been transplanted and had flowered in Italy as well.[5] Early in the century, however, Italy had begun to rediscover its native voice in the frottola and villota. Because of their basically fragmented and sectional character, reduced to a stereotype never reached by the contemporary chanson, for example, they were not especially endorsed by the composers from the North, even when working in Italy. But ultimately the *Oltremontani* responded to the need of the Italians to create a specifically Italianate art, and helped their southern colleagues to fashion not a frivolous secular music, but one worthy of the skills and craft of their northern heritage. The hybrid by-product, which appeared for the first time in the late 1520s, was the madrigal, one of the earliest objects of musical Mannerism. The frottola and villota played their part in the initial phase of the form, as did the Parisian chanson, but what raised the madrigal from the frottola-canzone genre to the realm of high art, and which softened the evidence of its humble (musical, not social) origins, was the invasion of Flemish polyphony.

Two distinct views with respect to the inception of Mannerism have been proposed by Hauser and Shearman,[6] and each, despite their seeming

[4] Leo Schrade's book on Monteverdi approaches these matters from a slightly different angle in its two initial chapters.

[5] It is interesting to note that music's *ars perfecta* of the early Cinquecento was predominantly defined by Northern currents, while the classic style of early sixteenth-century painting was exclusively Italian.

[6] Hauser, *Mannerism* (New York, 1965) and Shearman, *Mannerism* (Middlesex, 1967). The following additional works also discuss this complex but important stylistic question: Friedländer, *Mannerism and Anti-Mannerism in Italian Painting* (1957); Sypher, *Four Stages of Renaissance Style* (1955); Blunt, *Artistic Theory in Italy* (1956); Gombrich, Smyth, and Shearman in *The Renaissance and Mannerism*, in Acts of the Twentieth International Congress, II (1963); Briganti, *La maniera italiana* (1961); Bousquet, *Mannerism* (1964); Wurtenberg, *Mannerism* (tr. from German, 1963); Rowland, *Mannerism—Style and Mood* (1964). The assessment of the role of music in Shearman's *Mannerism*, pp. 96–104, though brief, is helpful. Two of the most provocative articles relative to the nature and scope of Mannerism in music are by Robert Wolf: 'The Aesthetic Problem of the "Renaissance",' in *Revue Belge de Musicologie*, IX (1955), pp. 83–102, and 'Renaissance, Mannerism, Baroque: Three Styles, Three Periods,' in *Les Colloques de Wégimont*, IV (1957), pp. 35–59. Don Harran's excellent article

opposition, carries a seed of truth. The sub-title of Hauser's provocative study describes Mannerism as 'The Crisis of the Renaissance and the Origin of Modern Art', and his position is summed up in the dictum: 'The development of mannerism marked one of the deepest breaks in the history of art, and its rediscovery implies a similar break in our own day.' Shearman, however, in his illuminating monograph has pointed to Mannerism as a 'logical sequel' to the High Renaissance, and judges that 'One of the most characteristic things about Mannerism is that its birth was ideally easy and attended by no crisis.' That the High Renaissance provided the foundation upon which the Mannerist spirit could flourish is undeniable. That the birth was easy points only to the unartificial relation to the source and the quality of the nourishment. Like all spirited children, however, the ultimate conflict with the parent was as inevitable as it was natural.

The madrigal, then, as the step-child of the motet and the orphan of the frottola, emerges as the Mannerist vehicle *par excellence*, even in preference to the chanson which could be similarly viewed in certain particulars.[7] Initially, however, it should be emphasized that anti-classic features, which in themselves are characteristically held to be Mannerist, typically live side-by-side with, and are counter-balanced by, elements totally classic in tone, and it is often precisely this confrontation which sparks the Mannerist flame. Just as the several ingredients in a single work are not all of the same order, it is not surprising that a composer will strike, from work to work, now one posture now another, so that a given artist's output may not be viewed as uniformly Mannerist. This accounts for much of the difficulty in defining the limitations of a stylistic concept which, because of its basically personal character, has always been somewhat elusive. As the Mannerist approach is alternately fanciful and anxious, superficial and tortured, there are inevitably a number of highly individual modes of expression to be found within its compass. The essential ambivalence, however, which pervades all Mannerism, is created in the madrigal out of the confrontation and conjunction of Northern and Italian currents.

' "Mannerism" in the Cinquecento Madrigal?' in *Musical Quarterly*, LV (1969), p. 521, appeared too late to be taken into account in the present discussion, as did J. Haar's 'Classicism and Mannerism in 16th-Century Music,' *The International Revue of Music Aesthetics & Sociology*, I (1970), pp. 55–67; M. Maniates' 'Musical Mannerism: Effeteness or Virility? in *Musical Quarterly*, LVII (1971), pp. 270–93; and C. Palisca's 'Ut oratoria musica: the Rhetorical Basis of Musical Mannerism,' in *The Meaning of Mannerism*, ed. F. W. Robinson & S. G. Nichols, Jr. (Hanover, N. H., 1972), pp. 37–65.

[7] Cf. *Chanson and Madrigal, 1480–1530*, ed. by James Haar; particularly 'Les Goûts Réunis, or the Worlds of the Madrigal and Chanson Confronted,' pp. 88–138, by Daniel Heartz.

The Elements of Mannerism

The term *maniera* is the nearest contemporary equivalent which can be culled from the Cinquecento; the word *manierismo* is a later invention.[8] *Maniera* refers to style, usually with the connotation of good style, even stylishness. It was used in a more or less complimentary fashion by Vasari with reference to the painter's copying of the most beautiful elements, particularly of the human figure, and combining them to make the most perfect whole. This courtly brand of Mannerism dominates the musical as well as the artistic scene until the mid-point of the century when Dolce and others use the term in a derogatory manner to refer to the monotonous uniformity with which this ideal was applied.[9] The theorists' censure of the increasingly routine application of specific rhythmic and contrapuntal figures in the work of the madrigalists may be cited as a musical analogue. The similarity between these two sixteenth-century attitudes is significant, especially since Dolce and Galilei already presage the Seicento use of the word from which later concepts of Mannerism stemmed. Bellori, the chief artistic critic to give voice to these views in the seventeenth century, in his turn anticipated the nineteenth-century view of *maniera*, namely as a vice that had been responsible for the decline of Cinquecento painting. To the Romantics the decline was not only inevitable but involuntary, a necessary sequence to the achievement of an *ars perfecta*.[10] Even today it is difficult to suppress the pejorative implication of the word. But while much of Mannerist art is patently mannered, all mannered art is not Mannerist. The confusion and near equation of 'Mannerist' with 'mannered' has proven to be one of the most serious stumbling blocks to a true appreciation of the idea.[11]

While the *ars perfecta* of the High Renaissance supported a reasonably

[8] By the historian Luigi Lanzi (1792).

[9] Dolce, *Dialogo della pittura* (Venice, 1557), republished in Paola Barocchi, *Trattati d'arte del cinquecento fra manierismo e controriforma* (Bari, 1960–1), I, p. 196.

[10] Craig Smyth, 'Mannerism and Maniera' in *The Renaissance and Mannerism*, Acts of the Twentieth International Congress, II, pp. 175, 177.

[11] In addition Mannerism has come increasingly to be viewed as a recurring phenomenon involving an anti-classic reaction, yet dependent in part upon selectivity and reliance upon its immediate past, prizing difficulty and preciosity as well as artificiality, affectation, and refinement. As such we might well speak of various 'manneristic' phases in history. But while it may be possible to defend a theory of cyclic patterning in any history, this view of 'the manifestation of a rebellious, expressionistic "constant of the European spirit"' (Smyth, 196–7) does not help to define a particular stylistic period and will not be considered here. Apel's use of the term 'manneristic' for the complicated rhythmic style of the late fourteenth century is a case in point. Cf. Hauser, *Mannerism*, pp. 355 ff for a discussion concerning the idea of recurring mannerist traits.

marked stylistic diversity between repertoires, the Mannerist spirit endorsed the application of increasingly varied means toward a collection of different musical ends. This variety, which is now held to be inherent in Mannerism, has led to the recognition of forces essentially Mannerist in tone as early as 1520. Thus the concept, which earlier was held not to apply before the midpoint of the century, has now been extended backward to include the figures Pontormo and Rosso Fiorentino in painting. Similarly in music the rise of the madrigal in the 1520s and 1530s in Florence and Rome provides a convenient parallel, not only chronologically but also geographically.[12] But if Mannerism was initially an Italian invention, it developed almost simultaneously outside its borders. In painting, the advent of Mannerism in France was not only localized but was accomplished almost solely by the transplant of Italian artists to Fontainebleau from Florence (Rosso) and Mantua (Primaticcio). In music, however, Mannerism not only fostered a cross-fertilization between the French chanson and the Italian madrigal, but, more interestingly, frequently inspired new and indigenous solutions. While developments in France were pursued somewhat more fitfully than in Italy and lack the sense of continuity normally requisite to label them a movement, it is proper to suggest that the variety inherent in Mannerism is determined not only by its chronological breadth, but to an extent by geographical distinctions, and results in artworks of diverse musical surfaces and highly divergent emotional intents.

Let us be specific. If elements of any art are to be judged typically Mannerist, in part because of their ornamental and elegant qualities as well as for the bravura apparent in their execution and the density of their application, music has a rich repertoire, of both Italian and French provenance, from which to mine such properties: the intricate, sometimes spastic, figurations of the *canzon francese*, together with the ascendent interest in ornamentation as a virtuosic conceit; the rhythmic, farcical, and onomatopoeic effects of the Parisian programme chanson which emphasize detail at the expense of any narrative consideration; the metrical asymmetries of the *musique mesurée* composers, artificially distilled from involved disputation concerning ancient and Italian literary practice; or the endless rhetorical figures in the madrigal from its earliest phase to its most mature creations. But there is another side to Mannerism, which is nourished continuously throughout the period, and is of greater importance for subsequent develop-

---

[12] Cf. Frank d'Accone's numerous articles as well as his series, *Music of the Florentine Renaissance*; David Sutherland's *Francesco Layolle*, (Ph.D. dissertation, University of Michigan, 1967); and especially Don Harran's 'Some early examples of the madrigali chromatici' in *Acta Musicologica*, XLI (1969), p. 240.

ments in the art. This is a capacity to create new and expressive sonorities—at first perhaps conceived partly in accordance with a theoretical subscription of Antiquity, but later adopted to the task of textual reflection in a manner far more affective than the decorative figures so characteristic of the madrigal. This was a discovery which was to prove of far-reaching importance, and eventually transcended the Mannerist period which gave it birth.

It may be concluded that the original association of 'style' with the word 'maniera' provides the fundamental ingredient for a definition of Mannerism. While 'style' in this instance connotes especially the meanings associated with taste and elegance, the emphasis upon contrivance becomes increasingly central as the century progresses, suggesting not only the familiar characterization of Mannerism as the 'stylish style' but underlining its tension-bearing elements. Early Mannerism's proclivity for combining variety with selectivity, individuality with suavity, and contortion with coolness, not only creates a diversity hardly imaginable by the High Renaissance, but sows the seeds for a later language, more enlivened and personal, that remains Mannerist in spite of what some see as an almost disqualifying emotional energy.

Nothing could better illustrate this Mannerist attitude than the selective adaptation and development of an extremely limited body of knowledge concerning the ancient world.[13] The chromatic movement in music, for example, openly received its initial impetus from its knowledge of the chromatic genera of the Greeks, much as the Mannerist painter moved directly under the guidance of antique relief.[14] Similarly the speculation of the academies was characteristically fed by a perusal of the ancients. But the imprecision which necessarily accompanied their interpretations gave the practising artist sufficient leeway to forge a language which was as individual as it was dependent. Thus Vicentino's essentially theoretical, contrived, and non-committal chromaticism is gradually, yet relatively quickly, absorbed by composers with a more urgent message and is transformed from an ancient artifice into a living expression without turning Baroque.

Clearly related to this is the artist's preoccupation with style, which causes him to be more concerned with the way he expresses his idea than with the

[13] While the cult of the classics, the revival of interest in the remote past, had been endorsed by the Humanists before a Mannerist phase ever developed, and although the inspiration provided by the ancient world set the wheels in motion later in the century for the discovery of monody, which led directly to the Baroque, it is also central to the definition of Mannerism that it relied heavily upon an idealization of the antique.

[14] Cf. Craig Smyth, 'Mannerism and *Maniera*' in *Acts of the Twentieth International Congress of the History of Art*, vol. II: *The Renaissance and Mannerism*, pp. 185-8.

idea to be expressed. This does not imply that he is unconcerned with his subject, that there are no recurrent themes which the Mannerist favours; but the themes which serve him best are those which admit a wide range of personal responses as well as a large catalogue of references from the arcane to the obvious. While he retains identifiable portions of a classic language as a mode of speech, and while he may have strong ties with his immediate past, the Mannerist no longer considers the canon of nature immutable. He may, in fact, strive for the 'unnatural'—not just to be perverse, but because it serves his artistic purposes more directly.[15] Subjectivity replaces objectivity, the personal vision of the artist counterbalances the scientific view of an ordered universe, and irrationality, if it does not snuff out the rationality of the High Renaissance, achieves a new status and stands proudly alongside it.

Nature and Genius

While the ancient doctrine of nature's unsurpassable perfection was re-iterated by Zarlino as late as 1558,[16] contemporaneously there were other forces which helped to create a new climate. Dolce suggested in 1557 that 'if the artist, correcting [nature's] imperfections, would "surpass nature," would render her fairer than she is, he must be guided by a study of the faultless antique. For the antique is already that ideal nature for which the painter strives and "the ancient statues contain all the perfection of art".'[17] Two important considerations emerge: (1) Nature is surpassable; (2) the Antique has become the ideal or second nature. The idea that the individual artist was capable of outstripping both Nature *and* Antiquity, a further step, was proclaimed by Vasari with reference to Michelangelo.[18]

The 'imitation of nature' as an artistic theory never embodied a single, simple point of view. Thus, it is possible to imitate nature in at least two basic ways, which through modification can result in a set of modes of imitation. Nature can be imitated: (1) either through a slavish copying of

---

[15] See Friedländer, *Mannerism and Anti-Mannerism*, p. 6, for an impressively clear view of the Mannerist painter's relation to nature.

[16] See particularly Schrade's 'Von der "Maniera" der Komposition der Musik des 16. Jahrhunderts,' in *Zeitschrift für Musikwissenschaft*, XVI (1934), 3–20; 98–117; 152–70; also Johnson's *The Sacred Music of Cipriano de Rore*, (Ph.D. dissertation, Yale University), pp. 260–4, and A. Carapetyan, 'The Concept of "Imitazione della Natura" in the Sixteenth Century' in *Journal of Renaissance and Baroque Music*, I (1946), pp. 47ff.

[17] Rensselaer W. Lee, 'Ut Pictura Poesis: The Humanistic Theory of Painting,' *Art Bulletin*, XXII (1940), p. 205, quoting Dolce, *Dialogo della pittura* (first ed. 1557), p. 190 of the 1735 Florence edition.

[18] Vasari, *Lives*, ed. by G. Milanesi (Florence, 1878–81), IV, 13.

appearances, or (2) through an incorporation of its essential qualities, typically with an emphasis on balance, order, harmony, and beauty. It is apparent that painting, for example, can make greater use of the first type than music, though music too has periodically found its voice as a 'copyist'. It is obviously the second type which affords the main opportunity for 'imitation' in all the arts, especially in the more abstract disciplines of music and architecture.

In sixteenth-century music we find an ascendant Mannerist interest in the more superficial level of imitative copying represented in the composer's reaction to the individual word. White and black, long and short, rising and falling, *canto* and *sospiro*, sorrow and joy—all found their appropriate musical counterparts. As a detail technique, this led occasionally to extraordinary musical results, which, in extreme cases where a single word was treated out of context, were not only inappropriate but ludicrous. This approach to the imitation of nature was endorsed throughout the Cinquecento by even the most responsible theorists,[19] though indulgence in it was also often decried.[20]

In seeking to go beyond the level of detail technique, the composer began to mirror the larger sentiments of the text and to create a new and expressive vocabulary. This development ultimately affected every element, rhythm, melody, harmony, and texture. It is generally conceded to have received its most striking early endorsement from Rore around the mid-point of the century, and is traceable as a continuing aesthetic not only through the remainder of the sixteenth century, but into the Baroque as well.

The separate and distinct modes of viewing a single concept, the *imitazione della natura,* by the classic masters of the High Renaissance, the Mannerists, and the emerging Baroque personalities, thus account in large measure for the fundamental conceptual changes which emerged in each of these periods: (1) While all three sought to re-inforce Nature through an imitation of one kind or another, Josquin's *ars perfecta* was inevitably seen as an approximation to Nature's perfection, and his classicism reflective of Nature's balance, order, harmony, and beauty. (2) Similarly, the Mannerist in trying to carry out a goal of a more personalized *imitazione della natura* contrived and devised solutions which were anti-natural as seen from the vantage point of the High Renaissance. His reliance upon the Antique as the ideal or second nature is partially responsible. In addition his use of graceful pose and studied

[19] Zarlino, *Istitutioni* (1558), IV, Cap. 32: 'In qual maniera le Harmonie si accomodino alle soggette Parole' and Vicentino, *L'antica musica* (1555), IV, Cap. xxix: 'Modo di pronuntiare le sillabe lunghe et brevi sotto le note: et comme si dè imitare la natura di quelli, con altri ricordi utili' are good examples.

[20] Doni, *Trattato della Musica Scenica* (1635), II, 73; see p. 170 of the present volume for the relevant passage.

gesture introduced tensions which were allowed to stand unresolved in the service of a Nature which also created imbalances; the strained effect, seen from one point of view as anti-natural, was seen by the Mannerist as a kind of faithfulness to Nature now under the artist's control. Only the stress which was placed upon the concept of *lo sforzato* and concentration of ideas relative to it could be construed as unnatural, not the idea itself. (3) On the other hand, Galilei, while also supporting the idea of a new and more humanly expressive music, sensed that this Mannerist art was in crisis because of a textural condition untrue to Nature, which stemmed from the inherent incompatibility of polyphony with the first-person emotionalism of the madrigal. In an effort to resolve this, monody was born.[21]

Ultimately the value which the Mannerist began to place upon the creative personality intensified, even exaggerated, the creator's individuality and power, so that now he operated 'not in imitation of Nature but on the basis of Nature already conquered in works of art.'[22] The artist no longer needed to fear the proclamation that an *ars perfecta* had been achieved, for it was always possible to set up a new ideal, to devise a new conceit. This recognition allowed the late sixteenth-century artist to build upon, destroy, or modify the tenets of the classic definition with a clear conscience. The potential crisis inherent in Glarean's statement of 'inevitable decline' was thus openly faced, and, if not totally dissolved, at least satisfactorily accommodated. The artist's personality is recognized; the concept of style as willful personal creation is born!

It may be that in ascribing perfection to Josquin, Glarean implied the idea of genius. But he had failed to hint at the presence of a *terribilità* which his contemporaries saw in Michelangelo. It was Doni (1594–1647), theorist and scholar, who first pointed to the 'contrast between counterpoint as a craft and dramatic music as the creation of genius.'[23] After pointing to the arid canons of Soriano, Palestrina's disciple, he concludes:

21 Robert Wolf, in 'Renaissance, Mannerism, Baroque: Three Styles, Three Periods,' *Les Colloques de Wégimont*, IV (1957), pp. 35–59, has proposed that this resolution of the polyphonic crisis was a Mannerist achievement, not a Baroque one, and toward this end suggests that the period to around 1635 is best considered Mannerist. From this point of view the *seconda prattica* may be directly equated with Mannerism. At this same colloquium Denis Stevens suggested that the true Baroque might be labelled a *terza prattica*. The adoption of such a terminology would permit a continuity of meaning compatible with Monteverdi's use of the term *seconda prattica*, which encompassed the music from Rore on, and allow for the textural changes which transpired during this period.

22 Shearman, *Mannerism*, 48.

23 E. Lowinsky, 'Musical Genius—Evolution and Origins of a Concept' in *Musical Quarterly*, L (1964), p. 338. In this two-part article Lowinsky has brilliantly traced the concept of musical genius to its source, and he emphasizes that the recognition of the

Gesualdo, Prince of Venosa, on the other hand, who was truly born for music, and with a gift for musical expression, and who could clothe with his musical gifts any poetic subject, never attended, as far as one knows, to canons and similarly laboured exercises.[24] Such should be, then, the genius of the good composer, particularly of that genre of musical compositions which bring to life all inner affects of the soul with vivid expression.[25]

Recognition of the composer's genius is thus associated with the development of an expressive style first attained in the Age of Mannerism. It assumed man's capacity to conquer Nature and attain an indisputable technical perfection. When he transcended the mastery of craft and infused its application with a powerfully individual control and an unmistakable, sometimes even eccentric, personal vision, his genius was recognized.

Gesualdo and Mannerism

It would be imprudent to argue that all music written in the period following the High Renaissance should be labelled Mannerist. Indeed, the basic ingredients of the classic style continued to be used to such an extent that we can correctly speak of two compositional approaches. We may borrow Monteverdi's distinction between a *prima* and a *seconda prattica* which, appearances notwithstanding, is only partially a chronological one. He tells us that by masters of the former he means Ockeghem, Josquin, la Rue, Mouton, Crequillon, and Gombert, and by the latter Marenzio, Wert, Luzzaschi, Rore, Gesualdo, and only finally Peri and Caccini. The omission from either list of Palestrina—a name which has often been held synonymous with late sixteenth-century style—may reveal Monteverdi's awareness of lingering *prima prattica* elements at a time when the *seconda prattica* was already well under way.[26]

In spite of the first use of the term *seconda prattica* as late as 1605, it should be obvious that Monteverdi's intention was not to announce the advent of

---

idea in the Renaissance is one of the features that helps to distinguish this period from the Middle Ages.

[24] A point picked up more than a century later by Charles Burney, who, however, censured him on this point.

[25] Doni, *Lyra Barberina* (Florence, 1763), II, 129–30, Chap. XLV: *Delle qualità naturali, e artificiali, che si richiedono nel Compositore di queste Musiche sceniche,* as translated in Lowinsky, 'Musical Genius', 339, together with the original text.

[26] Cf. Jerome Roche, 'Monteverdi and the *Prima Prattica*' in *The Monteverdi Companion,* ed. by D. Arnold and N. Fortune (London, 1968), pp. 167 ff.

an exclusively Baroque practice thereby. That is to say the coiner of the term considered that it applied to music from Rore on. If the line of demarcation between *prima* and *seconda prattica* in the sixteenth century is more difficult to draw than that between *stile antico* and *stile moderno* in the seventeenth century, it must be recognized that the Cinquecento had its special forms for each of these styles. Admittedly, the chanson and motet, which had had an illustrious history, initially contributed heavily to the formation of the madrigal, and ultimately those stylistic features which were developed in the madrigal were partly transferred back to *prima prattica* forms so that the formal lines of demarcation no longer adequately served to delineate the stylistic polarization. It must also be admitted that while the presence of certain gestures highly characteristic of Mannerism in no way deterred Monteverdi from including Rore, Luzzaschi, Wert, and Gesualdo in his list of *seconda prattica* composers, there can also be no doubt that there was a fervour and intensity in their music which he recognized as pointing directly toward what we have come to call the Baroque. The emotional content had begun to outstrip the conventions inherent in the form.[27]

Gesualdo has been considered the perfect example of the musical Mannerist because many of the currents normally associated with that movement are so clearly recognizable in his writing. Yet it is obvious that, if only because of his chronological position, other composers must be credited with establishing the foundations of Mannerism. In Italian secular music alone we may recall the repetitious use of the rhetorical figures, the textural contrasts, the mild chromaticism, the *note nere* style and quiet agitation of countless pre-Gesualdine madrigals—all of which reflect a cooler emotional climate than Gesualdo's tortured world but which are also qualities totally Mannerist in spirit. Gesualdo shares with El Greco and other late Mannerists an ardour not found in their earlier counterparts. Shearman has summed it up nicely:

> The capacity of artists to manipulate for their own ends forms invented in a different spirit is one of the facts of life that helps to explain how Mannerism grew out of the earlier Renaissance. Then, in turn, Mannerist forms were re-used as Mannerism was dying by artists whose passion and sensuousness essentially distinguished them. El Greco is one very obvious case, and Bellange is another. . . . The madrigals of Carlo Gesualdo, Prince of Venosa, fascinate us for this

---

[27] A comparison of Rore's *Calami sonum ferentes* with Monteverdi's *Non morir, Seneca* (from *L'Incoronazione di Poppea*) provides vivid testimony of Rore's continuing influence across formal boundaries.

very reason—because they tremble, as it were, on the brink of one or the other commitment.[28]

The date and individuality of Gesualdo's art, however, have too long encouraged us to parry its stylistic identification, to neutralize it to the point of non-epochal association, and to reduce it to the level of the ultra-personal, or the aberrant. With the features of Mannerism currently delineated with increasing clarity, the time is ripe to measure Gesualdo's music against them. Initially we may take note of the aristocratic character of all Mannerist art. Music specifically written for the court and reserved for its consumption could command the services of the finest performers of the day. It is no surprise that the Mannerist composer writes not only 'new music,' incorporating the most recent speculative advances of the academies and the theorists, but also 'virtuoso music'—music for virtuoso listeners as much as for virtuoso performers. Gesualdo's music qualifies in this respect as pure Mannerism.

A scrutiny of the music also yields a catalogue of specific features which are indisputably Mannerist. (1) Perhaps first of these is his choice of texts. Here he requires only a few verses replete with key words to trigger a musical response. The madrigalists' preference for texts of high literary quality had always been intermittent, and by Gesualdo's time anonymous distillates which served the composer's purpose directly had become commonplace. While texts by poetic luminaries continue to appear with some frequency, there was increasingly less need for poetry of such power that it could stand independent of its musical setting. Additionally, for all its repetitive thematic qualities, the text is often ambiguous or difficult to follow syntactically. This is not an accident. To the Mannerist, whatever his field, 'unambiguousness seemed over-simplification.'[29] Hence, clarity of textual meaning is invariably less important than the quality of stress and strain or the associative expressive musical response. To this end Gesualdo prefers texts that abound in oxymora and other imagery which are capable of contrasting musical treatment. (2) This leads to a disruptive musical style, characterized by alternations of the diatonic allegro and the chromatic adagio—akin to the familiar 'juxtaposition of irreconcilable elements'[30] typically associated with Mannerism in the visual and literary arts. (3) The chromatic side of this style itself has both a rational and an irrational dimen-

[28] Shearman, *Mannerism*, pp. 174–5.
[29] Hauser, *Mannerism*, p. 6.
[30] Cf. Maria Rika Maniates, 'Mannerist Composition in Franco–Flemish Polyphony' in *Musical Quarterly*, LII (1966), pp. 1–36, for observations of this 'manneristic' quality in music of the *ars perfecta*.

sion, i.e., it includes harmonic progressions which can be reconciled with an older modal order or a developing functional system, as well as many others which are difficult to explain by any theoretical system devised before or after. All seven sharps and six of the seven flats are used, which also allows an extension of the melodic element, including chromatic and other novel intervals. The spark for this development had been lit by Vicentino, and he in turn had been inspired by his view of ancient Greek practice, a thoroughly Mannerist propensity. (4) As a result of such extensions, portions of many works vacillate tonally, and clearly defined cadences are lacking for considerable stretches of time. Floating tonality, or key drifting, sometimes replaces true modulation. Thus, the tonal situation, too, has a characteristically Mannerist ambiguity. (5) The finished product, the madrigal, though brief and limited in subject, is marked by a density of idea, complexity of relationship, and persistent diversity born of a reflection of attendant literary *meraviglie*. The result is an overload. Precisely because abundant gesture and allusion is accompanied by compactness of form, the clarity and precision of countless details are ultimately rendered obscure by their very profusion in so tight a space. Yet the fascination resides not only in the labyrinthine dimension of such a tiny cosmos but also in its flickering irridescence and tentative stability.

In order to better understand this seeming paradox, we would do well to note on how narrow a front the old order had been attacked. It will be recognized that with the exception of a few telling melodic idiosyncrasies, Gesualdo's voice-leading is quite classical; his introduction of dissonance is more often than not traditional; his chromatic style, though admittedly often extreme, accounts for only a relatively small portion of a given piece. His irreverence in tonal matters is, likewise, not so great as has often been suggested, particularly in light of the care with which he handles tonality in relation to form. While his contrasts in tempo can surely be viewed as a heightening of an idea suggested much earlier in the Renaissance, a corollary contrast between diatonic and chromatic, homophonic and contrapuntal, emphasizes the issue and compounds the effect. The resulting diversity of texture must be seen as the essential anti-classic feature of Gesualdo's style. Its disruptive force, perhaps above all other qualities, suggests how intense was his rejection of the classic polyphonic continuum.

A further departure from the Netherlands model is shown by the piling up of entrances in imitation,[31] the frequent modification of the imitative

---

[31] While this may be observed occasionally even in Josquin's *ars perfecta* and later in the works of such relatively conservative composers as Crecquillon and Clemens non Papa, the feature is exaggerated by the madrigalists of the late sixteenth century.

subject in its working out, even to the point of unrecognizability, and the extension of the vocabulary of melodic intervals, in both imitative and non-imitative contexts.

Invariably such gestures reflect the composer's newly developed concern for the word and of his search for expressive means to portray it. The early madrigalists' concern for the text had led to results that were remarkable for their stylishness and variety, but which were less notable for depth of emotional intent. The fervour of the late madrigal is increasingly measured not only by the temperature of favoured sentiments but also by their compulsive reiteration. Alternatively flatulent and vulnerable, their unstable and irrational ecstasy is hammered into a dull echo. Yet the excessive urgency of the late madrigal is not only Mannerist but results from a logical extension of features inherent in the early phase of the form.

The Mannerist character of Gesualdo's work has been defined largely with reference to his madrigal production. And this is a logical first place to look. But it seems especially appropriate to look also at Gesualdo's sacred music, and the *Responsoria* in particular, because of the indubitable role that the force of the Counter-Reformation had upon the development of late Mannerist philosophy.[32] If, as suggested by both Hauser and Shearman, there was a natural antipathy between Mannerism and the Counter-Reformation, the former preferring embellishment and contrivance and the latter directness and lack of complication, in certain ways they displayed a decided compatibility. Thus the homophonic chromatic style, which may be described as an adornment of the diatonic, is marked by difficulty and artificiality, and yet is well suited to the demands of textual projection and clarity. In addition, the erotic secular fantasies of the madrigal are repeatedly transformed by Gesualdo into ecstatic visions of Marian worship, the dolorous sighs of unrequited love into the mournful cadences of the Passion story, and amorous agonies into scriptural utterances which reflect a personal sense of guilt and an unspeakable desperation. If the Counter-Reformation was to be served more faithfully by impulses developed in the Baroque, surely it may be claimed that certain late Mannerist composers, parallel in stylistic position to Tasso and El Greco, were influenced in their sacred writings by the Counter-Reformation without being converted into totally Baroque artists.[33] If, too, in music Mannerism is best defined through its approach to secular topics because of a greater fitness to function and stylistic permissiveness, there is no reason why we should not apply it to

[32] Hauser, *Mannerism*, pp. 71 ff.
[33] Cf. 'Tridentine Ideals and Post-Council Practice,' pp. 263–6.

the grey areas, both instrumental and sacred, wherein it came only partially to reside.[34]

It is doubtful that the period of Mannerism can any longer prudently be labelled a colourful intermission somewhere between the Renaissance and the Baroque, or considered the coda to a more prominent, more clearly defined age, parallel in position, individuality, and weight to the *Style galant* or the *Rococo*. The enormous strides and import of the stylistic pursuits undertaken during this time were of such dimension that this era is destined to achieve an identity clearly distinguishable from that of the periods which preceded and followed it. Consequently, its most significant figures will loom not as momentary revolutionaries or as simple dilettantes who presaged in an elementary way a new aesthetic; rather they will be seen as independent figures who released some of the most artful and stylish impulses, and, later, fashioned a catalogue of the most expressive nuances which the art of music had attempted to that time. Just as it is impossible to conceive of the Baroque appearing hard on the heels of the High Renaissance, so is the idea of an Age of Mannerism helpful in providing the framework for a logical stylistic development. Both the Renaissance and the Baroque gain thereby in clarity without being deprived of their fundamental character and force.

[34] A term too broadly defined, of course, can be useless or, worse, misleading. But the music historian has already experienced an extended frustration over an attempt at a too narrow description of the term *musica reservata*. Interestingly enough, one of the most perceptive writers on the subject of this dilemma has suggested the possibility of equating this term with Mannerism directly. Cf. Palisca, 'A Clarification of "Musica Reservata",' in *Acta Musicologica*, XXXI (1959), p. 159. 'Reservata—A Problem of Musical Mannerism' in H. Kaufmann's *The Life and Works of Nicola Vicentino*, MSD II (1966) develops the idea even further.

CHAPTER FIVE

∽✹∾

Text and Form

G ESUALDO was a composer who created principally to a text. It
is therefore imperative to establish the textual basis of the madrigal,
the principal object of his attention. A detailed survey of the
madrigal's textual development is, of course, beyond the scope of this
study.[1] Nevertheless, it is important to indicate something of the change
in the relation of text to music which took place in Italian secular music
after the beginning of the sixteenth century, before devoting our attention
to the texts Gesualdo himself set and to their influence on the musical form
of his madrigals.

Poetic Form

Textually the term 'madrigal', like the term 'frottola', was used in both a
generic and a specific sense. Thus the frottola as a class included the frottola,
strambotta, capitolo, ode, sonnet, etc., and the madrigal also took in a
variety of poetic forms such as the sonnet, the ottava stanza, the canzone,
and the ballata.[2] All of these forms were developed in the early madrigals,
but some are more relevant than others for the madrigals of Gesualdo.

The Canzone

The poetic form of the canzone is basically strophic. It varied from two to
nine stanzas in length, each of which duplicated the measure and rhyme
scheme of the initial stanza. A non-rhyming, undivided stanza form was

---

[1] See especially Einstein, *The Italian Madrigal*, pp. 166–246, regarding 'The Madrigal
and Poetry'; also Hersh, *Verdelot and the Early Madrigal* (Ph.D. diss., Univ. of California, 1963), pp. 48–104. The best overview of the text in the early madrigal is to be
found in Don Harran's (*alias* Hersh) 'Verse Types in the Early Madrigal', *JAMS*,
XXII, 1 (1969), pp. 27–53.

[2] Cf. Pier Enea Guarnerio's *Manuale de versificatione italiana* (Milan, 1893) for a rigorous
treatment of the Italian lyric forms which follow.

possible, which in some instances approached the free madrigal, but this was less popular as a literary form than the type of canzone, cultivated especially by Petrarch and Boccaccio, in which the stanza was divided into two parts. The first section, the *fronte*, contained paired verse groups called *piedi*. Each *piede* could contain couplets, tercets, quatrains, or longer groups. The rhyme need not be symmetrically repeated in each *piede*; thus in a pair of tercets the rhyme scheme might be ABC/BAC. But, though the syllabic lengths (seven and eleven-syllable lines were favoured in all Italian poetry) could vary within each *piede*, between members of a pair of *piedi* the arrangement was typically uniform, even when the rhyme scheme was varied, as aBC/bAC.[3] The second section, called *sirima*, could be treated as a single unit, divided into two *volte*, or, more commonly, could consist of a succession of rhymed couplets. There was usually a connecting rhyme (called *chiave*, *concatenazione*, or *unita*) between the last line of the second *piede* and the first line of the *sirima*, e.g. *piedi*: abC/abC, *sirima*: cDdeE. Intercalated verses which rhyme with some line of a *piede* were possible, as was the placement of the connecting rhyme link in the interior of the *sirima* and not at its beginning. Petrarch's twenty-nine canzoni were models of the greatest importance for sixteenth-century poets, and by extension for the sixteenth-century madrigal, particularly in its earliest phase.

By Gesualdo's time, however, the structured canzone stanza was already out of vogue. Canzoni texts are found only in the first two volumes of Gesualdo's madrigals, and even these few examples take considerable licence with the formula. Only one is quite clearly a canzone. It is the opening two-part madrigal of Book I, *Baci soavi e cari*. The *prima parte* comprises the *piedi*: abC/abC, and the *seconda parte* is the *sirima*: c dee Dff. The symmetrical verse length of the tercets of the *piedi* and the connecting rhyme line (c) of the *sirima* will be noted. Only a few other madrigals utilize some sort of canzone structure. *Gelo ha Madonna* (I, 5) contains the *piedi*: Ab ab, and the *sirima*: CcB. The departures from the norm will be quickly noted: the lack of symmetry in the length of line in the *piedi*, and the presence of a single couplet in the *sirima*. The connecting rhyme, B, comes at the end instead of at the beginning, but this is a possible variation of the standard formula. In other examples the connection with canzone form is even more tenuous.

The Ballata

The ballata also had provided a usable poetic vehicle for the early madrigal.

---

[3] Lower case letters designate seven-syllable lines; capitals indicate eleven-syllable lines.

It consisted of three parts. (a) An opening *ripresa*, two to four lines in length, was generally limited to two rhyme-endings; when only two lines are involved, they invariably rhyme. (b) The *mutazioni*, comparable to the *piedi* of the canzone, also varied in length from two to four lines. (c) The final section was the *volta*, which was frequently linked with the preceding *mutazioni*, in the manner of the *sirima* of the canzone. But, more importantly, it not only contained a rhyming connection with the opening *ripresa* but also frequently recapitulated whole verses from it.

Only three Gesualdo madrigals can lay claim to ballata structure. The first one is *Non mi toglia il ben mio* (II, 20). It is necessary to see the entire text in order to view its fundamental design, the rhyme-ending formula being inadequate to express its content.

> Non mi toglia il ben mio
> Chi non arde d'amor come faccio io!
> Se non è ingiusto Amore,
> Io sol avrò di la mia Donna il core.
> Dunque lasci il ben mio
> Chi non arde d'amor come faccio io!

The poem might be diagrammed thus:

> Ripresa: aA
> Mutazioni: bB
> Volta: aA

Here the connection between *ripresa* and *volta* goes beyond the rhyme link and includes the textual recapitulation typical of the ballata.

The only other madrigals of Gesualdo which show the influence of ballata structure to any degree are *Donna, se m'ancidete* (III, 20) and *T'amo, mia vita!* (V, 21). This is revealed largely by the reappearance of a portion of the text of the *ripresa* in the concluding *volta*, in the former case in inverted order. Other examples are so far removed from the standard patttern that any resemblances must be considered coincidental approximations of the form within the framework of the more fluid madgrial.

The Multi-Stanza Canzone and Sestina

While the sixteenth-century madrigal composer decidedly preferred the monostrophic ballata to the polystrophic, he was periodically drawn to the lengthy multi-stanza canzone. It lent itself naturally to various treatments according to the composer's desire for a longer or shorter text. This was also true of the sestina. The single canzone or sestina stanza was, of course, frequently set, but quite often a complete sestina or six, eight, or more stanzas of a canzone would be set to music in a madrigal of as many parts. Although composers of the middle part of the century and later continued to write canzone and sestina cycles,[4] these became increasingly the exception. Neither is represented in the works of Gesualdo.

The Sonnet

The sonnet, the ultimate Petrarchian conceit, toward the end of the century comes similarly to be viewed as too extensive a form, just as it had been in the early phase of madrigal development. It achieved a considerable favour in the central period of the madrigal following Willaert's example. The structure of the sonnet suggested by the rhyme scheme abba/abba/cde/cde (with optional endings as cdc/dcd, etc.) naturally invited the separation of the final two tercets into a second part. And this was accepted as the solution of the form for the composer as long as the genre continued to be composed. Set as the almost exclusive form in the early works of Rore, for example, it is virtually abandoned in his later period.[5] The single sonnet set by Gesualdo in all the six books is by his friend Tasso. It is *Mentre Madonna il lasso fianco posa* of Book I, and is treated as a madrigal of two *partes*, with the final *terzetti* reserved for the second part in the traditional manner.

The Madrigal

Though many of these elaborate literary forms at one time or another intrigued the Cinquecento composer, the form that ultimately captured his fancy, from around 1530 and especially after 1550, was the new madrigal. Its poetic form was inspired by the freedom inherent in the unstructured canzone stanza.[6] Consisting of alternating heptasyllabic and hendecasyllabic lines, the form prescribed neither the number of lines, nor a principle for the alternation of seven- or eleven-syllable units, nor the rhyme scheme. While it could be as long as fifteen lines, it was normally considerably shorter, and

---

[4] The *Vergine* cycles by Rore and Palestrina, with eight and eleven stanzas respectively, are notable examples.

[5] Nuernberger, *The five-voiced Madrigals of Cipriano de Rore* (Ph.D. dissertation, Univ. of Michigan, 1963).

[6] This is not to say that they are the same thing. Harran, op. cit., p. 52, concludes, 'The popular notion that the madrigal is none other than the *canzone* reduced to a single stanza does not hold up to critical examination ... madrigals and *canzoni* represent two separate verse types, structurally irreconcilable.'

the less lengthy versions were particularly favoured in the late phase of the madrigal. And while virtually any pattern of rhymes was possible, varying from a species of canzone stanza with no rhyme at all to neatly arranged groups of paired couplets, the norm is to be found somewhere between the two extremes. The form was thus relatively terse but flexible.

The madrigal of the second half of the sixteenth century thus offered a wide range of constructional possibilities, and it is not too surprising that this was Gesualdo's chosen form, or that he 'rarely set a sonnet and never a canzone, a sestina, or any other cycle.'[7]

The madrigal of two *partes* is the most extensive idea to be employed by him, and is utilized with undiminishing interest in the first four volumes. The two-part madrigal does not, however, imply a text of greater than normal length. The larger musical proportions result largely from a more generous working-out of the text through repetition and variation.[8] Thus a seven-line madrigal may be divided into two sections of three and four lines respectively, rather than set as a single unit (IV: 7–8, 9–10, 16–17, 20–21). The spatial freedom thus obtained is apparent. There are four two-part madrigals (eight out of twenty numbers) in Book I; six two-part madrigals (twelve out of twenty) in Book II; six out of twenty in Book III, and twelve out of twenty-one in Book IV. In the last two books he suddenly abandons the idea almost completely. Book V contains only a single pair; Book VI none at all.

It is pointless to suggest that Gesualdo was incapable of sustaining the more developed requirements of a madrigal sequence. His musical language, by its very nature, was alien to the extended text. It will be noted that he uses madrigal texts as short as four lines (I, 9: a complete madrigal, not a *prima* or *seconda parte*) but never longer than eleven (VI, 13). Rore, by contrast, never sets a text shorter than an ottava stanza in his five-voice madrigals.

The flexibility of the madrigal form stems from its capacity to expand or contract not only the total number of lines employed but also their syllabic quantities. That is to say, while a madrigal line typically contained seven or eleven syllables, the patterning resulting from the juxtaposition of these two lengths was markedly heterogeneous. An analysis of the six books of madrigals reveals a truly amazing repertoire of patterns. The multiplicity of schemes defies systematic codification. Even the custom of ending with an

[7] Einstein, op. cit., p. 691.

[8] See especially pp. 140–2 concerning Gesualdo's penchant in this regard as compared to A. Gabrieli, Marenzio, Wert, and Caimo in their several settings of Guarini's *Tirsi morir volea*.

eleven-syllable line in order to clinch the epigrammatic point is by no means always observed.

Rhyme schemes likewise encompass an unusual variety of types. From the third book onward, however, texts of an even number of lines show a preference for pairing—aa bb cc, etc. Texts of an uneven number frequently begin with an initial unpaired line, or *capoverso*, e.g. a bb cc dd. Book IV shows a marked preference for this scheme. Other patterns abound, occasionally showing the influence of *ottava rima* (ab ab ab cc) or *terza rima* (aba cbc dcd), but more frequently that of the freer canzone rhymes.

Musical Form

The Verse/Phrase

The question of musical form relates directly to the topic of textual form. From the inception of the madrigal the association of the verse or poetic line—the textual unit—with that of the phrase—the musical unit—had been fundamental. That is to say, a verse of text was normally set to a phrase of music, and the verse/phrase unit became the module out of which the madrigal was constructed. Zarlino stated in unmistakable terms that the cadence articulates not only the structure of the music but also the syntax of the text, and he warns that the cadence, which identifies the phrase, should not conflict with the textual structure.[9] It is not surprising that some licence was taken with this concept: a musical formation responding to the half-verse was not uncommon, as was the elision of verses in a single musical statement. On the other hand, when in the early madrigal the half-verse or the double-verse temporarily became the textual unit for musical purposes, strong textural contrast between half-verse phrases was uncommon, just as similarity of texture was prevalent in double-verse elision.

In his first two books of madrigals Gesualdo generally adheres to the verse/phrase unit as a formal building block, as in *Sento che nel partire* (see Ex. 12), but even in these early volumes he occasionally exercises considerable freedom with the idea. *Se per lieva ferita* (II, 4; see Ex. I), for example, obscures the relationship of text and music in several ways: (1) Two voices announce the first line of text, but this textual unit is not reinforced by a cadence, and before they have completed their statement voices three and four enter intoning the second verse, 'Onde te stessa offendi'. (2) The verse/phrase, while not defined by a harmonically-supported cadence, is neverthe-

---

[9] Zarlino, *Le Istitutioni harmoniche* (1558), III, cap. 53, 221: trans. by G. Marco and C. Palisca (Yale, 1968), 141–2.

less clearly set off as a melodic and rhythmic unit in the first three measures through the introduction of rests at separate points in all voices. (3) The cadence, delayed until bar four, is further weakened not only by its rhythmic position and duration, but also by the failure of all voices to subscribe to it textually, the third verse, 'Cosi dogliosa', being introduced in two voices in the preceding bar. This relatively moderate treatment can largely be accounted for by the influence of the motet upon the madrigal, particularly through the use of staggered entrances and phraseological dove-tailing. The importance of the motet for the madrigal, as it moved away from the more rigid association between verse and phrase which characterized the

Ex. 1

Prima Parte

frottola, canzone, and early madrigal, toward the more flexible relationships of the mature madrigal, cannot be over-estimated.

Gesualdo's treatment of the semi-verse, especially in his later volumes where each half of the verse is frequently set with strongly contrasting textures, shows his Mannerist capacity for swift and unexpected change, for 'juxtaposition of irreconcilable elements' even within the context of the verse/phrase. *Beltà, poi che t'assenti* (VI, 2) clearly illustrates the identification of the musical phrase with the half-verse (verse two), double-verse elision (verses three and four), and the single word (the final word of the madrigal).[10]

> Beltà, poi che t'assenti,/
> Come ne porti il cor,/porta i tormenti./
> Chè tormentato cor può ben sentire
> La doglia del morire,/
> E un'alma senza core/
> Non può sentir/dolore./

Elsewhere, his penchant for fashioning musical phrases which reflect the semi-verse or even the single word can be observed in the short-breathed openings of *Non è questa la mano* (II, 13), *Moro o non moro* (III, 2), *Non t'amo* (III, 11), and *Moro e mentre sospiro* (IV, 12; Ex. 2). These passages show how far this practice, applied as early as Rore,[11] had already eroded the basic verse/phrase module in Gesualdo's first volumes. Its continuing presence, even emphasis, in his last volumes elevates the gesture to the rank of a major stylistic point in Gesualdo's music.

Ex. 2

---

[10] For additional discussion of this principle at work in Book VI see the analysis of *Io pur respiro*, pp. 173–5.

[11] Cf. Claude Palisca, *Baroque Music,* pp. 13–16.

Larger Structural Features

The basic formal building-block, the verse/phrase, having been thus defined, it remains to be stated how textual and musical ideas were deployed in the madrigal to delineate larger formal sections. Close-quarter repetition, or immediate repetition of short textual fragments, was of course not uncommon from the beginning of the form, and even larger sectional repeats akin to the *formes fixes* or repetition patterns reflective of rhyme-endings in the manner of the early frottolists were occasionally pressed into service. As composers became ever more sensitive to the emotional demands of the text, however, they relied less heavily upon pre-fabricated repetition schemes. In the works of Gesualdo the through-composed approach to the madrigal is basic. But this does not imply that the composer never indulges in large-scale musical repetition. In fact there are only a few through-composed pieces with no sizeable repetition. Four pieces from Book I can be so classified; nine from Book II; seven from Book III, etc.—never more than half the madrigals in any book.

The early madrigalist often permitted the text to determine the sequence of his musical material, sometimes in a relatively primitive manner. For example, the composer accepted the pairs of *piedi* as suitable for identical musical treatment. Such choices reflected syllabic symmetry and/or identity of rhymes, not identical text or sentiment. Since the schematic canzone, as opposed to the freer variety, occurs so infrequently in the works of Gesualdo, its potential influence upon the sequence of his musical ideas is minimal. But in the few instances where this textual form occurs, he consciously

reflects it in his music. Thus *Baci soavi e cari,* which constitutes the two
tercet-*piedi* of a canzone text, abC/abC, receives a musical setting which
highlights this divisional structure: abC‖: abC: ‖. *Tirsi morir volea* is similarly
treated.

The three ballata-like texts set by Gesualdo also reflect the most
important structural element of this poetic form, that of the textual reprise.
In *Non mi toglia il ben mio* (II, 20) the musical repetition is more extensive than
in *T'amo mia vita!* (V, 21) because of the more extensive restatement of the
ripresa, but in the case of *Donna se m'ancidete* (III, 20) the inverted textual
reprise evokes music only faintly suggestive of the original setting. In each
case the identity of musical and textual material in no way violates Gesualdo's
preference for finding an individual musical reflection for each portion of the
text. That is to say, there is no repetition of a given musical idea to a
different text in the manner of the Quatrocento *formes fixes* or as a reflection
of the rhyme scheme as in the post-*formes fixes* chanson and early madrigal.[12]
The canzone treatment, mentioned above, is more clearly reminiscent of
earlier practice in this regard.

Almost nowhere else in Gesualdo's work is musical material reset to a
different text.[13] The one exception in all the madrigals, besides the two
canzone texts already mentioned, is *Luci serene e chiare* (IV, 1). Einstein
compares its musical structure to the bar form, although its poetic arrangement in three tercets, aBB/aCC/bDD, also resembles the canzone. The
syllabic symmetry of the three parts will be noted, as well as the connecting
rhyme link of the third section. The initial two tercets are here set to the
same music, without the excuse in the typical canzone of identical rhymes.
Whatever Gesualdo's reasons for affording this lovely madrigal such a
treatment, it stands as a thing apart in the final four books.

The single sonnet set by Gesualdo, Tasso's *Mentre Madonna il lasso fianco
posa,* receives the classic treatment as defined by Willaert and respected by
most composers of the form thereafter: the initial quatrains are separated
from the final tercets to form a madrigal of two *partes.* Yet he does not, as
some composers before him, engage in musical repetition between quatrains
or tercets, but adopts instead a through-composed plan.

Within the framework of the less stereotyped madrigal proper, musical
repetition occurs most frequently at the end of the piece, resulting in a

[12] See Brown 'The Genesis of a Style: The Parisian Chanson' and Rubsamen 'From
Frottola to Madrigal' in *Chanson and Madrigal, 1480–1530,* ed. James Haar (1964).

[13] Even the *Responsoria,* which are characteristically repetitive and dominated by
formulae, do not violate this principle. Only the chant-like *Miserere* and *Benedictus*
together with the *Salmi delle compiete* receive a devotional understatement through
the use of modified musical repetition to several different stanzas.

kind of musical ABB. This familiar scheme frequently resulted from the repetition, either exact or slightly modified, of music set to the final couplet of the text. This can be observed in Gesualdo's madrigals throughout, as for example in the first two books, I: 3, 11, 15, 19 and II: 5, 6, 8, 10, 15, 19. The idea is not, however, restricted to the repetition of the final couplet. It may encompass the restatement of as many as four lines out of a total of five, as in *Bella Angioletta* (I, 20), here also reflecting the structure of the poetic rhyme by separating the unrepeated *capoverso*, thus A‖:bBcC:‖; and as few as a single line, as in *Danzan le Ninfe* (I, 18), here ignoring the rhyme of the final distich: EFG‖:G:‖. But it must again be emphasized that the same music is never used in such cases for a different textual sentiment.

Some of the repeated sections naturally involve slight or moderate variation, as witness the discussion of Example 9. But a majority of examples involve little or no change at all as in *Son si belle le rose* (I), *Candida man* (II), *Languisco e moro* (III), *Arde il mio cor* (IV), *Asciugate i begli occhi* (V), and *Beltà poi* (VI).

Repetition of the opening section of a madrigal, while less common than repetition of a closing section, does often occur, as in *Quanto ha di dolce Amori* (I, 2) (the *seconda parte* of the canzone *Baci soavi*) where the connecting rhyme link and first half of the *sirima* are repeated: ‖: c/dee:‖ Dff. Book IV particularly favours repeating the opening section. This may appear by itself, as in *Mentre gira costei* (IV): ‖: abB:‖ cc dd ee; or in the two-part *Ecco, moriro dunque-Ahi, già mi discoloro* (16–17): ‖:abB:‖—CC dD, the two rhymed couplets which comprise the *seconda parte* being through-composed. Or it may be combined with a closing repetition as in *Arde il mio cor* (18): ‖:Abb:‖:cc:‖; or, to cite a later example, *Chiaro risplender suole* (VI, 5): ‖:aa:‖BbcC‖:dD:‖. The musical repetition does not however always reflect the rhyme scheme. *Si gioioso mi fanno* (I, 10), whose rhyme pattern is Ab Ab Cc, is divided ‖:AbA:‖:bCc:‖ to make a pair of balanced musical halves. But the musical division does no violence to the syntax, even though a separation of the final distich would have been more logical from the standpoint of the concluding textual quotation.

The fifth and sixth books, containing Gesualdo's most mature works in the form, show an increasing preference for the totally through-composed structure, and repetitions are normally limited to the final distich or the final verse. This does not rule out, obviously, his continued use of varied or unvaried repetition of the word or semi-verse, a compositional practice observable from his earliest works, especially in passages containing pungent harmonic movement. At the same time Gesualdo increasingly favours asymmetrical linkage between poetic verse and musical phrase which results in Manneristic disruptions, stresses the sense of difficulty, even unnaturalness, in the forging of musical formal ideas, and intensifies the tension bearing elements witnessed elsewhere in contrasting harmonic and rhythmic formations. In general the late madrigal composer is only moderately interested in reflecting the larger sectional features of the older poetic schemata, is increasingly attracted to tampering with the previously near-inviolate identity of verse and phrase in setting the freer constructions of the new madrigal stanza, and allows his own musical form to be largely determined by the sentiment of his text.

Poetic Subjects

When composers themselves began increasingly to try their hand at fashioning the numerous Petrarchan conceits into texts for their own use, as we must believe that Gesualdo repeatedly did, the product was frequently an empty shell made up of recurrent motifs and endless clichés. There is no need to pretend that most of Gesualdo's texts are anything but artless copies of more expensive models, yet it is necessary to stress how little the routine character of these creations affected the composer's capacity for musical originality.

The repertoire of topics in the madrigal had never been large. Yet the variety of subjects had continued to diminish to such an extent that, by Gesualdo's time, texts were made up of a highly restricted number of sentiments repetitively couched in a language that was openly *poesia per musica*. Earlier the basic themes of courtly love had been taken over by Petrarch from the troubadours, but expressed in a manner more direct, less obscure than the Provencal poets. With Petrarchism, the imitation of Petrarch, this simplicity early begins to disappear, and a return to a more complicated dialectic and recondite syntax becomes increasingly apparent.[14] By the late phase of literary Mannerism, which was spawned by Petrarchism in Italy, the presence of imagery, contrast, and textual strain were so prevalent, that any art form which mirrored this condition, as the musical madrigal did, was destined itself to reflect something of the same abstruseness and complexity.

Though pastoral topics are represented in both early and late volumes,[15] they are not especially favoured. Texts which focus primarily on parts of the

---

[14] Hauser, *Mannerism*, p. 303.
[15] Cf. *Questi leggiadri odorosetti fiori* (I, 16), or *Quando ridente e bella* (IV, 23).

anatomy also occur only infrequently.[16] Whatever the text, it is largely influenced by a small range of prevalent motifs, particularly those based upon the elements of contrast and oxymoron which allow the composer an opportunity to paint with bold and expressive gestures. The pleasure-pains, the bitter-sweets, the dolorous sighs and the rapturous breathing, and especially death in life and life in death—these are the tediously recurrent expressions which the composer seemingly demands in his texts.[17]

Ardita Zanzaretta (VI, 13), dealing with a little mosquito settling on the bosom of the beloved, is virtually the only madrigal in Gesualdo's output to touch obliquely upon a note of humour. The earlier subject of a tiny poem by Tasso, here the anonymous poet has robbed the tale of its charm and emphasized words such as 'stringere' (to squash) and 'morte' to the point of absurdity. Though we can be grateful for the textual relief, the death music of this madrigal has been appropriately described by Aldous Huxley as 'a concentrated version of the love-potion scene in *Tristan*.'[18] The tonal language is the same as, and the ultimate destiny of the insect—which the lover gladly shares—is set to music as poignant and affective as that used to depict the death cries of the Saviour on the cross in the *Responsoria*.

There is a single *madrigale spirituale* in the six volumes, *Sparge la morte al mio Signor nel viso* (IV, 11). While it may be that 'Good Friday was celebrated in Gesualdo's chapel' with such music,[19] elsewhere he cultivates these sentiments within the framework of the *Sacrae Cantiones* or the *Responsoria*.

Viewed as a whole the texts have a generally monotonous ring, and because of the potency of the language which Gesualdo invents as a musical response, one can agree with Einstein that 'It is impossible to sing three such pieces one after the other without being seized by a sort of nausea or musical sea-sickness, for the dose is too strong and the unsteadiness too prolonged.'[20]

Yet one must suggest that the difficulty is attributable not so much to the over-richness of the music (there is considerable musical variety within the six books) as to the uniformity of the textual subjects. The recurring sentiments of the madrigalist's text, though clearly required for expressive reasons, are nevertheless a weakness. This is true not only of Gesualdo but

[16] The eyes in *Mentre, mia stella, miri* (I, 14), *Del bel de' bei vostri occhi* (III, 5) or *Occhi, del mio cor vita* (V, 9); the bosom or breast, in *Son si belle le rose* (I, 19), or *Deh, coprite il bel seno* (V, 16); or a mole, as in *Caro, amoroso neo—Ma se tale ha costei* (II, 1–2).

[17] The satire of Giraldi Cinthio's *Hecatommithi* (1565), cf. Einstein, op. cit., p. 187, tells us that the threadbare character of this entire *poesia per musica* was well recognized even in his time.

[18] Huxley, 'Gesualdo: Variations on a Musical Theme' in *On Art and Artists*, p. 300.

[19] Einstein, *The Italian Madrigal*, p. 708.

[20] Ibid., p. 715.

also of other composers in the last quarter of the century. Ultimately we must admit that the source of this weakness is the original model, Petrarch. Even Bembo, to whom much was owed and on whom much would be blamed, only emphasized, distilled, and popularized an Italian legacy. These textual limitations are one of the principal reasons for the eventual demise of the musical form. They were only partially contributory, however. Another cause was the conflict between the first-person textual sentiments of the madrigal and their anomalous expression in multi-voiced polyphony. This induced an expressive crisis. The solo madrigal was the first step in its resolution. Thereafter it was only a short distance to monody and the opera.

The Problem of Textual Identification

In light of Gesualdo's known and intimate connection with the most important poetic personalities of the time, and Torquato Tasso in particular, it is disappointing that we are able to attribute to them so few of Gesualdo's texts. In a letter to Gesualdo of 10 December 1592[21] Tasso says that he had by that time provided more than forty texts for Gesualdo's express use, and on 16 December[22] of the same year he announces that he is sending an additional five. It is impossible to determine exactly how many texts Tasso may have composed for Gesualdo, but the casualness with which such poems were created is implied in the first of these letters when Tasso declares that 'I herewith send you ten additional madrigals. I would have sent you a much larger number, but having lost them like money, and perhaps in much the same manner, I am forced to re-do them.'[23] Yet Tasso also says that he attempted to fashion his product to the requirements of the composer. Speaking of a new group of madrigals which he is sending to Gesualdo, he states, 'The first, *which are exactly of the character and style which you desire*, possess no rare qualities.'[24] (My italics.) Elsewhere he says: 'Once again I send ten madrigals following the others, begging that you will excuse the poverty of talent, the infirmity of nature, and adversity of fortune; yet despite the difficulties of my present state and in order to comply with the wishes of Your Excellency, I am compelled to adopt new forms, as is suitable

[21] *Lettere*, vol. V, ed. C. Guasti, no. 1427: 'Ma in tutto devono essere stati sino a questa ora più di quaranta.'

[22] Ibid., no. 1428.

[23] 'Le mando diece altri madrigali; e n'avrei mandati in molto maggior numero: ma avendoli perduti come i danari, e forse per l'istessa cagione, sono stato costretto a rifarli.'

[24] Ibid., no. 1428: 'I primi, che sono a punto in quel soggetto ch'ella desidera, non hanno cosa alcuna d'esquisito.'

to the poet, who, according to Aristotle, must be either divine or of an amenable nature.'[25]

Thirty-six *Madrigali per musica ad istanza di Don Carlo Gesualdo, prencipe di Venosa* by Tasso have survived, and we may assume that they belong to the group completed by the end of 1592.[26] Curiously, of this group Gesualdo set only a single text, *Se cosi dolce è duolo*, which was composed about this time as it belongs to the collection anonymously printed prior to 1594. Why he did not set others would be difficult to say. Their length is to Gesualdo's taste,[27] their mood appropriately limited to amorous conceits, and their movement generously, if not uniformly, given to peripeteia. Equally curious is the fact that Gesualdo completely ignores one of the most important works of Tasso repeatedly used by other composers, the renowned *Gerusalemme liberata*.

The poems of Tasso which Gesualdo did choose to set are from a variety of sources. Two are from the *Rime per Lucrezia Bendidio: Mentre Madonna il lasso—Ahi, troppo saggia*[28] and *Non è, questa la mano—Fè tien face o saetta*,[29] poems which date from 1561–2 and 1585. Two are from the *Rime per Laura Peperara*, dating from 1563–7: *Se taccio, il duol s'avanza*[30] and *Felice primavera —Danzan le ninfe oneste*.[31] And three are from the *Rime d'occasione o d'encomio: Se da si nobil mano*[32] (1565–79); *Caro, amoroso neo—Ma se tale ha costei*[33] (date uncertain); and *Bella Angioletta*[34] (1579–82). A single text comes from the *Rime amorose estravagante: Gelo ha Madonna il seno*[35] (date uncertain).

The texts which have been accounted for are as follows:

Text	Book	Author
Baci soavi (prima parte)	I, 1	Guarini
Quanto ha di dolce (seconda parte)	I, 2	Guarini
Com'esser può ch'io viva	I, 4	A. Gatti
Gelo ha Madonna il seno	I, 5	Tasso
Mentre Madonna il lasso (p.p.)	I, 6	Tasso
Ahi, troppo saggia (s.p.)	I, 7	Tasso
Se da si nobil mano	I, 8	Tasso

[25] Ibid., no. 1423: 'Le mando ancora dieci madrigali appresso gli altri, pregandola che scusi la povertà de l'ingengno, l'infermità de la natura, e l'infelicità de la fortuna; per la quale malagevolmente al mio stato, ma per compiacere a Vostra Eccellenza, mia sforzerò di trasmutarmi in nuove forme, com' è conveniente al poeta; il quale, per opinione d'Aristotile, o deve esser divino, o di pieghevole ingegno.'

[26] *Rime*, vol. I of *Opere*, ed. by Bruno Maier (Milan, 1963), nos. 464–99.

[27] 15 of 9 lines; 14 of 7 lines; 3 of 10, and single examples of 6 and 11 lines.

[28] *Rime*, ed. B. Maier, no. 89.　　[29] Ibid., no. 47.　　[30] Ibid., no. 166.　　[31] Ibid., no. 196.

[32] Ibid., no. 571.　　[33] Ibid., no. 602.　　[34] Ibid., no. 735.　　[35] Ibid., no. 333.

Tirsi morir volea (p.p.)	I, 12	Guarini
Frenò Tirsi il desio (s.p.)	I, 13	Guarini
Mentre mia stella	I, 14	Tasso
Questi leggiadri	I, 16	Celiano
Felice primavera! (p.p.)	I, 17	Tasso
Danzan le Ninfe (s.p.)	I, 18	Tasso
Caro, amoroso neo (p.p.)	II, 1	Tasso
Ma se tale ha costei (s.p.)	II, 2	Tasso
Se cosi dolce è il duolo (p.p.)	II, 7	Tasso
Ma se avverrà ch'io moia (s.p.)	II, 8	Tasso
Se taccio, il duol s'avanza	II, 9	Tasso
O come è gran martire (p.p.)	II, 10	Guarini
O mio soave ardore (s.p.)	II, 11	Guarini
Sento che nel partire	II, 12	d'Avalos
Non è, questa la mano (p.p.)	II, 13	Tasso
Nè tien face o saetta (s.p.)	II, 14	Tasso
Voi volete ch'io mora	III, 1	Guarini
Dolcissimo sospiro	III, 19	Pocaterra
Luci serene e chiare	IV, 1	R. Arlotti
T'amo mia vita	V, 21	Guarini
Occhi del mio cor vita	V, 9	T. Molza (?)
O chiome dorate	P	G. Marino

Tasso and Guarini predictably dominate the scene, while Petrarch, Sannazaro, and Ariosto are totally absent. *Occhi del mio cor vita,* which was set earlier by Marenzio, has been tentatively attributed by Engel to the poetess-philosopher-singer, Tarquinia Molza,[36] and *O chiome dorate,* which appears in Gesualdo's posthumous collection of six-voice madrigals of 1626, is the only setting of a text by Giambattista Marino that I have been able to locate.[37] Arlotti, Pocaterra, Celiano, Gatti and d'Avalos likewise are repre-

---

[36] This text was set by Marenzio in Bk. III à 5.

[37] See G. Marino, *Poesie varie,* ed. B. Croce (1913), p. 66: *O chiome erranti, o chiome dorate.* It will be remembered that Marino, who was born in Naples in 1569, contributed two sonnets in his youth lamenting the murders of Maria d'Avalos and the Duke of Andria.

sented by a single madrigal.[38] One day the authors of additional poems, either slightly or drastically altered, may be discovered, but there is no reason to believe that many future identifications will be made, particularly in view of factors which will be presently discussed.[39]

Sento che nel partire underscores, however, the danger of relying solely on *capoversi* for purposes of identification. A comparison of the original d'Avalos poem, as set by Rore, with the version utilized by Gesualdo is revealing:

Rore

Anchor che col partire
Io mi sento morire
Partir vorrei ogn'hor ogni momento
Tantè il piacer ch'io sento
De la vita ch'aquisto nel ritorno,
E cosi mill'e mille volt'il giorno
Partir da voi vorrei
Tanto son dolci gli ritorni miei.

(Although when we part
I feel as if I were dying,
I would like to part always, every moment,
So great is the pleasure I feel
In the life that I acquire when I return;
And so a thousand, thousand times each day
I would like to part from you,
So sweet are my returns.)

Gesualdo

Sento che nel partire
Il cor giunge al morire,
Ond'io, misero ognor, ogni momento

[38] I am indebted to Anthony Newcomb for the identification of the Arlotti and the Pocaterra texts, the former of which he made on the basis of a letter from Fontanelli to Arlotti (15 February 1590; Bibl. Estense, MS alpha G. 1, 8) which reads in part: 'Questa sera alla musica cantandosi il Madregale Luci serene e chiare, et lodando il Sr. Gio: Bardi le parole S.A. ha detto che sono dell'Arlotti, huomo solito a far buone cose in questo genere, . . .' *Dolcissimo sospiro* is among the poems printed in *Due Dialoghi della Vergogna* by Annibale Pocaterra (Reggio, 1607).

[39] MacClintock's comments (*Giaches de Wert, Life and Works*, p. 55, fn. 9) with respect to the identification of Wert's texts is comforting: 'It might be thought that since so many contemporary poetic anthologies have survived, the task of identification would be easy. Quite the contrary. This writer has examined over 156 anthologies with most discouraging results.'

Grido: 'Morir mi sento,
Non sperando di far a voi ritorno,'
E cosi dico mille volte il giorno.
Partir io non vorrei,
Se col partir accresco i dolor miei.

(I feel that upon departure
My heart is at the point of death,
Wherefore, I, wretched one, always and at every moment
Shout: 'I feel I die
Not hoping that I shall return to you,'
And thus I speak a thousand times a day.
I would fain not leave,
If by leaving I increase my pains.)

Gesualdo has not tampered with the rhyme scheme and has even retained the last word of every line. Additionally the line lengths are the same (7,7,11,7; 11,11,7,11). For the rest, he alters the text in a way that is not particularly in keeping with his general inclination toward verses which stress oxymora, ambiguity and textual strain. As will be noted, the point of the d'Avalos[40] text is reversed in Gesualdo's adaptation. The momentary anguish upon departure which turns to joy upon the thought of return becomes in Gesualdo's version an unrelieved cry of distress. Elsewhere, however, he exhibits a penchant for peripeteia and a mastery of textual chiaroscuro worthy of his characterization as the 'composer of the oxymoron.' Such an early text as:

Se cosi dolce è il duolo,
Deh, qual dolcezza aspetto
D'imaginato mio nuovo diletto!

(If grief is so sweet
Pray, what sweetness I await
From my imagined new delight!)

[40] Alfonso d'Avalos, Marchese del Vasto, known to madrigalists as the author of the most celebrated madrigal of the times, *Il bianco e dolce cigno*, was a member of the illustrious Neapolitan family to which Venosa was connected through his first fateful marriage: he was the paternal grandfather of Maria d'Avalos; see p. 4. *Anchor che col partire*, also by d'Avalos, was set by Rore, Caimo, Cimello, etc.; Rore's setting, his most famous madrigal, is parodied as well by Vecchi in his *Amfiparnaso*, by Gabriello Puliti in the form of a mascherata à 3, by Andrea Gabrieli as a three-voice 'Giustiniana' and by countless others in arrangements for lutes and other instruments. Cf. Ferand, '*Anchor che col partire*, Die Schicksale eines berühmten Madrigals (Cipriano de Rore),' in *Festscrift K.G. Fellerer zum sechszigsten Geburtstag* (1962), pp. 137–54.

is typically Gesualdine. The brevity of the rhyme (the *prima parte* of a two-part madrigal) which he has adapted from Tasso is also significant, since it has been contended that he abandoned the major poets, and Tasso in particular, out of need for brief texts saturated with oxymora, which ultimately he either fashioned himself or had someone close at hand compose. In support of this thesis it may be suggested that while he set selections from Tasso in his early career, a time when he was also in personal contact with the poet, his later adoption of anonymous verses reflects not only his special textual requirement but a respect for Tasso in leaving his lines un-molested.

Textual abbreviation and alteration by his contemporaries was, however, not so uncommon as might be supposed. More than one composer was known to have mutilated the rigid form of the sonnet by severing the final tercets. With Luzzaschi, for example, the 'textual problem is difficult because he not infrequently alters, grafts two texts together, and changes the text to suit his needs.'[41] Luzzasco's unidentified text, *Itene mie querele*, which is virtually the same as Gesualdo's *Itene o sospiri* (V, 3), shows a loosening of the rhyme scheme compared with Gesualdo's more symmetrical pairings.

> Luzzaschi:
> Itene mie querele
> Precipitose a volo
> A lei che m'è cagion d'eterno duolo.
> Ditele per pietà ch'ella mi sia
> Dolcemente crudele,
> Non crudelmente ria
> Ch'i dolorosi stridi
> Cangerò lieto in amorosi stridi.

> Gesualdo:
> Itene, o miei sospiri
> Precipitate 'l volo
> A lei che m'è cagion d'aspri martiri.
> Ditele, per pietà, del mio gran duolo;
> C'ormai ella mi sia
> Come bella ancor pia,
> Che l'amaro mio pianto
> Cangerò, lieto, in amoroso canto.

[41] Arthur G. Spiro, *The Five-Part Madrigals of Luzzasco Luzzaschi* (Boston University, Ph.D. dissertation, 1961), p. 101.

The obfuscated order and substitution of verses in the anonymous *Deh*, *(s)coprite* as used by Nenna and Gesualdo provides further evidence of this textual malpractice.

Nenna

Deh, scoprit'il bel seno
Ch'invido vel ricopre,
Si ch'io vegghegia di Natura l'opre.
Ah, nol scoprite, no, ch'io vengo meno
E l'alma non avezza
A tanto ben, ne morria di dolcezza.

Gesualdo

Deh, coprite il bel seno,
Che per troppo mirar l'alma vien meno!
Ahi, nol coprite, no, che l'alma avezza
A viver di dolcezza
Spera, mirando, aita
Da quel bel sen, che le dà morte e vita.

Thus, notwithstanding the madrigalists' reputed preference for poetic texts of literary quality, Gesualdo is not unique in his textual habits, other well-known composers similarly grafting and abbreviating texts to their taste. We would do well to remember that the very features which we ascribe to Gesualdo's music, even though frequently associated with texts of indifferent merit, were inspired by his literary contemporaries, including the great Tasso himself, whose texts are 'shorter than the madrigals of the first part of the century,' and 'allow even more play to the oxymora and . . . give an even sharper "point" to the final couplet.'[42]

Gesualdo's approach to the text is symptomatic of a trend on the part of all madrigalists in the second half of the sixteenth century. It places a premium upon the expressive quality and stylistic sophistication of the musical idea, at the expense of literary merit. This view is, indeed, central to the Mannerist aesthetic. It is worthy of note that Rore's late madrigals not only abandon the formalistic ideal of the early works, namely the sonnet, but also abandon Petrarch to a large extent. While the madrigals of Marenzio, for example, continue to set the stanzas of Tasso, Guarini, Sannazaro and, surprisingly, even Dante in his final two volumes (Books VIII and IX, 1598

[42] Einstein, op. cit., p. 210.

and 1599),[43] the anonymous text is an important *option* in his later works.[44] Gesualdo's textual choices endorse this trait. In the twilight of the madrigal the simple pastoralisms of the earlier part of the century give way to a hyper-sensitive, oblique style—a style that is compact yet melodramatic, personal but difficult. Petrarch and Sannazaro are gradually replaced by the Mannerist poets, Tasso and Guarini, and, at the very end, Marino, who ultimately crosses the bounds of Mannerism and becomes such a special case that the imitation of him leads to Marinism. The essences, the emotional clichés of these several special cases lent themselves so readily to distillation by the anonymous pen, that a considerable quantity of *poesia per musica* was forthcoming, fashioned in many instances, assuredly, by the composers themselves. Those few texts in Gesualdo's mature style which are attributable to known poets differ little either in tone or quality from the prevalent anonymous rhymes, and the suggestion that madrigals which lack literary quality 'are either the work of unimportant composers or secondary work by more important men'[45] does not provide a totally accurate picture of the state of affairs in the late phase of the form.

[43] Engel, *Marenzio*, p. 227. See also Einstein's 'Dante on the Way to the Madrigal,' in *MQ*, XXV (1939), p. 142.

[44] W. Richard Shindle confirms this judgement with respect to Macque in a private communication: 'Macque's poets are Petrarca, Bernardo Tasso, Torquato Tasso, Luigi Alamanni, Bembo, Erasmo Valvasori, Sanazarro, Moscaglia and Fabio Petrozzi. The majority of his madrigals are anonymous. It is interesting to note that Guarini does not appear on this list.'

[45] Kerman, *The Elizabethan Madrigal*, p. 3.

CHAPTER SIX

The Madrigals: Books I & II

THE form most consistently cultivated by Gesualdo was the five-voice madrigal. Of the seven books of madrigals only one, the posthumous collection of 1626, developed the madrigal *a sei*. There are three excursions into the six-voice medium in the earlier volumes, the last piece of Book III and the last two (actually a single madrigal of two parts) of Book IV. Otherwise six-voice polyphony is reserved by Gesualdo for two sacred collections, the *Sacrae Cantiones in sex vocibus* of 1603 and the *Responsoria* of 1611.

As the seventh book of madrigals has come down to us incomplete,[1] six madrigal collections remain to be considered. They are best treated in pairs, partly because of their dates of first publication and partly because of matters of style.

It will be remembered that the first two books both appeared in the year of the celebration of Gesualdo's second marriage and were brought out by the ducal printer, Vittorio Baldini, who had issued the two books of wedding poems. This was not however their first appearance. Scipione Stella, who edited the two Baldini publications, tells us in a foreword to the second book that this volume had already appeared in print earlier under the pseudonym Gioseppe Pilonij.[2] While no copy of this print is known to have survived, it may be accepted therefore that Book II of the 1594 set was actually the first to appear, and it is interesting to note that in the score edition of the complete set of six volumes which appeared in 1613 its editor, Simone Molinaro, has reversed the order of 1594, thus re-establishing the original sequence. The order determined by Molinaro and maintained by most modern editors will be adhered to in the present discussion.

Both of the first two volumes enjoyed a modest but continuing popularity despite, or perhaps because of, what critics today would call the lack of an

[1] Only a single Quinto part-book survives in the Civico Museo Bibliografico Musicale in Bologna. A facsimile of this volume is printed in Vol. X of the complete works (Hamburg, 1967).
[2] See p. 56.

adventurous style.[3] Yet the basis for a true understanding of Gesualdo's language lies in these early collections. Later critics, overly concerned with explaining or denouncing the harmonic wizardry of the last volumes, would have done well to acquaint themselves with the music of the first two books. From even a brief perusal of their contents it becomes clear that the composer of the mature chromatic works did not stumble onto a few provocative harmonies at the keyboard and amateurishly set them to paper. Rather he developed his style gradually from relatively conservative beginnings.

Contrapuntal Foundations

To be sure, Venosa's early madrigals do more than establish evidence of his control of a traditional contrapuntal language, but in light of the greater harmonic orientation of many of his later works, it is especially important for us to note the sureness of the craft in order to comprehend his ultimate posture. There can be no question that Gesualdo knew and had studied the classic masters extensively, and in spite of a few traits which are openly personal, the care he exercised in voice-leading reveals a composer well versed in the traditions of contrapuntal practice.

In these first two books the continuing transformation of imitation as a structural technique is apparent. The cramped entrances, as in *Candida man* (II, 15) with its compressed announcement of the initial subject in its plain and inverted forms together with a second idea, are far removed from the stately expositions of the classic motet.

Ex. 3

[3] Book I was reprinted in Naples in 1603, 1604, 1608, and 1617. Book II was reprinted in 1603, 1607, and 1616 (Venice, Gardano). See Vogel, *Bibliothek*, pp. 289–92, where, of course, *Libro primo* is labelled *Libro secondo* and vice versa.

Gesualdo was not the first to indulge in such licences. Others had earlier used imitative transformation and stretto expressively—Josquin occasionally, and later Crecquillon and Clemens non Papa, in the motet; Luzzaschi; to an extent Vicentino,[4] and certainly Rore and Marenzio in the madrigal. Compare the beginning of Marenzio's *Scaldava il sol* (Book III *à 5 v.*, 1582) with Gesualdo's *Candida man*, above.

Ex. 4

Such compression and variation occurs in the motet more frequently in an interior position. As an opening statement it becomes increasingly characteristic of the madrigal.

Elsewhere Gesualdo demonstrates his mastery of traditional contrapuntal practices, including imitation in pairs. Even his handling of the homophonic-declamatory idea reveals a knowledge of contrapuntal craft for which he is not normally given credit, especially in his employment of double counterpoint, either in close-quarter or widely separated repetitions. As an example of the former type, the final section of *Tirsi morir volea* is remarkable.

Ex. 5

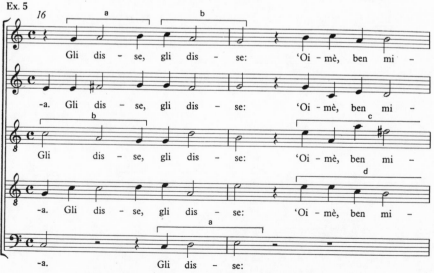

[4] N. Vicentino, *Opera Omnia*, ed. by H. Kaufmann, p. vii.

The passage is later repeated with the same interchanges. At one point, however, at bars 26–27, corresponding to the earlier bars 17–18, the repetition of figure *c* is retained in the same voice instead of being transferred, but with this startlingly angular result.

Ex. 6

... oi -mè ben mi – o, oi -mè ben mi – o,

Viewed as a juxtaposition of two *c*s, the melodic figure is tame enough; seen from the non-contextual view of *a*, the difficulty of the vocal requirement is revealed.

While double conterpoint was used as early as Obrecht and Josquin, it did not receive its first comprehensive theoretical discussion until Zarlino (1558).[5] Even in the madrigal melodic interchange was frequently limited to a simple substitution between inner parts, as in Rore's *Non è lasso* (Ex. 7).[6]

Ex. 7

32

- ta È che del mio mo - rir ____

È che del mio mo - rir se

È che del mio mo - rir se

È che del mio mo - rir

È che del mio mo - rir

35

È che del mio mo - rir se -

È che del mio mo - rir se - te con-

È che del mio mo - rir se - te

È che del mio mo - rir se -

È che del mio mo - rir se -

[5] Vicentino's *L'antica musica ridotta alla moderna prattica* (1553), Lib. IV, Cap. 34, 'Modo di comporre il contrapunto copia, overo compositione doppia,' contains a slightly earlier discussion. It has been inferred from this that the principle of double counterpoint was codified by Adrian Willaert, the teacher of both Vicentino and Zarlino.

[6] In *Madrigali à 5 v.* (1574).

This is akin to medieval *stimmtausch* and results in virtually no alteration of sound. In the opening of the same madrigal, interchange between parts involving transposition (the two appearances of *c* in Ex. 8), though indeed qualifying as bona fide invertible counterpoint at the octave, also provides only minor colour variation without harmonic change.

Ex. 8

When, however, the lowest voice is involved in this manoeuvre, and especially when bass and soprano exchange with each other, there is not only a difference in colour or melodic content, but a complete harmonic reorientation.

Example 9 from the last madrigal of Book I, *Bella Angioletta,* a piece whose rhyme and repetition scheme is A‖:bBcC:‖, shows this. It also displays Gesualdo's use of the device as a variation factor in the repetition of larger sections. Not only do the outer voices exchange positions in the second statement of the B verse, but the material is otherwise modified by the introduction of a chromatic inner voice.

Ex. 9

Luzzaschi went further than most previous composers in the frequency with which he applied genuine double-contrapuntal technique, which may be found throughout his entire production.[7] Yet while Gesualdo's use of double counterpoint may reflect a knowledge of Luzzaschi's practice, it need not derive directly from it, for all the masters of the late madrigal— Rore, da Monte, Marenzio, Wert—repeatedly demonstrated their control of the technique. An aspect of Gesualdo's contrapuntal prowess which has not often been discussed before,[8] the technique is observable in approximately half the madrigals of the first book and somewhat fewer in the second. Found in considerable concentration in these early books, it was also to serve well in his chromatic style.[9]

Some Comparisons

In searching to establish Gesualdo's relation to earlier madrigalists, it would be logical to look amongst those composers who had previously set texts included in his first volumes. *Tirsi morir volea* (I, 12–13) affords such an opportunity.[10] The complete text of the Guarini dialogue contains twenty-one lines:

> Tirsi morir volea,
> Gl'occhi mirando di colei ch'adora,
> Quand'ella, che di lui non men ardea,
> Gli disse: Oime ben mio,
> Deh non morir ancora,
> Che teco bramo di morir anch'io.
>   Frenò Tirsi il desio,
> C'hebbe di pur sua vit'alhor finire;
> Ma sentia morte in non poter morire
> E mentre'l guardo suo fiso tenea
> Ne begl'occhi divini;
> E'l nettare amoroso indi bevea;
> La bella Ninfa sua, che già vicini
> Sentia i messi d'Amore,
> Disse, con occhi languidi e tremanti:
> Mori cor mio, ch'io moro.
> Cui rispose il Pastore:

[7] Spiro, op. cit., 109.

[8] W. Weismann, 'Die Madrigale des Carlo Gesualdo' in *Deutsches Jahrbuch der Musik-wissenschaft für 1960*, pp. 14–15, examines this characteristic briefly.

[9] Cf. Exx. 16, 17, 18, 40, 41.

[10] I wish to thank Mr. James Anthony for his scorings of the Marenzio and Wert compositions as part of a seminar project.

Et io, mia vita, moro.
Cosi moriro i fortunati amanti,
Di morte si soave, e si gradita,
Che per anco morir tornaro in vita.

The following comparative chart reveals that of five well-known composers of the second half of the sixteenth century who set the madrigal all but two set the lengthy text complete. Even Caimo sets the entire poem except for two lines (verses 18 and 19). Gesualdo, on the other hand, sets only the initial nine verses. Yet his setting is musically the longest except for Marenzio's. In the opening nine lines the other composers write one-third to one-half the amount of music composed by Gesualdo.[11]

	No. of voices	No. of verses set	No. of parts	Total bars	Bars used to set first 9 verses
Marenzio (1580)	5	21	3 (29, 30, 16)	75	37
Wert (1581)	7	21	1	51	20
Caimo (1584)	5	19	2 (30, 33)	63	31
A. Gabrieli (1587)	6	21	1	49	35
Gesualdo (1594)	5	9	2 (36, 32)	68	68

For all the brevity of Gesualdo's text he has divided it into a madrigal of two parts, the *seconda parte* beginning at 'Freno Tirsi il desio'. This division is reminiscent of Marenzio's work, the only one of the other four settings to begin a second section at this point, and both composers emphasize the opening section through extensive repetition. Marenzio's part two, however,

[11] This comparison is of bars of $\frac{4}{2}$ time with respect to original time values. The number of $\frac{4}{4}$ measures in Einstein's edition (Marenzio, *Sämtliche Werke*, 1929), which also uses original note values, are thus halved, and the $\frac{6}{4}$ barring according to the Molinaro edition of 1613 in the two opening measures of Gesualdo's setting, for example, is similarly adjusted.

is much longer textually (12 lines as opposed to Gesualdo's 3 lines) although
it is slightly shorter musically (30 measures compared with 32), and he
separates the final three lines into a *terza parte*. Gabrieli and Wert both set
the complete text as a single-part madrigal.

From this comparison a fundamental distinction emerges between
Gesualdo and his immediate predecessors and indicates an essential ingredient of his style. He is in one way more concerned with his text and in
another less so. He is more alert to the possibilities of savouring, through
extension and re-working, the textual climate of a given moment, less
concerned with preserving the poetic integrity of the original. The considerable variety achieved in thus extensively re-working the textual
element is often associated with the contrapuntal practices discussed in
relation to Ex. 5.

The element of dialogue inherent in *Tirsi morir volea*, which is highlighted
especially in the settings by Gabrieli and Wert (for six and seven voices
respectively) through contrast of upper and lower voices, is virtually ignored
by Gesualdo, either in the interest of expressiveness or in order to use
spatial contrast solely as a colouristic device. For those sections involving
direct speech Gesualdo employs a homophonic, highly declamatory style,
which contrasts upper and lower registers in the repetition of short phrases
but not so as to match the text. Contrasts of tempo, however, achieved
through written-out ritenutos and faster imitative episodes, forecast a
stylistic feature that he was to employ to the end. When later his language
becomes progressively more chromatic, his chromatic and diatonic idiom
will divide precisely along the lines of such tempo changes. For the present
it is important to observe the trait in non-chromatic surroundings.

Several other madrigals in the first two books utilize texts set earlier by
well-known madrigalists. Guarini's *Baci soavi*, the opening piece of Book I,
appeared also in Monteverdi's first book of madrigals of 1587. Gesualdo's
setting of this text was the only early madrigal of his to be repeatedly cited
by writers in the seventeenth and eighteenth centuries. At first glance it
may seem a singularly uninteresting choice, but closer examination reveals
the reasons for the special admiration that Padre Martini, for instance,
expressed in his *Saggio* of 1775. It discloses Gesualdo's remarkable capacity,
even at this early stage, for motivic unification and development. For all its
formal cohesiveness, moreover, *Baci soavi* is not without its expressive
moments, and stands comparison with Monteverdi's setting. Although
Monteverdi's piece appeared in 1587 and Gesualdo's in 1594, it will be
remembered that the latter had appeared earlier under a *nom de plume*. Thus
it seems probable that the two settings are very nearly exact contemporaries.

One passage in the Monteverdi work noted[12] for its prolonged and intense
string of suspensions (Ex. 10), finds the following counterpart at the same

Ex. 10

textual point in Gesualdo's setting.

Ex. 11

[12] Denis Arnold, *Monteverdi Madrigals*, p. 13.

Both composers have responded to the text with a similar tempo and
texture together with an accumulation of dissonances. In Gesualdo's case
there are not only suspensions but other unusual dissonance formations (★)
as well.[13] Melodic interchange between the two outer parts will also be
noted: melodic flow and harmonic function match flawlessly. The octave
skip in an interior voice is also characteristic of many cadences of the first
three books[14] and to an extent later.

Although mild degree inflection occurs throughout the two early books,
only one madrigal gives much hint of the composer's ultimate and characteristic bent, any clue of things to come harmonically. This is the madrigal
Sento che nel partire, a variation of the text *Anchor che col partire*. The most
striking part is the opening. For all the occasional chromatic usage of Rore,
Caimo, Vicentino, Marenzio, and Lassus before this time, few can claim a
passage so rich in pathos as the following.

Ex. 12

[13] The dissonance at ★ could be viewed as resulting from the suspension of the two
lowest voices; when their resolution (F & A) occurs, however, the upper voices have
moved on to suggest D6. The immediately following beats confirm this genesis of
the dissonance with a more classic resolution of the Bassus in relation to the stationary
upper parts. It would be difficult in any event to consider the intervals of the fourth
and sixth as a consonant fourth figuration in light of their approach. Genesis aside,
the harmonic sonority at ★ underscores the increasingly independent use of the
seventh chord and its inversions, here c_3^4, during this period.
[14] Cf. Bk. II: 7, 9, 15, 16, 17.

This is a miracle worthy even of the later Monteverdi. It is in fact reminiscent of the solo style, and could easily be performed with a single voice singing the top part and the remaining ones reduced to an instrumental accompaniment. Note how in bar four the dotted half-note in the soprano against the rests in the lower voices suggests the quality of a monodic air. It does not require much imagination to hear a resemblance between this excerpt and the opening passage of Monteverdi's famous lament, *Lasciatemi morire*. Appearing in print some fourteen years before the latter, could it be that Monteverdi knew of this work?

While Gesualdo's piece may or may not have served as a spiritual model for Monteverdi in this instance, earlier settings by Rore and Caimo of *Anchor che col partire* established a treatment that Gesualdo could hardly have overlooked. Yet he did not, like certain other composers, indulge in melodic diminutions of Rore's soprano,[15] and neither Rore nor Caimo can have suggested the emotional tone of his piece.[16] Rore's opening, for example, is bland by comparison:[17]

Ex. 13

And Caimo's setting of the phrase 'Io mi sento morire' seems almost flippant:[18]

Ex. 14

[15] I. Horsley, 'The Diminutions in Composition and the Theory of Composition,' *Acta Musicologica* (1963) XXXV, pp. 133–4.

[16] Ernest T. Ferand, '*Anchor che col partire*. Die Schicksale eines berühmten Madrigals [Cipriano de Rore],' *Festschrift K.G. Fellerer zum sechszigsten Geburtstag 1962*, pp. 137–54.

[17] Einstein, *Italian Madrigal*, III, p. 112.   [18] Einstein, op. cit., p. 214.

-re Io mi sen-to mo-ri - re

All three, however, reflect an ABB musical scheme which stems from a syntactical rather than a rhyme division of the text: aaBbc‖:CdD:‖. Thus the last repeated section begins in each case at the words 'E cosi dico mille volte il giorno', with a considerably heightened rhythmic movement. Gesualdo is closer to Caimo here, for in both the rhythmic quality changes more radically than in Rore. The return to a slower tempo likewise occurs at the identical location, 'Partir da voi vorrei' in Rore and Caimo, 'Se col partir' in Gesualdo. Gesualdo tacks on a small coda and closes with an intervallic conceit that was to become a habit in later years: Quintus and Altus exchange notes of resolution producing a melodic diminished fourth in the Altus. Note also the double pedal-points in Cantus and Tenor, a feature also developed in later works, as well as the chromatic inflection in the Altus expressive of the text 'accrescoi dolor miei'.

Ex. 15

- cre - sco i do - lor mie - - i.
-sco i do - lor mie - - - i.
mie - - - - - - i.
do - lor mie - - - - i.

What other influences are visible in the early style of Gesualdo? Einstein relates Gesualdo most directly to Luzzaschi:

> Gesualdo is to Luzzasco about what Tintoretto is to Titian or El Greco to Tintoretto; from the outset he goes further harmonically, his motifs are less simple and 'diatonic', he avoids pairing his voices. But fundamentally the two styles are the same. In both there is the same breaking up of the piece by rests in all the voices, both have the same

motet-like exposition in close imitation and the same epigrammatic brevity.[19]

In the light of Gesualdo's known admiration for Luzzaschi it is somewhat disappointing to find that Luzzaschi's madrigals are not more adventurous. It will be recalled that Fontanelli wrote in February 1594, 'He says that he has abandoned his first style and has set himself to the imitation of Luzzaschi, a man whom he greatly admires and praises although he says that not all of Luzzaschi's madrigals are equally well written.' Knowing that Gesualdo's first two books had been completed at this time, we would expect the indebtedness to be observable in Books III and IV. This is not so, however. If the 'two characteristics that remain throughout his [Luzzaschi's] artistic career are his rigid adherence to the poetic line and his use of melodic interchange of parts,'[20] it is in his first two books that Gesualdo comes as close to Luzzaschi's style as he ever will. It is true that as early as *Quivi sospiri* (Book II, 1576) Luzzaschi had composed chromatic passages worthy of Gesualdo's admiration, but the work is not typical of the collection. Luzzaschi's Book IV (1594) also contained madrigals, if not totally Gesualdine in complexion by a later standard, at least melodically expressive and occasionally harmonically audacious. (*Dolorosi martir, fieri tormenti*[21] displays some of the more adventurous traits of this collection.) The rhythmic posturing, so characteristic of Gesualdo's later style, is not forecast however.

While melodic interchange, varied repetition of textual units and the breaking up of the piece by rests is intermittently characteristic of both composers, as is a mildly chromatic bent and a common penchant for epigrammatic brevity, all of these points are found in varying degrees, in other madrigal composers of the period.[22]

Fontanelli's letter of 23 May 1594 indicates that Gesualdo saw in Luzzaschi a man of such accomplishments that he was 'the only enemy' he feared, that the others he laughed at.[23] This probably comes a good deal nearer to giving us a hint of the Gesualdo-Luzzaschi relationship than his earlier suggestion that he was turning away from his first style toward a new one modelled directly after Luzzaschi. Ingredients of the latter's art do appear in Gesualdo's creations from the time of his stay in Ferrara. But the

[19] Einstein, op. cit., p. 703.
[20] Spiro, p. 109.
[21] Einstein, op. cit., III, pp. 257–61.
[22] Gesualdo's occasional obvious dependence upon Marenzio, for example, has been noted, as at the end of the second section of his *Baci-soavi e cari—Cibi della mia vita*, where one voice leads and a pair of voices follow. Cf. Einstein, op. cit., p. 697.
[23] See p. 63.

competitive element, the desire to prove himself as a composer of the first rank (something totally unheard of for a man of his station) undoubtedly contributed to his selection of Luzzaschi as his 'enemy'—Luzzaschi was simply the most forceful and respected composer in Ferrara, where Gesualdo had gone to take a new wife. We must also keep in mind that Gesualdo's opinions regarding Luzzaschi come to us through an intermediary, Fontanelli, who may have had his own reasons for exaggerating what he had heard or confecting what he had not.

Before final judgements are in order, however, a fuller assessment of Luzzaschi's music must be undertaken, starting with a complete edition of his works. In any event, Gesualdo's first publications are firmly linked with the Italian madrigal tradition of the sixteenth century. What he creates would have been impossible without Rore, Marenzio, and Wert, as well as Luzzaschi, and it is as important for us to be aware of this foundation in such works as *Tirsi morir volea*, as to see a hint of things to come in *Sento che nel partire*.

CHAPTER SEVEN

The Madrigals:
Books III & IV

Backgrounds

THE third and fourth books of madrigals were largely written during Don Carlo's relatively continuous sojourn in the city of Ferrara from 1594 to 1596, but partly also during his six-month return to Gesualdo in the second half of 1594. Book III appeared on 19 March 1595 (reprints: Venice, 1603, 1611, 1619), Book IV in 1596 (reprints: Venice, 1604, 1611, 1616). The initial publications of 1595 and 1596 included an editorial preface by Hettore Gesualdo and appeared under the auspices of the ducal printer Vittorio Baldini. The later Venetian printings were all under the imprint of Gardano, and this long-standing association presumably stemmed from Gesualdo's visit to that city as early as 1594.

The music of these volumes, especially Book IV, marks the appearance of a new and decidedly personal language. The temptation to consider the traumatic events of Gesualdo's first marriage as largely responsible for the later development of his art is specious, if only because similar artistic aims were cultivated by other contemporaries (Nenna, Macque, etc.) whose emotional balance has never been held in question. It is more logical to relate these stylistic changes to his musical and artistic associations at Ferrara. Not that there was a single source, a particular model that can be cited to explain the direction the music of the Prince now takes. The turn was obviously stimulated by a composite group of influences involving creative personalities, performing artists, and instrumental resources. It is fruitless to speculate about the nature of Gesualdo's creations had he never journeyed to Ferrara, but almost certainly the atmosphere there served as an important catalyst in the early formation of his highly original artistic personality. At the same time it would be unwise to ignore the possibility of certain Neapolitan ingredients in his development, even in the third and fourth books. Macque and Nenna loom especially large in this connection, and their relation to Gesualdo will be discussed later in detail.

Transitions

In his third and fourth books of madrigals Gesualdo naturally retains many
of his initial compositional habits, although occasionally with less insistence
than before. Double counterpoint continues to appear, but much less
frequently. There are changes even here, however, which indicate that
Gesualdo was not content to accept it as a static technique. In *Ed ardo e
vivo* (III, 13), for example, we can observe the standard melodic exchange
altered by a subtle rhythmic displacement in an interior voice which
likewise suggests imitation between it and the soprano. The characteristic
homophonic texture of such a passage is thus modified in a manner which
stems naturally from the stretto-like imitation of the passage between these
two sections.

Ex. 16

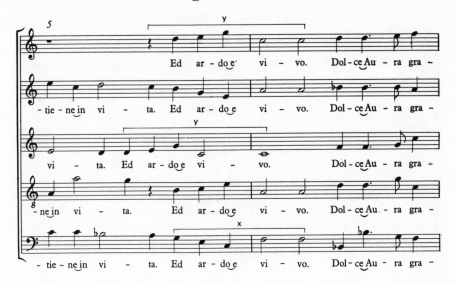

In *Io tacerò* (IV, 3) another variant can be observed. The Bassus in the repeated section (Ex. 17, bar 9) draws first from an interior voice and then from the top voice while the Cantus adopts the Bassus entire:

Ex. 17

And in *O sempre crudo Amore* from the same book Gesualdo demonstrates his capacity to meet the hazards of free triple-counterpoint in a chromatic context:

Ex. 18

It will be noticed that *y* ends in a three-note figure which outlines the interval of a seventh. This is a common feature of many of Gesualdo's melodies from now on. It is found in descending form, as in *Ahi, dispietata e cruda* (III, 6):

Ex. 19

or in ascending form, as in the following remarkable passage from *Non t'amo* (III, 11) where a motif outlining the seventh alternates with a compressed variant outlining the sixth at bars 18–19.

Ex. 20

Non t'amo (Ex. 20) contains a number of additional features noteworthy in light of future practice. (1) In bar 16, a phrase begins with a six-four sonority. (2) In bar 17, a six-four is used in the manner of a consonant fourth, but coupled with a 'consonant ninth'. (3) In bars 21–24, a chromatic complex is repeated at the fifth below, predictably at an affective textual point, 'Ahi, non si puo morire.'

Figurations similar to Exx. 19 and 20 are to be met elsewhere, e.g. in the sacred repertoire (*Responsoria*, Sabbato Sancto, I and IX). More unusual intervals are also to be found in this book, which displays a freedom barely intimated in the first two volumes. Not only do we witness the diminished fourth at the cadence in *Sparge la morte* (IV, 11) in the manner of *Sento che nel partire* (Ex. 15), or diminished and augmented fifths, but also in the previously cited *Non t'amo* a descent of a minor ninth at the final cadence in lieu of the expected minor second.

Ex. 21

Such melodic gestures are not, however, completely without parallel. Marenzio's *Solo e pensoso*,[1] a madrigal otherwise notable for the extended melodic chromaticism of the Superius, contains a downward leap of a minor ninth in the Bassus (Ex. 22a), and the substitute voice-leading of Ex. 15 resulting in a diminished fourth was used by Wert as early as his first book (1558).

Ex. 22a

[1] Printed in Torchi, *L'arte musicale in Italia*, II, pp. 228–9. Original appearance in *Nono Libro de Madrigali a cinque voci* (Venetia: Gardano, 1599).

Other vocal lines of exceptionally wide range and expressive intervals occasionally exhibited in the madrigals of Marenzio and Wert mirror or prefigure Gesualdo's style. This is amply demonstrated in the opening measures in the four lowest voices of Marenzio's *Solo e pensoso* (1599):

Ex. 22b

and in the Bassus of Wert's vocally demanding setting of the same text (1581).[2]

Ex. 22c

The following earlier examples from Rore may suggest an even more direct antecedent. Ex. 22d is from *Se'l mio sempre voi* (1550), Ex. 22e from *Da le belle contrade* (1566).

Ex. 22d

Ex. 22e

Elsewhere expressive melodic intervals and contrapuntal ingenuity blend to produce powerful and graphic statements. *Cor mio, deh, non piangete* (IV, 9; Ex. 23) provides a spectacular example of melodic interchange between two motifs containing drooping melodic skips of sevenths, while a free voice joins them at the cadence with a diminished fifth in a reflection of the word 'languir'. This cannot be dismissed as mere 'madrigalism'. It is a bold new

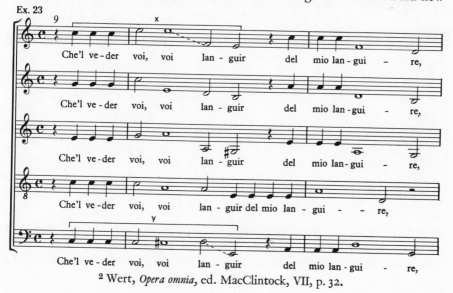

Ex. 23

[2] Wert, *Opera omnia*, ed. MacClintock, VII, p. 32.

vocal style, pliant, expressive, fantastic, which springs not from an extreme harmonic practice but from expressive extensions of the melodic element.

Unusual intervallic treatment of the word 'languire' can be seen in a number of madrigals, as in *O mal nati messagi* (III, 9; Ex. 24) or later in *Languisce al fin* (V, 10).

O mal nati messagi (Ex. 25) also exhibits an especially forceful and insistent dissonance chain in its opening measures, while other pieces of both collections

yield an extensive list of felicitous dissonances, such as the unprepared seventh in the final cadence of *Moro o non moro* (III, 2):[3]

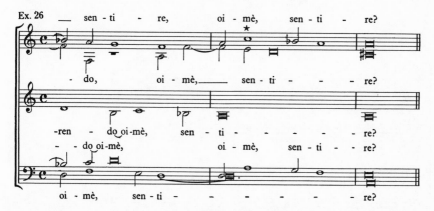

More unusual is the employment of a sixth-chord succession as an opening statement in a chromatic-melodic context garnished by suspensions as in *Ahi, già mi discoloro* (IV, 17).

[3] Note, however, that the seventh in the soprano is classically prepared and resolved in relation to the alto.

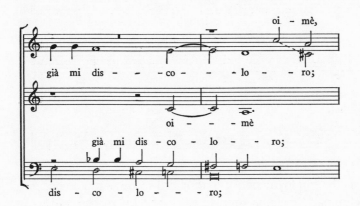

The presence of successive chords of the sixth is common throughout
Gesualdo's production. It may point to a specific knowledge of the works of
Rore and Wert,[4] but this feature is equally observable in many other composers of the fifteenth and sixteenth centuries. Particularly typical of the
mature Gesualdo is the employment of a figure in parallel motion over a
pedal-point, sometimes with sustained parts in both outer voices enclosing
the moving inner parts. This occurs as early as Book III, as at the cadence of
Veggio, si, dal mio sole (Ex. 28), where the syncopated rhythmic figuration also
unveils the dissonance potential (★) of this sliding harmonic device.

[4] The editors of the complete works of these two composers both single out the
characteristic use of the sixth-chord style. See Cipriano Rore, *Opera Omnia,* ed. by
Bernhard Meier, III, pp. v–vi; Giaches de Wert, *Collected Works,* ed. by Carol
MacClintock, I, p. i.

Ex. 28

As characteristic as the chromaticism are the smaller gestures, such as the last two notes on the text 'oimè' in Ex. 27 above, where a cross-relation occurs between the soprano and alto on the last beat (C–C♯). This is typical of a kind of movement which Gesualdo increasingly employed to create not only harmonic tension (Ex. 27, bar 8, third beat: C–D–E sounding simultaneously) but also modal ambivalence. In the same example, the single notes on the word 'Ahi' for the two lowest parts in the opening bar, and again in bar three, reflect his continuing infatuation with the rest as an agent of textual emphasis.

Other madrigals throw additional light on his developing chromatic vocabulary. The final cadence of *Or, che in gioia credea viver contento* (IV, 7) is as extended an example of melodic chromaticism as can be found up to this time in Gesualdo's output, containing in the Cantus a succession of seven descending semitones:

Ex. 29

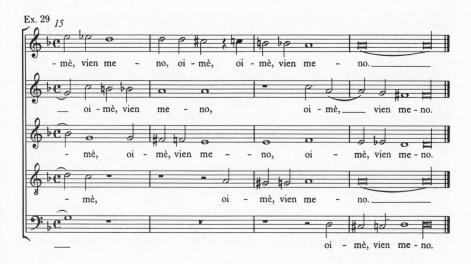

The scalar presentation of chromatic notes is, however, less important than their invasion of all parts of the polyphonic complex. Notably different from the simple chromatic scale in one voice in Marenzio's *Solo e pensoso* (Ex. 22a, b), the passage more readily recalls the style of Rore's *Calami sonum ferentes*.

On the other hand passages like the opening of *Ecco, morirò dunque* (IV, 16; Ex. 30)[5] and the close of *Arde il mio cor* (IV, 18; Ex. 31) contain as many harmonic surprises as melodic ones.

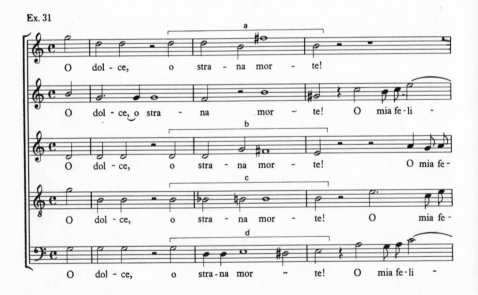

[5] For principles of harmonic progression involved in this passage, see the discussion in Chapter 8, p. 204.

The latter passage, in addition to qualities of tonal ambivalence, illustrates Gesualdo's mastery of harmony at the service of a specific contrapuntal requirement. The phrase 'O dolce e strana morte' is set to the chord progression G–B♭6–e–B6–E. The opening third-relationship and especially the ensuing tritone progression are noteworthy in the light of the text.[6] The modified repetition of the phrase three bars later is somewhat less audacious harmonically in view of the demands of the final cadence (D–C–c–a6–E–A). Comparative harmonic analysis of the two passages shows the remarkable way in which the *melodic* events virtually dictate the *harmonic* outcome. Here Gesualdo, whose skill in melodic interchanges we have already witnessed in his first two books, conceives one of his finest masterstrokes. Reading from top to bottom, the initial arrangement *a–b–c–d* reappears in inverted order as *d–c–b–a* without a single intervallic adjustment in any voice—a truly striking display of contrapuntal craft, especially in view of the ravishing, though appropriately differing, harmonic results.

Finally, it must be noted that, for all his harmonic audacity, the tonal outline of this passage is tightly focused. The phrase 'O dolce, o strana morte' opens initially on G major and cadences on E major.[7] The repetition of the idea at the final cadence begins on D and cadences on A major. The opening levels of the two settings (G, D) as well as the closing levels (E, A)

[6] As to the analytical appropriateness of referring to such a passage as a tritone progression, however, see p. 182.
[7] I refer here to chords, not keys.

emphasize the fifth-relation. And importantly, this repetition at the dominant permits Gesualdo to end at precisely the tonal level which he requires for a close, the piece having begun in a, cadenced on A at the end of the first large section, and now concluding on A at its final cadence. If the chromatic-melodic fluxions and surprising harmonic progressions initially appear to be the result of compositional chance or creative caprice, we will do well to remind ourselves of Gesualdo's invariable control over the larger tonal complex.

The closing passage from *Arde il mio cor* also embodies one of the innumerable examples that earned for Gesualdo the epithet 'the composer of the oxymoron,' and reflects his delight in setting texts dealing with the bittersweet or abounding in references to pleasure-pain. 'O dolce, o strana morte!' ('O sweet, o strange death!') the poet intones, and Gesualdo answers with a sweet and strange music.

CHAPTER EIGHT

The Madrigals: Books V & VI

THE fifteen-year gap between the appearance of the fourth and fifth books of madrigals is puzzling. We know that Gesualdo had not remained totally inactive during this period since he had published two books of *Sacrae Cantiones* in 1603. Yet it might still be logical to suppose that the pause before his last two madrigal volumes represents a genuine incubation period for the development of the stylistic features of his most mature creations.

The first printing of Book V, in 1611, contains information which is unusually rich, not only because it suggests an answer to this dilemma, but also because it focuses as in no other source upon Gesualdo's psyche. Only the Alto, Quinto, and Basso parts survive in a unique copy in the Biblioteca della Conservatorio di San Pietro a Majella, Naples, but the dedication page is perfectly preserved. It has not been previously reproduced, even by Vogel or Einstein.[1]

> To His Most Illustrious, His Most Excellent
> Don Carlo Gesualdo, Count of Consa, Prince
> of Venosa, etc., My Lord and Most Respected Patron
> That humble and modest desire, which by nature has been given to Your Excellence to keep your rare musical compositions hidden from public applause as much as possible, has now thankfully been put aside and deemed to be overly contrived. It was with labour that the work was born to light, and its great delight has been enjoyed only domestically, without looking forward to the benefit of the press, which is already declared to be an enemy to the taste of Your Excellence. Yet this has caused

> [1] All'Illustrissimo et Eccellentissimo Sig.
> Don Carlo Gesualdo, Conte di Conso,
> Prencipe di Venosa &c. Signore & Padron
> mio Colendissimo.
> Quell'humile, e modesto desiderio, che dalla natura è stato dato à V.E. di tener'le sue rare compositioni musicali quanto più si possa celate alli publichi applausi, è venuto troppo disaiutato dal molto artificio, e gratia loro; poichè à pena uscito il parto à luce, e gustata solo domesticamente la gran vaghezza di esso, senza aspettarsi il beneficio della stampa dichiarata gia nemica del gusto di V.E. hà cagionato, non solo, che alcuni mossi da sincero desiderio di goder cose si eccellenti, habbino usata sottile industria per haverne qualche ritratto, tale, quale poteva uscire anche da

not only that some people, moved by a sincere desire to enjoy such excellent works, have used a subtle astuteness to obtain some copies which could fall even into dishonest hands, but also that certain composers with this opportunity have wished to make up for the paucity of their own talent through fraudulent means, attributing to themselves many beautiful passages of the works and innovations of Your Excellence, such as has happened in particular to this fifth set of your marvellous madrigals. Therefore, the world after having avidly waited for the duration of fifteen years from the time when they were composed, and I, having waited for ten years exercising the due obedience necessary to your commands, have made the effort to keep them at home. After having seen that my efforts were in vain and moved by the compassion of seeing such rare compositions fall into the hands of such dishonest people (like very precious jewels embedded in lead), I have resolved to be worthy of Your Highness with the exercising of charity and of justice by way of the press, trusting that Your Excellence, yielding to the minor part of your distaste, will approve this matter in good spirit instead of scorning the ardour of your most faithful but lowly servant. In order that you might graciously deign to pardon me of any excess which you have endured, and thus taking a fresh new look at your works which are free from the fraud of others, to you I offer and dedicate this printing, and it is with profound reverence that I bow to you. At Gesualdo on the twentieth of June, 1611.

> Most humbly and devotedly,
> Don Gio: Pietro Cappuccio

The dedication to the sixth book, which is dated 25 July 1611, only a month after Book V, repeats the basic sentiment of the one to Book V, and states that its contents were 'composed in the same years as those of the fifth book,' that is as early as 1596.[2] The long delay was due purportedly to

---

scorrette mani, ma che certi compositori con questa commodità habbino voluto supplire con fraudolente arte alla scarsezza del lor proprio ingegno, attribuendo à se stessi molti belli passi delle opere, e inventioni di V.E. si come è particolarmente avvenuto à questa quinta muta de'i suoi maravigliosi madrigali. La onde dopo essere stato il mondo avidissimamente aspettandoli per lo spatio di quindici anni, da che sono stati composti, & dopo haver' io già per lo spatio di dieci con l'essercitio dell' obbidienza devuta à suoi commandamenti, fatto forza per ritenerli in casa, e visto finalmente esser vana ogni mia deligenza, mosso da compassione di veder' si rare compositioni andar per le mani di alcuni cosi scorrette, e come incastrate in piombo gioie si pretiose, mi son risoluto di voler' meritare con l'essercitio della carità, e della giustitia per mezo della stampa, confidando che l'Ecc. Vostra con rendersi al minore de doi disgusti sia più tosto per approvare in questa parte in buon zelo, che per isdegnarsi dell'ardire di questo suo fedelissimo se ben minimo creato. Et accioche in ogni caso ella si pieghi più gratiosamente à perdonarmi qualsivoglia eccesso, che vi fusse, rimirando i suoi parti liberati dalle altrui fraudi à lei medesima offerisco, e dedico questa impressione, e con profonda riverenza me le inchino. Di Gesualdo à 20. di Giugno 1611.

DI V.E.   Humilissimo, & devotissimo creato
                                          Don Gio: Pietro Cappuccio.

2 The dedication to Book VI, which is given only incompletely in Vogel, reads: 'Questi madrigali della sesta muta furono composti da V.E. nelli medesimi anni, che furono quelli della quinta; e perciò questi ancora sono stati aspettati con grandissimo desiderio dal mondo si lungo tempo, & hanno corso l'istessa fortuna con quelli, in andar per

Gesualdo's distate for publication, but this does not make a totally convincing story in light of the two volumes of motets which Cappuccio himself edited and saw into print in 1603. It also seems unreasonable that this sizeable group of virtually unprecedented masterworks should have been born within a few months of the publication of Book IV. Yet spread evenly over the period 1596–1611, the forty-four madrigals of these two collections would average slightly less than three madrigals per year, an equally improbable rate of production. A more respectable quantity, and a realistic mixture of secular and sacred works, emerges for this period if we view the total production of three volumes of motets and three volumes of madrigals (Books V, VI, and the posthumously published volume of six-voice madrigals).

It is unfortunate that we shall probably never be able to date these late works with the precision which the resolution of certain questions demands. While there is no reason to insist that the complete contents of Books V and VI were composed as late as 1609–11 (1609 marks the earliest appearance in print of any madrigal from these two collections), it is strange that Gesualdo should claim that these two volumes of madrigals were written as early as fifteen years before. That this is Gesualdo's own testimony we need not doubt, for there can be little question that Don Gio: Pietro Cappucio, probably one of the Capuchin friars of Gesualdo's Santa Maria delle Grazie, is merely the Prince's mouthpiece. The clue to the need for such a declaration lies in the charge that certain composers, lacking sufficient natural talent, had attributed to themselves many beautiful passages from Gesualdo's works which had circulated privately though unprinted. Gesualdo would have us believe that it is this situation which has moved him to publication. There are several implications, and we shall be forced to consider certain of the more unseemly possibilities later on with respect to the productions of other Neapolitan composers.

Whatever the complete story, it is clear that Gesualdo went to great trouble to bring out these volumes, for he brought the Neapolitan printer Gio. Jacomo Carlino to Gesualdo and set up a press in the feudal castle expressly for this purpose.[3] Why he would have done this can only be

---

le mani d'alcuni trascritti infedelmente, & in patir furti di molti belli passi loro: onde io per le istesse cagioni, che mi mossi a mandar alla Stampa quelli, mando hora in luce questi, & con l'istessa confidenza, che V.E. sia almeno per far gratioso passagio di questo mio nuovo ardire, vengo a presentarglieli, & con profonda riverenza bacio à V.E. le mani. Di Gesualdo à 25, di Iuglio, 1611. Humilissimo & devotissimo creato, Don Gio: Pietro Cappuccio.'

[3] G. Fumagalli, *Lexicon Typographicum Italiae* (Florence, 1905), 173, places Carlino in the

surmised, but the legendary accuracy of these collections produced under Gesualdo's watchful eye suggests only a partial answer. The note of paranoia, struck in the preface to Book V, suggests an additional reason for maintaining such surveillance over the production of these volumes, which include the *Responsoria* of 1611 in addition to the two books of madrigals. Furthermore, it is interesting to note that there were no additional printings or re-printings by other presses during Gesualdo's lifetime.

Books V and VI were published separately only once more, in the years 1614 and 1616 respectively. The qualification 'separately' is important, for all six volumes were collected together and printed by Giuseppe Pavoni of Genoa in a score edition prepared by Simone Molinaro, Maestro di Cappella of the Cathedral of Genoa. The rather slim number of printings of the separate madrigal books, when compared to those of other leading madrigal composers of the period, indicates that Gesualdo's works were not widely distributed (the difficulty of the music of the later collections would have precluded their easy acceptance in the ranks of amateurs). Nevertheless the music was known and admired to the extent that connoisseurs of music and students of the art recognized the study value that such a collection would have.

Gesualdo was virtually unique among the composers of his time in being honoured by the appearance of a collected edition of his madrigals. Rore's two books of four-voice madrigals were the only comparable works to have been published in this format in 1577. Eitner says that 'Just as Rore's two books were printed in score, a completely extraordinary undertaking for that time, so were the Prince's. Rore did it, however, for the sake of his students and its study value, the Prince because he could afford it.'[4] Both conclusions seem unwarranted in view of the probability that neither composer had anything to do with their respective publications. Rore almost certainly did not as he died in 1565, while the 1613 Gesualdo edition was executed not by a press under the Prince's supervision, as with the first printings of Books V and VI, but by Simone Molinaro, a Genoese lutenist and composer who was noted for his cultivation of the best music of his period. The appearance of the six volumes not only in score, but together, implies that the collection was conceived as a unity. This they became only upon Gesualdo's death, which implies a publication date sometime between

---

castle at Gesualdo in 1611, at Tricarico in 1613. See also M. Cosenza, *Biographical and Bibliographical Dictionary of Italian Printers and of Foreign Printers in Italy from the Introduction of the Art of Printing into Italy to 1800* (Boston, 1968).

[4] Eitner, *Quellen-Lexikon*, Bd. IV, 220.

8 September and 31 December 1613. Furthermore, it is noteworthy that nowhere in the extensive list of commands and bequests of Gesualdo's will is there to be found a single item relating to the posthumous publication of his own works. This is particularly interesting in light of the belated publication of his six-voice madrigals in 1626 as well as the other miscellaneous works which never found their way into print.

★ ★ ★

Music historians are prone to point to the last two books of madrigals as anthologies of Gesualdo's wanton and depraved style, and not infrequently suggest that there is a definite cleavage between the musical manners of these pieces and those that had been written before. At the same time there is frequently the tacit implication that they must be viewed as the result of the last stages of a severe neurosis. But while we can be reasonably certain that the Prince's personality manifested strongly neurotic, even psychotic, elements, which increased in intensity throughout his life, we should not fail to notice the extent to which the most audacious moments of these later madrigals are anticipated in earlier volumes. It is thus important to follow the progress of Gesualdo's style from the first books to these admittedly fantastic compositions. Precedents for virtually every musical gesture of the last two books are to be found in his earlier collections. The difference lies in the proportion and the concentration of such ideas. It is a relatively simple matter to describe these madrigals as a series of musical details, but we are at a loss to explain their spell-binding effect. Reduced to the analytical language of contrapuntal usage, to the citation of unprepared dissonances, invertible counterpoint, cross-relations, unusual melodic intervals, suspension chains, degree inflections, chromatic non-functional harmony, and a rich modulatory vocabulary, it is not surprising that the music loses its essential spirit. For while all of these traits can indeed be found in the music, it is the special mixture, the blend of otherwise isolated phenomena which yields the true magic ingredient of his style. The daring posturing, side by side, of seemingly immiscible elements is the essential sign of Gesualdo's Mannerist personality. His unerring instinct alone permits the successful juxtaposition of these several ingredients in a highly delicate balance which seems always to suggest the possibility, nay probability, of an architectural collapse. When the edifice continues to stand, the result is frequently breathtaking.

In the discussion of the first two books, emphasis was naturally placed upon Gesualdo's relation to the earlier madrigal tradition, especially with respect to contrapuntal skills and his approach to familiar texts. The third and fourth books continue to show many of the same traits while often introducing novel gestures and unexpected turns. In books five and six, however, certain issues implicit earlier now become more apparent, and require a fuller treatment. The relation of music to text, an ubiquitous topic in any appreciation of the madrigal, remains of primary importance. Extensions in the use of dissonance and counterpoint call for an assessment of his dazzling harmonic style, particularly in the light of the history of chromaticism and the requirements of tonality and the cadence. Thus studied, these traits, which will not be so systematically treated in the works which remain to be discussed, will be understood as the essential markings of this noble genius.

Text and Music: Disruption and Contrast

Despite Gesualdo's development of a highly personal and affective style, which sought to capture not just the letter but the spirit of the text, he nevertheless continues in his final works to make use of the conventional madrigalisms that reflect a single word literally. Gesualdo was noted however for stressing the expressive nature of such figurations and avoiding eye-music and other empty symbolisms. In his *Trattato della Musica Scenica*, Doni writes:

> The error consists in this: that instead of expressing or imitating the complete concept, given in an appropriate melody, they set about to express the separate words, and in this they believe consists the true imitation of the word, as they call it, even if it be an extremely clumsy method of imitation, and much too affected. And still almost all seem to fall for this, believing to have demonstrated great skill; whereby the word which signifies length, duration, continuation, and the like, will use notes so long that it is death to listen to it. And if they wish to set such words as denote height or speak of the sky, the stars, and like things, they will suddenly search out the high notes, or those placed high upon the staff; and if on the contrary they speak of 'to sink', 'to descend,' 'to lower', etc., or mention the Inferno, they will have the voice plummet the depths to the lowest note of the scale. And furthermore, which is worse, if they come upon the word 'sigh' or 'to sigh', they will scrupulously interrupt this same word with a sort of pause,

which is given with a sigh, the like of which can in no way be excused, although the Prince himself has used it.[5]

The final sentence significantly implies that the Prince of Venosa was above such a practice, and the expressive as opposed to the symbolic nature of his musical gestures is indeed invariably apparent. Yet writers eager to connect the music with the life have gone so far as to see in the graphic setting of a 'sospire' or 'respire' reflections of Gesualdo the asthmatic. In countless madrigals by other composers[6] the short phrases, the small number of notes in any part before the appearance of a rest show a predilection for the breathless style. More often than not, however, previous treatment of the word 'respiro' (to breath) or 'sospiro' (to sigh) had been limited to the use of a rest just before the appearance of the word, as a kind of catchbreath. Gesualdo's treatment is more drastic, breaking up the syllables of the word itself with a rest. Such word-splitting is virtually non-existent in the five-voice madrigals of Marenzio or Rore, and rare, as well as less dramatically handled, in the works of Wert.[7] In Gesualdo it appears as early as Book III, in *Dolce spirto d'Amore*, and *Sospirava il mio core*, the latter example introducing the idea as an extraordinary opening statement.

Ex. 32

[5] Doni, Tome II, p. 73.

[6] Cf. Exx. 76 and 81.

[7] It is impossible to make absolute judgements about these composers without the complete works at hand. Fortunately, *opera omnia* for all three are on the way. See Wert's Bk. VII, no. 11, bars 19–24, for an effective splitting of 'sospir'. (I am grateful to Carol MacClintock for information regarding this piece.) For an interesting

Itene, o miei sospiri (V, 3), which also makes use of *sospiri interrotti*, is of additional interest because it was also set in a slightly altered version by Gesualdo's professed mentor, Luzzasco Luzzaschi.[8] It is one of the few madrigals of Luzzaschi besides *Quivi sospiri* to disclose a progressive harmonic vocabulary. A comparison of the opening phrase in the two settings is instructive. Both begin in a similar declamatory fashion. But note Gesualdo's attention to the key word in his text (missing in Luzzaschi's version). The phrase is pulled apart with two rests in all parts, before as well as after the first syllable of 'sospiri', while Luzzaschi takes the phrase all in one breath. The most crucial point, however, relates not to the strikingly graphic setting of a particular word, but rather to the basically disruptive potential of Gesualdo's Mannerist vocabulary, which not only reflects a violent reaction against the steadier rhythmic flow of *ars perfecta* polyphony but adopts harmonic surprise as a concomitant feature.[9]

---

example of Marenzio's treatment of the word 'sospir' in a six-voice madrigal (*Baci, soavi*, Bk. V), see Engel, *Marenzio*, p. 173. For other evidence of syllable splitting in a composer before Gesualdo (albeit not in a madrigal and not with relation to the word under consideration), see Coclico, *Consolationes Piae Musica Reservata* (1552), ed. M. Ruynke (EDM 5), 15, at 'Rugiebam a ge-mitu cordis meil'; also G. Renaldi (1576) and G. B. Mosto (1578) in the opening of their settings of *Quiri sospiri*. Nenna, perhaps predictably, provides a Gesualdine treatment of 'sospirata' in *Sospir che dal bel petto* (*Libro Primo* à 4 v.).

[8] In Einstein, *The Italian Madrigal*, III, p. 262.
[9] See p. 130, p. 185 fn. 32, and pp. 225–6.

Ex. 33

a) Luzzaschi

b) Gesualdo:

At the same time this example emphasizes an increasingly prominent feature of the period: whereas the early madrigalists almost slavishly equated the musical phrase with the poetic line, now the musical idea corresponds to the semi-verse or even to the single word. Witness the opening of *Io pur respiro* (VI, 10).

Ex. 34

The early madrigalists would have set the entire first line ('Io pur respiro in cosi gran dolore') as a single musical phrase, or at most as a pair of semi-verse phrases of similar texture.[10] Gesualdo divides the text into two distinct musical ideas, the first atomized by syllabic disjointment, the second lubricated by linear chromaticism. In this setting, all the lines (except lines 3 and 6) are broken into more than one musical phrase, and line 7 into as

[10] For a discussion of how Rore uses the semi-verse to generate the musical phrase, see Claude Palisca, *Baroque Music*, pp. 13–16.

many as three. The verse endings Gesualdo tends to respect as logical phrase points, but occasionally, as with the early madrigalists, they are passed over and elided with the beginning of the next line in a textual enjambment (lines 1–2, 3–4).

> Io pur respiro/in cosi gran dolore
> E tu pur vivi,/o dispietato core?/
> Ahi, che no vi è più spene
> Di riveder/il nostro amato bene!/
> Deh, morte,://danne aita,/
> Uccidi questa vita!/
> Pietosa/ne ferisci,/e un colpo solo/
> A la vita dia fin/ed al gran duolo./

Gesualdo's attention to the single word, either as the occasion for a complete musical phrase (as 'pietosa' in verse 7, above) or as the source of internal details, serves to remind us of an essential ingredient of his style. In spite of a general wariness of the more obvious madrigalisms, it is precisely the quality of certain words—the wildly exuberant 'gioia's' (VI, 19, 22, 23, for example), the roller-coaster 'cantare's' (VI, 22), the soaring 'volo's' and 'fuggire's' (VI, 7, 22), and the tripping 'scherzan's' (VI, 19, 23)—which provides the contrast of melody and tempo to the lugubriously haunting 'io moro's' (about half of the madrigals use the word in some form)[11] and the oxymoron-laden phrases such as 'dolcissimo il languire'.[12]

No example could illustrate this point more markedly than the following extraordinary passage from *Ardo per te* (VI). Following a diatonic and contrapuntally buoyant setting of the word 'gioia', a harmonically ravishing passage is launched on the text 'dolcissimo il languire' beginning on C♯ and ending on D. As a stroke of confirmation he repeats, only now beginning on B and ending on C. The level of the repetition (earlier he had preferred repetitions at the fourth or fifth), the tonal movement from beginning to end of the phrase, and the sonorities which are as dissonant as they are chromatic, are all stylistically progressive as well as aurally effective. The homophonic texture and the dotted rhythms of the section which follows (bar 26) resemble music at the same formal point in other madrigals.[13]

[11] While it is true that the word 'morir' (to die) has an erotic double meaning in sixteenth-century Italian poetry (as in English poetry for the period), Einstein's observation that 'for Gesualdo "death" and "pain" always have their full literal meaning' is essentially true. Of course, many a line such as the final verse of *Mercè grido* (V) is openly erotic. [12] I. Horsley, 'The Diminutions in Composition and the Theory of Composition', in *Acta Musicologica*, xxxv (1963), pp. 133–4. [13] See I, 9; II, 4, 5, 7, 8; III, 9; IV, 6; VI, 2.

Ex. 35

The basic character of the example, that of a swift and striking contrast according to the most extreme implications of the text, is a feature which has disturbed many a critic of Gesualdo's style. Cecil Gray, one of the most ardent appreciators of his music wrote, for example, that 'the most conspicuous fault of all Gesualdo's work lies in its stylistic inequality. He seldom succeeds in reconciling his harmonic manner with the traditional polyphonic style, and perpetually oscillates between the two.'[14] He points out that Marenzio's smoother style did not suffer from this. Fault or not, Gray here touches upon an essential ingredient in Gesualdo's music. But while contrast is indeed the cornerstone of his art, and the irreconcilable dualism fundamental to his Mannerist personality, it would be a mistake to suggest that it is unique to his music. There had been ample precedent throughout the madrigal's development, and it was already inherent in some of the earliest ventures of the *note nere* technique as utilized by Arcadelt and others.[15] The use of the ℃ time signature for such pieces implied a slightly slower tactus than ₵ and provided greater space for the working out of contrasted rhythmic formations. While this distinction was not always consistently applied, it was known to Glareanus and endorsed by a line of madrigalists from Verdelot and Arcadelt to Rore, Monte, and[16] Lassus. A late recognition of this dualism is reflected in the barring employed in Simone Molinaro's score edition of 1613.[17] Here the intermittent shifting from 6/2 to 4/2 to 4/4

[14] Gray, *The History of Music*, pp. 97–8.
[15] See James Haar, 'The *Note Nere* Madrigal,' *JAMS*, XVIII (1965), pp. 25–41; Don Harran, 'Some early examples of the madrigali chromatici,' *Acta Musicologica*, XLI (1969), p. 240.
[16] For a quotation from a Monte madrigal which illustrates this point see Reese, *Music in the Renaissance*, p. 407.
[17] See p. 45, fn. 22.

is in direct relation to the note values involved: the slower sections are cast either in 6/2 or 4/2, the faster sections with small note-values in 4/4.[18]

To an extent it is possible to view this Mannerist dualism of texture, tempo, and harmony as an important bequest to the Baroque. Bukofzer reminds us that the Baroque doctrine of affections was not unknown to the Renaissance, as witness the rhetorical figures of both the madrigal and the motet. However, as Bukofzer continues, 'The two periods actually operated under the same principle, but they differed fundamentally in the method of application. The renaissance favoured the affections of restraint and noble simplicity, the baroque the extreme affections ranging from violent pain to exuberant joy. It is obvious that the representation of extreme affections called for a richer vocabulary than had been required before.'[19]

According to this description, Gesualdo's music would hardly qualify as Renaissance in character. His is not a style of restraint and noble simplicity but one of extreme affections—a style, as we have witnessed, ranging from 'violent pain to exuberant joy.' If his style persistently vacillates between the diatonic-melodic allegro and the chromatic-harmonic adagio, it is not because he was incapable of amalgamating his materials into a unified whole, as Gray suggests, but because his musical language sprang from an exaggerated sensitivity to the emotional tone of the text. This in turn demanded a heightened capacity for making a striking and swift musical response to a whole catalogue of affects. In Craft's words, Gesualdo is, as a Mannerist *par excellence*, the master of *lo sforzato*—the strained effect.

The most famous of all Gesualdo's madrigals, *Moro lasso* (VI, 17), dramatically illustrates this quality. The piece begins with an expansive homophonic gesture employing eleven of the twelve chromatic pitches to the text 'I die, alas, in my grief.' For the more neutral text which follows, 'and he who can give me life,' he shifts to a faster tempo (complete with the required sixteenth-note melisma on 'vita') in a diatonic style such as might have been written by any madrigal composer of the period. The mood again changes with the verse, 'Ah, but slays me and does not wish to give me aid.' The madrigal ends with the expected twist, a textual inversion epitomizing the unresolvable dilemma: 'Oh dolorous fate; the one who can give me aid, ah, gives me death.' It is obvious that the more adventurous harmonic passages would be impossible in a faster tempo either for listener or performer; hence any smoothing out of the stylistic dichotomy in such sections

---

[18] Cf. p. 45, fn. 22. For a discussion of this question with respect to Gesualdo's sacred music, see pp. 273–6. Note also Ex. 57 where an accelerando from whole notes to half to quarter (and later eighth and sixteenth) is reflected in three different metric lengths in as many measures: 6/2, 4/2, 4/4.

[19] Bukofzer, *Music in the Baroque Era*, p. 5.

is virtually precluded. But it should be equally apparent that these extra-ordinary episodes are not mere harmony exercises and that a true appreciation of their meaning must stem from a knowledge of the text which they reflect. This mirroring of the text, both the spirit and the letter, produces the element of exaggerated contrast central to the Mannerist rhetoric, as distinct from the rather more unified, more dispassionate idiom of the Early and High Renaissance. Rore may have been one of the first to exploit the changing mood of the text and move away from the relatively constant mood and technique of the early madrigal,[20] yet by comparison to Gesualdo he had barely tapped the idea.

As important as Rore for this aspect of Gesualdo's technique was that segment of the madrigal production of the 1570s and particularly the 1580s which increasingly exhibited a new virtuosity associated with, if not born solely of, the developing expertise of the *concerto di donne* at Ferrara. In the animated sections a highly melismatic style in growing measure infiltrated all the voices of the polyphonic complex in tightly compacted episodes. This in turn resulted in exaggerated contrasts between those sections marked by fioratura and those which were not.[21] Gesualdo's first three books are relatively devoid of this feature. The final three volumes, however, pursue this advancement of the 1580s relentlessly.

Gesualdo and the Dissonance

The harmonic interest in Gesualdo's work lies not only in his chromaticism but also in the use of prepared and unprepared dissonances.[22]

Ex. 36

[20] Reese, *Music in the Renaissance*, p. 330.
[21] Newcomb's *The Musica Secreta of Ferrara in the 1580s* (Ph.D. dissertation, Princeton, 1970), develops this thesis brilliantly.
[22] The sources are: (a) *Se la mia morte brami* (VI, 1), bars 8–9; (b) *Io parto* (VI, 6), bars 26–28; (c) *Se la mia morte brami*, bars 21–22; (d) *Mille volte il dì* (VI, 7), bars 4–5.

Considering the quotations above, however, one will recall that the seemingly audacious 'unprepared' 4–3 suspension of Ex. 36b was known also to earlier madrigalists such as Arcadelt.[23] The use of a ninth with a fourth in the manner of a double upper-auxiliary in the same example is also less revolutionary than the ninth used in conjunction with a seventh in Ex. 36c where the seventh is resolved by skip.[24] Ex. 36d contains elements of the conventionally prepared $^6_5$ coupled with degree inflection and double-contrapuntal manipulation, a collection of traits partially analogous to the formations of Ex. 40.

Other dissonance formations common to the *prima prattica* are occasionally pressed into service by Gesualdo in a manner that belies their origin. Of these none is more striking than his use of the minor six-five dissonance approached through chromatic inflection as in *Ardo per te* (Ex. 35, bar 21, 3rd beat; bar 24, 3rd beat). Compare its stupefying power there with the more neutral, Palestrinian use of the same sonority in Ex. 36d. A multiple dissonance fashioned from a triple syncope, even when all members are approached and quitted by step (cf. Ex. 53c, bars 19 and 21), can similarly carry a most telling effect. Not infrequently a classic handling of dissonance is entwined in a chromatic fabric.[25], [26]

Ex. 37

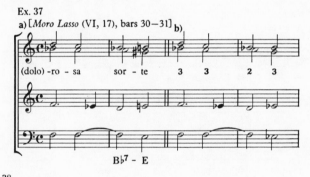

Ex. 38

[23] Reese, *Music in the Renaissance*, p. 322.

[24] For a similar treatment of the seventh in Marenzio, see his *Cosi nel mio parlar* (*Nono libro à 5 v.*, 1599) in Einstein's 'Dante im Madrigal,' *Archiv für Musikwissenschaft* III (1921), p. 418, bar 4, superius.

[25] See Carl Dahlhaus, 'Zur chromatischen Technik Carlo Gesualdos' in *Analecta Musicologica*, Bd. 4 (1967), pp. 81–82.

[26] See p. 184, Ex. 40.

The puzzling movement in the second measure of Ex. 37a could be seen from a later harmonic point of view as a progression from a Bb major 7th chord to an E major triad. In the second bar of Ex. 38a, the first two beats could similarly be analysed as a movement from a B minor to an F major triad.[27] Both progressions, thus viewed, disclose a tritone root-movement. The reduction formulae of Exx. 37b and 38b, however, suggest that both passages are generated contrapuntally. Gesualdo's introduction of chromatic semitones in each instance is only a mildly unconventional licence reflecting the contrapuntal theory of the time, which considered B and Bb (Ex. 37a) and F and F♯ (Ex. 38a) as contrapuntally identical. Both pairs of examples involve prime intervals, not seconds, which interact classically in the formation of suspension figures: in the first example, a 2–3 suspension between the uppermost voices; in the second example, a 4–3 suspension chain between the two lower voices.

Less explicable as an extension of the *prima prattica*, however, are passages such as the unprepared seventh and $^{6-6}_{4-4}$ at the opening of *Gia piansi nel dolore* (VI, 22).

Ex. 39

Ample precedent for the use of unprepared dissonances had already been established, however, in a flourishing *seconda prattica*. Vicenzo Galilei's unpublished counterpoint treatise of 1588 provides perhaps the clearest contemporary statement concerning the use of dissonance.[28] Here he claims

---

[27] Cf. J. Clough, 'The Leading Tone in Direct Chromaticism: From Renaissance to Baroque' in *Journal of Music Theory*, I (1957), p. 17, which views the passage thus. Cf. also C. Dahlhaus, op. cit., p. 81.

[28] See Claude Palisca's 'Vincenzo Galilei's Counterpoint Treatise: A Code for the *Seconda Pratica*' in *JAMS*, IX, 2 (1956), pp. 81–96.

the validity for expressive purposes of a wide range of suspension figures, tritone movements, inflected resolutions, accented and unprepared dissonances. While he purported to sum up the experience of his own contemporaries (and like Cesare Monteverdi accorded Rore the role of founder of the new practice), he claimed a degree of originality in his examples which he predicted would be widely imitated. There is nothing to indicate that Gesualdo knew this treatise, but he assuredly knew the music which kindled its spirit. Although Gesualdo employs unprepared dissonances periodically throughout his entire production (cf. Ex. 11), they appear more frequently in his late works. Significantly both Marenzio and Monteverdi explored similar formations in the same decades as Gesualdo, and a number of lesser lights, including Nenna and Macque, also discovered the charm of the unprepared dissonance at precisely this time and repeatedly exploited its potential.

Double Counterpoint

While the ravishing harmonic element of Gesualdo's last books is of such force that it tends to overshadow their contrapuntal aspect, there is no doubt of the presence of a genuine, essentially diatonic contrapuntal style, used principally as a foil to the more adventurous harmonic sections. Paradoxically, however, the harmonic sections themselves are frequently most readily explained in terms of contrapuntal procedures (as in Exx. 37 and 38 above). Gesualdo's use of double-counterpoint, for example, while seemingly more suited to relatively diatonic surroundings (cf. Exx. 5 and 9) and less frequently employed in his last works, nevertheless provides a basis for many of his most advanced harmonic constructions. We have witnessed this as early as Book IV (Ex. 31), where the tritone relation of roots in the chromatically complex progression $G–B_6^b–e–B_6–E$ may be better viewed in the context of an initial statement of quadruple counterpoint which leads two bars later to the appropriate cadential harmony, $C–d–a–E–A$. The first of these two conjunctions of vertical sonorities, then, does not reflect of harmonic logic so much as look forward to imminent contrapuntal events.

Similar gestures in his final volumes demonstrate that the logic of double counterpoint can occasionally not only override the demands of harmonic coherence, but also fashion unusual inversions. Note the exchange of a $_3^5$ for a $_4^6$ sonority in the following interplay of double-counterpoint from *Ancide sol la morte* (VI, 15).

Ex. 40

Other examples[29] of double-counterpoint from his last volumes fluctuatingly draw on several voices to fashion the transposed reappearance of an initially discrete idea.[30]

Ex. 41   *Se vi duol* (V, 8)

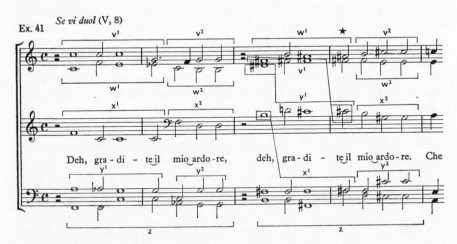

[29] See also *Mille volte il di* (VI, 7), bars 4–5; *Io pur respiro* (VI, 10), bars 24–25; *Moro lasso* (VI, 17), bars 29–33.

[30] The interval of transposition, a tritone, is unusual even for Gesualdo. Dahlhaus, op. cit., p. 93, convincingly suggests that the more classic origins of the passage may be witnessed by reading bars 3–4 up a semitone at the perfect fifth: B–F♯ then

Tonality and Cadence

Passages like the final cadence from *Mercè grido* (Ex. 42)[31] depart from prior models, not so much from the point of vertical structure or harmonic conjunction as of melodic direction. A short, ambivalent three-note motif proceeds variously: F♯–G–G♯, C♯–D–C, E–F♯–F, C♯–D–B, or G–A–F♯. Undoubtedly it was moments such as this that prompted earlier critics to describe Gesualdo as a 'cavalier stumbling about in a maze of modulation.'[32]

Ex. 42

But for all this audacity, his final cadences, his points of tonal definition, are characteristically strong. In the preceding example, despite the striking cross-relation between the G″ on the penultimate note in the superius and the final note G♯′ in the quintus, and the tonal ambiguity in the approach

becomes C–G at the beginning of the passage, connecting smoothly with the end of bar 2; and the chord of C♯ at the end of bar 4 becomes D, which progresses convincingly to the a of bar 5.

[31] See Ex. 67a for a comparison between Gesualdo's and Nenna's setting of this text.

[32] The separation of the motif from its restatement by rests highlights the emphasis upon the small textual unit. This we have met before, as in Gesualdo's *Io pur respiro* (see p. 174), and it is a habit which he shares with Nenna, as seen in the final cadence to his *Vuoi tu dunque partire* (IV, 6); cf. Istituto Italiano per la Storia della Musica, *Monumenti* II, vol. I, p. 118. For a provocative discussion that would provide a classic foundation for such seemingly capricious movements, see Jackson, 'On Frescobaldi's Chromaticism and Its Background,' *Musical Quarterly*, LVI (1971), pp. 263–6.

to the cadence, the ultimate moment of repose is harmonically sure and tonally decisive, V6–I.

One of the central and at the same time most debatable problems in Gesualdo's art is that of tonality. Two primary considerations for testing the tonal character of any work have traditionally been (1) pitch correspondence between the beginning and end of a piece; and (2) evidence at the cadences, especially sectional and final ones, of a network of inter-related keys. With respect to the first point Gesualdo's spectacular harmonic posturing might seem to preclude any attention to such factors, and one might almost be tempted to let the question pass. Interestingly enough, however, the tonal correspondence between outer extremities is as a rule so high that one can say that Gesualdo begins and ends in the same 'key'.[33] The exceptions are virtually non-existent if one is willing to look beyond the first chord of a piece. For example, although *Moro lasso* ends in A while appearing to begin in C♯, the first cadence settles on a with an unmistakable V7–I progression (Ex. 43):

That composers of later centuries came to recognize such opening procedures as not only theoretically valid but aurally convincing is demonstrated with the first bars of Beethoven's First Symphony. Similarly, while *Deh, come invan sospiro* (VI, 9; Ex. 44) begins with a G sonority, the initial cadence on E provides the first tonally decisive evidence and forecasts the final cadential level of the piece. This, moreover, is in spite of an unsettling e7 which is left hanging at the end of the first bar, but which acts as a quasi-secondary dominant with respect to the opening chord of the next bar (e7–a$_4^6$–E).

---

[33] Keiner suggests that Gesualdo shows a preference for beginning a madrigal with a key that stands in a tonic, subdominant, or dominant relation to the final key. Marshall is correct in suggesting that this relationship applies more rigorously to the key used at the first cadence.

Ex. 44

Deh,   co-me in-van   so-spi - ro

Deh,   co-me in-van   so-spi - ro

Deh,   co.-me in-van   so-spi - ro

It would be possible to question the genuine correspondence between tonal levels at beginning and end in some other examples. But exceptions aside, the tonal foundation of a piece can generally be discovered by reference to the first and last chords, without a momentary suspension of judgement as in the preceding examples. It could be argued, however, that tonal identity at beginning and end may mean little if there are few or no conforming signs throughout the course of a work. Significantly, however, Gesualdo demonstrates his knowledge of the importance of tonality to form, and while there may be considerable tonal vacillation within a piece, at the crucial formal points he typically gives an important tonal signal.

While *O dolce mio tesoro* (VI, 8) is one of the few pieces from that book which, even by extended reasoning, cannot be held to conform to the principle of tonal identity at beginning and end, the key relationships at the structurally important points provide a guide to the composer's itinerary. Cast in an ABB design, the madrigal begins in C and comes to rest in the key of a, with a raised third at the end of the A section; the ensuing B section begins in e and closes in E.[34] Relative minor and fifth relationships, classic even by later standards, unify the piece tonally, dictate the progress of events, and lend a cohesiveness which might otherwise seem lacking if one only looked at the initial and final chord, C major and E major. An analogous principle operates in the earlier volumes which contain a number of madrigals of two *partes*. These pieces are invariably wedded by a tonal bond, the final cadence chord of the *prima pars* normally being either the tonic or the dominant of the opening of the *seconda pars*.

With respect to the final cadence, the vocabulary of basic types is not large: authentic (V–I), plagal (IV–I), and Phrygian formulae account for a

[34] It can be argued that the tonal level of the final cadence, with its strong tendency to end on C, the opening key of the piece, is capricious in its ultimate movement to E. Yet, whether seen as a denial of a C–C plan or as a confirmation of a C–a–e–E scheme, the tonal metamorphosis has a logic that cannot be denied.

vast majority of them, but there is an enormous variety within these types. In all six books[35] root movement by thirds is found only once (*Luci serene e chiari*; IV, 1) at the final cadence though it occurs more frequently at internal cadences.[36] Not infrequently, however, a cadence which would appear to be approached by a third ultimately discloses itself as plagal, as witness Ex. 46. The first book utilizes the authentic formula almost exclusively, and while later books gradually employ more varied and sophisticated types, this pattern is to be found in more than three-quarters of the final cadences of all the madrigal volumes. Gesualdo's preference, mentioned earlier, for approaching the cadence over a pedal-point leads him to favour a plagal sound, as in *Deh, come invan sospiro* discussed above. Degree inflection may invade this formula in a single part, as in *Languisce al fin* (V, 10; Ex. 45), or in all parts as in *Io pur respiro* (VI, 10; Ex. 46),[37] without compromising the ultimate resolution. Indeed, a chromatic linear approach frequently gives the impression of helping to secure the tonal goal as the several voices gradually lock into place.

Ex. 45   *Languisce al fin*

[35] Anderson in *The Cadence in the Madrigal of Carlo Gesualdo* labels three other cadences as being approached by thirds: IV, 10 (heard as a–E, although appearing as C–E); III, 10 (see explanation relating to Ex. 46); and VI, 5 (see Ex. 49a).

[36] Frequently, however, internal cadences which are approached by thirds are traditional half cadences which link firmly with the ensuing phrase. Thus in *Io parto* (VI, 6), bars 15–16, the cadence c6–E ends with an air of expectancy which is resolved naturally in the A major triad at the beginning of the next phrase.

[37] While the ultimate plagal effect is, of course, identical in both cases, the approach to the Bassus pedal-note by a descending third (G–E), in Ex. 46, or by an ascending

Ex. 46

Similarly the Phrygian cadence can appear in a relatively diatonic fabric or, more frequently in the later books, in a highly inflected one replete with extravagant intervals, as in (a) *Occhi del mio cor vita* (V, 9; Ex. 47a) or (b) *Mille volte il di* (VI, 7; Ex. 47b).

---

second (D–E), in Ex. 45, is a differentiating pre-cadential factor. The use of the seventh above the tonic pedal before settling on the plagal formula in Ex. 46 is temptingly suggestive of the late Baroque tonic-seventh sonority prior to a flirtation with the subdominant at the final cadence.

Ex. 47a)

In his elucidation of the Renaissance origins of functional tonality Lowinsky sees[38] Gesualdo as something of a distraction along the main line of tonal development during this period, but he quite correctly attributes to Gesualdo a paradoxically important role in this same evolution. Regarding Gesualdo's lack of influence upon an evolving tonality, Lowinsky says of the madrigal *Languisce al fin*:

[38] *Tonality and Atonality*, pp. 43–46.

Beginning and ending a composition on the same note or chord loses significance in view of a harmonic art based on widespread elimination of the cadence as an organizing principle. . . . Not a single authentic cadence appears in the work. To cancel in each phrase the tonal implications of the preceding phrase, to create a state of tortured suspense, to refuse the searching mind any place to rest—these are the most definite tendencies discoverable.[39]

While his description of this particular piece is essentially correct, it should be stressed that elsewhere the tonal cadence is an important factor in delineating form in Gesualdo's music. Even in this very madrigal internal cadences revealing dominant (vii°–I and V–I) influence are to be found (cf. bars 4, 8–9, 19), and the final cadence, while not qualifying as an authentic one, is indeed an urgently tonal one (Ex. 45).

The force of the authentic cadence in resolving foreign tonal flirtations and securing the prescribed pitch level is dramatically illustrated at the close of *Moro lasso*. In the final three bars of the piece eleven of the twelve notes are employed—not as a direct chromatic-melodic statement, but in a ravishing harmonic-contrapuntal complex. For all its chromatic twistings, it is interesting to note that the cadence is an authentic V–I formula in the opening key of the piece (cf. Ex. 43). Viewed either from the point of view of sixteenth-century practice (featuring the consonant fourth) or of later harmonic functional usage, the ultimate cadential release is classic.

Ex. 48

[39] Ibid., p. 43. For an enlightening examination of the opening subject of *Languisce al fin* and the close of *Moro lasso* (Ex. 48), see Jackson, 'On Frescobaldi's Chromaticism and Its Background,' *Musical Quarterly*, LVII (1971), pp. 263–6.

Furthermore, in his sixth book of madrigals, where we might expect to find tonal forces suspended more than at any other place, no less than seventeen of the twenty-three pieces end with an authentic cadence. Of the remainder two are plagal (8, 10) and four are Phrygian (5, 6, 7, 9). Two of the Phrygian cadences are atypically approached (5, 9); one (Ex. 49a) transposed over a double tonic-dominant pedal, the other (Ex. 49b) using the under-second (root position) form for the penultimate chord against a dominant pedal.

Ex. 49a)   *Chiaro risplender suole*

b) *Deh, come invan sospiro*

Note particularly how the second of these Phrygian solutions inspires a descending minor seventh in the next to top voice. This is akin to the results witnessed in Ex. 47, where voices exchange notes of resolution. Here it is prompted additionally, of course, by the desire to avoid parallel octaves with the ascending bass line of an unorthodox Phrygian formation.

One of Gesualdo's most unusual final cadences is that for *Asciugate i begli occhi* (V, 14).

Ex. 50

N

The semitonal descent in the Bassus suggests a modified Phrygian formula and the movement of the upper voices recalls Ex. 49a, but closer observation discloses the later resolution of a clearly formed and subtly stressed Neapolitan sonority against a tonic-dominant pedal in the outer voices. The clash of the E♭ against the D harmony, however, recalls a similar confrontation at the outset of the piece (Ex. 53a, bar 2, third beat)—a sound which Gesualdo surely intended to be remembered.[40]

While Gesualdo's final cadences are invariably clear tonally, his alarming rate of 'modulation' frequently tends to cancel out any sense of tonal security. In *Beltà poi* (VI, 2), for example, numerous changes of 'key' level appear in a piece that takes only two minutes to perform: g B C♯ g D B♭E♭ g–E♭ d‖ B♭ F B♭ g EB–B♭ f a g. Significantly, each of these levels is not described with the same degree of clarity through strong cadential definition.

[40] For a similar approach to the final cadence in a setting of the same text by Nenna, see Ex. 68c.

The movement at the beginning of the piece (Ex. 60) from g to B is clear enough through the introduction of a half cadence at the end of the first phrase; but the shift to C♯ is approached cadentially through a root movement of thirds which is less convincing, and the establishment of this tonal level is achieved primarily through the phrase structure and the fact that the chord is followed by a rest in all voices.[41] The remainder of the first half of the piece moves almost imperceptibly from key to key, sometimes with a mild cadential force, as with the two vii° chords in root position which define the keys of B♭ and E♭ at bars 11–12 and 13 respectively, at other times with no sense of cadence at all, as at bars 14–18. Due to a lack of cadential clarity, there is more often a sense of tonal drifting than of actual modulation.

But even in such a kaleidoscopic 'modulatory' world the central tonality is reinforced through reference to primary keys at the structurally most important cadence points, and the opening and closing of the two main sections of *Beltà poi* disclose key choices (g–d‖:B♭–g:‖)[42] made with obvious care. In view of the thoughtfulness, freshness, and even conclusiveness of many of Gesualdo's modulatory schemes, it is difficult to agree with Einstein when he said:

> Every chord is tested, every transposition permitted. But the little modulations from C major to G, such as occur in the canzonette of Ferretti or Orazio Vecchi, point the way to freedom and the future, and are worth more historically than all Gesualdo's audacity.[43]

Accidentals and Chromaticism

The traditions of *musica-ficta* which utilized the sharp primarily to create the leading-tone, required only three sharps in theory or practice from the Ars Nova to the Cinquecento. Even after the eight ecclesiastical modes had been theoretically expanded to twelve by Glarean, these three sharps could assume the total burden: Dorian, Mixolydian, and Aeolian were served by C♯, F♯,

[41] A discussion of the internal cadential patterns of Gesualdo's *Io parto* (VI, 6) is undertaken in Rowland's *Mannerism—Style and Mood*, pp. 42–46, and in Chart C, p. 101. This is not very helpful, however, as a number of the cadences are mistakenly identified. The general discussion relating to Manneristic qualities is more useful. More complete and accurate in relation to the cadence question is J. Anderson's *The Cadence in the Madrigals of Gesualdo*, (Ph.D. dissertation, Catholic Univ., 1964), although he does not stress the plagal quality of cadences similar to Ex. 46.

[42] The musical repetitions in the last two volumes stem from a restatement of the last three lines of text, as in V, 11, 13, and VI, 4, 21; the final couplet as in V, 3, 5, 14, 15 and VI, 2 (*Beltà poi*), 20, 23; or the last line only as in V, 7, 16 and VI, 8, 9, 18. Compare this with treatment in the earlier volumes, Chapter V, pp. 121–2.

[43] Einstein, *The Italian Madrigal*, p. 717.

and G♯ respectively; Phrygian did not require D♯, as it achieved a semitonal effect by approaching the tonic from above (F–E); leading-notes for Lydian and Ionian were inherent in the diatonic, modal system.

The harmonically conservative masters of the last part of the sixteenth century, such as Victoria, Palestrina, and Lasso, normally use an accidental vocabulary no larger than that of the Trecento, two flats and three sharps. Even the incipient chromaticists Rore and Marenzio make only peripheral additions to the basic list of accidentals.[44] Two facts are deducible: (1) it is unnecessary to increase accidentals beyond two flats and three sharps in order to provide the pitches sufficient to most melodic and harmonic requirements of the period; (2) further extensions of the accidental vocabulary result generally from the demands of extended modulation or abrupt transposition, and to a much lesser extent non-harmonic activity.[45]

It is largely for this reason that the repertory of sharps and flats employed by Gesualdo is so much greater than any of his predecessors. He extends the list of sharps to the complete complement of seven, though on the flat side, while he fails to incorporate only the last flat (F♭), the fifth and sixth flats G♭ and C♭ are rarely employed. On the sharp side only the seventh sharp, B♯, is so sparsely utilized. A table of accidentals employed in the three most chromatically adventurous volumes provides a synopsis of relative usage (see p. 196). The approximately equal length of the three volumes (IV, 21 madrigals; V, 21; VI, 23) permits an accurate comparative view between volumes.

The reasons for Gesualdo's adoption of certain accidentals are not hard to find. His addition of the last four sharps to the standard vocabulary of three sharps can be seen in virtually every case to have resulted from a desire to produce the major third of a major triad, and by inference it might be added because the major triad is capable of a dominant as well as a tonic function. Hence, D♯ appears primarily as the third of a B major triad, A♯

---

[44] Rore adds A♭, occasionally D♭, D♯, A♯; Marenzio uncommonly uses A♭, D♯, rarely A♯, D♭. Cf. Kroyer, *Die Anfänge der Chromatik*, p. 149.

[45] This is true, of course, only to the extent that the composer is unconcerned with making distinctions, thoroughly developed only somewhat later, between the melodic tendency of a sharp to rise and a flat to descend. Even Gesualdo will misspell, by later standards, a German sixth chord, as in *Io pur respiro* (VI, 10), bar 24, in an ascending melodic movement, G–A♭–A. But see also *Se tu fuggi* (V, 20), bar 17, where an ascending line, C–D♭–D, indicates a dissonant six-five figuration, whereas the use of a C♯ would have suggested a chromatic passing-note interpretation. Such considerations of chord-spelling notwithstanding, Gesualdo's extraordinary care and accuracy in the notation of accidentals is exemplary and was remarked upon by more than one of his contemporaries. For a discussion of the principles of accidental application see Gesualdo, *Sämtliche Werke*, vol. VII, *Responsorien*, ed. by Glenn Watkins, Editorial Notes.

Table of Accidentals
in Gesualdo's Last Three Books*

Accidental	IV	V	VI	Total
G♯	52	112	151	315
D♯	7	46	57	110
A♭	11	22	33	66
A♯	2	24	23	49
E♯	—	8	17	25
D♭	—	5	16	21
G♭	—	1	2	3
B♯	—	1	1	2
C♭	—	—	1	1
F♭	—	—	—	—

* The tabulation does not count the repetition of accidentals before consecutive notes of the same pitch in one and the same voice.

as the third of a F♯ major triad, E♯ as the third of a C♯ major triad, and B♯ as the third of a G♯ major triad. None of these sharps is ever used as the root for any kind of triad. The three flats that are either missing or infrequently employed are most readily conceivable as thirds of a minor triad, and all except G♭ would make most unusual roots.

While Gesualdo's most extreme harmonic passages show a decided though not exclusive preference for sharps,[46] passages of extended melodically oriented chromaticism show a greater balance of interest between sharps and flats. Harmonic exploration via the sharp stands in pointed contrast to the early sixteenth century modulatory probes primarily through the use of flats, initially suggested by the introduction of the flat in order to avoid the melodic or harmonic tritone. Further development of the idea led naturally to exploration through a spiral of flats. This we see not only in such exceptional early examples as Josquin's (?) *Fortuna d'un gran tempo*[47] (1501) or Willaert's *Quidnam ebrietas*[48] (1519) but also as the basis of Lowinsky's 'secret chromatic art' of a later decade. As an agent more of modulatory adventure than enrichment of a palette of harmonic progressions, such practice in the use of accidentals nevertheless significantly helped prepare the way for harmonic explorations independent of classic modulatory schemes, and undoubtedly helped free the mind to consider the application

[46] See pp. 204–6 for the contrapuntal-cadential origins of many of these progressions.
[47] Printed in Hewitt's *Odhecaton*, p. 375; the problem discussed in Lowinsky's 'The Goddess Fortuna in Music,' *MQ*, XXIX (1943), 45.
[48] Cf. Levitan's 'Adrian Willaert's Famous Duo "Quidnam ebrietas",' in *TVNM*, XV (1938), p. 166; also Lowinsky's 'Adrian Willaert's Chromatic "Duo" Re-examined,' in *Tijdschrift voor Muziekwetenschap*, XVIII (1956), pp. 1–36.

of sharps as well as flats in new and bold contexts not directly related to time-honoured *musica ficta* practice.

Many of the modulatory passages in the works of Gesualdo reflect an extension of the practice of the madrigalists of an earlier decade. Thus Marenzio's *O voi che sospirate*, the classic example of the 1580s, looks extraordinary to the eye (particularly with respect to the enharmonic notation) but sounds surprisingly conventional to the ear because the modulations are diatonically achieved. Few inflected chromatic passages occur, though accidentals abound. Similarly, the use of accidentals as remote as the fifth sharp (A♯) and the fourth flat (D♭) may be noted in less than half a dozen bars in Gesualdo's *Mille volte il di* (VI, 7; Ex. 51) with only two instances of degree inflection (cantus, bars 39–40; altus, bar 46).

Ex. 51

That this passage was the object of transposition is suggested by suppressing all of the flats from bar 43 to the end. The result is a totally convincing piece of diatonic counterpoint. The note which initially triggered the movement to the flat side is the A♭ in the Bassus of bar 43. Had the flat not been notated, *musica-ficta* practice of an earlier period might well have lowered it in any event. The resulting spiral of flats, once the A♭ is undertaken, is reminiscent of Lowinsky's 'secret chromatic art'. Gesualdo's exit from the maze is swift and effected by the only melodic inflection (D♭–D♮) of the passage. The rescue is none too soon as the composition comes to a close on the very next chord through a Phrygian cadence. The movement toward the sharp side in bar 40, through the introduction of chromatic inflection in the Cantus, could similarly be halted with efficacious results. The Bassus of bar 41 would then be obliged to introduce a B♭, however, and thereby suggest a movement toward Gesualdo's own solution of bars 43–47.

Contemporary evidence confirms that similar passages were indeed considered to have been transposed. Giovanni Battista Doni suggests that the first two bars of the following passage from *Mercè grido piangendo* (V, II; Ex. 52) is a transposition from C Lydian to C♯ Lydian.[49]

49 Doni in his designation of the C mode as Lydian discloses his aesthetic ties with Vicentino and others from the midpoint of the century who, in adopting whatever they could of Greek manners in an outward display of their admiration of antiquity, reckoned the modes beginning on E, descending. Thus the E scale was Dorian, D Phrygian, C Lydian. Doni's passage reads thus: 'In iis verbis "morrò dunque tacendo" ubi in diversam plane speciem melos mutatur, videlicet in harmoniam Lydiam (siquidem tonus hypothematicus seu fundamentalis Dorius sit) quae omnibus

Ex. 52

While linear inflection is a part of Gesualdo's grammar, he never indulges in extensive melodic chromaticism in long note-values like that employed by Marenzio in his *Solo e pensoso* (Ex. 22a, b). Such practice, recognizably, is not the Prince's style; the slow unfolding of Marenzio's chromatic superius in relation to the swifter motion of the other diatonic parts does not permit the intensity of harmonic shift that Gesualdo characteristically demands, and the extensiveness of the idea excludes the possibility of a disruptive musical language ever sensitive to the changing demands of the text. Chromatic melodic ideas occur, however, as early as the second book in *Sento che nel partire* (Ex. 12), but no more than four semitones in a row are to be found there. Although by the fourth book Gesualdo's chromatic melodic habits have developed to the point of employing a succession of seven descending semitones (Ex. 29), this is as extensive a treatment as he ever affords the idea. Occasionally melodic chromaticism may also be used with a short motif in an imitative context as at the end of *Dolcissima mia vita* (V, 4), or as at the close of *Mercè grido* in a less predictable, twisting chromatic variation (Ex. 42).

To any catalogue of chromatic usage in Gesualdo's music should be added the conflicting sound of the false relation. He particularly liked to utilize this feature in an approach to the cadence, either in a framework of changing harmony or as a pitch conflict over the same root.[50]

Chordis signum ♯ usurpat, quam partem si quis vulgaribus syllabis ut re mi fa etc. recte enuntiare potuerit—nisi novam clavem seu systema adhibeat—nae ille magnam rem praestabit.' Cf. Ambros, *Geschichte der Musik*, Bd IV (1909), p. 203; Dahlhaus, op. cit., p. 93. Cf. also Ex. 67c for a similar treatment of this same text by Nenna.

[50] The strength, originality, and sureness with which Gesualdo handles the false relation makes us wonder at so recent a criticism as the following by Einstein, *The Italian Madrigal*, p. 696: 'Where the *nobile dilettante* betrays himself is in certain awkward and clumsy details—the overcrowded voice-leading, the clashing of the voices, which betrays a strangely defective ear, the insensibility toward false relations, an insensibility characteristic of the whole century, though especially of the time before 1560. In his own time Gesualdo is not surpassed in this by any of his colleagues.'

Ex. 53 a)

b)

c)

Ex. 53 (a) is taken from *Asciugate i begli occhi* (V), (b) from *Dolcissima mia vita* (V), and (c) from *Mille volte il di* (VI). In Ex. 53c, the conflict between B♭–B and E♭–E is emphasized through the drop of a diminished fourth in the approach to the second pitch each time. The principle of confirmation through transposed repetition, here at the fifth below, is also demonstrated.

In all, the range and subtlety of Gesualdo's chromatic art is without any real precedent. Individually most of his fanciful notions may have been anticipated by other madrigalists, but through the sheer concentration of these ideas, poised and balanced in the most fragile way, Gesualdo forged a language which juxtaposed the chromatic with the diatonic in a variety and intensity not matched by any of his predecessors. Neither the intrepid Caimo,[51] the youthful Lasso, nor the audacious Vicentino exploited the idiom much beyond the illustration of a theoretical idea; Marenzio, Luzzaschi, and Rore pursued the manner rarely, though with some mastery, and elsewhere only Nenna, Macque, and a few of their Neapolitan contemporaries developed the style with success. The originality and boldness of Gesualdo's chromatic style is also intimately connected with matters of harmonic progression and inversion characteristics. How this is so remains to be discussed.

Harmonic Progression

The difficulty in providing an incisive description of Gesualdo's harmonic manner stems in large part from a stylistic ambiguity. He utilizes elements of the two well-known contrapuntal styles which preceded and followed him, and at the same time adds ingredients associated with neither.[52] From the previous discussion of the cadence we have seen that Gesualdo's art, like that of his predecessors, was indebted to functional harmonic principles. In the interior of the phrase, as well, we can find harmonic progressions which either confirm a sense of key or endorse a logical sequence of events without unsettling details. A succession of dominant relations is by no means uncommon even in the last volumes.

[51] Cf. Patricia Brauner's *Gioseppe Caimo, "Nobile Milanese"* (Ph.D. dissertation, Yale University, 1970) for further information about this fascinating figure.

[52] Ferdinand Keiner's 1914 Berlin dissertation on Gesualdo employed a consistently anachronistic analytical language. While George Marshall's dissertation devoted to the study of the harmonic laws in Gesualdo's madrigals is much clearer and quite useful, Carl Dahlhaus's 'Zur chromatischen Technik Carlo Gesualdos,' *Analecta Musicologica*, Bd. 4 (1967), is the most penetrating study of the question to date.

Ex. 54a)

Ex. 54 (a) is taken from *Occhi del mio cor vita* (V, 9), (b) from *Ma tu, cagion* (V, 18), and (c) from *O dolce mio tesoro* (VI, 8).

Even in passages involving relationships of a chromatic third, a surrounding functional terrain is often apparent (Ex. 54c).

Relatively strange to twentieth-century ears unconditioned to the sound is the downward progression of two major triads whose roots are a major second apart, although this progression is clearly reconcilable with earlier modal practice. Such triads are frequently stressed through separation by rests, especially at the opening of a composition, but often continue quickly to a functional cadence, as in *Mercè grido*.

Ex. 55

The role of the A major triad in *Mercè grido* is at first sight uncertain. The progression B–A might be regarded as a V–IV, harking back to a common device of many earlier Renaissance composers. If so, E is readily recongizable as the tonal goal, reached after a brief flirtation with G. Alternatively, however, the establishment of G as a secondary tonal plateau allows us to view the phrase beginning after the first rest (A–f$\sharp^0_6$–G) as V/V–vii$^0_6$–I. A new definition is thereby given to the A major triad, and, particularly because of the rest, its relation is stressed to the events which follow, as opposed to those which precede. The choice of G as the key of the second phrase ('Ma chi m'ascolta?') confirms this view of the tonality of the first. Such harmonic manoeuvring demonstrates Gesualdo's understanding of the usefulness of secondary dominants in establishing temporary tonal centres— an idea which plays a notable role in his vocabulary of harmonic progressions.

But while dominant as well as secondary dominant relations abound in all volumes from the first to the last, it would be misleading to imply that there are no difficulties in trying to reconcile Gesualdo's concept of harmonic progression with the principles of harmonic function. The modal, non-functional system of the Gothic and Early Renaissance periods provides a wealth of diatonic progressions that defy reconciliation with the tonal principles of the seventeenth century. Such passages in Gesualdo, together with the various chromatic constellations and floating modulatory schemes that eschew any functional tonal orientation, make Gesualdo's language a curious, though remarkably fascinating, mixture, capable of being identified now with Renaissance, now with Baroque practice.

Analytical approaches reflecting the influence of these two practices have been periodically undertaken.[53] It is natural, because of the harmonic individuality and chronological position of this music, that its relation with incipient Baroque practices should be studied first. Yet while this has occasionally led to satisfactory results, there are questions which remain unresolved. Lowinsky's expressions 'floating tonality' and 'triadic atonality' reflect this continuing dilemma.

Those passages in which the roots move by thirds, with chromatic inflection in at least one voice, have proved to be analytically tantalizing.[54] Dahlhaus has proposed that certain of these progressions derive contrapuntally from the juxtaposition of a pair of Phrygian cadences.[55]

Ex. 56

The progression (E–c6) occurs at the juncture of these cadences. The diatonic semitones (A–G♯ and F–E; G–F♯ and E♭–D) are inherent in the cadences; the chromatic semitones (G♯–G and E–E♭) occur at the enjambment of the two formulae. Together they result in parallel chromatic tenths between Alto and Bass.

Gesualdo frequently uses this progression by thirds in isolation,[56] but

---

[53] John Clough, 'The Leading Tone in Direct Chromaticism: From Renaissance to Baroque' in *Journal of Music Theory*, I, 1 (1957), pp. 2–21, attempts to establish a basis for determining which of Gesualdo's direct chromatic progressions are compatible with Baroque tonal function.

[54] In the following discussion I have found Dahlhaus's 'Zur chromatischen Technik Carlo Gesualdos,' *Analecta Musicologica*, Bd. 4 (1967), invaluable. Ex. 61a is his, and others are prompted by his insights.

[55] See Dahlhaus, op. cit., p. 78, for the discussion of an analogue in the response *Tristis est anima mea*.   [56] Cf. V, 9, bar 44; V, 11, bar 29 for typical examples.

he employs it in larger sequences as well. The opening of *Moro lasso*, for example, is clearly analogous to Ex. 56, though with the initial chord of the series (b6) suppressed.

Ex. 57

While the phrase closes with an authentic cadence and a break in the chromatic descent in the bass voice, a continuation of the Phrygian formula (g6–a) would have led to the same tonal goal.[57] In any case the ultimate arrival at a is securely prepared and contrapuntally suggested.

In addition to the Phrygian cadences, there are other formulae which, though varied, help to establish a norm for harmonic progression in Gesualdo's music. Walther Dürr,[58] opposing Clough's theory of root progression, has stressed that the chromaticism of the late sixteenth century had a secure foundation, both melodic and contrapuntal, traceable to the 'regola delle terze e seste' of the fourteenth and fifteenth centuries. This provided for the introduction of an accidental to ensure that a harmonic third on its way to the perfect fifth, or a sixth on its way to the perfect octave, would be

---

[57] It would also have provided a B♭, the only one of the twelve pitches missing from the phrase. The segment G6–E7–a, which replaces g6–a, is another progression often found in Gesualdo's madrigals, as witness the discussion relative to Exx. 58, 59, 61b.

[58] W. Dürr, 'Zur mehrstimmigen Behandlung des chromatischen Schrittes in der Polyphonie des 16. Jahrhunderts' in the *Kassel Kongressbericht* (1962), p. 138.

major. Marchettus of Padua[59] includes the following example in his *Lucidarium* under the sub-heading '*De semitonis chromatico.*'

Ex. 58

In the second half of the sixteenth century, the leading-tone function of the chromatic semitone continued to be endorsed, frequently with several harmonic concomitants.

Ex. 59

Patterns *a* and *c*, above, could be expanded by the chord in brackets into a chain of two authentic cadences. Once more, as in the case of the Phrygian chain, the conjunction of two authentic cadences spawns a chromatic mediant progression, with a potential pair of chromatic melodies in parallel sixths (analogous to the parallel tenths of Ex. 56). The realization of this potential depends upon the nature of the second chord in each case, as with the Ab and Bb of example *a*.

The masterful opening of *Beltà poi* (VI, 2) may be seen as a variant of the three-chord model of Ex. 59a. Not only is the general tonal movement identical, but where a substitute chord structure is employed, the root of the missing formula-chord is to be found in the soprano. Gesualdo's substitutes are pattern *b* for *a* at x; pattern *c* plus a dominant alternation (D–G–D6) at y; and a dominant substitution (B–E, instead of B–G♯) at z, which is itself equivalent to the first three chords of the four-chord model of example *a*.

[59] Gerbert, *Scriptores III*, p. 74.

Ex. 60

In *y*, above, the dominant-tonic portion of the harmonic formula is interrupted by a rest. In other instances the insertion of a rest contributes not only to Gesualdo's disruptive style, but highlights, through isolation, the chromatic third-relation of the Ex. 59a formula. Thus the following passage from *Itene, o miei sospiri* (Ex. 61a) is reducible to the sequence of Ex. 61b:

Ex. 61a

Ex. 61 b)

Hence rather than emphasizing, through the phrase structure, the harmonic
plan G–c, A–d, B–e, Gesualdo artificially converts it into the pattern G,
c–A, d–B, e.[60] At the same time he achieves an effective and expressive
reflection of the text.

While the root relationships are of unavoidable interest and unmistakable
originality, there are other features in Gesualdo's late madrigals which are
equally adventurous and which contribute as significantly to the sense of
'progression'. *Resta di darmi noia*, one of Gesualdo's most praised works,[61]
combines many of these notable traits.

The use of only two chords at the opening of the piece, followed by a rest

Ex. 62 a)

[60] Cf. Dahlhaus, op. cit., p. 88.

[61] Cf. especially Doni's remarks, p. 256. Hawkins, *A General History*, III, p. 213, similarly
observes: 'Doni speaking of the fourth madrigal in the sixth book, "Resta di darmi
noia," calls it "quell' artificiosissimo Madrigali del principe"'; and indeed it well
deserves that epithet; for being calculated to express sorrow, it abounds with
chromatic, and even enarmonic (sic) intervals, indeed not easy to sing, but admirably
adapted to the sentiments.'

in all voices, alerts us to the ensuing breathless style. There follows a dominant link with the opening of the next bar (D–g), which leads to the startling harmonic movement g–E♭7–(e)7–c♯°–G$^6_4$–B. Three prominent events take place: (1) a striking use of chromatic third-relation at the cadence; (2) the Cantus' approach to a harmonic seventh by skip (★); and (3) the use of a six-four chord which does not resolve to five-three over the same bass; indeed, the bass drops out altogether as the harmonic shift to B major takes place. In every way the third point, the six-four sonority, is the most outrageous event in the entire progression, not only because of its 'resolution', but because of its approach. The immediately preceding chord, c♯°, possesses a strong urge to move to D; had Gesualdo satisfied this cadential urge before making the shift of a third to B, he would have provided the listener with a well-anchored springboard for the ensuing harmonic leap. What he actually wrote goes a step further. The musical suspense coupled with its unexpected harmonic release creates a passage which must rank high in the history of music for its dazzling and calculated musical effect. The following reduction of the opening may disclose the origins of the passage, but it also robs the music of its magic.[62]

Ex. 62b

While the second-inversion triad is used less commonly than the first-inversion or root-position triads, it is nevertheless treated in a variety of ways most of which are common to functional harmony, e.g. auxiliary six-four, passing six-four, and cadential varieties. In addition, however, less familiar types occur, as demonstrated above, and some of the most startling passages in all Gesualdo stem from extraordinary and atypical usages of this sonority.[63]

A concluding remark regarding *Resta di darmi noia*. The opening passage, which we have discussed, is repeated—a practice previously noted in other eventful harmonic passages. Here, however, the repetition is not made at a level he would have chosen in his earlier books, but at the major second

---

[62] Other equally striking usages of six-four sonorities abound in Gesualdo's music, as at the opening of *Tu piangi, o Filli mia* (VI, 3), and are a marked characteristic of the mature master. See also the discussion of Ex. 40.

[63] Marshall, op. cit., pp. 55–60.

above. While this may seem a capricious choice, it will be noticed that it allows the strongest possible link with the conclusion of the preceding statement: the first statement ends on B major, the new statement begins on E major. A fundamental point has been repeatedly made, concerning Gesualdo's seemingly audacious and irresponsible harmonic manner. If we view only the small unit, the minute detail, the single progression, we may admire his venturousness, yet wonder at his lack of harmonic logic. Seen from a broader perspective, we can see how often the smaller harmonic niceties provide an interior spice which is blended and ultimately subordinated to the requirements of a larger tonal plan—his daring typically dissolving into perspicacity.

If formulae do not predominate in Gesualdo's harmonic rhetoric, they do exist, and help to establish the semblance of a norm. Harmonic surprise in any period is related to expectation; and while we cannot claim to know all that the Renaissance ear anticipated, or attribute to it a fully developed sense of harmonic function, the extent of the adoption of certain formulae allows us to guess something of its aural habits. The isolated chromatic third-relationship, for example, must have sounded as freshly to the Cinquecento ear, tutored in normally diatonic modal polyphony, as it does to the ear conditioned to the implications of Baroque harmonic function, just as melodic chromaticism must have been heard as a colouring of the diatonic church modes.

In sum, Gesualdo vastly increased the repertoire of usable accidentals. In so doing he seemingly did more to enlarge the harmonic than the melodic vocabulary. Yet while his choice of unusual melodic intervals is frequently related to basic harmonic considerations, he must also be seen as a composer willing to apply an enlarged repertoire of linear devices to fresh contexts. Conversely his bold harmonic style can be seen to spring for the most part from a conservative but sure control of the contrapuntal element, a classic sense of voice-leading. An awareness of both factors allows us to appreciate his sensitivity not only to the harmonic root relationships but also to the weight and surprise of inversion formations.[64] In this last point Gesualdo stands apart from the chromatic practice of most other composers before him, who as a rule showed an unrelenting preference for root positions in their most progressive passages. While Gesualdo's harmonic building

---

[64] We no longer need to support the idea that it was Rameau who first developed a theory of chord inversions. Lippius, *Synopsis musicae novae* (1612), and Campion, *A New Way of Making Foure Parts* (1613), both speak directly on the subject in Gesualdo's time. Cf. particularly Dahlhaus's 'Die Entwicklung der Akkordtheorie' in his important study, *Untersuchungen über die Entstehung der harmonischen Tonalität* (1968), pp. 104 ff.

blocks are principally major and minor triads, he seldom makes prolonged use of triads in root position and clearly shows a preference for greater variety. He seems especially aware of the harmonic weight of chordal inversions, and employs them in an extremely sensitive and refined way. Compare, for example, the simple and relatively primitive use of root position sonorities in the following passage by Lassus (from the Prologue of *Prophetiae Sibyllarum*), which is otherwise somewhat audacious,

Ex. 63

or this by Vicentino,[65]

Ex. 64

[65] *Non s'incolpi la voglia* (Book V, 1572), bars 17–22. In *Collected Works*, ed. by H. Kaufmann, p. 81.

to the opening of *Moro lasso* (Ex. 43) or *Resta di darmi noia* (Ex. 62a). A
similar refinement is frequently observable in the works of other members
of the contemporary Neapolitan circle and is impressively evident in the
polyphonic madrigals of Sigismondo d'India.[66] As an ingredient in the
development of a new tonal language, with far-reaching implications, this
feature of Gesualdo's style has not been sufficiently stressed.

Lowinsky's recent exposition of the chromatic movement in the late
sixteenth century not only as a counterthrust to tonal consolidation but also
as an agent for the expansion of that concept—i.e. as a supplemental as
well as an opposing force—is helpful in reviewing Gesualdo's stylistic
position and in fixing a meaning for many of the harmonic developments of
the Mannerists.[67] It is of particular importance, because upon its validity
depends our ability to regard Gesualdo as a composer of some relevance to
the period which followed. In one sense Gesualdo is indeed, as Kerman says,
the creator of 'stillborn fantasies'; but in another he may be considered a
composer whose harmonic vision helped to open new possibilities for the
Baroque.

[66] See Ex. 81, bar 2.
[67] Lowinsky, *Tonality and Atonality in Sixteenth-Century Music,* pp. 43–46.

CHAPTER NINE

The Late Style: Models and Successors

WE have seen that the resemblances between Gesualdo's style and that of his best-known predecessors, Marenzio, Wert, Rore, Caimo, and especially Luzzaschi, ultimately related more to the larger issues—form, textual quality, and madrigalism, and only partially to expressive nuance. These composers do not share to any great extent the idiosyncratic gestures peculiar to Gesualdo's personality, the harmonic and rhythmic daring and the exaggerated emotionalism. Even so the question remains whether in the smaller details Gesualdo stands in any demonstrable relation with one or more of his contemporaries.

Pomponio Nenna

The association of Gesualdo with Pomponio Nenna has been continually stressed from the seventeenth century to our own day, but curiously Nenna's music has until now been virtually ignored. To define the relationship, it has been necessary to look at all his music, and in the process to score much of it for the first time.[1] The significance of Nenna's music for Gesualdo's art was soon apparent.

Nenna's first appearance in print in 1574 suggests a sufficient disparity in age between him and Gesualdo to permit a teacher-pupil relationship (and also strengthens the conjecture of 1550–5, as opposed to 1560, as a probable birthdate for Nenna). Nenna's association with the Gesualdo court, however, dates from a period, 1594–9,[2] seemingly too late to have allowed him much of a formative influence upon the writings of the Prince.

[1] See *Istituto Italiano per la Storia della Musica, Monumenti II*, Vol. I, for Books I and IV of Nenna's madrigals *à 5*.
[2] Cf. Romano Micheli's *Musica vaga et artificiosa* (1615), Preface.

On the other hand Gesualdo, after departing for Ferrara in February 1594 for his marriage to Eleanora d'Este, had already returned to the south by May of that year. Correspondence from Fontanelli assures us that Gesualdo composed regularly during this period. Although he was no doubt partially under the spell of Ferrara at this time, his stay there had amounted to no more than three months. At Gesualdo he stayed six months, at a time that coincided with Nenna's residency. Thus, if Nenna's influence at this date cannot be guaranteed, its possibility cannot be rejected. As Gesualdo's new style does not show itself until his fourth book of 1596, it is tempting to believe that Nenna (as well as Luzzaschi and other things Ferrarese) had a hand in its development.

It would be helpful if it were possible to document beyond question the dates of Nenna's productions, but first editions are rare or non-existent. The following list of his extant madrigal collections tells the story:

Primo libro à 5	1582,[3] 1617
Quarto libro à 5	1609, 1617
Quinto libro à 5	1603, 1612
Sesto libro à 5	1607, 1609, 1614, 1618
Settimo libro à 5	1608, 1609, 1613, 1616, 1624
Ottavo libro à 5	1618
Primo libro à 4	1613,[4] 1621

The most significant clue is the appearance of the fifth book as early as 1603. The fourth book, which shows a drastic stylistic change from the relatively conservative language of book one, must therefore antedate by at least six years the sole edition of it that survives. Equally frustrating is the absence of books two and three, which could well have introduced for the first time the progressive features found in the fourth book. But most puzzling and tantalizing of all is the *Primo libro à 4*, which contains five texts set by Gesualdo. Because of stylistic connections between settings of the same text by the two composers, the original dating of this particular collection is

[3] Nenna dedicated his *Primo Libro de Madrigali à 5 v.* (Venice, Gardano, 1582), to Fabrizio Carafa, Duke of Andria, the lover of Donna Maria d'Avalos and the Prince of Venosa's victim.

[4] A 1613 edition of this set of madrigals was cited by Fétis as well as by Mischiati in his more recent article on Nenna in *MGG*. The location of a surviving copy is mentioned by neither, and it is not listed in Vogel or in Ernst Hilmar, 'Ergänzungen zu Emil Vogels "Bibliothek der Gedruckten Weltlichen Vocalmusik Italiens, aus den Jahren 1500–1700"' in *Analecta Musicologica*, Bd. 4 (1967), pp. 154–206. Earlier in the century a copy was in the library of Daniel Fryklund in Hälsingborg, Sweden. Photographs of the title page and dedication were provided by him in 'Musik-bibliografiska Anteckningar' *Svensk Tidskrift för Musikforsning* (1928). I am grateful to Mr. Keith Larson for bringing information of the Fryklund copy to my attention.

crucial.[5] There is evidence to suggest that the entire set of madrigals may have been written as many as nine or ten years prior to the earliest edition. *S'io taccio* and *La mia doglia*, adjacent items (18 and 19) in the 1621 edition, had appeared side-by-side in Alessandro di Costanzo's *Il primo libro d'madrigali à quattro voci* of 1604. This is not a first edition either, as we learn from the title page: 'Novamente ristampato ad istanza di Giacomo Voltaggio di Trapani, con la gionta d'alcun altri.' There are five madrigals in this collection not by Costanzo: three at the end by Dentice which are clearly marked as 'newly added,' and the two by Nenna (not so labelled) sandwiched into the middle of the collection. It is therefore evident that the Nenna pieces were written prior to 1604, and by extension it may be surmised that this holds true for the complete contents of his *Libro primo à 4*. The appearance of ten of the madrigals from this collection in MS Magl. XIX. 106bis of the Biblioteca Nazionale di Firenze supports this theory. They are the first ten pieces of the 1621 edition, in the same order as they appear there. Becherini[6] dates the manuscript, which also contains a group of twelve ricercars by Macque,[7] from the second half of the sixteenth century. Both Macque and Nenna were publishing as early as the 1570s and 1580s, and while the style of these four-voice Nenna madrigals suggests that they followed the first book *à 5 v.* of 1582, the style of the fourth and fifth books (pre-1603 and 1603 respectively), which are the next preserved sources, indicates that the works included in this manuscript could have come from the twenty-year interim which is a blank for us today.

A list of texts set by both Gesualdo and Nenna (see p. 216) suggests several hypotheses.

The four texts which Nenna shares with Gesualdo's Book V are noteworthy in light of Gesualdo's comments in the Preface to that volume.[8] Of the four, two (*Deh, coprite* and *Mercè grido*) come from Nenna's Book V of 1603, and were thus published eight years prior to Gesualdo's pieces. A similar claim can be made for Nenna's *Tu segui* (Book IV, pre-1603). The stylistic connection between their settings of these three texts suggests the possibility of further imitation in other instances where parallel verses were used.

[5] The title page of the 1621 print discloses that it is not only a reprint but one subjected to considerable editorial re-working: 'Novamente ristampati, & con ogni diligenza corretti, Con 'Aggiunta del Basso Continuo da Carlo Milanntio.'

[6] *Catalogo dei manoscritti musicali della Biblioteca Nazionale Firenze*, p. 41.

[7] These Macque ricercars are *unica* and have not been examined or discussed to my knowledge. They are not mentioned or included by Watelet, *Monumenta Musica Belgicae*, IV, or cited by Clercx in *MGG* in the article on Macque.

[8] All the Nenna madrigals which share texts with Gesualdo appear in a modern edition by the author in Pomponio Nenna, *Madrigali* (Penn. State Music Series, 1973). None-such H-71277 records most of the music in performances based upon this edition.

Texts set by Gesualdo and Nenna

Text	Nenna	Gesualdo	Resemblance
Tu segui, o bell'Aminta (Clori)	IV	VI, 20	Yes
Itene miei sospir(i)	IV	V, 3	★
Deh, (s)coprite	V	V, 16	Yes
Merce grido	V	V, 11	Yes
Se non miro io mi moro (S'io non miro non moro)	VI	V, 2	★
Si gioioso mi fanna	VIII	I, 10	★
Ahi dispietata	I à 4	III, 6	No
Ancide solla morte	I à 4	VI, 15	Yes
Candida man	I à 4	II, 15	★
Qual fora à donna	I à 4	V, 6	Yes
Asciugate i begli occhi	I à 4	V, 14	Yes
S'io taccio il duol	I à 4	II, 9	See Ex. 66

★ Indicates that these texts are totally different in spite of similar or
identical textual incipits.

The similarities between two settings vary in scope and mode. On
occasion it is primarily in the sharing of a small but vivid detail, as in the
opening of *Deh, coprite* (Ex. 65), where texture and rhythm are identical.[9]

Ex. 65

Deh, co-pri-te jl bel se - no, Che per trop -

Deh, co-pri-te jl bel se - no, Che per trop-po mi-

[9] For Alfoso Fontanelli's setting of this text, from *Secondo libro de madrigali à 5 v.* (1604),
see Ex. 78a.

In one instance, at least, it is possible to suggest that borrowing of a trenchant idea occurs in association with a different madrigal and text. In *S'io taccio il duol*, for example, which we know from Costanzo's collection of 1604, the borrowing is apparent not in Gesualdo's early madrigal of the same name but in his *Dolcissima mia vita* of Book V.

Ex. 66

a) Gesualdo, *Dolcissima mia vita*

b) Nenna, *S'io taccio il duol*

At other times, identical texts develop phrase by phrase with corresponding textural changes, and often with similar rhythmic patterns. Thus Gesualdo's setting of *Mercè grido* (Book V, 1611) develops phrase and texture according to Nenna's setting which had appeared as early as 1603 (Ex. 67). Nenna's reflection upon the words 'Morrò dunque tacendo' (Ex. 67c) results in a passage that is singularly Gesualdine not only because of the harmonic progression, but also because of the repetition and transposition involving melodic interchange, here double counterpoint at the octave.

Ex. 67
a)

Ma chi m'a-scol - ta, ma chi m'a-scol - ta?

Ma chi m'a-scol - ta, ma chi m'a-scol - ta?

b) Gesualdo:

Ahi las - - so

Ahi las - so

Nenna:

Ahi las - - so

Ahi las - so

c) Gesualdo:

Mor - rò, mor - rò dun - que ta - cen - do, Mor - rò, mor-

Mor - rò, mor - rò dun - que ta - cen - do, Mor - rò, mor-

Occasionally both textural plan and adoption of detail go hand in hand. Note Nenna's opening as well as his approach to the final cadence in *Asciugate i begli occhi* (Ex. 68), and compare it with Gesualdo's. In Nenna's final cadence (Ex. 68c) the use of the untransposed Phrygian highlights the semi-tonal clash (last two chords: F major over E pedal) inherent in the modal choice, and may disclose the origins of Gesualdo's solution (last two chords: E♭ major over a D pedal).

Nenna's setting of *Ancide sol la morte* (Ex. 69) similarly has many details in common with Gesualdo's, none more telling than at 'Io morendo per te' (Ex. 69b). Here Nenna not only employs double counterpoint in the upper two voices, but also introduces an excruciating minor six-five dissonance made more pointed by its approach. Although Gesualdo also employs a minor six-five dissonance in the contrapuntal repetition, Nenna's approach to the figure via double chromatic inflection (as well as parallel fifths!)[10] is more reminiscent of Gesualdo's *Ardo per te* (Ex. 35).

[10] This would not have constituted a contrapuntal violation, since the chromatic semitone, as opposed to the diatonic semitone, is a prime interval. See the discussion on pp. 182–4.

While the boldness and originality of such passages encourages us to suspend our analytical judgement, it is worth noting that Nenna frequently eschews continuation in the same manner once such a nugget has been mined. The comparison of a complete madrigal by the two composers typically demonstrates Nenna's preference for a terser, less diffusive and capacious style.

Since all but Nenna's eighth and final volume of madrigals for five voices had been published by the year 1608, and the most relevant part of that repertoire by 1603, Gesualdo could have adopted certain details in his collections which appeared for the first time in 1611. Even the inclusion of Gesualdo's *T'amo mia vita* (Book V) in an anthology of 1609 does not alter the fact that most of Nenna's productions appeared in print before Gesualdo's. In view of this it is not difficult to divine the motives behind the Preface to Gesualdo's Book V (see p. 165). He knew that without the claims of that preface many of the mature works of Luzzaschi, Macque, Nenna, and even Marenzio (whose *Cosi nel mio parlar* and *Solo e pensoso*, for example, appeared as late as 1599) would enjoy a published chronological advantage; with them his works could assume chronological priority in one of the madrigal's most feverishly productive decades. But to believe that the last two books of madrigals were composed by 1596 is to conclude that Gesualdo fashioned all six volumes within five years, the last four within two or less. We should remember that the cautious language of Books I and II was barely enlarged in Book III (1595), the first volume from his Ferrara period. Not until 1596 in Book IV do we have the first signs of things to come. It seems improbable that the virtually unprecedented miracles of the two final collections were created at white heat in the next few months and that the composer then, for all intents and purposes, closed his secular workshop for the remaining fifteen years of his life.

It would be just as easy to contend that Nenna's productions had been created earlier and held up along the way, since we have none of his music printed between 1582 and 1603. As his first madrigal volume appeared in 1582, it is logical to assume that the missing second and third volumes had been composed by the time of his appearance at Gesualdo in 1594, twelve years later. While Book V did not appear until 1603 (and Book IV at an uncertain earlier date), it seems probable that the period 1594–9, when Nenna was at Gesualdo, saw the creation of these books. Gesualdo says that his own unpublished madrigals were kept back for domestic consumption. Could it not be that Nenna's music was also closeted during this period for the same reason?

The seed of suspicion cast by the accusations of Gesualdo's preface need not be over-nourished. No one is mentioned by name (Monteverdi-Artusi, Vicentino-Lusitano, Gagliano-Effrem and others also demonstrate a wavering distaste for explicitness). Gesualdo's unspecific reproof to *certi compositori* (plural) for copying beautiful passages from his works may well have been intended for the group of minor composers (Lacorcia, Genuino, etc.) who belonged to his circle and who after the turn of the century created a small but colourfully chromatic repertoire.[11] Yet he may well have had Nenna and other established composers in mind.

Luzzaschi and Macque

A list of Gesualdo's texts set also by Luzzaschi, who had died in 1607, and by Macque, who lived until 1614, is intriguing in this regard.

Text	Macque[12]	Gesualdo
Gelo ha Madonna	II à 5, 1587	I, 1594
Ahi, disperata vita	IV à 5, 1599	III, 1595
	I à 6, 1576	
Tu segui	VI à 5, 1613	VI, 1611
Questi leggiadri	Madr. and Nap.	I, 1594
	à 6, 1581	
Son si belle	III à 4, 1610	I, 1594

[11] See pp. 227 ff.

[12] I am at a loss to explain the remark by Suzanne Clercx in 'Jean de Macque et l'evolution du Madrigalisme,' *Festschrift Joseph Schmidt-Görg zum 60. Geburtstag* (1957), p. 78,

Text	Luzzaschi	Gesualdo
Mentre gira	II à 5, 1576	IV, 1596
Luci serene e chiare ⎱	—	IV, 1596
Lucente e chiara ⎰	II à 5, 1576	—
Da l'odorate	III à 5, 1582	II, 1594
O come è gran martire	III à 5, 1582	II, 1594
Itene, o miei sospiri ⎱	—	V, 1611
Itene mie querele ⎰	VI à 5, 1596	—
Cor mio benche	VI à 5, 1596	P, 1626
Giote voi col canto	VII à 5, 1604	V, 1611
Tirsi morir volea	VII à 5, 1604	I, 1594
Di bei colori	VII à 5, 1604	P, 1626
Non è questa l'Aurora	VII à 5, 1604	P, 1626

Neither list, admittedly, is so directly revealing as Nenna's, but there are some undoubted parallels in light of the general style and date of certain of their productions. Macque's *Ahi, disperata vita*, while a different text from Gesualdo's, possesses a chromatic manner in the 1599 setting as extravagant and virtuosic as any he ever wrote. The book of 1599 'is remarkable in every way. The Macque of the "Durezze" style is present in each and every madrigal in this book, and each madrigal is individual. The experimentation of the 1599 volume is tempered and yet somewhat more intensified in the later books of 1610 and 1613.'[13] Furthermore, Macque's *Tu segui*, set by both Nenna and Gesualdo, contains dissonance patterns at 'ch'arde Sol d'amore' worthy of either of his Neapolitan colleagues.

Amongst the Luzzaschi pieces the only texts set by Gesualdo in his final collections belong to his Book V, cited specifically as the principal object of piracy. Of the two, *Itene mie querele* alone could have been the source of Gesualdo's irritation.[14] It had been printed as early as 1596 when Gesualdo

---

fn. 53: 'Il n'est pas san intérêt d'observer que De Macque avait choisi, dans l'oeuvre du Tasse, les mêmes textes que Gesualdo: *O come è gran martire, Sento che nel partir, Quella arpa felice, Baci soavi e cari, Gelo ha madonna il seno, Questi leggiadri, Bell'angioletta, Ahi disperata vita, Tu m'uccidi o crudele, Se tu fuggi io non resta/* . . . Il serait utile de comparer les versions respectives des deux musiciens.' Amongst the texts listed only *Gelo ha madonna* is, to my knowledge, by Tasso; *O come*, and *Baci soavi* are by Guarini, *Questi leggiadri* by Celiano, and *Ahi disperata vita* is a completely different text. Questions of textual authorship aside, I know of no settings by Macque of *O come*, *Sento che, Quella arpa, Baci soavi, Bell'angioletta, Tu m'uccidi*, or *Se tu fuggi*.

13 I am grateful to Prof. W. Richard Shindle who lent me his scorings of all of the Macque items and provided the information quoted above.

14 Luzzaschi's *Giote voi col canto* bears no resemblance to Gesualdo's setting. Cf. Spiro, op. cit., 101, for a comparison of the texts; 193, for the music.

was in residence at the Ferrara court. By claiming that his own *Itene, o miei sospiri* dated from the same year, his challenge of Luzzaschi seems almost pointed. Whichever piece was created first, the modelling is uncontestable.[15] Remembering Gesualdo's earlier reference to Luzzaschi as the only enemy he feared, it could be argued that the sentiment of the preface is at least in part directed at him.

Unless we are to claim, however, that all the chromatic wonders of the period 1590–1610 came to light under the inspiration of Gesualdo's example, originality must be allowed in the works of others who repeatedly demonstrated a capacity to handle progressive elements with ease. Yet for all the attention showered on Luzzaschi by Gesualdo personally (or so Fontanelli tells us), there is little evidence to indicate that he learned his chromatic-rhythmic lessons directly from him. The well-known *Quivi sospiri* and *Itene mie querele* are unusual products and stand almost alone in Luzzaschi's output. One could as well claim Rore as a direct influence by virtue of his *Del la belle contrade* or *Calami sonum ferentes* (equally atypical works of this master). In a word neither Rore or Luzzaschi were inveterate chromaticists, and while there are other ingredients involved that make it dangerous to ignore their relationship to Gesualdo, it is difficult to view them as prime models. Both Macque and Nenna, on the other hand, were personal associates both in Gesualdo and Naples prior to the appearance of Gesualdo's third book. Macque's first book of madrigals appeared in 1576 and Nenna's in 1582. Their seniority as published composers suggests strongly that, as the two major composers in residence at Gesualdo, they would have been responsible for instructing the talented local prince at least in the rudiments of composition. While we cannot unequivocally maintain that Macque and Nenna developed as chromaticists themselves before the 1590s, there is no reason to insist that they in turn were introduced to such manners by Gesualdo. The fact that Nenna's Books II and III,[16] written during the period of the late 1580s and 1590s, and Macque's[17] entire production between 1579 and 1599, are either missing or incomplete, currently presents insurmountable obstacles to the satisfactory solution of this question. But

[15] See Einstein, *The Italian Madrigal*, III, p. 262, for Luzzaschi's *Itene mie querele*; pp. 130, 173 of the present book for a comparison of the two *Itene* texts.

[16] Mr. K. Larson informs me that after an intensive search of older bibliographies and catalogues of music he also found not a single reference to Nenna's second and third books of five-voice madrigals.

[17] W. Richard Shindle writes in a personal communication regarding Macque's *Madrigali à 4, à 5, et à 6* (1579) that 'In the book of 1579 the more colorful tendencies of Macque begin to appear. . . . Touches of chromaticism that will be intensified later on are present as well as tendencies for irregular resolution.'

we might conclude that these three figures very probably nourished one another's sensibilities. The possibility cannot be denied either that it was the senior musicians who led the way or that they in turn were influenced by their protégé.

★ ★ ★

In spite of Gesualdo's sensitivity to the question of originality, a trait increasingly characteristic of the Renaissance artist, ultimately we must openly acknowledge what he also knew: other contemporaries were busily engaged in fashioning chromatic hybrids with more than occasional success, a practice dating from the 1550s. While Gesualdo pursued the idiom more relentlessly and may have more consistently struck gold, he epitomized rather than invented a movement. The spirit of competition in setting similar or identical texts could easily have induced a person of Gesualdo's nature to lay too broad a claim for what he must have viewed as a personal style. In light of the essential individuality of these masterpieces, however, Gesualdo need not have worried about the judgements of posterity.

One final connection between Nenna and Gesualdo resides in the non-madrigal repertoire of the two men. Both composers' most significant sacred music was a cycle of Responses for Holy Week; Nenna, in fact, composed two such cycles—one of them published in 1607, four years before the appearance of Gesualdo's set. Of the three composers, Luzzaschi, Macque, and Nenna, the last can most convincingly be viewed as a *piccolo* Gesualdo. That he may have provided the direct nourishment for many of Gesualdo's mature masterworks, takes nothing away from Gesualdo's indebtedness to Rore, Luzzaschi, and others. It does suggest, however, that not all of the shaping forces in his last years were from Ferrara, and that talent, in figures such as Nenna and Macque, established a climate close at home which was both progressive, original, and of signal importance in the formation of Gesualdo's final creations.

Minor Neapolitan Figures

If it is tempting to propose Nenna, Macque, and Luzzaschi as composers of stature sufficient to have influenced Gesualdo's productions in one way or another, there is a group of lesser Neapolitan composers whose style was in varying degrees related to Gesualdo and in many instances, surely, indebted to his example. Their music is virtually unknown today, having been lost in the shadows of their illustrious associates. A few of them, however, display a boldness which, though obviously derivative, is nevertheless marked by an amazing sureness of application. In some instances, one wonders what posterity's judgement of them might have been if more of their works had survived. While the list could be extended, the following composers seem the most important:

Agostino Agresta is represented by only a single book of madrigals, a *Libro Primo* (Naples, Vitale, 1617). The contents are generally routine for the period, but *O come è gran martire*, set by Gesualdo in his Book I, makes use of occasional degree inflection. *Io penso e nel pensar* introduces novel and highly mannered proportional complexities which, while appearing theoretical as well as anachronistic, may well be an attempt by the composer to suggest expressive tempo variability. Two madrigals had appeared in anthologies of 1606 (Copenhagen, Waltkirch) and 1609 (Napoli, Gargano et Nucci). The earlier of these, *Caro dolce*, opens thus:

Ex. 70

Scipione Dentice wrote five books of madrigals all in five voices. Book I (Naples, Cancer, 1591), dedicated to the Duke of Ferrara, survives in only two parts, Alto and Basso, while Book III (Naples, Carlino & Pace, 1598), dedicated to Leonora d'Este, Principessa di Venosa, survives only in the

Alto part. Book II (Venice, Gardano, 1596), Book IV (Naples, Pace, 1602), and Book V (Naples, Sottile, 1607) survive complete. Book IV contains a setting of *Deh come in van*, set by Gesualdo in Book VI, which displays moderate but interesting degree inflection, as does *O longamente sospirato in vano* in the same collection.

Francesco Genuino composed at least five books of madrigals. Only Book Two (Naples, Sottile, 1605) survives complete, and I have not seen it. Of the remaining collections Book Three (Naples, Carlino, 1612) is remarkable for a highly inflected style, evidenced by the surviving parts, as in the following excerpts from the Alto of *Io rido amanti*.

Ex. 71

mi - se - ro,   mi - se - ro, mi - se - ho - ra vi - va pian-gen - do

Of even greater interest is a setting of *Beltà poi che t'assenti* (Ex. 72) from the same collection. Although the Quinto is missing, the entire madrigal presents a point of comparison with Gesualdo's composition on a similar text.[18] While it is far less daring than Gesualdo's and appears to resemble it only marginally in its handling of texture, it clearly belongs to the contemporary chromatic orbit of the Neapolitans.

Ex. 72

[18] Only the first two lines of text are the same, however. Compare Genuino's text in Ex. 72 with the version used by Gesualdo, p. 119.

His remaining collections survive even less completely, but the inclusion of other Gesualdo texts such as *T'amo mia vita* in Book Five (Naples, Carlino, 1614) and *Tu segui o bell' Aminta* in the *Nuova Scelta di Madrigali di Sette Autori* (Naples, Carlino, 1615) is worthy of note.

Scipione Lacorcia wrote at least three books of madrigals of which only the last two survive. Book Two (Naples, Carlino, 1616) contains pieces by F. Lambardi and Luca Valente as well; Book Three (Naples, Vitale, 1620) includes settings of *Non è questa* and *Ancidetemi*, both conservatively treated by Gesualdo, and two additional works by Hettore della Marra which exceed in harmonic boldness anything else in the collection, as witness the opening of his *Occhi un tempo mia vita*.

Ex. 73

Both volumes, however, demonstrate that Lacorcia was one of the most progressive spirits of the Neapolitan school, and further investigation should prove these books to be chromatic wonderlands. The opening of his *Langue Clori* from Book Three is representative.

Ex. 74

Camillo Lambardi, maestro di cappella at the Annunziata in Naples, has left us two volumes of madrigals. *Primo libro à 4 v.* (Naples, Carlino, 1600) has a setting of *Io tacerò*, which Gesualdo had set in his Book IV (1596), but it does not follow the earlier piece even in general outline and altogether lacks its pungent details. It begins as follows:

Ex. 75

The entire first volume is otherwise tame and harmonically non-progressive. This holds true as well for the *Secondo libro à 4 v.* (Naples, Gargano, 1609) though features of rhythm and phrase common to the late madrigal link him with Gesualdo in a general way. The opening of the Cantus in *Ite sospir ardenti* is illustrative.

Ex. 76

Giovanni Vincenzo Macedonio di Mutio, Cavalier Napolitano, introduces a mild but expressive harmonic style in *Piangete occhi dolenti* of his *Primo libro à 5* (Naples, Vitale, 1603) which is dedicated to Scipione Dentice. This trend is further developed in a few works of the second book (Naples, Carlino, 1606) but the two volumes are not especially remarkable for the period.

Two anthologies of madrigals from 1609 and 1615 bring together many of these Neapolitan musicians and thus fashion a semi-official link between them. The first is *Teatro de Madrigali à 5 v. de diversi eccelentissimi musici Napolitani* (Naples, Gargana et Nucci, 1609) which includes the works of Agresta, Cerretto, S. Dentice, Effrem, Francisco and Camillo Lambardi, Macque, de la Marra, Gesualdo, and others. The second collection is entitled *Nuova scelta di Madrigali di sette autori* containing works by Dentice, Genuino, Nenna, Stella, Pecci, Fontanelli (*senza nome*), and Gesualdo. Of the seven all but Pecci and Fontanelli are Neapolitans. The stylistic relation of both to this circle, however, is demonstrable;[19] furthermore both shared a place of honour alongside Gesualdo in Monteverdi's list of *seconda prattica* composers.

Alfonso Fontanelli, diplomat and *gentiluomo* to the Este dukes for most of his life, is cited by Einstein as a composer whose madrigals epitomize the Ferrarese style. His presence here in almost exclusively Neapolitan company is worthy of note. The anonymity which marks his two books of madrigals (*Madrigali, senza nome, à 5 voci*) may well have been prompted by the initial publication of Gesualdo's Book I under a pseudonym.[20] Fontanelli's first book (Ferrara, Baldini, 1595) contains an elaborate and laudatory preface by Horatio Vecchi in its second printing (Venice, 1603). Vecchi tells us that the praiseworthiness of these works is doubled if one realizes that Fontanelli, a nobleman, composes '*per ricreatione, & non per professione*'. Vecchi's judgement is not overdrawn even without the qualifier, for madrigals from this collection such as *Moro e de la mia morte*, *Io parto e nel partire*, and *Si che s'io viss' in guerra* (Ex. 77a, b, c) are carefully shaped and spiced with a harmonic and rhythmic invention which, considering their date, must surely have impressed Gesualdo himself.

[19] See Denis Arnold's article on Pecci in *MGG*.

[20] The hypothesis seems especially plausible since *Com'esser può mia vita* is openly attributed to Fontanelli in *La gloria musicale di diversi Eccelentiss. Autori a cinque voci* of 1592.

Ex. 77

a)

The second book (Venice, Gardano, 1604; repr. 1609) contains some of his
best work including masterful settings of *Deb coprite'l bel seno* (Ex. 78a) and
Qual saria Donna (Ex. 78b), both texts set by Gesualdo and Nenna. Here are
the opening bars of Fontanelli's settings.

Ex. 78a

ma vien me - no,   deh co - pri - te'l bel se - no, che per trop -

l'al - ma vien me - no,   deh co - pri - te'l bel se - no, che per trop -

deh co - pri - te'l bel se - no, che per trop -

- po mi - rar l'al - ma vien me - no,   l'al - ma vien me - - no!

- po mi - rar   l'al - ma vien me - no,   l'al - ma vien me - no!

- po mi - rar   l'al - ma vien me - - - no!

Ah, no'l co - pri - te,   non,   ah no'l co - pri - te, non,

Ah, no'l co - pri - te,   non,   ah, no'l co - pri - te, non,   che

Ah, no'l co - pri - te,   non,   ah no'l co - pri - te, non,

che l'al-ma a-vez - za   a   vi - ver di dol - cez - za

l'al-ma a-vez - za   a   vi - ver di dol - cez - - za

Ex. 78b

Deh coprite'l bel seno appears in Gesualdo's Book V and in Nenna's Book V (1603). Fontanelli's opening phrase is similar to both in texture and rhythm, '*l'alma vien meno*' shares Gesualdo's descending chromatic figure, and '*Ah, no'l coprite, non*' suggests Nenna's treatment. The texts used by Gesualdo and Nenna are markedly different (see p. 131), but Fontanelli's is identical to the one used by Gesualdo. Possibly Fontanelli knew both pieces, as Nenna's had been published the year before, and Gesualdo would have us believe that his work had also been composed by this time. Yet it could be Gesualdo who knew the settings of Nenna and Fontanelli and borrowed his text directly from the latter. It should not be forgotten that Gesualdo's first prolonged contact with Nenna in 1594 found Fontanelli in their company. While it would seem unlikely that Nenna's influence was important in Fontanelli's 1595 collection, a few of the more adventurous pieces there, in addition to those of 1604 which invite comparison, may well owe a debt to him as well as to Macque and Luzzaschi.[21] His final development, if this is the appropriate term for such a limited production, may indeed reflect Neapolitan as well as Ferrarese associations.

A relationship between Fontanelli and Pecci more specific than the one suggested by Monteverdi may be seen by comparing the opening of Fontanelli's setting of *Era l'anima mia* of 1604 (Ex. 79a) with that by Pecci in his Book Two of 1612 (Ex. 79b).

Ex. 79
a)

[21] In addition to the texts which he shares with Gesualdo and Nenna, Fontanelli also shares *lo vò piangendo—Si che s'io viss' in guerra* (see Ex. 77c) and *Padre del Ciel* with Macque. Fontanelli did not set a single text used by Luzzaschi.

Pecci's harmonic idiom never moves closer to Gesualdo's than in this madrigal, which may be judged decidedly atypical. Banchieri, however, had linked the names of Pecci, Fontanelli, Gesualdo, and Monteverdi as early as 1609 in his *Conclusioni nel suono dell'organo*[22] while speaking of their common ability to reflect their texts. Elsewhere it will be noted that Pecci set three Gesualdo texts in his book of *Canzonette à 3 con B.C.* of 1607 (*O come è gran martire, Voi volete ch'io mora* and *Cor mio, deh, non piangete*) and three more in his second and final book of five-voice madrigals of 1612 (*O chiome erranti, Donna se m'ancidete,* and *Dolcissimo sospiro*). Although these works only hint at the progressive qualities of other contemporary Neapolitans, Monteverdi rightly labelled him one of the *seconda prattica* composers. The opening of *Dolcissimo sospiro* (Ex. 80a) is thus familiar in its use of repetition involving transposition and melodic exchange, while an interior phrase in *Se di veder* (Ex. 80b) from the same collection fuses linear chromaticism and parlando declamation in a way more reminiscent of Wert and Sigismondo d'India (Ex. 80c from *Ottavo libro de'madrigali,* 1624) than of Gesualdo.

22 Pp. 58–60.

Ex. 80 a)

Ex. 80b)

Ex. 80c)

Sigismondo d'India

In summary, there is a sizeable coterie of composers whose relation to Gesualdo and Nenna appears unmistakable. A more complete assessment of the late Neapolitan madrigal school will assuredly reveal new and perhaps unexpected connections amongst a group of colourful but now forgotten minor masters.

We are no longer dealing with a minor figure in Sigismondo d'India, however. One of the most powerful and innovatory composers of early monody, he continued to compose polyphonic madrigals throughout his life. When this parallel production is examined in more detail, we shall no doubt discover further evidence of the relevance of the late madrigal (and Gesualdo in particular) to early monody. The opening of d'India's *Mercè grido* from *Il Terzo Libro de Madrigali à 5 v.* of 1615 (Ex. 81)[23] reveals many expressive and textural similarities with Gesualdo's and Nenna's settings of the same text (Ex. 67).

[23] The continuo line, essentially a basso seguente in Exx. 80c and 81, is omitted in these two excerpts.

Ex. 81

The six-four sonority at 'piangendo' is mind-boggling, and a clear challenge to his Neapolitan contemporaries.[24] His slightly later setting of these same verses for solo voice and continuo of 1618 (Ex. 82) adopts certain melodic details from his own polyphonic version, while effecting a change of texture and the transference of expressive aims to an only partially new form.

[24] d'India's setting of another Gesualdo text, *Ecco, moriro dunque—Ahi già mi discoloro* (Book VII, 1624) suggests a similar awareness of his predecessor, though in less dramatic terms. The collection unfortunately survives minus the alto part.

Ex. 82

In the *Madrigali a cinque voci* (1638) of Domenico Mazzochi, which Einstein calls the 'last milestone' in the history of the form, Gesualdo's example lingers on. Not only does Mazzochi occasionally demonstrate his chromatic bent but he publishes his madrigals simultaneously in score and in parts and openly states his admiration for Gesualdo's notational precision. In the postscript to his *Dialoghi e Sonneti* (1638) he reinforces the connection of several of the figures mentioned above, saying that Gesualdo, Pecci, Luzzaschi, Nenna, and Macque share a common precision in the placement of accidentals. Perhaps Einstein was correct when he stated that in the history of the unaccompanied polyphonic madrigal 'Gesualdo is really an end', and that Mazzochi, for all his conscious modernity, 'retains a certain connection . . . with the ideals of the sixteenth-century madrigal; in taking leave of it, he pays it a tribute.'[25]

[25] Einstein, *The Italian Madrigal*, p. 872.

CHAPTER TEN

✒

The Sacrae Cantiones

THE only reference to any of Gesualdo's sacred works before the twentieth century is in a letter from Fontanelli to Duke Alfonso stating that the Prince had been busy writing and had composed, in addition to several madrigals, a motet and an aria.[1] Heseltine was one of the first to mention their existence, but he did not examine them and was correct in stating at that time that his fame as a composer rested entirely upon his madrigals.[2]

Gesualdo's first sacred publications were printed in 1603 in Naples by Constantino Vitali under the editorship of Giovanni Pietro Cappucio. They were two volumes of *Sacrae Cantiones*, one in five voices, the other in six and seven voices. Although Gesualdo had written three six-voiced madrigals in his third and fourth books, the *Sacrae Cantiones* in six and seven voices is his first collection to make extensive use of this texture. Both the motet volumes are entitled *Liber primus*, signifying the difference in texture between the two books. But if their titles seem to imply that they are the first of a series, there is no evidence that other such collections were ever printed.

Of the three books of Gesualdo's sacred music that were published in his lifetime—the third was a volume of Responsoria for Holy Week printed in 1611—only the book of *Sacrae Cantiones* in six and seven voices has come down to us incomplete. Four out of the six parts are preserved, but the Bassus and Sextus have been lost. This volume of motets cannot be entirely dismissed even though it is defective.[3] Certain details of harmony and melodic structure, which can be deduced from the surviving parts, do sustain or enlarge our former view of Gesualdo. But his achievement in the field of contrapuntal artifice is displayed in this collection as in no other preserved source. In two instances strict canonic procedures are indicated, and happily supply for us one of the missing parts in each case. In the motet *Da pacem* the Tenor is marked 'Canon in Diapente'; the Quintus of *Assumpta*

[1] See p. 65.   [2] Gray & Heseltine, p. 82.
[3] Published as Bd. IX of the complete works (Ugrino Verlag).

est Maria contains the marking 'Canon in Diapason et Diapente' resulting in 'ex una voce tres'. The resolution of the canon (the rhythmic distance for which is clearly given by a *signum congruentiae*) in the first instance reveals the missing Sextus part, and in the latter both Sextus and Tenor are derivable. The Tenor, however, is also written out as a *Resolutio* in its appropriate part-book. The number of missing voices in each case is thereby reduced to one, the Bassus.

In these strict canon motets a striking confirmation is discernible of Gesualdo's knowledge of the works, and workings, of the earlier masters. A survey of the sacred anthologies of the sixteenth century discloses, for example, that among the fifteen or so settings of *Da pacem* which found their way into the printed motet collections of the period, at least four involve canons: Martin Agricola, *4 voc. ex 2* (1567); Anton Brumel, *4 voc. ex 2* (1545); Pierre de la Rue, *4 voc. ex duabus* (1540); and Philip Verdelot, *4 voc. ex una* (1545). Even Josquin's (?) *Missa Da Pacem* involves strict canonic use of the same material utilized by Gesualdo. We can surmise that Gesualdo's acquaintance with the music of many of these composers came during his stay at the Este court where he had access to a renowned music library. Both Anton Brumel and Josquin had even lived in Ferrara for a period. The concept of canon either in mass or motet, especially earlier in the century, was not so extraordinary as to call for special comment; considering, however, the late date of these pieces and the fact that canon occurs nowhere else in Gesualdo's entire output, it is logical to assume that he was attracted to this technique after coming across a specific model or group of models.

One additional piece stands apart from the others in this volume. The original Index to the collection shows that the last motet, *Illumina nos*, is the only one of the set that was conceived in seven voices. Again the Bassus and Sextus are missing, but fortunately the Septima pars survives, and hence only two, instead of three, parts are lacking. It was these three pieces which are less incomplete than the others in the collection which Igor Stravinsky chose to embellish.[4]

Quite apart from Stravinsky's additions these canonic pieces are of more than routine interest because they belie Gesualdo's past reputation. Battista Doni[5] actually praised Gesualdo for not relying upon canonic technique and

---

[4] *Illumina nos* was completed in April 1957, *Da pacem* and *Assumpta est Maria* in Venice, September 1959.

[5] *Appendice a' Trattati di Musica*, Cap. XVII, 47 (not 177 as stated by Burney): 'Il Principe di Venosa per il contrario, ch'era nato propriamente per la Musica, con l'espressione di melodia poteva vestire qualsivolgia concetto, non attese ami, che si sappia a Canoni, e si fatte sofisticherie.' See p. 105 for a further discussion of the complete passage.

indicated that those who did (Soriano, for example) were forced to it out of a lack of originality.[6] While canon is more characteristically associated with the contrapuntal achievements of the *ars perfecta* composers, it is interesting to note that Romano Micheli devotes the major portion of his *Musica vaga et artificiosa* (1615) to the illustration of canonic enigmas, and that Sigismondo d'India in his motets of the same period likewise makes use of the device. The sense of *difficoltà* (a property admired by all Mannerists) as well as the quality of perfection inherent in the canonic idea may explain its occasional attractiveness to these composers.

Elsewhere in this incomplete collection pieces such as *O Oriens, splendor, Ardens est cor meum*, and *Ne derelinquas me* preserve an outline, particularly melodic and contrapuntal, sufficient to add to Gesualdo's reputation as a composer of sacred music.

Of the music that has come down to us intact, it may be observed that the book of motets in five voices appears on the surface to hark back to an earlier style of sacred polyphony.[7] Any doubt of Gesualdo's ability to manipulate the intricacies of diatonic polyphony can be quietened by a glance at these works. There are in addition occasional glimpses of the more advanced harmonic utterances of the mature composer, so that Einstein is forced to speak of 'distortions and want of style' and of places 'when the harmony becomes almost a gesture in its chromaticism and its clashes,' as in *O vos omnes*. But even he must admit that there are passages 'full of truth, depth and reverence, full of harmonic assurance and beauty, full of awareness of the expressive value of chords, both on the brilliant side and on the somber.'[8] There are few precedents in sacred music before this date for passages as harmonically expressive as the following from *Ave, dulcissima Maria*.

Ex. 83

6 Burney, *A General History of Music* (1776), p. 220, fn. g, quotes Doni and replies, 'He is, however, always struggling at fugue and imitation.'

7 The motets in five voices were first brought to the attention of the musical world in 1934 when Guido Pannain edited fourteen of the nineteen motets contained in that

Hei, mihi, Domine is a model of clarity, relying on a basically diatonic vocabulary to express the highly personal text that must have had a special meaning for the Prince of Venosa:

> Hei mihi, Domine, quia peccavi
> nimis in vita mea! Quid faciam,
> miser? ubi fugiam, nisi ad te,
> Deus meus? Miserere mei, dum
> veneris in novissimo die.
>
> (Woe is me, O Lord, because I
> have sinned greatly in my life!
> What shall I do, poor wretch? Where

---

collection: *Istituzioni e Monumenti dell'Arte Musicale Italiana*, V, pp. 221–73. It has been solely on the basis of the incomplete edition of this one volume that any information has been available concerning Gesualdo's sacred output until the recently published edition of the complete works brought out the entire sacred corpus under the editorship of the present writer (Ugrino Verlag, Bds. VII, VIII, IX, X).

[8] Einstein, *The Italian Madrigal*, p. 694.

shall I flee, except to thee,
my God? Have mercy upon me until
thou comest on the Last Day.)

The harmonic language at 'Quid faciam, miser?' is far from audacious, yet its poignancy is as keen as it is simple, and the repetition, reminiscent of the madrigals, underlines it.

Ex. 84

A comparison with a setting of the same text by Vicentino, in one of the few sacred works by him that has been preserved, illustrates the more incisive directness of Gesualdo's style as compared with Vicentino's version, which is equally contaminated with accidentals.[9]

Ex. 85

[9] Vicentino, *Opera Omnia*, p. 134, ed. H. Kaufmann.

In Gesualdo's setting a brief, contrasting fugal excursion occurs immediately to the words 'ubi fugiam nisi ad te'.

Ex. 86

and at the arrival of the text 'Miserere mei' he clears the boards with a rest in all voices as if to announce that a passage of special urgency is imminent. The simplicity of the fan-like motion of the outer voices against a dominant (fifth of the chord) in an interior voice is deceptive in its appearance. In its full context it is a cry of lamentation rarely equalled in the sixteenth century.

Ex. 87

Peccantem me quotidie contains another setting of the same text, and it is in many ways one of the most disquieting passages in all Gesualdo's music. Here the affective opening gives way to a passage of tortured chromaticism which 'offers the mind no place to rest.' This is not the breathless, short-phrased world of the late madrigal but a chromatic continuum conducive to a state of vertigo. Who knows how a future generation will hear this music—not to mention how Gesualdo's own did?

Ex. 88

The choice of texts in the volumes of *Sacrae Cantiones* is revealing. Just as his madrigals continually emphasize the images of despair, suffering, and death (both erotic and real), the motets stress their Latin counterparts. Anyone inclined to connect Gesualdo's texts, which, as Einstein says, 'consist of nothing but cries of anguish, self-accusation, and repentance,'[10] with his life will find ample evidence here. Recall the text of *Hei mihi*: 'Woe is me, o Lord, because I have sinned greatly in my life.' Consider in addition *Reminiscere miserationum tuarum*: 'Remember, o Lord my God, thy tender mercies and thy lovingkindnesses, and remember not the sins of my youth,' or *Peccantem me quotidie*: 'Because I sin daily and do not repent, the fear of death disturbs me, for in hell there is no redemption. Have mercy upon me, my God, and save me.' The ancient Lamentations text *O vos omnes*, set frequently during the sixteenth century, receives one of the most strikingly personal treatments it has ever received. It occurs twice more in the *Responsoria*, and it is significant that it is additionally set as an independent motet: 'All ye that pass by, attend and see if there be any sorrow like unto my sorrow.'

[10] Einstein, op. cit., p. 692.

Another group of texts, which may be classified as prayers of intercession, recall the altar painting of Santa Maria delle Grazie in Gesualdo. In the five-voice set four are prayers to the Virgin Mary and an equal number are addressed to her in the six-voice collection. In the latter volume there is also the All Saints motet, *Gaudeamus omnes*, as well as one for St. Francis, *Franciscus humilis et pauper*. Gesualdo's devotion to St. Francis will be remembered both from the painting and the last will and testament. Of the altar painting Einstein remarks, 'This is a painting with a secret personal content, and the same holds true for these motets; it is as though personal suffering and personal anguish sought purification, relief, and "objective" expression. This characteristic attitude stands out when we compare Gesualdo's motets with those of his Neapolitan contemporaries.'[11]

Yet one Neapolitan, Scipione Stella, member of Gesualdo's wedding cortège to Ferrara in 1594, provides a comparison for Gesualdo's motets, not so much from a point of musical style as in the matter of textual choice. Stella, who not only edited the Baldini publications of the Prince's first two books of madrigals but was also a composer himself, produced a motet collection, dedicated to Duke Alfonso II, in 1595 while he was still in Ferrara. The contents of this volume, which likewise issued from the presses of Baldini, is striking for the large number of texts which it has in common with Gesualdo's two volumes of 1603. Of the twenty motet texts utilized by Stella, Gesualdo set fourteen; four in his five-voice set and ten in his set of six and seven-voice pieces.

Stella, *Motectorum,* 1595	Gesualdo, *Sacrae Cantiones,* 1603
Verba me auribus percipe	XIII à 6
O bone Jesu, è purissime Iesu	
Sana me Domine, & sanabor	III à 6
Domine Deus meus in te speravi	
Virgo benedicta esto mihi adiutrix	I à 6
Peccantem me quotidie, et non me	X à 5
Illumina faciem tuam	XVIII à 5
Deus qui corda fidelium	
Beata es virgo Maria	
Ad te levavi animam meam	XVII à 6
Beata Mater, et intacta virgo	XVI à 6

[11] *The Italian Madrigal*, p. 692. For a comparative glance at the sacred polyphony of Mayone, Trabaci, Nenna, and others, see *Istituzioni e Monumenti*, V, ed. Pannain.

Precibus et meritis beatae Maria	XIII à 5
Sub tuum praesidium confugimus	
Veni sanctae Spiritus reple tuorum	VIII à 6
Ne derelinquas me Domine	XV à 6
Per viscera misericordiae Dei nostri	
Ave sanctissima Maria	IV à 6
Exaudi Domine vocem meam	XII à 5
O sacrum convivium	IX à 6
Adoramus te Domine Iesu Christe	X à 6

It seems clear enough that Stella's five-voice collection of 1595[12] served as an impetus, even a textual source, for Gesualdo's later motet productions. That the connection does not extend to the music is perhaps disappointing, but the fact is that parody, a technique we might be prepared to find in his motets, plays little if any part in these works. A volume of hymns by Stella (1610) does however contain a few items that will later offer a point for comparison in the discussion of Gesualdo's *Responsoria*.

We find two contrasted appraisals of Gesualdo's sacred style (based of necessity on an examination of only part of the motets *à 5* as none of the other music was available to either of them) offered by Redlich and Einstein. The former states, 'Somewhat in contrast to Monteverdi's fundamental stylistic differentiation between madrigal and religious music, no true stylistic contrast separates Gesualdo's motets and Responses from his madrigals, at most a contrast of basic tempo, which prefers the ₵ time-marking for sacred music.'[13] Einstein remarks, however, 'What is more, Gesualdo distinguished carefully between the secular and sacred styles. This is evident even in externals, for without exception his madrigals have the time-signature C and thus stand in four-four time, while the recently reprinted motets are all in the *misura di breve*. In addition to this, the freedom or fluctuation of the tempo in his madrigals is carried to an extreme, just as it is in Marenzio, though Gesualdo's unit is even smaller than Marenzio's —where Marenzio uses the half note, Gesualdo uses the quarter. Yet in the motets the uniformity of the tempo is hardly ever disturbed.'[14] Both writers are partially correct, but Einstein comes nearer the truth when he notices the mutually exclusive and absolutely consistent use of C and ₵ for madrigal and motet respectively. The usage of the former for the new *note nere*

[12] Incompletely preserved, minus Cantus, in the British Museum.
[13] Redlich, article on 'Gesualdo' in *Music in Geschichte und Gegenwart*.
[14] *The Italian Madrigal*, p. 692.

madrigal, as early as Arcadelt, had signalled an important stylistic development. Glareanus tells us that the C-sign connotes a somewhat slower tactus than ₵ when used for an entire piece.[15] This was useful for the madrigal, where greater latitude in matters of tempo was required because of the considerable emphasis placed upon contrasts between fast and slow motion, frequently within a short space of time. By adopting a slightly slower tactus, the *note nere* sections could maintain their relatively quicker pace without undue strain upon the fabric of the music. In the more even tempo and textured music of the motet, this need was less felt, and the C-sign thus reflects not only a consideration of tempo but also a greater uniformity of texture.[16] But just as there are madrigals that show little of this contrast, there are, conversely, motets which make use of the idea, and in Gesualdo's strongest harmonic passages he invariably uses the texture and tempo of madrigal practice, namely the homophonic adagio. The distinction between motet and madrigal often resides rather in the absence of an ensuing tempo change in the motets, while textural contrast remains typical. But, although far less commonly, even the tempo may change with the texture, as in the madrigals. The examples illustrating the texts 'Quid faciam, miser' and the ensuing 'ubi fugiam nisi ad te' illustrate this possibility (Exx. 84, 86).

The larger formal schemes of the *Sacrae Cantiones* vary, but Robert Craft accurately classifies them into two general types: 'The first of these is the "sacred song" of uninterrupted polyphony in which, straight through, rectilinearly, and with hardly a silent beat, a simple motive and one or more subsidiary motives are developed. . . . The second form is more sectional. It begins homophonically, goes on to a longer polyphonic section, and concludes by repeating either the first or the second sections, but with significant changes.'[17] The through-composed form is far more common, while there are also pieces involving exact repetition schemes. In the book of motets *à* 5 we can observe Gesualdo's favourite pattern of the madrigals, ABB, the two B sections being absolutely identical in pieces such as *Ave, dulcissima Maria, O vos omnes*, and *Precibus et meritis beatae Mariae*.

In spite of certain audacious harmonic passages that have been cited, Gesualdo's sacred music tends to be more diatonic than his secular. At the same time this diatonic language occasionally incorporates a concentration of dissonances worthy of the most advanced madrigals. The following passage from Gesualdo's *O Crux benedicta* is illustrative.

[15] Glareanus, *Dodecachordon* (Basel, 1547), III, viii, quoted in Sachs, *Rhythm and Tempo*, p. 223.
[16] James Haar, 'The *Note Nere* Madrigal,' *JAMS*, XVIII, 1 (1965), pp. 22–41.
[17] Gesualdo–Stravinsky, *Tres Sacrae Cantiones* (London, 1960), Preface by Robert Craft.

Ex. 89

As the long-note cantus firmus had been virtually abandoned by Gesualdo's time, it is not surprising that it is rarely encountered in his works. There are only three works in his entire sacred output which make a clear and marked use of this procedure. Two of them are in the *Sacrae Cantiones* for six voices, and predictably are the ones involving canons, the *Da pacem* and the *Assumpta est Maria*. Indeed, it is the cantus firmus itself which is subjected to canonic treatment. The sole example in the *Responsoria* is to be found in *Astiterunt reges* (Sabbato Sancto, VII). Additional evidence of reliance upon Gregorian materials in a paraphrase fashion is sparse, but in a few instances the opening motif of a motet suggests the chant associated with its text. Gesualdo's approach to the motet, inherited from the High Renaissance but at the same time reflecting the new expressive power won in the realm of the madrigal, provides a significant rapprochement between the speech of these two worlds.

SACRAE CANTIONES à 5 v.

1. Ave, Regina coelorum			Not LU 1864
2. Venit lumen tuum	An ★	Epiphany, 2nd Vesp.	LU 463; AR 312
3. Ave, dulcissima Maria			
4. Reminiscere miserationum tuarum	In ★	Lent, 2nd Sun., Mass	LU 545; GR 111
5. Dignare me, laudare te	Ve		AM 1181, 1182
6. Domine, corda nostra			
7. Domine, ne despicias			
8. Hei mihi, Domine	Re ★	Off. Dead, Matins	LU 1791; AR 165
9. Laboravi in gemitu meo			
10. Peccantem me quotidie	Re ★	Off. Dead, Matins	LU 1797; AR 171
11. O vos omnes	An AV SR Re	Holy Sat. (M, L); Sept. 15	LU 737, 1634v, 1632, 727
12. Exaudi, Deus deprecationem	Ps	Wednesday at Compline	LU 294; AR 144
13. Precibus et meritis beatae Mariae			
14. O Crux benedicta	An	Sept. 15; Feast Dolours	LU 1631; AR 839
15. Tribularer si nescirem			
16. Deus refugium			
17. Tribulationem et dolorem inveni			
18. Illumina faciem tuam	Com ★	Septuagesima Sunday, Mass	LU 501; GR 76
19. Maria, mater gratiae	Va	Marian Hymn	LU 1863

SACRAE CANTIONES à 6 e 7 v.

1. Virgo benedicta			
2. Da pacem Domine	Va ★★	For Peace	LU 1867; AR 144*
3. Sana me Domine			
4. Ave sanctissima Maria			
5. O Oriens splendor	An ★	Gr. Ant., Dec. 21	LU 342; AR 236
6. Discedite a me omnes			
7. Gaudeamus omnes	In	Mass, Nov. 1; All Sts.	LU 1724; GR 647
8. Veni Creator Spiritus			
9. O sacrum convivium	An	Corpus Chr.; 2nd Vesp.	LU 959; AR 98* 535
10. Adoramus te Christe	SR	May 3 at Sext.	LU 1458; AR 703
11. Veni sponsa Christi	An ★	Common of Virgins, 1st Vesp.	LU 262[8], 1209; AR 577[20]
12. Assumpta est Maria	An ★★	Aug. 15, 2nd Vesp.	LU 1605; AR 822
13. Verba mea	AV, In		GR 395, 312
14. Ardens est cor meum	An		AR 466
15. Ne derelinquas me	In		GR 118 (not LU 302, An)
16. O Beata Mater			
17. Ad te levavi	In	Mass, 1st Sun. Advent	LU 318; GR 1
18. Franciscus humilis	AV	Mass, Sept. 17	LU 1643; GR 602
19. O anima sanctissima			
20. Illumina nos	An		AR 327

ABBREVIATIONS

Sources

AM	*Antiphonale Monasticum pro diurnis horis,* Desclée et Socii, 1934.
AR	*Antiphonale Sacrosanctae Romanae Ecclesiae,* Desclée et Socii, 1949.
GR	*Graduale Sancrosanctae Romae Ecclesiae,* Desclée et Socii, 1948.
LU	*Liber Usualis Missae et Officii pro Dominicis et Festis,* Desclée et Socii, 1942.

Category of Chant

An	Antiphon	In	Introit	SR	Short Response
AV	Alleluia Verse	Ps	Psalm	Va	Varia
Hy	Hymn	Re	Responsory	Ve	Versicle

Other Symbols

★★ Chant extensively quoted ★ Chant incipit suggested

CHAPTER ELEVEN

❧

The Responsoria

Form and Style: Liturgical Backgrounds

ALTHOUGH Gesualdo's character as a composer has until recently been known to us only from his madrigals, the somewhat larger view now afforded by the knowledge of his sacred works and two instrumental pieces does not materially affect our picture of him as a composer working within the framework of the older forms. The madrigal he inherited from a line of distinguished predecessors from Festa and Arcadelt to Rore and Marenzio, and the motet in its various guises had had an even longer history. Yet neither the madrigal nor the motet implied a rigid formal design. The madrigal could change its shape for expressive purposes, and this same quality infused the motet also with a new life at a moment when it might otherwise have outlived its usefulness.

While the response may be classified as a motet, it is the only one of the main categories for which Gesualdo wrote which had a fixed design, an aBcB scheme in which aB represents the Response proper and c the Versus. Not that Gesualdo resisted repetition in the other forms of madrigal and motet. But their appeal for him as expressive vehicles stemmed largely from their formal flexibility and their textual variety. That his style does not crumble under the rigid schematic restrictions of the Responsoria is therefore of special interest.

Because Gesualdo's forms were inherited, previous historical assessments of his music have tended to place him with the Renaissance and to see him as a figure whose daring harmonies, strange and imaginative as they were, nevertheless led to a dead end and ultimately vanished without influence upon the ensuing Baroque. Einstein, for example, can say that his music was 'not based upon clear harmonic perception and hence not fully absorbed by the main stream of development.'[1] But it is fair to suggest that this feeling is conditioned by the contention that the madrigal as a form effectively

---

[1] Einstein, *A Short History of Music*, p. 60.

perished with the emergence of the Baroque,[2] and by the failure to trace harmonic expansion and textural contrast into the following century.

Gesualdo's lack of influence is attributed by Redlich largely to formal considerations:

> The limited effect in the seventeenth century which was the lot of Gesualdo's chromatic experiments which finally ended up a blind alley, is explained by the intensely, increasingly hostile mien of the composer towards the basso continuo and the instrumentally accompanied monody around 1600 . . . Gesualdo's obstinate concentration on the 5-voice unaccompanied madrigals and the unaccompanied motets, at a time which embraced instrumentally accompanied monody and the dramatic cantata, is alone responsible for the all too short span of influence which was allotted to his music.[3]

This is not a totally unfair assessment; indeed, if influence is to be judged in terms of the quantity of later music which sounds like Gesualdo, it could be argued that he was one of the least influential composers in history. On the other hand we should guard against the tendency to see connections only within the framework of a particular genre, and to attribute importance only to music which engenders a repertoire of copies. It may require a degree of imagination to establish a chain of influence between the intense expressivity of Gesualdo's madrigals and the dramatic qualities of the secular Italian cantata or the accompanied solo madrigal.[4] But while Gesualdo did not write in these forms, and did not pour his ideas into moulds which at this distance we have come to call 'baroque', this did not prevent observers such as della Valla, Doni, or Kircher from seeing his true import in relation to Seicento developments.[5] The drama of Gesualdo's music, whether it be the personal drama of his madrigals impregnated with love, death, and guilt, or the not-so-impersonal drama of the Passion motets, may be less Baroque for not having been cast as opera and oratorio respectively. Yet the essential quality stems not from external form but from internal speech. Gesualdo was absorbed by the dramatic potential of music, and the fact that he did not write in any of the new dramatic forms (we have evidence which suggests that he may have written in the new solo style, but nothing has been preserved) shows only that his formal preferences did not change. His sense of contrast, his unprepared dissonances, his intense chromaticism,

[2] An unwarranted one in any case. Cf. Gloria Rose, 'Polyphonic Italian Madrigals of the seventeenth century,' *Music and Letters*, XLVII (1966), p. 153.

[3] Article on 'Gesualdo' in *MGG*, V, p. 44.

[4] See Palisca's *Baroque Music*, pp. 48–50, for a discussion of the influence of Gesualdo upon Sigismondo d'India's solo madrigal style.   [5] See Chapter 13, pp. 299–301.

and his visionary harmonic flights, however, point to the seventeenth century and beyond.

In his *Responsoria* for Holy Week, however, there are several factors that demand consideration apart from the larger questions of period style. Though the responsory form itself was inherited and had shown signs of an increasing popularity as a motet form during the sixteenth century, the liturgical responsory cycle had not been frequently set. Compositional solutions to problems of larger musical designs had been faced relatively early in the fifteenth century in the Mass Ordinary, but the large cycles of Mass Propers and Hymns for the church year, were not set until the early sixteenth century in the works of Isaac and Festa respectively.[6] In the Holy Week repertoire the two Petrucci collections of Lamentations of 1506 are not sufficiently systematic or complete to qualify as true cycles. Morales was one of the first, if not the first, so to set the Lamentation cycle, toward the middle of the century.[7]

Complete settings are more frequently encountered during the second half of the century, and Palestrina composed not one but four Lamentation cycles. The Tenebrae Responsoria cycle has a close and intimate connection with the Lamentation group, for the Lamentation texts comprise the first three lessons of the first Nocturne for each of the last three days of Holy Week. The Responsoria follow not only the first three, but all nine of the lessons which make up the hour of Matins, and this holds true for Maundy Thursday, Good Friday, and Holy Saturday (the Latin designations are *Feria Quinta*, *Feria Sexta*, and *Sabbato Sancto* respectively). With nine response texts on each of these days, a complete cycle comprises twenty-seven responses. Composers have frequently set two additional items belonging to Tenebrae. They are the Canticle of Zachary, *Benedictus Dominus Deus Israel*, which closes Lauds, and Psalm L, *Miserere mei Deus*, which opens it on each of the three days.

With the exception of Bernardo Pisano's creations of *c.* 1520,[8] the first

---

[6] This is not meant to ignore the formidable achievements in the field of Proper settings in the early history of polyphony.

[7] For a transcription and discussion of Morales' Lamentations see the author's *Three Books of Polyphonic Lamentations of Jeremiah, 1549–1564* (Ph.D. dissertation, University of Rochester, 1953).

[8] Eighteen responses for Tenebrae by Pisano have survived, and there is reason to believe that he composed the remaining nine for use on Maundy Thursday as well, making his contribution exceptional not only for its date but because of its completeness. Cf. F. d'Accone, 'Bernardo Pisano, An Introduction to His Life and Works' in *Musica Disciplina*, XVII (1963), pp. 131–4. The music may be found in *Music of the Florentine Renaissance*, vol. 1: Bernardo Pisano, *Collected Works*, CMM (1966), ed. by F. d'Accone.

Holy Week responsory cycles were attempted shortly after the mid-point
of the sixteenth century, though the large number of twenty-seven responses
kept most composers from achieving a complete set. Even abbreviated cycles
were relatively rare. They include Victoria's Holy Week volume of 1572,
with a group of Responses often designated as a complete cycle but actually
containing only eighteen such pieces. There are also cycles by Paolo
Ferrarese (1565), Ruffo (1586), Ingegneri (1588), Zallamella (1590), Camillo
Lambardi (1592), Scipione Dentice (1593), Mauro Panormitano (1599),
Pomponio Nenna (1607; 1622), Lodovico Viadana (1609), and Marco da
Gagliano (1630).

Potentially the service of Tenebrae is one of the most dramatic of the
entire church year. The rubric for the service reads: 'At the end of each
Psalm of Matins and of Lauds, one of the fifteen candles is extinguished on
the triangular candlestick before the altar, the candle at the top being left
lighted.'[9] And by the end of the service each evening, 'fourteen of the candles
of the triangular candlestick having been extinguished as has already been
explained, the one at the top of the triangle alone remains lighted. During
the Canticle *Benedictus* the six candles on the altar are likewise extinguished
one by one, from each side alternately, at every second verse, so that by the
last verse all are extinguished. All other lights and lamps in the church are
also put out. During the repetition of the Antiphon *Traditor* the lighted
candle is taken from the top of the candlestick and hidden behind the altar
at the Epistle side.' The prayer *Respice, quaesumus Domine* follows. 'At the
end of this Prayer, a noise is made by knocking on the stalls of the choir
until the lighted candle re-appears from behind the altar. All then rise and
retire in silence.'[10]

The unimpassioned directions recited here cannot conceal the drama
inherent in this ritual. As the service abounds in texts of great poignancy
and beauty, it would be natural to assume that composers throughout the
period would have responded with their most powerful vision and highest
emotional tone. The typical reaction, somewhat at odds with these expecta-
tions, will be discussed presently. As this music is destined for use at one
of the most important celebrations at that time in the church year, two
questions should be discussed first: (1) what restrictions of musical language
were implicit in the composition of sacred works, particularly in light of the
just concluded Council of Trent (1545–64), and (2) what further precedents
existed regarding an appropriate style for Holy Week?

[9] *Liber Usualis* (Tournai, 1952), p. 621.
[10] Ibid., pp. 652–3.

Tridentine Ideals and Post-Council Practice

The first point demands a consideration of the role of music in relation to the Counter-Reformation, a question which has only recently been clarified. The mythology that had grown up around these events is well known. We are told how polyphonic music was almost abandoned by the church in the deliberations of the Council of Trent in its last years; how Palestrina or Kerle or other worthy figures composed music so sublime that the hearts of the ruling fathers were melted and church polyphony was saved; how, having finally admitted the continuance of polyphony, the attempt to define an appropriate musical style emphasized a clear and correct declamation of the text.

There are several pieces of musical evidence which corroborate the view that some heed was paid to the last-mentioned requirement of the Council, even that the suggestion constituted an admonition to composers to restrict themselves to the homophonic and syllabic styles in their task of providing a fitting declamation for the text. Vincenzo Ruffo, who accepted the appointment as *maestro* at the Cathedral in Milan in 1563 (the last year of the Council of Trent and the one in which the most important considerations relating to music took place), was one of the key figures in this question. Stationed in Milan, his association with Carlo Borromeo was natural enough. Borromeo, although Archbishop of Milan, spent a large portion of his career in Rome, particularly during the Tridentine years, supervising the work of reform, acting as secretary to his uncle Pope Pius IV, and through his personal example serving as a guiding light to many during these problematic times. This important figure, who was Carlo Gesualdo's uncle, has been described by Pastor:[11]

> It was not, however, only by his decrees that Borromeo exercised an incalculable influence upon the future. . . . The Council of Trent had laid upon the bishop and placed in his hands the whole work of restoring the Church. It was therefore of an importance that can never be over-rated that in the Cardinal of Milan a man was given to the Church who showed by his own example how the decrees of the Council ought to be carried out in practice, and how much could be accomplished by their full application. That which at first sight appears to be a dead letter in its prescriptions, becomes a living reality in the work of Borromeo. He is the model of a Tridentine bishop, in whom the Council becomes a thing of flesh and blood.

[11] Pastor, *The History of the Popes*, XXI, p. 86.

He had gone to Rome only in 1560 and his rise in the papal hierarchy had been meteoric. On 22 January he was named papal Secretary of State; on 31 January he was elevated to cardinal, and on 22 February he was appointed Archbishop of Milan *in absentia*.

His continuing relation with Milan, particularly with reference to the musical scene there, has been detailed in an important study which cites two highly relevant letters from Borromeo to Monsignor Ormaneto in Milan written on 20 January and 31 March 1565.[12] The first emphasized a Tridentine precept soon to be familiar: 'I would like you to speak to the master of the chapel there and tell him to reform the singing so that the words may be as intelligible as possible, as you know is ordered by the Council . . .' But the second contains a surprise: 'I shall await Ruffo's Mass; and if Don Nicola [Vicentino] who favours chromatic music should be in Milan you can also ask him to compose one—thus by the comparison of the work of many excellent musicians we will better be able to judge this intelligible music.'

We know that Ruffo brought out a collection of masses in 1570 subtitled *Concinate ad Ritum Concilii Mediolani*, another set of four '*novamente composte seconda la forma del Concilio Tridentino*' in 1580 and in 1592 the *Missae Borromeae*; all were written with the intention of pleasing Rome in its search for works which avoided secular models or technical display and allowed the text to be heard with perfect clarity.[13]

Of greater interest is the reference in Borromeo's letter of 31 March to the solicitation of a mass in a chromatic style by Vicentino. This casts a new light on the views that Borromeo in particular (and by inference the Church as a whole) held in relation to the kind of music which might satisfy the requirements of the council. As Lockwood has put it, 'In 1565 it must have been perfectly well known to Borromeo, as to any musically literate person, that Vicentino heralded the most progressive, indeed radical advances in contemporary music. Certainly Borromeo was aware of Vicentino's point of view, for he specifically calls him "don Nicola della musica Cromatica".'[14] While Lockwood is not willing to conclude decisively that 'the cardinal foresaw the possibility of receiving a Mass composed in the chromatic manner,' recalling Vicentino's sharp attack a decade before on irreverent sacred music, there is no reason to think the possibility at all unlikely. The chromatic manner by its very nature tends towards the homophonic, at most lightly polyphonic style, and the introduction of chromaticism would in no

[12] Lewis H. Lockwood, 'Vincenzo Ruffo and Musical Reform after the Council of Trent,' *MQ* (1957), XLIII, pp. 348–9. The translations of the letters are by Lockwood.
[13] Reese, *Music in the Renaissance*, p. 490.   [14] Lockwood, op. cit., p. 350.

way, as Borromeo undoubtedly understood, stand in the way of a careful declamation of the text, the principle at the heart of the Tridentine reform. In saying 'thus by the comparison of the work of many excellent musicians we will better be able to judge this intelligible music,' Borromeo seems to suggest that the precept of clarity might well be in keeping with several different modes of musical expression.[15]

Unfortunately there is no evidence that Vicentino ever wrote any masses at all, and it may be questioned whether or not Borromeo's invitation was ever extended to him. Such a mass, had it ever been written or had it survived, would provide an extremely interesting document. There is one piece of sacred polyphony from the pen of this same Vicentino that suggests the style which such a Mass might have adopted. Interestingly it is also a Tenebrae text, a setting of the cry 'Jerusalem, convertere ad Dominum Deum tuum.' Appearing initially in Vicentino's *L'antica musica* of 1555, its intensely chromatic style is unprecedented in sacred music before this time.[16]

The possibility of a chromatic style in keeping with the Tridentine injunctions casts a new light upon Gesualdo's *Responsoria*. While it is possible to argue that at this time the 'courts were steadily becoming the arenas of progressive musical activities, in sharp contrast to the strongholds of conservatism maintained by the Church in matters musical,'[17] Borromeo's pronouncement and his nephew's creations suggest that this view is in need of at least partial modification. On the surface it might appear that Gesualdo's *Responsoria*, and even certain of the *Sacrae Cantiones*, are the result of an approach too personal to reflect adequately the demands of the corporate Church. It has even been suggested that an affective approach to sacred music is contrary to the ideal of the church before the Baroque.[18] If this is so, then we must recognize that the sparks of the Baroque had already been ignited in the Age of Mannerism.

What Borromeo hinted at in relation to music he also stated with reference to architecture. He was in fact the only person to apply the Tridentine decrees to the problem of architecture, and in his *Instructiones Fabricae et Supellectilis Ecclestiasticae* of 1572 he concerned himself in considerable detail with the problems of church building. 'The book centres

---

[15] It can additionally be argued that if Ruffo's response to the injunctions of the council were considered models, they proved to be relatively ineffective in influencing others to embrace this simple style, and it will be remembered that Ruffo himself ultimately abandoned it as a too restricted, unpliable formula.

[16] See H. Kaufmann, 'The Motets of Nicola Vicentino' in *Musica Disciplina*, 15 (1961), 167–85. Note especially the motet *Heu mihi Domine* in Vicentino's *Opera Omnia*, ed. by Kaufmann, p. 133, in light of the discussion of Gesualdo's setting of the same text in this book, pp. 248–9.

[17] Redlich, *Monteverdi*, p. 46.   [18] Einstein, *The Italian Madrigal*, p. 692.

around one idea which is typical of the Counter-Reformation and which was to be of even greater significance in the seventeenth century: that the Church itself and the services held in it must be as dignified and as *impressive* as possible, so that their splendour and their religious character may force themselves even on the casual spectator.'[19] The astute Borromeo seizes upon a singularly potent weapon when he encourages both music and architecture to espouse what he refers to as an ancient tradition of ecclesiastical splendour and demands that musicians, architects, and priests shall combine to promote it. It is not enough to act out an Order of Worship, which has been prescribed, ordered, and made canonical; the Act of Worship must be made to glow with an emotional zeal that will enrapture (hence, capture) the heart of man. The approaches to Reason engendered by Humanism and adopted by the Reformation are to be dissolved in a spiritual and mystical experience. The arts made an enormous contribution by accepting a major share of this responsibility together with other prominent agents such as the Jesuits and the Oratory. It is fascinating that Gesualdo's great-uncle, Pope Pius IV, was one of the early figures to support this movement.

Seen in this light Gesualdo's sacred music, and especially the *Responsoria et alia ad officium hebdomadae sanctae spectantia*, if not a pure product of the Counter-Reformation spirit is more than marginally indebted to it. In the intimate climate of Gesualdo's *Responsoria*, we are impressed by a sense of personal involvement that is in harmony not only with the dicta of Borromeo and the interior agonies of Ignatius, but also with the predominating individuality characteristic of the tortured spirit of the late Mannerist genius. By 'late' Mannerist I mean to distinguish the products of figures like Gesualdo and El Greco from their earlier Mannerist counterparts, who had stressed elegance, stylishness, difficulty, and a preference for the arcane over matters of emotional content. There is no doubt that the late Mannerist still qualifies as Mannerist through his retention of earlier Mannerist gestures, but to them he has now added a spiritual power and depth of expression that are antipathetical to the central movement. If a semblance of anxiety and tortured expression can be spotted in the mainstream of Mannerism, this hyper-emotionalism is very frequently no more than contrivance, not the inward reflection of genuine feeling. The outward manner of El Greco and Gesualdo is Mannerist; the inner spirit is already becoming Baroque in its expressive power.[20]

[19] Anthony Blunt, *Artistic Theory in Italy, 1450–1600* (Oxford, 1956), p. 126.
[20] John Shearman, *Mannerism* (London, 1967), 174–5.

Renaissance Traditions of Holy Week Polyphony

In view of the inherent drama of the service as well as the textual poignancy of the Lamentations and Holy Week Responsoria, it is not difficult to understand why Gesualdo, or any late Renaissance composer, would have been attracted to the writing of Tenebrae polyphony. Yet, paradoxically, there had been no precedent for Tenebrae music of a highly emotional tone. A perusal of Lamentation items from the late fifteenth century (Petrucci published two volumes of Lamentations in 1506 with contributions by Agricola, de Orto, Tinctoris, Werbecke, Tromboncino, etc.)[21] to the mid-sixteenth century discloses a decided preference for studied simplicity. In an earlier investigation of Lamentations, I determined that Gardano, Fevin, Sermisy, La Rue, Carpentras, Festa, Arcadelt and Morales advanced little from the conservative Lamentation style of the Petrucci anthologies.[22] Only Crequillon introduced a more active polyphony to any great extent. Of note, too, is the unadventurous use of accidentals in this often homophonic, at most slightly polyphonic music. The adoption of an uncomplicated texture in relation to contrapuntal as well as harmonic matters marks this repertoire as traditionally solemn and grave.

This is true for the entire liturgies of Holy Week and Lent. Schrade has remarked how strange it is that such plaintive exclamations as the *O vos omnes* ('All ye that pass by, behold and see if there be any sorrow like unto my sorrow')

> did not at once call forth an echo as piercing as the original voice. In fact, the echo was late in forthcoming, whether it issued from the Improperia, the Lamentations, or the Passion; and well it may be that the liturgical restrictions imposed by the mournful season prevented the musician from matching his force of expression with the force of the theme. . . . During the whole period of the Renaissance, then, the very theme which like none other was fraught with pathos failed to find commensurate expression for reasons other than artistic, yet not for want of masterly minds.[23]

Even Rore, the composer of affective madrigals, is no more than an uninvolved commentator in his Passion. Outside the Holy Week liturgical

[21] A modern edition of most of this material appears in *Mehrstimmige Lamentationen aus der ersten Hälfte des 16. Jahrhunderts*, ed. by Günther Massenkeil (Mainz, 1965).

[22] Glenn E. Watkins, *Three Books of Polyphonic Lamentations of Jeremiah, 1549–1564* (Ph.D. dissertation, University of Rochester, 1953; Univ. of Rochester Microcard Press, 1954).

[23] Schrade, *Tragedy in the Art of Music* (Harvard, 1964), pp. 94–5.

cycles, however, in the occasional motet dealing with the subject of Christ's suffering, the Renaissance composer retrieved his capacity to mirror the pathos of the text. Yet Gesualdo reveals his most acutely expressive nature not in the individual motet but in the *Responsoria pro hebdomadae sanctae*.

Among the composers of Holy Week response cycles Camillo Lambardi (1592), Scipione Dentice (1593),[24] Pomponio Nenna (1607; reprinted 1622), and Marco da Gagliano (1630) share a distinct personal link with Gesualdo as contemporary Neapolitans. The *Responsoria* of Lambardi and da Gagliano, however, contribute little toward a new climate for Tenebrae, and only the former, by virtue of its date, could have been known to Gesualdo before he composed his own *Responsoria*. The one composer of the group who might have served as a model is the Neapolitan Nenna.[25] But even here we feel Gesualdo's greater personal commitment, and witness the potential confusion between 'the sufferings of the dying Christ (and) those of the composer himself. We sense that Gesualdo, the creator of those endless pleasure-pains in his madrigals, has seized here upon the ultimate vehicle for self-flagellation.'[26] The knowledge of his personal life which makes this picture plausible is also paradoxically in harmony with the Jesuit injunction for the artist not only to participate in the re-enactment of the scenes of the Passion but also to sense these horrors himself.[27]

Gesualdo's settings of *O vos omnes* undoubtedly would have satisfied Schrade's call for a musical statement as piercing as the original text. At the very outset of the response it will be noticed, however, that the introduction of the pathetic quality is in no way at variance with the Tridentine proclamations favouring textual lucidity.

[24] Dentice's cycle, which is chronologically well placed as a potential influence, I have not examined.

[25] There are two complete settings of Tenebrae responses by Nenna, both of which appeared posthumously in 1622. *Istituzioni e Monumenti*, V, ed. Pannain, contains a few items from the five-voice collection. The four-voice set presents a double cycle, one for Christmas as well as Easter. Gaetano Gaspari in his *Catalogo della Biblioteca del Liceo musicale di Bologna*, vol. II (1893), p. 136, states: 'Fin dal 1607 cominciaronsi a veder musiche del Nenna, trovandosi in detto anno impressi da Gio. Battista Sottile in Napoli dei *Responsorii di Natale et di Settimana Santa a 4 voci*.' This implies an earlier edition from a different press for the four-voice collection; both of the 1622 editions issued from Ottavio Beltrano, Naples. Although I am not aware of an extant copy of this 1607 edition, the existence of a Holy Week cycle by Nenna published prior to Gesualdo's set suggests further stylistic connections between these two figures. From what I have been able to determine from my own scorings of the four-voice responses, however, it appears that they are much simpler and less well developed than Gesualdo's.

[26] Einstein, *The Italian Madrigal*, p. 694.

[27] Blunt, *Artistic Theory*, p. 136.

Ex. 90

Most of the harmonic trademarks of Gesualdo's mature style appear in the *Responsoria* though they are somewhat more diatonic than the late madrigals. Compared to the *Sacrae Cantiones*, however, the *Responsoria* are more consistently chromatic and utilize a more uniformly colourful harmonic vocabulary. At the outset of the above example the cross-relation D–D♯ in two different voices as well as the series of harmonic third relationships are typically Gesualdine. Chromatic melodic inflection occurs later in the piece at 'sicut dolor meus' in a highly expressive manner, together with a cadential pattern often found in Gesualdo's madrigals.

Ex. 91

The similarity between Gesualdo's five-voice motet and six-voice response on this same text is notable, particularly at the opening and close (the final thirteen bars of both are identical). Of greater interest, however, is a setting by Scipione Stella, Neapolitan organist at the Annunziata from 1583 to 1593, whose motet collection of 1595 we have considered earlier. Stella's *O vòs omnes*[28] appeared in his *Hymnorum ecclesiasticorum* of 1610, while Gesualdo's two settings appeared in 1603 and 1611. The question of precedence aside, a comparison of the opening of either of Gesualdo's pieces with Stella's will disclose conspicuous similarities; likewise Stella's treatment of the words 'si est dolor' at bar 33 recalls the six-five dissonance in Gesualdo's *Hei mihi Domine* at 'Miserere mei' (Ex. 87, bar 37). The opening of the *Stabat mater*

---

[28] Printed in *Istituzioni e Monumenti*, V, pp. li–liii. I have scored additional hymns from this collection and find many of great beauty and simplicity. Further indication of Stella's progressive nature is suggested by his ownership of an archicembalo, which he undoubtedly played; cf. Doni, *Compendio del Trattato* (1635), 5, 20.

which also appears in this hymn collection leaves little doubt that further investigation of Stella's works should prove rewarding. Together, the works of Stella, Nenna, and Macque have much to tell us, not only about the activities of a Neapolitan school at this time, but in particular about its contribution to the late Mannerist style. While there have been a few pilot studies,[29] the need for further work is acute.

Form and Tonality

The sudden rhythmic contrasts characteristic of Gesualdo's madrigals appear as well in the *Responsoria*, but the formal schema of the responses, *aBcB*, also offers opportunity for contrast in larger blocks. Most frequently this is achieved not so much through changes of tempo but through alternations in density to an extent not encountered in his madrigals. There are examples of a relatively unrelieved use of six voices throughout an entire piece, but this is quite rare. More often we see some reduction in the number of voices in the versus, *c*, in relation to the number employed in B. The opening *a* may utilize the same or a lesser number of voices than B, never more; that is, the B section invariably employs the densest texture. There are occasional examples of Response-Versus-Response with no sub-division of the Response into *aB*, such as *Caligaverunt oculi mei*, as well as others which disclose a fuller pattern, *aBcBa*, like *Ecce quomodo* and *Sepulto Domino*.

The contrast in densities is paralleled by tonal contrasts which similarly highlight the schematic formulae. Considering the strong urge toward having the same tonality at the beginning and end of a madrigal, it might be expected that Gesualdo would do likewise within the considerably more rigid responsory design. Surprisingly, he does not do so with any degree of consistency. Of the nine pieces for *Feria Quinta* five begin and end on the same tonal level; only three do so in *Feria Sexta*, and the same number in *Sabbato Sancto*. The overall percentage is too small to be considered a working principle.

While Gesualdo does not completely ignore all tonal considerations in the *Responsoria*, he often takes delight in contrasting adjacent formal units

[29] *Istituzioni e Monumenti dell'Arte Musicale Italiana*, vol. V: *L'Oratorio e la Scuola Musicale di Napoli*, ed. by Guido Pannain (Ricordi, 1934); Joseph Burns, *Early Neapolitan Keyboard Music* (Ph.D. dissertation, Harvard Univ., 1953); Roland Jackson, *The Keyboard Music of Giovanni Maria Trabaci* (Ph.D. dissertation, Univ. of California, 1964). Studies in progress on Macque by Shindle (Indiana University) and on Nenna and the Gesualdo circle by Larson (Harvard University) should illuminate the scene considerably.

through highly dramatic choices of key. Even in the *Vinea mea electa*, for example, where the tonal level of beginning and end is the same, we can observe his penchant for such contrasts. Here the normal response pattern is extended to *aBcBa*, and the opening and closing key level for each section is:

$$
\begin{array}{ccccc}
a & B & c & B & a \\
\hline
\text{F–F} & \text{D–G} & \text{g–D} & \text{D–G} & \text{F–F}
\end{array}
$$

The strongest contrasts occur between the opening *a* and *B* and at the return from *B* to *a* at the end. Otherwise, the relationship of beginning and end of the interior sections is confined to the opposite mode or the dominant (this is not to imply that no other key levels are suggested internally). The following patterns suggest the variety of tonal contrasts Gesualdo achieves elsewhere.

	a	B	c	B
Velum templi:	B♭/g–D	F–D	A–A	F–D
Jerusalem, surge:	G–A	e–E	e–C	e–E
Recessit pastor:	e–E	e–G	a–C♯	e–G

While it is apparent that Gesualdo understands the strength of the dominant and relative minor relationships and uses them frequently, in the *Responsoria* he feels little compulsion to make each piece a self-contained tonal unit. Tonality is not required to contribute to a quality of conclusiveness in the manner demanded by the single motet or madrigal. The feeling of tonal suspension or inconclusiveness is not only appropriate to the open-ended character of the responsory cycle but is in keeping with its function. In this regard it will be noticed, however, that the last piece, the ninth, for each of the three days always begins and ends in the same key, hence providing the necessary note of finality.

Text, Texture, and Figuration

While the potential of tempo contrast is neither so consistently nor so radically employed in the *Responsoria* as his secular works, there are never-theless some striking instances as in the versus of *Astiterunt reges* at the text 'et populi meditati sunt inania?' ('why have the people devised vain things?') or at a similar spot in the final response *Sepulto Domino* at the text 'petierunt illum.' Invariably such usage springs from the text and is akin to the familiar procedures of the madrigalist. A single passage from one of the most familiar texts, *Tristis est anima mea*, will illustrate the point and at the same time allow a reassessment of a statement made by Einstein regarding what he saw as a difference in the attitudes of Nenna and Gesualdo. Speaking of Gesualdo's greater involvement with his textual subject, he concludes,

> This is evident above all in his renunciation of all external, visual appeals to the imagination, of all that his time considered 'picturesque,' a trait in which he differs from Nenna who, to retain the same example (*Tristis est anima mea*) sets the word *fuga* as a 'fuga' in the reproach of Jesus, at *Vos fugam capietis*. . . . He failed to experience—or else ignored —the graphic or visual components. Gesualdo . . . as a member of the high nobility had received the education of his class and had undoubtedly read and understood Vincenzo Galilei's mocking diatribes against 'eye-music' and other forms of symbolism. In all his work there is hardly a single example of this sort.[30]

Einstein, not knowing the *Responsoria* of Gesualdo (although he knew *of* them) unwittingly chose an unfortunate example. At the text 'Vos fugam' (Ex. 92) Gesualdo not only illustrates the text with a 'fuga', but does so in a way that makes Nenna's word-painting seem anaemic by comparison (Ex. 93).

Ex. 92

<hr />

[30] *The Italian Madrigal*, pp. 694–5.

Note in addition to the scurrying figure at 'fugam' the snare laid at the end of the phrase on the word 'capietis' in a frenetic rhythmic stretto, and compare this with Nenna's treatment.

Ex. 93

Even Lassus' setting of the same passage (Ex. 94), singled out by Schrade as an example of the poignant tone of which the late Renaissance composer was capable, is still heavily reliant upon the gestures of the old *ars perfecta*.

Ex. 94

The point involved is almost too clear to require comment. While both Nenna and Lassus absorb the word 'fugam' into a gentle phrase of smooth-flowing imitative polyphony, Gesualdo sets off the word 'Vos' with a block chord and precisely at the word 'fugam' engages us in a frantic musical flight. One could almost miss the point in the music of Nenna and Lassus; Gesualdo puts the text into such bold relief that we are obliged to follow it.

After the 'Vos fugam' section, the text continues 'et ego vadam immolari pro vobis' ('and I shall go to be offered up for you').[31] The music once more responds to the emotional climate of the text with an intensely chromatic passage that must rank as one of Gesualdo's finest. This is openly affective as opposed to the greater literalness of the preceding passage.

Ex. 95

[31] For a discussion of the harmonic movement at this point, cf. p. 204 ff and Dahlhaus, op. cit., p. 78.

If Gesualdo does not mirror the text so slavishly, on a word-for-word basis, as the earlier madrigalists, his adoption of the principle is still to be found even in his sacred music. Consider the following text (*Feria Sexta*, II):

> Velum templi scissum est
> Et omnis terra tremuit:
> latro de cruce clamabat, dicens:
> Memento mei, Domine, dum veneris in regnum tuum.
> ℣: Petrae scissae sunt, et monumenta aperta sunt,
>   et multa corpora sanctorum, qui dormierant,
>   surrexerunt.

> The veil of the temple was rent
> And all the earth shook:
> The thief from the cross cried out, saying: Lord,
>   remember me when Thou comest into Thy kingdom.
> ℣: The rocks were rent and the graves opened,
>   and there arose many bodies of the saints that were
>   dead.

At 'the veil of the temple was rent,' we find a series of plummeting lines;

Ex. 96

'tremuit' is mirrored by a quivering, undulating figure (Ex. 96); a quality of
serenity suddenly prevails (Ex. 97) at the plea of the thief to be remembered
('Memento mei, Domine'); and at the 'rocks were rent' a series of falling

Ex. 97

figures suggests the rending of the earth (Ex. 98). The intervals in the series of imitative figurations are subjected to ever-changing distances in their fall, ending at the cadence with a descent of a diminished fourth in the topmost voice.

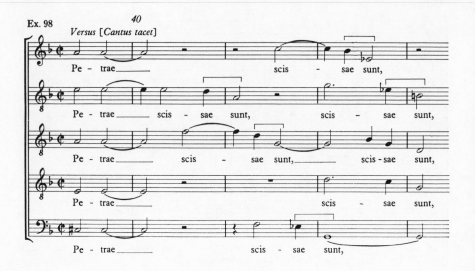

Virtually every word capable of literal or affective treatment is so set, and the versus ends (Ex. 99) on the text 'surrexerunt' with an unearthly sense of elevation.

Harmony and Dissonance

It will be noticed that at least part of the poignancy stems not only from chromatic habits but also from the occasional and pungent use of dissonance, as in the dark chordal opening of *Tenebrae factae sunt*[32] which is followed by unusual dissonance treatment particularly in the lowest voice.[33]

Ex. 100

[32] Note the similarity between the opening of this response and the madrigal *O tenebroso giorno* (V, 19).

[33] The dissonance stems from the consonant fourth figure in bar 4 now subjected to invertible counterpoint.

The unprepared sevenths at 'Quia non est inventus qui me agnosceret' in *Animam meam dilectam*,[34] are similarly poignant.

Ex. 101

[34] Note the similarity of this use of dissonance with the final cadence of Nenna's *Ecco, o mia dolce pena*, bars 78–81 (Book IV, 4; pre-1603).

On the other hand Gesualdo's masterly control of a harmonic design built solely from triads is manifest throughout the collection, as in *Vinea mea electa* at 'Quomodo conversa es.' The reason for the triadic purity of the opening verse becomes apparent in the ensuing phrase. By reserving the use of non-harmonic material for 'amaritudinem' (bitterness) and 'crucifigeres', he fashions a powerfully graphic image.

> Vinea mea electa, ego te plantavi:
> Quomodo conversa es in amaritudinem,
> ut me crucifigeres, et Barabbam dimitteres?
>
> (O my chosen vineyard, I planted thee:
> How art thou turned to bitterness,
> that thou shouldest crucify me,
> and release Barabbas?)

Replete with vivid and incisive visions, the texts of the *Responsoria* inspired Gesualdo to some of his most intensely beautiful, sublime, and terrifying music. Though cast in the guise of a Responsoria cycle, its completeness provides a telling of the Passion story, and within the history of that form it must stand as one of the earliest examples in which music rose to the challenge of the emotion inherent in the text. This is not to say that within the frame of the Holy Week cycle (as Victoria) or the individual passion text (Lassus) there are not examples of great beauty in the Cinquecento. But the note of pathos and tragedy which rings from virtually every line of these scriptures had never before been caught with such a vision. Perhaps it was not possible before the expressivity inherent in the distortions and disproportions of a Mannerist language had been developed and infused with a personal warmth. Once achieved, this newly won power was destined not to be pursued within the framework of the older motet, but to complement and feed the emotional sensibilities of a new age.

CHAPTER TWELVE

~⚬~

Miscellanea

A FEW of Gesualdo's previously published madrigals, particularly those of the earlier volumes, were also included in the anthologies of the time.[1] Other collections include items by Gesualdo which appeared nowhere else. *Psalms of Compline* by Gesualdo are to be found amongst psalms by various Neapolitan composers published by Ottavio Beltrano in 1620 (*Salmi delle Compiete de diversi Musici Neapolitani*), and two canzonette by him appear at the end of Pomponio Nenna's eighth book of madrigals of 1618. So far as is known, this accounts for all of the Prince's music that found its way into print.

Canzonette

The canzonette are typical examples of the frequently charming but unpretentious pieces of a rather lightweight character that appeared under this name in the second half of the sixteenth century and the first decades of the seventeenth. Both of Gesualdo's contributions in this form, *All'ombra degl'allori* and *Come vivi cor mio*, conform to the typical strophic design of the genre with four stanzas cast in a two-part design. The first section in each case discloses a homophonic-syllabic style, and the second a lightly contrapuntal one which is only mildly imitative. The opening of *All'ombra degl'allori*, for all its simplicity, nevertheless manifests Gesualdine harmonic manners, particularly in the contrast between the F major and A major of the first two phrases. The A major triad in turn launches a series of triads

---

[1] *Novi Frutti Musicali Madrigali a cinque voci di diversi excellentissimi Musici* (1610), contains the double madrigal *Se cosi dolce è l'duolo-Ma s'avverra* (Bk. II) and *Mentr, mia stella* (Bk. I). *Teatro de Madrigali a Cinque Voci. De diversi excellentiss. musici Napolitane* . . . (1609) includes works by Cerretto, Dentice, Effrem, C. Lambardi, Fr. Lambardi, Macque, Mayone, and Trabaci, as well as *T'amo mia vita* from Gesualdo's Bk. V, two years before its appearance in 1611. *Nuova Scelta di Madrigali di Sette Autori* . . . (Carlino, 1615) contains *Com'esser puo ch'io viva*, *Son si belle le rose*, and *Bell'Angioletta* from Bk. I. Lambardi, F., *Il Secondo Libro de Villanelle, à 3, à 4, et à 5* (1618), includes madrigals from Bk. I.

which function as dominants (A–D–G–C–F) and ultimately return to the F level. The basically conservative character of the canzonette is evident at a glance.

Ex. 102

The intimate connection between Nenna and Gesualdo has been stressed, and as the canzonette appeared only in Nenna's madrigal collection of 1618, it may be that they were included by him as a memorial to the Prince. It is similarly possible that they were early works of Gesualdo which Nenna had saved.[2]

Psalms of Compline

The *Salmi delle compiete* is the only printed piece of Gesualdo provided with a basso continuo, but it is no more than a *basso seguente* and is almost certainly an editorial contrivance. Basso continuo parts of an identical nature exist for the gagliarda which will be discussed shortly, as well as for a few madrigals which appear in a manuscript at Christ Church, Oxford. Musically, the style of the Psalms is simple, with essentially the same music set to the three verses and a *Gloria*. The subtle changes which occur in the repetition of the unelaborate texture are similar to those which occur in the recitation formulae of the *Benedictus* and *Miserere* at the end of the *Responsoria* collection. Repetition brings with it expectation; in such a scheme even the slightest alteration of rhythmic, harmonic, or melodic idea stands out with clarity and can become a thing of delicate beauty.

[2] See p. 65, for a possible dating of this work.

Ex. 103

In te Do — mi — ne spe — ra — vi non con —

B.C.

—fun — dar in ae — ter — — — num in iu — sti — ti — a

tu — a li — be — ra_____ me._____

E — sto mi — hi in De — — um pro — tec — to —

—rem et in do — mum re — fu — — — gi — i ut

sal — vum me fa — ci — as.

The textual source for Gesualdo's piece is Psalm xxx, 1–2, 5. That *alternatim* performance was implied may be assumed by reference to the chant formula associated with Psalm lxx which shares the identical opening verses. There we see the text 'Esto mihi in Deum' labelled as verse 3, although it belongs to the second half of verse 2 in the Vulgate. It is equally apparent that a plainchant *Sicut erat* following the *Gloria Patri* must be supplied at the conclusion in performance.[3]

The Naples Gagliarde Manuscript

Two manuscript sources which have only recently been investigated in detail reveal other music of an instrumental character that can be ascribed to Gesualdo. The first of these is MS 4.6.3. of the R. Conservatorio di San Pietro a Majella in Naples, consisting of four part-books, three of which bear the label *Gesualdo/Manoscritto 1600/Gagliarde à 4/per sonare le viole*. The collection opens with a *Sinfonia* whose title is supplemented with the indication *Sonata antica*. This is followed by the ten gagliarde referred to in the cover title, and other pieces, both vocal and instrumental, some with definite ascriptions (Stella, Gio. Maria Sabini, T. Marchii d'Arpe, etc.), others anonymous. The arrangement in part books suggests a performance by an instrumental group, but other information, to be discussed presently, indicates the possibility of a wider instrumental choice.[4]

In the manuscript, 'Principe di Venosa' is written at the top of the last of the set of ten gagliarde, and it is the only one of the set to carry a specific attribution to Gesualdo.[5] Although it is a strong temptation to deduce that

---

[3] I am indebted to Prof. Denis Stevens for calling this to my attention. He additionally observed in a private communication that 'There is a hint of a psalm tone in the alto line, but in view of the prevailing tonality I think the best solution would be to use Tone 4 with the E ending.'

[4] Watelet in his edition of some of these same pieces as they appear in Br. Mus. Add. 30491, *Monumenta Musica Belgicae*, 4e Jaargang, suggests organ solo or viols as equally appropriate. An especially valuable discussion of the contemporary practice, including limitations, occurs in Bottrigari's *Il Desiderio*. For an excellent English translation see the one of Carol MacClintock in *MSD*, 9 (1962).

[5] An abbreviation that might pass for 'G^do' appears at the top of the Tenor part only in Gagliarda Nona. In addition, the word 'corna', written on each of the four parts of the first piece, has lent itself to a piece of fanciful interpretation (Columbia Record ML 5341): an allusion, possibly, to Gesualdo cuckolded, for in the *Informatione presa dalla Gran Corte della Vicaria* relating to the investigation of the motives for Gesualdo's murder of his first wife and her lover, reference is made to the house of Gesualdo as 'casa Gesualdo corna'. However, the appearance of the word at the identical spot in each part in the interior of the piece suggests that probably an instrumental indication was intended. Regarding the identification of Gagliarda Nona, see p. 289.

this ascription, coming at the end of the series, stands for the entire set, additional information renders this interpretation untenable. This is based largely on two gagliarde to be found in Br. Mus. MS Add. 30491.[6] Here they are ascribed to Giovanni de Macque, and the manuscript being in the hand of one of his pupils, Luigi Rossi, the ascription carries a special ring of authenticity. The first of these two gagliarde is identical to the *Gagliarda Seconda* of the Naples Conservatorio manuscript, and the second, while not identical to any particular one of the set, has features in common with all of them. Macque's claim to the *Gagliarda Seconda*, specifically, receives striking confirmation in the middle section of another piece attributed to Macque, a *Capriccio sopra un Sogetto*,[7] where the same thematic material is stated in an almost identical contrapuntal setting. Still another of the Gagliarde has recently been identified as a piece by the contemporary Neapolitan Trabaci.[8] The *Gagliarda Nona* of the Naples MS is identical with one to be found in Trabaci's keyboard book of 1603. Perhaps as important as the ascription is the identification of the work as a keyboard piece. This suggests that, in spite of the part-book arrangement of the gagliarde in the manuscript source, all of them could conceivably be so performed.

A part labelled 'B.C. del G. di Venosa' appears much later in the manuscript after a number of works by other composers. This part is identical with the lowest sounding voice of the gagliarda attributed to Gesualdo, and is the only gagliarda provided with a basso continuo. The location of this part at a later point in the manuscript, as well as its attribution, not only confirm that the piece (Ex. 104) is by Gesualdo, but also indicate it as a thing apart from the other gagliarde of the set. The first nine all have titles by number, *Gagliarda Prima*, *Gagliarda Seconda*, etc. The last one receives no number or formal designation (logically *Gagliarda Decima*), merely the ascription 'Principe di Venosa' in all four parts, intimating that it is not the tenth

Ex. 104

[6] A modern edition of thèse two gagliarde may be found in *Monumenta Musicae Belgicae*, 4e Jaargang (Berchem–Antwerp, 1938), p. 61.
[7] Ibid., p. 40.
[8] The author is indebted to Prof. Roland Jackson for this information.

gagliarda of a series but a separate one by Gesualdo appended to a series of nine.[9]

The final gagliarda also has stylistic features which set it apart, for while it resembles the earlier pieces of the group in rhythm, phrasing, and general character, the harmony, with its frequent chromatic-melodic shifts, bears an undoubted resemblance to Gesualdo's. The establishment of his

[9] Columbia ML 5341 recorded three from this group of gagliarde, not including, ironically, the one which is definitely ascribed to Gesualdo. This was recorded subsequently, however, on Columbia ML 5718.

claim to the final gagliarda alone has a corrective value in light of the title of the manuscript.[10]

Canzon francese del Principe

British Museum MS Add. 30491[11] has a collection of unusual pieces, one of which it is tempting to ascribe to Gesualdo. It is a *canzon francese* written on eight staves, the upper four containing the vocal model and the lower four a keyboard elaboration. The arrangement of the elaboration on four staves with a single part to a line need not suggest that the piece is for an instrumental ensemble.[12] The use of open score, or *partitura*, for keyboard works enjoyed a vogue among Neapolitan composers of this very period, and was especially convenient for the notation of highly contrapuntal pieces.[13] Characteristic manual figurations bear out the contention that this is a piece for keyboard instrument.

The central problem in connection with the work is one of identity. Neither the word 'Gesualdo' or 'Venosa' is to be found in the manuscript. The complete title reads: *Canzon francese del Principe*. A plausible identification, however, is to be found by referring to the contents of the collection as a whole. First of all, Br. Mus. Add. 30491 is in the hand of Luigi Rossi, pupil of Giovanni de Macque. Although there are a few vocal pieces at the end of the manuscript, the collection is otherwise devoted to instrumental compositions by members of the Neapolitan circle, Stella, Macque, Fabritio Fillimarino, Fr. Lambardi, Trabaci, etc. More specifically, the first three musicians of this list were, at one time or another, associated with the Gesualdo *accademia*. In this company 'Principe' would seem to admit but one identity. Other uses of the single word 'Principe' with reference to Gesualdo are to be found amongst seventeenth-century theorists.[14]

The discovery of a keyboard piece by Gesualdo, if this is what it is, is of interest beyond the mere progressive qualities visible at an initial glance. First it affords an opportunity to test one of the commonest explanations of

[10] This interpretation is corroborated by the manuscript analysis in the *Catalogo delle Opere Musicali Città di Napoli: Biblioteca del R. Conservatorio di Musica di S. Pietra a Majella* (Parma: 1934), 550–1.

[11] A number of keyboard works which appear in this manuscript are to be found in *Monumenta Musica Belgicae*, 4e Jaargang, ed. by Watelet, and in *Neapolitan Keyboard Composers (Circa 1600)*, ed. by Roland Jackson, *Corpus of Early Keyboard Music*, 24 (1967).

[12] The *Catalogue of Manuscript Music in the British Museum*, III, p. 495, for example, contains the entry regarding this piece: 'A string quartet apparently by Gesualdo.'

[13] Cf. Willi Apel, *Notation of Polyphonic Music*, p. 18.

[14] Cf. the final sentence from a passage by Doni, p. 171 and p. 300.

Gesualdo's style. From the writings of his contemporaries we learn that he was known as a virtuoso performer on several instruments, including the archlute, the theorbo, the chittarone, and possibly the archicembalo. From this information, later historians began to see a plausible source for some of the outlandish progressions in his madrigals, and Ambros was probably not the first to entertain the idea that the works of the master were not the result of speculation alone, but the 'result of practical exploration on the keyboard or the organ.'

While few today would suggest that harmonic explorations on the keyboard made Gesualdo lose sight of contrapuntal niceties, one can still ask whether there is evidence for keyboard influence on his vocal works, particularly in relation to his chromatic harmonies. Marshall, in a detailed study of temperament and tuning in Gesualdo's music, concludes that while the first four books of madrigals are conceivable within the framework of a mean-tone system, the final two books could have been created only from a view that encompassed equal temperament.[15] This implies that while all of the madrigals of the first four books could have been played on the harpsichord with its mean-tone tuning, the most mature works could not have been. This had led Keiner to suggest earlier that the late works were probably conceived on the archicembalo, 'which obviates the awkward chords of mean-tone temperament.'[16]

The piece is important less for what it lends to these theories however, than for what it reveals as a keyboard piece in its own right. Colourful harmonic sequences occur, but hardly of the character that one would expect from a knowledge of his madrigals. In fact, no examples of slow homophonic writing (the usual context for his daring harmonic ventures) exist in the work, and we find little evidence of the madrigalist's habit of lingering over the vertical element through a slower tempo or 'close-quarter repetition of materials. The piece is contrapuntal and sectional—as its title would lead us to suspect—and most of the main sections open with some version of the head motif in a variation-style canzone, a form to which Macque was contributing so significantly at that time.

Ex. 105

---

15 Marshall, *The Harmonic Laws in the Madrigals of Carlo Gesualdo* (Ph.D. dissertation, New York University, 1956), pp. 19–37.
16 Marshall, op. cit., p. 20.

The figurations which appear throughout the score are fantastic yet idiomatic, sometimes tossed imitatively among the different voices (Ex. 106),[17]

Ex. 106

sometimes striking a first note dissonant in relation to the sustaining harmony in the opposite hand (Ex. 107), and at other times beginning

Ex. 107

consonantly but engaging in narrow-range chromatic roulades such as, one suspects, could only have been conceived on, or through contact with, Vicentino's archicembalo (Ex. 108). A few basically polyphonic sections with

[17] Examples 106 and 109b contain corrections to the author's edition in Bd. X of the complete works (Ugrino Verlag, 1967)—corrections necessitated in Ex. 106 as the result of a printer's error, in Ex. 109b as the result of having consulted Prof. Roland Jackson's transcription in *CEKM*, 24 (1967) and corroborated by reference to the original manuscript.

Ex. 108

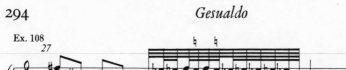

interesting chromatic alterations reflect Gesualdo the madrigal composer (Ex. 109), but they are rare. It is only through reference to other Neapolitan

Ex. 109 a)

keyboard works of the time that an accurate assessment of Gesualdo's *canzon francese* is possible. While it is not the sole keyboard piece of its kind, it is perhaps one of the most remarkable. As a parallel it is only necessary to cite the many astonishing works of Trabaci and Macque, and particularly the latter's *Stravaganze*, for those interested in searching out some of the most unjustifiably forgotten music of any period. (The beautiful *Seconda Stravaganza* of Macque which immediately precedes the Gesualdo canzone in the British Museum manuscript is a highly expressive miniature containing many details common to both pieces.) Needless to say, not all Neapolitan music was of equivalent interest, but the generally progressive quality of much of the music at this time in Naples has not been sufficiently stressed.

With sections of little or no elaboration standing juxtaposed to others of an enormously intricate and involved style, Gesualdo's score is visually reminiscent of Luzzaschi's madrigals for one, two, and three sopranos. Lacking the textual association which justifies the internal textural dichotomy in his vocal works, this piece may not be counted a complete success. But as a bizarre example of Mannerist instrumental music it is extremely fascinating. And as an early Neapolitan example of a keyboard canzona based upon the variation principle which was to influence Frescobaldi, it is of more than passing interest in the history of the form.[18] Finally, as a piece that permits us to view a corner of our composer's mind unhinted at in any other work it is supremely important.

A statement made by Blancanus in his treatise of 1615 to the effect that 'all singers and players on stringed instruments, laying aside that of others, everywhere eagerly embraced his [Gesualdo's] music' has led Redlich to suggest that a repertoire of instrumental works by Gesualdo has evidently been lost. This is doubtful, as the passage must refer to the possibility of playing the madrigals on the viols either alone or together with singers. While Gesualdo may have written other independent instrumental pieces, the contemporary habit of playing his madrigals on the viols is corroborated by Doni in discussing musical intermezzi. In his *Musica Scenica* he proposes that one adapt music to the character of the action. Thus 'after a happy act, one plays perhaps a pavane, or a ricercare which similarly expresses gaiety, on the viole da braccia, harp or cembalo. For a more moderate situation, one brings forth a lute or theorboe sonata; and for action of a melancholy nature one plays a madrigal of the Prince of Venosa on the viols.'[19]

[18] Willi Apel, 'Neapolitan Links Between Cabezon and Frescobaldi,' *MQ*, 1938 (24), 419–37.
[19] *Compendio del Trattato*, p. 112.

CHAPTER THIRTEEN

Epilogue: The Controversy

PERHAPS no composer in history has invoked such puzzlement or gathered such an uneven press over the centuries as Carlo Gesualdo. Surely no other composer of the sixteenth century has been involved in anything approaching a continuing controversy. True, even the greatest geniuses of times gone by have had to withstand criticism before being accorded their place in the pantheon, but seldom has the swinging pendulum of taste affected a composer's reputation so capriciously. It is worth asking how and why there has been so much divergence of opinion.

Critical judgement of Gesualdo over the past 350 years has focused on only half-a-dozen madrigals. They include works like *Moro lasso* and *Resta di darmi noia*, which are amongst his most provocative and original creations and would seem to be fair selections upon which to found an opinion. Yet the base they provide is too meagre in quantity and too stylistically particular for the establishment of a norm. Despite the small number, interest in them has not flagged, so that Gesualdo can claim to have received a considerable degree of attention over the years.

The centuries do not, however, agree on their estimate of the man. Nor can one predict a particular century's reaction to Gesualdo on the basis of its own stylistic habits; for an era which was especially attracted to counterpoint does not necessarily criticize him any more than a period noted for its chromatic bent universally praises him.

* * *

The seventeenth century, Gesualdo's own, differs from all later ones by its repeated and unswerving veneration of him. He was held up by writer after writer as a model, as a master of his age. The opinion has been commonly voiced that seventeenth-century judgement gave its unanimous praise out of deference to his princely rank. But, while this may have played a hand in a few instances, the evidence of criticism which continued to extol his virtues well after his death weakens the strength of the argument. On occasion the chronicler pays tribute to the fact that a nobleman should have progressed beyond the role of dilettante to such a degree of excellence. Tassoni even suggests Gesualdo's indebtedness to another royal personage:

> We can relate of James, King of Scotland, that he not only composed sacred music, but invented a new species of plaintive melody, different from all others; in which he was imitated by the Prince of Venosa, who, in our times, has embellished Music with many admirable inventions.[1]

Peacham in his *Compleat Gentleman* (1622) is probably more interested in citing Gesualdo's accomplishments as part of the refinement of the *uomo universale* and stressing the honour he brought to his rank than he is in making an evaluation of the man's music: 'The Duke of Venosa, an Italian prince, in like manner of late years hath given excellent proof of his knowledge and love of music, having himself composed many rare songs which I have seen'.[2] Cerone's remarks in his *El melopeo y maestro* of 1613 leave no doubt that this too is his point of view.[3]

But in addition to all of this rather correct reporting, there exists a sizeable testimony to the true affection and esteem in which he was held by his contemporaries both during his life and following his death. Thus we find Scipione Cerreto speaking in 1601, a good decade before the composer's death, of Gesualdo as 'inferior to no other composer, having discovered new inventions of composition adorned with thought and caprice so that all musicians and singers of the world have been given to marvel,' and concluding 'that certainly there ought to be a statue made in his memory not of marble but of gold.'[4] Only a few years later Giulio Cesare Monteverdi in the foreword to his brother's *Scherzi musicali* (1607), while attempting to put the critic Artusi in his place, makes abundantly clear the esteem in which Monteverdi held Gesualdo, and he begs musicians, 'following the

---

[1] *Pensieri diversi*, Lib. X, cap. xxiii. Cf. also Berardi, *Miscellanea musicale* (1689), p. 50. Burney in the eighteenth century challenges the assertions of Tassoni and Berardi which connect the style of Gesualdo with James's Caledonian airs. A certain confusion has been introduced into this alleged association by confounding James I of Scotland (1394–1437) with James I of England (1566–1625), the first Stuart monarch, who came to England as James VI of Scotland. There is no evidence, however, that the latter ever composed, though he was a person of modest literary ability. As a contemporary of Gesualdo the confusion was natural, but it was James I of Scotland to whom Tassoni undoubtedly referred. Although an accomplished musician and reputedly something of a composer, none of his music survives, and on chronological grounds alone Gesualdo's indebtedness to him appears specious.

[2] Strunk, *Source Readings in Music History*, p. 333.

[3] Cerone, *El melopeo y maestro*, p. 150.

[4] Cerreto, *Della prattica musica*, p. 154.

divine Cipriano de Rore, the Signor Prencipe di Venosa . . . Count Alfonso
Fontanella . . . and other gentlemen of that heroic school, to pay no attention
to nonsense and chimeras.'[5]

Blancanus in his treatise of 1615 offers an important critical view in the
first few years following Gesualdo's death, and in essence it is the most
uncompromisingly laudatory statement of the century—a fitting obituary,
as it were:

> The most noble Carolus Gesualdus, prince of Venusium, was the prince
> of musicians of our age; for he having recalled the Rhythmi into music,
> introduced such a style of modulation, that other musicians yielded
> the preference to him; and all singers and players on stringed instru-
> ments, laying aside that of others, everywhere eagerly embraced his
> music.[6]

In 1623 in a controversy recalling the Monteverdi-Artusi exchange
above, Muzio Effrem struck out against Marco da Gagliano, again holding
Gesualdo up as a model. We know that Effrem was particularly close to
Gesualdo, and by his own admission was for a long period associated with
him. It is only necessary to think of the innumerable passages in Gesualdo,
however, which are far more audacious than anything Gagliano ever penned,
in order to imagine what Effrem could have written as a *censure* against the
Prince had he so desired. The suggestion of Gagliano's ineptitude, however,
ultimately turns into a hint of plagiarism which recalls Cappucio's preface
to the fifth book of madrigals. Gesualdo would have been pleased by his
new defender.

> If my service for the most illustrious and most excellent Prince of
> Venosa over a period of twenty-two years, accompanied by the favour
> given me by His Most Serene Highness of Mantua by having honoured
> me with the responsibility of Maestro di Cappella in His Most Serene
> Camera, and ultimately the state of favour which I enjoyed from His
> Most Serene Highness, the Duke of Tuscany, by being enrolled among
> the number of his most gifted musicians—if all this has not moved you
> to believe that I am a musician, then the mistakes listed below will
> certainly do this, which have been found in your madrigals by young
> beginners anxious to learn the true rules of counterpoint, and con-
> firmed as mistakes by me. These young men were moved by justified
> indignation against you, because you have plainly torn to pieces the

[5] Strunk, op. cit., p. 408.
[6] *Chronologia celebrorum mathematicorum ad sec. Christi XVII*, sec. xvi.

fifth and sixth books of madrigals of the famous and highly admired
Prince [of Venosa].[7]

Vincenzo Giustiniani's *Discorso sopra la musica* (1628) makes a reference to
Gesualdo's contrapuntal prowess somewhat at odds with the remarks of
Doni ('he never aimed at Canons or such sophistry') and Burney ('he is,
however, always struggling at fugue and imitation').[8] But Pietro della Valle
(1586–1652), one of the most widely travelled men of the period, who
chronicled much of what he saw and heard, makes an even more surprising
evaluation which directly associates Gesualdo with two of the acknowledged
masters of the early Baroque style. After mentioning the revival of interest
in things Greek amongst many musicians of the latter part of the sixteenth
and early part of the seventeenth centuries, he concludes:

> The first good compositions which were heard in this form were *Dafne,*
> *Arianna, Euridice,* and other things from Florence and Mantua. The
> first who praiseworthily followed this path in Italy . . . were the Prince
> of Venosa who perhaps showed the light to all others in affective song
> (*cantare affettuoso*) and Claudio Monteverdi and Jacopo Peri in the
> works named above.[9]

That Gesualdo did not write operas and did not pour his ideas into forms
which at this distance we have come to call Baroque, did not prevent della
Valle from seeing his importance for an evolving style. Such assessments of
Gesualdo's position thwarted, to a large extent, the growth in music of a
critical position such as the art critics of the seventeenth century commonly
espoused. In spite of the Vicentino-Lusitano, Monteverdi-Artusi, and
Effrem-da Gagliano disputes, there is a curious absence of anti-Gesualdo
sentiment, *à la* Bellori,[10] which even partially blames him for the decline of
polyphony since Josquin. Specifically we do not find critics who, despising
Gesualdo, endorse Monteverdi as an alternative, in the manner that the
art critics supported the Caracci as an anti-Mannerist symbol.[11]

The most pertinent remarks of Doni are likewise those which directly
relate musical personalities whom we might hesitate to compare today.

---

[7] Vogel, 'Marco da Gagliano' in *Vierteljahrschrift für Musikwissenschaft* V (1889), p. 567,
 gives original Italian.
[8] Giustiniani, op. cit., ed. by C. MacClintock, *MSD* 9 (American Institute of Musicology, 1962), pp. 70–1.
[9] *Della musica dell'età nostra* (1640) in Doni, *Lyra Barberina* (1763), p. 251.
[10] See p. 99.
[11] Friedländer, *Mannerism and Anti-Mannerism,* pp. 47–83.

The proto-Baroque manifestations of Mannerism are thus underscored. Doni can be specific:

> . . . as for example the songs of the Prince are more varied in melody than those of Claudio [Monteverdi], while the latter's are more graceful in their rhythm.[12]

Later, in the midst of theoretical speculations, Doni makes another double reference.

> From these speculations of mine I have extracted a most true and useful maxim: that modern compositions marked with accidentals are not, as commonly held, a mixture of the Genera and the Modes. This position, which appears to some as a great paradox, is however as clear as the sun, and I believe that eventually it will be proved. Thus today one finds neither chromatic nor enharmonic compositions, except some few which have a mixture of chromaticism, as that most excellent madrigal of the Prince, *Resta di darmi noia*, and the *Lament of Arianna* of Monteverdi.[13]

It is noteworthy that Doni in speaking elsewhere of the expressive uses of chromaticism again cites *Resta di darmi noia* and the *Lamento d'Arianna* as especially affective examples. While Monteverdi's *Lament* is well known today, Gesualdo's piece, if known at all, is usually considered in an entirely different light. It is thus of no little significance that their contemporaries saw them as pieces of a similar expressiveness. We would do well to remember that the *Lament* appeared in at least three guises, including an unaccompanied madrigal and a continuo aria. Certain of Gesualdo's pieces too might enjoy such a double life, as we have pointed out. Recall particularly the opening of the early madrigal *Sento che nel partire* which is reminiscent of the Monteverdi piece both melodically and harmonically (Ex. 12).

As a final source for the period, Kircher's *Musurgia Universalis* from the mid-point in the century, shows something of the undiminished esteem in which critics held Gesualdo long after his passing.

> Another example is the work of the Prince of Venosa, who was the first, as all agree, to raise music to that degree of excellence which

---

[12] Doni, *Appendice a'Trattati di Musica*, cap. XVII, p. 63.

[13] Doni, *Compendio del Trattato*, p. 16. The reference here is obviously to the Vicentino–Lusitano dispute of 1551. Cf. Vicentino, *L'antica musica ridotta alla moderna prattica*, facsimile ed. E. Lowinsky, in *Documenta Musicologica*, Ser. I, No. XVII (1959), fols. 95–98v; also Kaufmann, 'A "Diatonic" and a "Chromatic" Madrigal by Giulio Fiesco' in *Aspects of Medieval and Renaissance Music*, ed. J. LaRue (1966), pp. 474–88.

certainly all muscians look up to and admire. Here in a certain madrigal of his, which begins 'Baci soavi, e cari,' he so expresses this amorous affect, following the example of nature, that nothing more could be desired.[14]

He later adds what might well serve as a summary of seventeenth-century opinion about Gesualdo.

Among the composers of this generation the Prince of Venosa seems deservedly to have snatched the palm from the others because of the excellence of this metabolical style, capturing the marvellous force of his genius and a new method in various madrigals which are extant everywhere. And we found none in the works preceding these madrigals to which we can send a reader.[15]

★ ★ ★

The 'Gesualdo controversy' was born in the eighteenth century and was largely inspired by the first English writers of music history. The non-English historians seem to reconfirm the attitudes and opinions of the seventeenth century. Thus Rousseau in his famous dictionary, known for its inclination toward barbed commentary, stated simply: 'His madrigals are full of knowledge and taste, being admired by all the masters and sung by all the ladies.' Likewise the illustrious Padre Martini, one of the most knowledgeable musicians of his age, held nothing but reverence for his earlier compatriot, and like Effrem a century earlier held up Gesualdo's works as models of their kind to the young student.[16]

In the year following the appearance of Martini's *Saggio*, Hawkins'

---

[14] Kircher, *Musurgia*, Lib. VII, p. 599; for additional references to Gesualdo see pp. 547, 586, 602, 608, 612.

[15] Ibid., p. 675.

[16] Martini, *Saggio*, Parte Seconda, pp. 237–8: 'Abounding in artifice and passionate expression is this madrigal (*Donna se m'ancidete*), the author of which harboured a predilection for a certain *morbidezza*, which was already beginning to be introduced in madrigal music at the beginning of the last century, the purpose of which was none other than to have emerge distinctly in his compositions, by force of extraordinary modulations, a strong and clear expression quite removed from the practice even of the more celebrated composers of his time, as can easily be recognized by comparing the madrigals of this author with those of Palestrina, Marenzio, Monteverdi and others of his contemporaries.' He likewise singles out Gesualdo for his skill in 'demonstrating the intermingling, the union of the parts and the dexterity with which they are disposed to give a place to imitation, which is to be met in abundance in all the works of this author.'

three-volume history and the first volume of Burney's *History of Music* appeared, the first of their kind in the English language. Although contemporary assessment of the two works tended to give the edge of approval to Burney, it must be remembered that Burney's remaining three volumes were not completed until 1789, and to a certain extent he relied upon the misadventures of Hawkins' enterprise in order to improve his own product. Over a decade elapsed between Hawkins' estimate of Gesualdo and the appearance of Burney's volume that dealt with the composer, thus permitting Burney a retort to Hawkins' evaluation. Hawkins' central argument is based largely upon the authority which he summons from seventeenth-century writers with citations from Blancanus, Kircher, Doni, Tassoni, and Beradi. He ventures the following rather brief, original appraisal.

> The distinguishing excellencies of the compositions of this admirable author are, fine contrivance, original harmony, and the sweetest modulation conceivable; and these he possessed in so eminent a degree, that one of the finest musicians that these later times have known, Mr. Geminiani, has been often heard to declare that he laid the foundation of his studies in the works of the Prencipe of Venosa.[17]

Burney's considerably longer statement, although quoting from earlier authorities, tends to amplify or challenge each of them. Through an examination of all critical opinion of the past pertaining to Gesualdo and through an investigation of the music itself, Burney proposes a re-evaluation.

> But no Neapolitan composer, of this high period, is mentioned with such unlimited praise, as Don Carlo Gesualdo, Prince of Venosa; it will be necessary, therefore, to stop and pay our respects to the abilities of this celebrated and illustrious Dilettante, in consideration of the honour he has done the art of which we are tracing the history.
>
> This Prince, whose fame has been extended by his musical productions more than by his high rank, though this rank will be found reciprocally to have added lustre to the compositions, was nephew to Cardinal Alfonso Gesualdo, Archbishop of Naples, and had his title from the place which gave birth to Horace, the *Venusium* of the ancients. . . .
>
> The numerous editions of these madrigals in different parts of Europe, and the eulogiums bestowed on the author by persons who

[17] Hawkins, *A General History*, III, p. 221.

rank high in Literature, as well as Music, made me extremely curious
to see and examine them. Gerard Vossius, Bianconi, Bapt. Doni,
Tassoni, and many others, speak of him as the greatest composer of
modern times; as one who, quitting the beaten track of other
musicians, had discovered new melodies, new measures, new harmonies, and new modulation; so that singers, and players on instruments, despising all other Music, were only pleased with that of this
Prince (Blancanus).

Tassoni tells us, that James I King of Scotland, had not only composed Sacred Music, but invented a new species of plaintive melody,
different from all others; 'in which he has been imitated by the Prince
of Venosa, who, in our times, has embellished Music with many
admirable inventions.' This assertion greatly increased my desire to
examine works in which so many excellencies were concentred [sic];
particularly as I had long been extremely desirous of tracing the
peculiarities of the national melodies of Scotland, from a higher source
than David Rizzio. But, in a very attentive perusal of all the several
parts of the whole six books of the Prince of Venosa's madrigals, I was
utterly unable to discover the least similitude [sic] or imitation of
Caledonian airs in any one of them; which, so far from Scots melodies,
seem to contain no melodies at all; nor, when scored, can we discover
the least regularity of design, phraseology, rhythm, or, indeed, any
thing remarkable in these madrigals, except unprincipled modulation,
and the perpetual embarrassments and inexperience of an Amateur,
in the arrangement and filling up of the parts. . . .

This illustrious Dilettante seems to merit as little praise on account
of the expression of words, for which he has been celebrated by Doni,
as for his counterpoint; for the syllables are constantly made long or
short, just as it best suited his melody; and in the repetition of words,
we frequently see the same syllable long in one bar, and short in
another, or the contrary; by which it is manifest that their just
accentuation was never thought of.

The remarks of Tassoni, if he meant otherwise, certainly must have
been hazarded either from conjecture or report; as is but too frequently
practised by men of letters, when they become musical critics, without
either industry or science sufficient to verify their assertions.

The Prince of Venosa was perpetually striving at new expression and
modulation, but seldom succeeded to the satisfaction of posterity,
however dazzled his cotemporaries [sic] may have been by his rank,
and the character he bore among the learned, who so frequently get

their musical information from tradition, that whether they praise or censure, it is usually *sans connoissance de cause*.

Dilettanti usually decide in the same summary way, with an additional prejudice in favour of their own little knowledge, and a disposition to censure whatever they are unable to acquire, be it science or execution.

Cicero has long since said, that 'it is not with Philosophy and Science, as with other arts; for what can a man say of Geometry or Music, who has never studied them? He must either hold his tongue, or talk nonsense.'

With respect to the excellencies which have been so liberally bestowed on this author, who died in 1614 [sic], they are all disputable, and such as, by a careful examination of his works, he seemed by no means entitled to. They have lately been said to consist in 'fine *contrivance, original harmony*, and the *sweetest modulation conceivable*.' As to *contrivance*, it must be owned that much has been attempted by this Prince; but he is so far from being happy in this particular, that his points of imitation are generally unmanageable, and brought in so indiscriminately on concords and discords, and on accented and unaccented parts of a bar, that, when performed, there is more confusion in the general effect than in the Music of any other composer of madrigals with whose works I am acquainted. His *original harmony*, after scoring a great part of his madrigals, particularly those that have been the most celebrated, is difficult to discover; for had there been any warrantable combinations of sounds that Palestrina, Luca Marenzio, and many of his predecessors, had not used before him, in figuring the bases, they would have appeared. And as to his *modulation*, it is so far from being the *sweetest conceivable*, that, to me, it seems forced, affected, and disgusting.

The following madrigal ('Moro lasso'), being the seventeenth of his sixth book, is presented to the musical reader as a specimen of his style, and harsh, crude, and licentious modulation; in which, the beginning a composition in A minor, with the chord of C sharp, with a sharp third, is neither consonant to the present laws of *modulation*, nor to those of the ecclesiastical tones; to which, as keys were not settled and determined on the fixed principles of major and minor, in the time of Venosa, composers chiefly adhered. But a more offensive licence is taken in the second chord of this madrigal than in the first; for it is not only repugnant to every rule of transition at present established, but extremely shocking and disgusting to the ear, to go from one chord to another in which there is no *relation*, real or imaginary; and which is composed of sounds wholly extraneous and foreign to any key to which the first chord belongs.

I have bestowed more remarks on this Prince of Musicians, and more time in the examination of his works than they perhaps now deserve, in order to furnish my readers with what seems, to my comprehension, a truer idea of their worth than that which partiality and ignorance have hitherto given.[18]

Of considerable interest is British Museum MS Add. 11588 which contains 'Madrigals, etc., in score, transcribed by *Dr. Charles Burney*, 54 items.'[19] Items 36–49 are exclusively from the five-part madrigals of Carlo Gesualdo and give us a reliable clue as to the works upon which Burney based his severe judgements. It is a remarkably varied sampling, including three pieces from the first volume of Gesualdo's madrigals, one from the second, one from the third, three from the fourth, none from the fifth, and five from the sixth. The margins are peppered with personal commentary. While he not infrequently transcribes whole madrigals in his study of Gesualdo, the seven opening measures of *Beltà poi che t'assenti* suffice for Burney. He breaks off at this point with a private caustic remark directed at Hawkins: 'Let the admirers of Venosa's "sweetest modulation conceivable" defend the following fragment of a madrigal (the 2nd, op. 6) in G minor.' Is it a coincidence that a twentieth-century admirer of Gesualdo, Igor Stravinsky, undertook to 'defend' precisely this madrigal as the final number in his *Gesualdo Monumentum ad CD annum*?

In addition to the evaluations of Burney, Hawkins, Martini, and Rousseau, light is thrown on the influence and circulation of Gesualdo's music at that time by accounts relating to the Academy of Ancient Music which flourished to the midpoint of the century in London. We learn from Hawkins, who was a member, that the taste of John Immyns, a leader of the Academy, 'was altogether for old music, which he had been taught to admire by Dr. Pepusch. . . . With these prejudices, it is no wonder that he entertained a relish for madrigals, and music of the driest style: Vincenti[n]o Ruffo, Orlando de Lasso, Luca Marenzio, Horatio Vecchi, and, above all, the prince of Venosa, were his great favourites. He was very diligent in collecting their works, and studied them with incredible assiduity.'[20]

---

[18] Burney, *A General History*, III, 217–22.
[19] *Catalogue of Manuscript Music in the British Museum*, vol. II, pp. 163–4.
[20] Hawkins, *A General History* (1776), V, pp. 350–1. A single item in MS Add. 31407 of the British Museum in the hand of John Immyns (item no. 14) does little to amplify our knowledge of his activity in this field—it is the first madrigal of the first book,

In view of the evidence it seems safe to assume that representative examples of Gesualdo's music were known to Pepusch, Immyns, Hawkins, and Burney, and that on occasions they were performed at the Academy. The mention of Geminiani's frequent attendance at these society meetings recalls Hawkins' remark regarding Geminiani's indebtedness to Gesualdo. It may be concluded that if Gesualdo's music did not enjoy an actual vogue in eighteenth-century England, it probably received more attention, at least in terms of performance, than at any period between Gesualdo's time and our own.

★ ★ ★

If taste were predictable, it might be reasonable to expect that the nineteenth century, one of whose major achievements was the development of an increasingly chromatic harmonic vocabulary, would have been sympathetic to Gesualdo's music, if not openly cordial. For a time twentieth-century historians tended to speak of Gesualdo's harmonies as anticipating Wagner's, and Heseltine even suggested specific parallels between passages from *Moro lasso* and *Die Walküre*. But while in certain externals his music does seem to presage various nineteenth-century idioms, this period's lack of sympathy for him should not surprise us.

The Romantics viewed the Mannerist movement as a vice responsible for the decline of Cinquecento art, a notion indebted to seventeenth-century thought. Any artistic personality highly representative of the period was thus likely to be denied their approbation. At the same time the aesthetic propositions relating to Mannerism in music remained if not unrecognized at least unassimilated. The critical reaction in music thus proved to be similar, if for somewhat different reasons, to those in painting and sculpture. In Winterfeld's classic study of G. Gabrieli which appeared in 1834, we meet the questioning mind of the nineteenth century, not quite sure of the attitude which it should assume—perplexed at certain aspects of the method, yet obviously drawn by the emotional quality of much of the music. His assessment of Gesualdo ends by admitting the difficulty of trying to explain much of it coupled with an open confession of the music's aural attractiveness.[21]

Baci soavi, which had appeared complete in Hawkins—except to demonstrate that in eighteenth-century Britain Gesualdo's madrigals were 'Englished' in the manner of *Musica Transalpina* (1588) for local consumption.

[21] Winterfeld, *G. Gabrieli*, zweiter Theil, pp. 94–7: 'One of their [Gesualdo's madrigals] conspicuous characteristics consists in the employment of sharply dissonant sound relationships, whose resolution when they appear in a harmonic context through

It was Fétis who suggested for the first time that at least some of the confusion in the mind of later musicians stemmed from attitudes developed after Gesualdo's day—later periods heard his music through ears conditioned to later styles and inevitably subjected Gesualdo's music to comparisons with their own music. That this is a common critical hazard is obvious, but in a style as bold as Gesualdo's it is a special danger, to which the nineteenth century, as well as Burney, succumbed. It is a welcome sight to find Fétis alluding to the source of the anxiety. Considering the paucity of the musical material available to him in making his judgements his position is remarkably sound and is less vacillating or apologetic than the writings of most of his contemporaries.

[Burney] found in [Gesualdo's madrigals] neither melody, nor rhythm, nor phraseological merit, and he was stunned at the false system of modulation, the perpetual embarrassments and the inexperience in the arrangement of the parts. This judgement, as severe as it is unjust, proves only that Burney did not understand the original thought which prevailed in the madrigals of the Prince of Venosa. All these pieces are of melancholic and sweet scenes, where the musician is dedicated, above all else, to the expression of the poetic meaning of the words, according to his individual manner of feeling. . . . The system of tonal succession employed by Gesualdo is not true modulation, because the harmonic element of tonal progression did not yet exist when he was writing; but these same successions are a part of his thought, and Burney was wrong to judge them by the ordinary rules.[22]

While Fétis is undoubtedly hasty in denying not only an incipient functional harmony but also the capacity for genuine modulation in Gesualdo's music,

---

unexpected melodic progressions, instead of soothing, only pierces the ear with an intensified harshness; namely by the juxtaposition of the strangest harmonies (even if they are independently euphonious) in which we fruitlessly search for an inner connection with the harmonic sense of that time. Also in the abundant employment of chromatic notes, which we later find used in a different connection and under another name: all, peculiarities which made their performance without minute preparation almost impossible for his associates. But because of its newness it had a charm which easily misled them to an overestimation of the music . . . While we wish still at the present time, more than 200 years after the cessation of his creative activity, to praise him as exemplary in his characteristic tendency, we are unable to justify it. But the first disclosure of every new life has a somewhat mysterious attraction, whose force, if we view Venosa's creations with unclouded eyes, will not be denied to us.'

[22] Fétis, *Biographie universelle des musiciens*, III, pp. 469–70.

he does alert us to the dangers which beset the historian concerned with problems of stylistic evaluation.

Other personalities of the century commented briefly on Gesualdo's musical style, but most of them tend to echo each other. Even an occasional show of enthusiasm for the music is usually tempered with the implication that Gesualdo's music sowed the seeds for a style which was to appear fully developed only in the nineteenth century.[23] The late Romantic spirit here strains to endorse the *maniera*, but still only in terms of its congeniality to the current practice of the day.

★ ★ ★

Giedion has said that 'Absolute points of reference are no more open to the historian than they are to the physicist; both produce descriptions relative to a particular situation.'[24] Thus our own interest in Gesualdo and Mannerism has flourished, perhaps predictably, at a time whose rupture with the immediate past is closely analogous to that which occurred in the late sixteenth century. Nevertheless, the variety of opinion amongst our most seasoned historians indicates that appreciation of Gesualdo's music may still be less than universal.[25] Except for the final stylistic label, Sachs has probably given us the most balanced account and struck the critical posture most commensurate with our current knowledge:

> Contemporaries admired these madrigals as the inspirations of a genius, just as much as the critics of the nineteenth century scolded them as the amateurish experiments of a 'cavalier stumbling about in a maze of modulation.' Today, we know that he was one of the great masters and one of the boldest pioneers. True, his modulation was 'illogical'; but only from the viewpoint of Rameau's harmonic system. It was not illogical as a floating harmony without a supporting thorough-bass. True, also that Gesualdo did not strictly confine his unwonted chromatics to underscoring the Tristanic pangs of death in his love songs, with their ever recurring *io moro's* (I die), or to other emotional climaxes. No doubt, Gesualdo overdid chromatics from sheer delight in eccentricity and abnormalcy. But, in this delight, he reflected one

[23] See particularly Ambros, *Geschichte der Musik*, IV, 192–5.
[24] Giedion, *Space, Time and Architecture*, pp. 5–6.
[25] For a generally enthusiastic view, see Leichtentritt's remarks in Ambros, *Geschichte*, IV, pp. 192–5, 205, 209; for a more negative account, see Newman, *A Musical Critic's Holiday*, pp. 209–14. For opinions by Einstein see pp. 199, fn. 50, 247, 259; by Redlich, p. 260.

of the traits of the Baroque age—the one that popular terminology denotes as 'baroque'.[26]

Whatever the judgements of past centuries on Gesualdo and the Age of Mannerism, they may help us not only to make our own estimate of the age, which can no longer prudently be labelled a volatile *fin-de-siècle* movement, but also to recognize our relation to it.

In the past the major stumbling block to an appreciation of Gesualdo's music has probably been the difficulty of reconciling a progressive style with a fading form. Yet was it not the adaptability of the madrigal which led initially to the solo style, and was it not the expressive qualities won in the polyphonic madrigal which directly served the early writers of opera? The Baroque did not altogether abandon counterpoint for a soprano-bass, two-line system, and the late sixteenth-century reconciliation of chromatic technique with the ancient systems of counterpoint was at least as important a bequest to the Baroque as the conception of monody. What the late madrigal did lack was the dimension for working out the human sentiments which were to appeal to a new age. Gesualdo's madrigals—aphoristic and epigrammatic distillates—frequently disturb because too much is compacted in too small a space. Yet ultimately, it is this density which emerges as the central ingredient and chief source of fascination.

Meanwhile, it is notable that the recent decades which witnessed the Gesualdo revival also testified to a quickening interest in El Greco, as well as in Pontormo, Rosso, and Parmigianino. They similarly signalled the codification, if not the birth, of the idea of Mannerism as a period of Triumph and not, as in a previous time, an age of Decline.[27] The appeal of this point of view for the future will ultimately be revealed; its attraction for our own time is already history.[28]

---

[26] Sachs, *Our Musical Heritage*, pp. 177–8.

[27] Rijksmuseum, Amsterdam, *Le Triomphe du Maniérisme Européen de Michel-Ange au Gréco*, Catalogue (1955).

[28] Wellesz has spoken for Schoenberg in 'Arnold Schönberg' in *Zeitschrift der Internationalen Musikgesellschaft*, XII (1910–11), p. 342, and 'The Origins of Schönberg's Twelve-Tone System,' The Louis Charles Elson Memorial Fund Lecture (Washington, D.C., January 10, 1957); Stravinsky and Hesse for themselves in the Preface and Postscript to this book; Huxley in 'Gesualdo. Variations on a Musical Theme' in *On Art and Artists* as well as in his cooperation with the production of several recordings devoted to the music of Gesualdo.

Postscript

Hermann Hesse, Nobel laureate, sketched the following poem★ shortly before his death, on hearing a recording of Gesualdo's music.

Einst vor tausend Jahren

Unruhvoll und reiselüstern
Aus zerstücktem Traum erwacht
Hör ich seine Weise flüstern
Meinen Bambus in der Nacht.

Statt zu ruhen, statt zu liegen
Reisst michs aus den alten Gleisen,
Weg zu stürzen, weg zu fliegen,
Ins Unendliche zu reisen.

Einst vor tausend Jahren gab es
Eine Heimat, einen Garten,
Wo im Beet des Vogelgrabes
Aus dem Schnee die Krokus starrten.

Vogelschwingen möcht ich breiten
Aus dem Bann, der mich umgrenzt,
Dort hinüber, zu den Zeiten,
Deren Gold noch heut mir glänzt.

Verses scribbled on a December night 1961 in something of a fever

Restless and desiring travel, awakened from a broken dream, I hear my bamboo whisper its melody in the night.

Instead of rest, instead of lying, it draws me from the beaten track to hasten away, to fly away, and to journey into infinity.

There was a home, there was a garden once, a thousand years ago, where on the bed of a bird's grave the crocuses peeped up from the snow.

Would I might escape on birds' wings from the spell which rings me round, back to those times that glitter still for me like gold.

★ Printed by permission of Suhrkamp Verlag © Suhrkamp Verlag Frankfurt um Main 1962

Bibliography

Adams, Ruth. *The Responsoria of Carlo Gesualdo* (M.A. Thesis, University of California, Los Angeles, 1957).

Aldimari, Biagio. *Historia genealogica della Famiglia Carafa* (Naples, 1691).

Ammirato, S. *Delle Famiglie nobili Napoletane* (Florence, 1580, pt. I; 1651, pt. II).

Anderson, John. *The Cadence in the Madrigals of Gesualdo* (Ph.D. dissertation, Catholic University, 1964).

Antolini, Patrizio. *Manoscritti relativi alla storia di Ferrara* (Ferrara, 1891).

Apel, Willi. 'Neapolitan Links Between Cabezon and Frescobaldi' in *Musical Quarterly*, XXIV (1938), pp. 419–37.

Archivio di Stato di Modena. *Inventario, Archivio Segreto Estense*, Sezione 'Casa e Stato' (Rome, 1953).

d'Arienzo, N. 'Un predecessore di Alessandro Scarlatti,' in *Gazzetta Musicale di Milano*, 1892.

Arlotti, Ridolfo. *Lettere*, Biblioteca Estense, MSS W.5, 6 (*olim* 11.*26); G.1,6 (*olim* IX. F, 17); M.5, 15.

Arnold, Denis and Fortune, Nigel, ed. *The Monteverdi Companion* (London, 1968).

Arnold, Denis. *Marenzio* (London, 1965).

Artusi, G. M. *Delle imperfettioni della moderna musica* (Venice, 1600).

Baldini, Vittorio, publ. *Diversorum poemata* (Ferrara, 1594).

Baldini, Vittorio, publ. *Rime di diversi Autori* (Ferrara, 1594).

Barbour, J. M. *Tuning and Temperament* (East Lansing, Mich., 1951).

Bellonci, M. *I segreti dei Gonzaga* (Florence, 1947).

Berardi, Angelo. *Miscellanea musicale* (Bologna, 1689).

Bialostocki, Jan. 'The Renaissance Concept of Nature and Antiquity,' Acts of the Twentieth International Congress of the History of Art: *The Renaissance and Mannerism*, vol. II (Princeton, 1963), pp. 19–30.

Blancanus, Josephus. *Chronologia celebrorum mathematicorum ad sec. Christi XVII* (Bologna, 1615).

Blunt, Sir Anthony. *Artistic Theory in Italy, 1450–1600* (Oxford, 1940).

Borzelli, Angelo. 'Notizia dei mss. Corona, ed il Successo: di Donna Maria d'Avalos principessa di Venosa e di Don Fabrizio Carafa duca d'Andria,' in *Rassegna scientifica, letteraria e politica*, anno II, nn. 5–6 (Paravia, 1891).

Borzelli, Angelo. *Successi tragici et amorosi di Silvio et Ascanio Corona* (Naples, 1908).

Bottrigari, Ercole. *Il Desiderio*, 1594; ed. by K. Meyer, 1924; trans. by C. MacClintock, Musical Studies and Documents 9 (American Institute of Musicology, 1963).

Boulting, William. *Tasso and His Times* (New York, 1907).

Bousquet, Jacques. *Mannerism* (New York, 1964).

Brantôme, Pierre de Bourdeilles. *Vies des Dames galantes*, ed. by Ludovic Lalanne (Paris, 1864).

Brantôme, Pierre de Bourdeilles. *The Lives of Gallant Ladies*, trans. out of the French by H.M. Subscribers only (1924).

Bukofzer, Manfred. *Music in the Baroque Era* (New York, 1947).

Burney, Charles. *A General History of Music* (London, 1776–89).

Burns, Joseph. *Early Neapolitan Keyboard Music* (Ph.D. dissertation, Harvard University, 1953).

Campanella, Thomaso. *Medicinalium juxta propria principia* (Lyons, 1635).

Campori, Giuseppe. *Gli artisti italiani e stranieri negli stati estensi* (Modena, 1855).

Capasso, Bartolommeo. *Torquato Tasso a Napoli* (1895).

Carapetyan, Armen. 'The Concept of *Imitazione della Natura* in the Sixteenth Century,' in *Journal of Renaissance and Baroque Music*, I (1946), pp. 47 ff.

Catone, Giacomo. *Memorie Gesualdine* (1840).

Cerone, Domenico Pietro. *El melopeo y maestro, tractado de musica theorica y practica* (Naples, 1613).

Cerreto, Scipione. *Della prattica musica vocale e strumentale* (Naples, 1601).

Clough, John. 'The Leading Tone in Direct Chromaticism: from Renaissance to Baroque,' in *Journal of Music Theory*, I, 1 (1957), pp. 2–21.

Choron, Alexander. *Principes de composition des écoles d'Italie* (Paris, 1816).

Consiglio, Alberto. *Gesualdo ovvero Assassinio a cinque voci. Storia tragici italiana del secolo xvi* (Naples, 1967).

Craft, Robert. 'Gesualdo, Prince of Madrigalists,' in *High Fidelity* (1961) and Columbia Record KL 5718/KS 6318.

Craft, Robert. 'A Journey with Gesualdo' with Columbia Record ML 5341/MS 6048.

Craft, Robert. Preface to Gesualdo-Stravinsky *Tres Sacrae Cantiones* (London, 1960).

D'Accone, Frank. 'Bernardo Pisano, An Introduction to His Life and Works' in *Musica Disciplina*, XVII (1963), pp. 115–35.

D'Accone, Frank, ed. *Music of the Florentine Renaissance*; vol. I: Bernardo Pisano, *Collected Works*, Corpus Mensurabilis Musicae 32 (1966).

Dahlhaus, Carl. *Untersuchungen über die Entstehung der harmonischen Tonalität* (Cassel, 1968).

Dahlhaus, Carl. 'Zur chromatischen Technik Carlo Gesualdos' in *Analecta Musicologica*, Bd. 4 (1967), pp. 76–96.

Disertori, Benvenuto. 'Un libro italiano su Carlo Gesualdo,' in *Rivista musicale italiana*, 45 (1941), pp. 20–4.

Doni, G. B. *Compendio del trattato de'generi e de'modi della musica* (Rome, 1635).

Doni, G. B. *Lyra Barberina* (Florence, 1763), ed. by A. F. Gori.

Doni, G. B. *Trattato della musica scenica* (Rome, 1635).

Dürr, Walter, 'Zur mehrstimmigen Behandlung des chromatischen Schrittes in der Polyphonie des 16. Jahrhunderts,' in *Kassel Kongressbericht* (1962), pp. 138ff.

Einstein, Alfred. Collection of Manuscript Scores, including scores of over 300 madrigal books, MS, Smith College; available on microfilm.

Einstein, Alfred. 'Dante on the Way to the Madrigal,' in *Musical Quarterly*, XXV (1939), pp. 142–55, 507–9.

Einstein, Alfred. *The Italian Madrigal*, 3 vols. (Princeton, 1949).

Einstein, Alfred. *A Short History of Music* (New York, 1938).

Engel, Hans. *Luca Marenzio* (Florence, 1956).

Equicola, Mario d'Alveto. *Genealogia delli Signori prencipi in Ferrara con breve trattato di loro Particolari gesti composta da Mario Equicola de Alveto dell'anno 1516*. Ferrara, Biblioteca Comunale Ariostea, MS Cl. II, n. 349.

d'Este, Alessandro. *Lettere*, Biblioteca Estense, Modena, MS F.6, 6 (*olim* 11, *21).

d'Este, Eleanora. *Contratto di matrimonio di Eleanora col Principe di Venosa in data 1593*, Biblioteca Estense, Modena, MS b. 376, fasc. 58/2011.

Ferand, Ernest T. '*Anchor che col partire*. Die Schicksale eines berühmten Madrigals (Cipriano de Rore),' in *Festschrift K.G. Fellerer zum sechszigsten Geburtstag 1962*, pp. 137–54.

Fétis, F. J. *Biographie universelle des musiciens*, 2nd ed., 8 vols. (Paris, 1860–5).

Florimo, Francesco. *La scuola musicale di Napoli e suoi conservatori*, 4 vols. (Napoli, 1880–2).

Fontanelli, Alfonso. *Lettere*, Archivio di Stato, Modena, Busta no. II (2769/65), no. 88 (3345/72).

France, Anatole. 'Histoire de Donna Maria d'Avalos et de Don Fabrizio, Duc d'Andria,' in *Le Puits de Saint Claire*, 4th ed. (Paris, 1895), pp. 271ff.

Friedländer, Walter. *Mannerism and Anti-Mannerism in Italian Painting* (New York, 1957).

Frizzi, Antonio. *Memorie per la storia di Ferrara*, 2nd ed. (Ferrara, 1848), iv.

Gasparini, Alberto. *Cesare d'Este e Clemente VIII* (Modena, 1959).

Geminiani, Francesco. *Guida Armonica, o Dizionario Armonico, being a Sure Guide to Harmony and Modulation* (London, 1742).

Gesualdo, Don Carlo. *Lettere,* Archivio di Stato, Modena; busta 1251–8, Napoli.

Gesualdo, Don Carlo. *Testamento di Carlo Gesualdi principe di Venosa, 1613 Septembre 3*; tre copi sempl. Archivio di Stato, Modena; busta 376, fasc. 2011/3.

Gesualdo, Don Carlo. *Sämtliche Werke,* 10 vols., ed. by Wilhelm Weismann and Glenn E. Watkins (Hamburg, 1957–66).

Giazotto, Remo. 'Poesia del Tasso in morte di Maria Gesualdo,' in *La Rassegna Musicale,* XVIII (1948), pp. 15–28.

Giazotto, Remo. 'Pianto e poesia del Tasso in morte di Maria Gesualdo,' in *Musurgia Nova* (Milano, 1959), pp. 157ff.

Giedion, Sigfried. *Space, Time and Architecture* (Cambridge, Mass., 1956).

Giustiniani, Michele. *Lettere memorabili* (Rome, 1675).

Giustiniani, Vincenzo. *Discorso sopra la musica,* ed. by C. MacClintock, Musical Studies and Documents 9 (American Institute of Musicology, 1962).

Gray, Cecil and Heseltine, Philip. *Carlo Gesualdo, Musician and Murderer* (London, 1926).

Gray, Cecil. *Contingencies and Other Essays* (London, 1947).

Gray, Cecil. *The History of Music* (New York, 1931).

Guarini, Marcantonio. *Diario di tutte le cose accadute nella nobilissima città di Ferrara principiando per tutto l'anno MDLXX sino a questo di et anno MDLXXXXVIII,* Biblioteca Estense, Modena, H.2, 16 (*olim* VIII.B.8).

Guerra, Scipione. *Diurnali* (Naples, 1891). A modern edition based on two seventeenth-century codices which treat the years 1574–1627.

Haar, James, ed. *Chanson and Madrigal, 1480–1530* (Cambridge, Mass., 1964).

Haar, James. 'The *Note Nere* Madrigal,' in *Journal of the American Musicological Society,* XVIII, 1 (1965), pp. 22–41.

Harran, Don. ' "Mannerism" in the Cinquecento Madrigal?' in *The Musical Quarterly,* LV, 4 (1969), pp. 521–44.

Harran, Don. 'Some Early Examples of the Madrigale Cromatico' in *Acta Musicologica,* XLI (1969), pp. 240–6.

Harran, Don. 'Verse Types in the Early Madrigal,' in *Journal of the American Musicological Society,* XXII, 1 (1969), pp. 27–53.

Hauser, Arnold. *Mannerism* (New York, 1965).

Hawkins, Sir John. *An Account of the institution and progress of the Academy of ancient music with a comparative view of the music of the past and present times* (London, 1770).

Hawkins, Sir John. *A General History of the Science and Practice of Music* (London, 1776).

Hersh, Donald. *Verdelot and the Early Madrigal* (Ph.D. dissertation, University of California, 1963).

Hibbard, Howard. 'The Early History of Sant'Andrea della Valle,' in *Art Bulletin*, XVII, 4 (1961), pp. 289–318.

Horsley, I. 'The Diminutions in Composition and the Theory of Composition,' in *Acta Musicologica*, XXXV, ii–iii (1963), pp. 124–53.

Huxley, Aldous. 'Gesualdo: Variations on a Musical Theme,' in *On Art and Artists* (New York, 1960).

d'India, Sigismondo. *Madrigali a cinque voci, Libro I*, ed. by Federico Mompellio, *I Classical Musicali Italiani*, vol. 10 (Milan, 1942).

Jackson, Roland. *The Keyboard Music of Giovanni Maria Trabaci* (Ph.D. dissertation, University of California, 1964).

Jackson, Roland. *Neapolitan Keyboard Composers, circa 1600*, Corpus of Early Keyboard Music 24 (American Institute of Musicology, 1967).

Jackson, Roland, 'On Frescobaldi's Chromaticism and Its Background,' in *Musical Quarterly*, LVIII (1971), pp. 255–69.

Johnson, Alvin. *The Liturgical Music of Cipriano de Rore* (Ph.D. dissertation, Yale University, 1954).

Kaufmann, Henry W. 'A "Diatonic" and a "Chromatic" Madrigal by Giulio Fiesco,' in *Aspects of Medieval and Renaissance Music*, ed. by Jan LaRue (New York, 1966), pp. 474–88.

Kaufmann, Henry W. *The Life and Works of Nicolas Vicentino*, Musical Studies and Documents 11 (American Institute of Musicology, 1966).

Kaufmann, Henry W. 'The Motets of Nicola Vicentino,' in *Musica Disciplina*, XV (1961), pp. 167–85.

Kaufmann, Henry W. 'Vicentino's Arciorgano; an Annotated Translation,' in *Journal of Music Theory*, V, 2 (1961), pp. 33ff.

Keiner, Ferdinand. *Die Madrigale Gesualdos von Venosa* (Leipzig, 1914).

Kerman, Joseph. *The Elizabethan Madrigal. A comparative study* (American Musicological Society, 1962).

Kiesewetter, R. G. *Geschichte der europäis-abendischen oder unsrer heutigen Musik* (Leipzig, 1834).

Kinkeldey, Otto. 'Luzzasco Luzzaschi's Solo-Madrigale mit Klavierbegleitung,' in *Sammelbände der Internationalen Musikgesellschaft*, IX (1907–8), pp. 538–65.

Kircher, A. *Musurgia Universalis* (1650).

Kroyer, Theodor. 'Die Anfänge der Chromatik im italienischen Madrigal des XVI. Jahrhunderts,' in *Publikationen der Internationalen Musikgesellschaft*, Heft IV (Leipzig, 1902).

Lellis, Carlo di. *Discorsi delle famiglie nobili del regno di Napoli* (1654–71).

Levitan, Joseph S. 'Adrian Willaert's Famous Duo: Quidnam ebrietas,' in *Tijdschrift der Vereeniging voor Nederl. Muziekgeschiedenis*, XV, 3–4 (1938–9), pp. 166–233.

Levy, Kenneth. 'Costeley's Chromatic Chanson,' in *Annales Musicologiques*, III (1955), pp. 213–63.

Litta, Pompeo. *Famiglie celebri d'Italia*, 1819.

Lockwood, Lewis. 'Vincenzo Ruffo and Musical Reform after the Council of Trent,' in *Musical Quarterly*, XLIII (1957), pp. 342–71.

Lowinsky, E. E. 'Adrian Willaert's Chromatic "Duo" Re-examined,' in *Tijdschrift voor Muziekwetenschap*, XVIII (1956), pp. 1–36.

Lowinsky, E. E. 'Echoes of Adrian Willaert's Chromatic "Duo" in Sixteenth- and Seventeenth-Century Compositions,' in *Studies in Music History* (Princeton, 1968), ed. Harold Powers, pp. 183–238.

Lowinsky, E. E. 'Matthaeus Greiter's *Fortuna*: An Experiment in Chromaticism and Musical Iconography,' in *Musical Quarterly*, XLII (1956), pp. 500–19; XLIII (1957), pp. 68–85.

Lowinsky, E. E. *Secret Chromatic Art in the Netherland Motet* (New York, 1946; repr. 1967).

Lowinsky, E. E. *Tonality and Atonality in Sixteenth-Century Music* (Berkeley, 1961).

Luzzaschi, Luzzasco. *Madrigali per cantare e sonare a uno, due e tre soprani* (1601), ed. by Adriano Cavicchi (Brescia, 1965).

Luzzaschi, Luzzasco. *Il quarto libro de' madrigali a 5*, 1594 (Einstein Manuscript Scores, XXIX, i, Smith College; microfilm).

Luzzaschi, Luzzasco. *Seconda scelta delli madrigali a 5*, 1613 (Einstein Manuscript Scores, XXIX, ii, Smith College; microfilm).

MacClintock, Carol. *Giaches de Wert, Life and Works*, Musical Studies and Documents 17 (American Institute of Musicology, 1966).

Maniates, Maria. 'Mannerist Composition in Franco-Flemish Polyphony,' in *Musical Quarterly*, LII (1966), pp. 17–36.

della Marra, Don Ferrante (Duca della Guardia nell'anno 1623). *Rovine di case Napolitane del suo tempo*, Biblioteca Nazionale di Napoli, MS X.A.A.8.

Marshall, George R. *The Harmonic Laws in the Madrigals of Carlo Gesualdo* (Ph.D. dissertation, New York University, 1956).

Marenzio, Luca. *Sämtliche Werke*, ed. by Alfred Einstein, in *Publikationen älterer Musik*, Jg. IV, Teil 1 and Jg. VI (1929–31). Includes only *Madrigali a 5*, Books I–VI. *Madrigali a 4*, 1585 (Einstein Collection, LXXII); *Madrigali a 4, 5 & 6*, 1588 (Einstein Collection, XXX, i); *Madrigali a 6*, lib. 1, 1581; lib. 2, 1584; lib. 3, 1585; lib. 4, 1587; lib. 5, 1591; lib. 6, 1595 (Einstein Collection, LXX, LXXIV, XXX, ii–iv, and XXI, i–ii).

Martini, Padre G. B. *Esemplare ossia Saggio fondamentale pratico di Contrappunto*, 2 vols. (Bologna, 1774–5).

Massenkeil, Günther. *Mehrstimmige Lamentationen aus der ersten Hälfte des 16. Jahrhunderts* (Mainz, 1965).

Massenkeil, Günther. 'Zur Lamentationskomposition des 15. Jahrhunderts,' in *Archiv für Musikwissenschaft*, 18 (1961), pp. 103–14.

Mei, Girolamo. *Letters on Ancient and Modern Music to Vicenzo Galilei and Giovanni Bardi*, A Study with Annotated Texts by Claude V. Palisca, Musical Studies and Documents 3 (American Institute of Musicology, 1960).

Merenda, Don Girolamo. *Memorie della città di Ferrara di don Girolamo Merenda Rettore della Chiesa di S. Biagio di Ferrara*, Biblioteca Estense, Modena, MSS H.3, 3 (*olim* IX.D, 2); G.P.28; VI.C.1; VII.C.1; VII.C.12; VIII.C.9.

Micheli, D. Romano. *Musica vaga et artificiosa* (1615).

Modestino, C. *Della dimora di T. Tasso in Napoli, 1588, 1592, 1594* (Naples, 1863).

Mompellio, Federico. *Sigismondo d'India* (Milan, 1957).

da Monte, Alessandro. *Storia di Ferrara dalle origini al 1643*, 3 vols., Biblioteca Estense, Modena, MSS Q.4, 6–8; W.6, 17–19 (*olim* VIII.H.1–3; VIII.A.17–19).Libro secondo carries the title, *Delle cose di Ferrara al tempo dei Duchi*.

Mutinelli, Fabio, ed. *Storia arcana e anedotica d'Italia raccontata dai Veneti Ambasciatori*, annotata ed edita da F. Mutinelli, 4 vols. (Venice, 1855–8).

Nenna, Pomponio. *Madrigali*, Books I and IV à 5 v., Istituto Italiano per la Storia della Musica, Monumenti II, vol. I, ed. by E. Dagnino (Rome, 1942).

Nenna, Pomponio. *Madrigals*, from Books V, VI, VII, VIII *à 5 v.* and Book I *à 4 v.*, ed. by Glenn Watkins, Penn State Music Series (University Park, Pa., 1973).

Newcomb, Anthony. 'Carlo Gesualdo and a Musical Correspondence of 1594,' in *Musical Quarterly*, LIV, 4 (1968), pp. 409–36.

Newcomb, Anthony. *The Musica Secreta of Ferrara in the 1580s*, (Ph.D dissertation, Princeton, 1970).

Newman, Ernest. *A Musical Critic's Holiday* (New York, 1925).

Nota dei musici del Signor Duca di Ferrara Alfonso II. Bibl. Civica, Ferrara, MS Racc. Antonelli, n. 474.

Nuernberger, Louis. *The five-voiced madrigals of Cipriano de Rore* (Ph.D. dissertation, University of Michigan, 1963).

Palisca, Claude V. *Baroque Music* (Englewood Cliffs, N.J., 1968).

Palisca, Claude V. *The Beginnings of Baroque Music: Its Roots in Sixteenth-Century Theory and Polemics* (Ph.D. dissertation, Harvard University, 1953).

Palisca, Claude V. 'A Clarification of "Musica Reservata" in Jean Taisner's "Astrologiae", 1559' in *Acta Musicologica*, XXXI (1959), pp. 133–61.

Palisca, Claude V. 'Science and Music,' in *Seventeenth Century Science and the Arts*, ed. by H. H. Rhys (Princeton, 1961).

Palisca, Claude V. 'Vicenzo Galilei's Counterpoint Treatise: A Code for the *Seconda Pratica*,' in *Journal of the American Musicological Society*, IX, 2 (1956), pp. 81–96.

Pannain, Guido. 'Note sui Responsori di Carlo Gesualdo da Venosa' in *Chigiana*, xxv, 5 (1968), pp. 231–7.

Pannain, Guido, ed. *L'Oratorio dei Filippini e la scuola musicale di Napoli*, vol. V of *Istituzioni e Monumenti dell'arte musicale italiana* (Milan, 1934).

Pastor, Ludwig Freiherr von. *The History of the Popes*, 40 vols., edited by Ralph Francis Kerr (London, 1952).

Pietri, Francesco di. *Historia Napoletana* (Naples, 1634).

Pirrotta, Nino. 'Gesualdo,' in *La Musica*, vol. II (Turin, 1966).

Prota-Giurleo, U. *La Musica a Napoli nel Seicento*, IV (Benevente, 1928).

Prota-Giurleo, U. 'Notizie sul musicista belga Jean Macque,' in *Report of the First Congress for the International Society for Musical Research* (Liege, 1930), pp. 191–7.

Ramazzini, Amilcare. 'I Musici fiamminghi all'corte di Ferrara: Giaches de Wert e Tarquinia Molza,' in *Archivio Storico Lombardo*, VI (1879).

Raymond, Marcel. 'Le Pléiade et la maniérisme', in *De Petrarque a Descartes*, 11–12 (1966–7), pp. 381–423.

Redlich, Hans. 'Gesualdo,' in *Musik in Geschichte und Gegenwart*.

Redlich, Hans. 'Gesualdo and the Italian Madrigal,' in *The Listener* (London, 18 Sept. 1952).

Reese, Gustave. *Music in the Renaissance* (New York, 1954).

Ricca, E. *La Nobiltà delle due Sicile* (1859–87).

Romei, Annibale. *Discorsi*. Reprinted complete in Solerti, *Ferrara e la Corte estense* (Castello, 1891).

Roncaglia, Gino. *La cappella musicale del Duomo di Modena* (Florence, 1957).

Rore, Cipriano de. *The Madrigals of Cipriano de Rore for 3 and 4 voices*, ed. by G. P. Smith (Smith College Music Archives, 1943).

Rore, Cipriano de. *Opera Omnia*, ed. by Bernhard Meier, Corpus Mensurabilis Musicae 14 (American Institute of Musicology, 1959–).

Rosini, Gio., ed. *Opere di Torquato Tasso* (Pisa, 1776–1855). Four letters from

Tasso to Gesualdo in Appendix to Vol. XVIII; also poems concerning murder of Maria d'Avalos and to Don Carlo, Vol. XXXII.

Rowland, Daniel B. *Mannerism—Style and Mood: An Anatomy of Four Works in Three Art Forms* (New Haven, 1964).

Sachs, Curt. *Our Musical Heritage*, 2nd ed. (New York, 1955).

Santi, Venceslao. 'La storia della *Secchia rapita*,' in *Memorie della Regia Accademia di Scienze*, Ser. III, vols. VI and IX, 1906, 1909. Particularly Ser. III, vol. IX, 'Memorie della Sezione di Lettere,' p. 317.

Schmidt, Günther. 'Grundsätzliche Bemerkungen zur Geschichte der Passionshistorie,' in *Archiv für Musikwissenschaft*, XVII (1960), pp. 100–25.

Schrade, Leo. *Monteverdi, Creator of Modern Music* (New York, 1950).

Schrade, Leo. 'Renaissance: the Historical Conception of an Epoch,' in *Kongress-Bericht Internationale Gesellschaft für Musikwissenschaft, Utrecht, 1952* (Amsterdam, 1953), pp. 19–32.

Schrade, Leo. *Tragedy in the Art of Music* (Cambridge, Mass., 1964).

Schrade, Leo. 'Von der Maniera der Komposition des 16. Jahrhunderts,' in *Zeitschrift für Musikwissenschaft*, XVI (1934), pp. 3–20, 98–117, 152–70.

Serassi, P. A. *Vita di Torquato Tasso*, 3rd ed., 2 vols. (Florence, 1858).

Shearman, John. *Mannerism* (London, 1967).

Smyth, Craig. 'Mannerism and Maniera' in Acts of the Twentieth International Congress of the History of Art: *The Renaissance and Mannerism*, vol. II (Princeton, 1963), pp. 174–99.

Solerti, Angelo. 'Un dramma d'amore a Napoli nel secolo XVI,' in *Gazzetta letteraria*, XII, 22 (Turin, 1888).

Solerti, Angelo. *Ferrara e la corte estense nella seconda metà del sec. XVI* (Castello, 1891).

Solerti, Angelo. *Musica, ballo e drammatica alla corte Medicea dal 1600 al 1637* (Florence, 1905).

Solerti, Angelo. *Le Origini del Melodramma* (Turin, 1903).

Solerti, Angelo. *Vita di Torquato Tasso*, vol. I (Turin, 1895).

Spaccini, Gio. Batt. *Cronaca Modenese di Gio. Batt. Spaccini (1588–1636)*, a cura di Emilio Paolo Vicini (Modena, 1911–19). Serie delle Cronache, Tomo XVI e XVII, of *Monumenti di Storia Patria delle Provencie Modenesi*. Original MS in the Archivio storico del Comune di Modena housed in the Biblioteca Estense.

Spiro, Arthur G. *The Five-Part Madrigals of Luzzasco Luzzaschi* (Ph.D. dissertation, Boston University, 1961).

Stravinsky, Igor and Craft, Robert. 'Gesualdo,' in *Conversations* (New York, 1959), pp. 33–4.

Stravinsky, Igor. *Monumentum pro Gesualdo ad CD annum* (London, 1960).

Stravinsky, Igor. *Tres Sacrae Cantiones,* completion of three motets by Gesualdo (London, 1960).

Strunk, Oliver. *Source Readings in Music History* (New York, 1950).

Summonte, Giovanni Antonio. *Historia della città e regno di Napoli* (Naples, 1601–43); 2nd ed. (Naples, 1675).

Sutherland, David. *Francesco de Layolle (1492–1540): Life and Secular Works* (Ph.D. dissertation, University of Michigan, 1968).

Sypher, Wylie. *Four Stages of Renaissance Style* (New York, 1955).

Tasso, Torquato. *Opere,* ed. Bruno Maier (Milan, 1963). *Rime* in vol. I.

Tasso, Torquato. *Opere,* ed. by Gio. Rosini (Pisa, 1776–1855). Poems concerning murder of Maria d'Avalos and to Don Carlo, in vol. XXXII.

Tasso, Torquato. *Lettere,* ed. C. Guasti (Florence, 1855). Letters to Gesualdo in vol. V.

Tassoni, Alessandro. *Paragone degl'ingegni antichi e moderni* (Bologna, 1830), cap. xxiii: 'Musici antichi e moderni,' p. 221.

Torchi, L., ed. *L'arte musicale in Italia,* 7 vols. (Milan, 1897–1908).

Torri, Luigi. 'Nei Parentali (1614–1914) di Felice Anerio e di Carlo Gesualdo Principe di Venosa,' in *Rivista musicale italiana,* XXI (1914), pp. 501–8.

Valdrighi, Luigi F. 'Cappelle, concerte e musiche di casa d'Este dal secolo 15 al 18,' in *Atti e Memorie delle RR. Deputazioni di Storia Patria per le provincie Modenesi e Parmensi* (Modena, 1884). Ser. III, vol. II, parte II, 416; Ser. III, vol. III, parte II, 507.

della Valle, Pietro. *Della musica dell'età nostra* in Doni, *Lyra Barberina,* vol. 2 (Florence, 1763), ed. by Anton F. Gori. Reprinted in Solerti, *Le Origini del Melodramma,* pp. 148ff.

Vatielli, Francesco. *Il Principe di Venosa e Leonora d'Este* (Milan, 1941).

Vedriani, Lodovico. *Historia dell'antichissima città di Modena* (Modena, 1666).

Vicentino, Nicola. *L'antica musica ridotta alla moderna prattica,* 1555; fascimile ed. by E. Lowinsky (Cassel, 1959).

Vicentino, Nicola. *Collected Works,* ed. by H. Kaufmann, Corpus Mensurabilis Musicae 26 (American Institute of Musicology, 1963).

Villarosa, Carlo A. *Memorie dei compositori di musica del regno di Napoli* (Naples, 1840).

Vogel, Emil. *Bibliothek der gedruckten weltlichen Vokalmusik aus den Jahren 1500 bis 1700,* 2 vols., (Berlin, 1892).

Vogel, Emil. 'Claudio Monteverdi,' in *Vierteljahrsschrift für Musikwissenschaft,* III (1887), pp. 315–442.

Vogel, Emil. 'Marco da Gagliano,' in *Vierteljahrsschrift für Musikwissenschaft,* V (1889), pp. 509–68.

Vossius, G. J. *De universae Mathesios natura & constitutione liber; cui subjungitur*

Chronologia Mathematicorum (Amsterdam, 1650), lib. 3, cap. 59, par. sign. 26.

Wade, Walter W. *The Sacred Style of Luca Marenzio as represented in his four-part motets, 1585* (Ph.D. dissertation, Northwestern University, 1958).

Walker, John. *Bellini and Titian at Ferrara* (New York, 1956).

Watanabe, Ruth. *Five Books of Italian Madrigals of the Late Sixteenth Century* (Ph.D. dissertation, University of Rochester, 1951; Univ. of Rochester Microcard Press, 1954).

Watkins, Glenn E., ed. *Gesualdo di Venosa, Sämtliche Werke*, Bds. VII, VIII, IX, X (Hamburg, 1959–66).

Watkins, Glenn E. *Notes* in 'Gesualdo, Prince of Madrigalists; A Tribute to His Amazing Life and Music,' Columbia Records KL 5718/KS 6318.

Watkins, Glenn E. *Three Books of Polyphonic Lamentations of Jeremiah, 1549–1564* (Ph.D. dissertation, University of Rochester, 1953; Univ. of Rochester Microcard Press, 1954).

Weismann, Wilhelm, ed. *Gesualdo di Venosa, Sämtliche Werke*, Bds. I, II, III, IV, V, VI (Hamburg, 1957–63).

Weismann, Wilhelm. 'Die Madrigale des Carlo Gesualdo, Principe di Venosa,' in *Deutsches Jahrbuch der Musikwissenschaft für 1960* (Leipzig, 1961), pp. 1–36.

Wert, Giaches de. *Collected Works*, ed. by Carol MacClintock in collaboration with Melvin Bernstein, Corpus Mensurabilis Musicae 24 (American Institute of Musicology, 1961–   ).

Wiora, Walter, ed. *Italienische Madrigale (Das Chorwerk*, I, v), 1930.

Wilde, R. H. *Conjectures and researches concerning the love, madness, and imprisonment of Torquato Tasso* (1842).

Winterfeld, Carl von. *G. Gabrieli und sein Zeitalter* (1834).

Wolf, Robert E. 'The Aesthetic Problem of the "Renaissance",' in *Revue Belge de Musicologie*, IX (1955), pp. 83–102.

Wolf, Robert E. 'Renaissance, Mannerism, Baroque: Three Styles, Three Periods,' in *Les Colloques de Wégimont*, IV (1957), pp. 35–59.

Zacconi, Lodovico. *Prattica di Musica* (1596–1622).

Zarlino, Gioseffo. *Istitutioni harmoniche* (1558), translated by G. Marco and C. Palisca (New Haven, 1968).

Zeri, Bruno. *Biagio Rossetti* (Turin, 1960).

List of Works

LIST OF SOURCES

Publications containing only works by Gesualdo

I. *Madrigali a cinque voci; Libro primo* (Ferrara: Baldini, 1594; Venice: Gardano, 1603, 1604, 1608, 1617; Naples: Nucci, 1617).

The original publication of this volume, a copy of which is no longer extant, appeared under the *nom de plume* of Gioseppe Pilonij. This suggests that, although it is referred to as *Libro secondo* in printings of 1603, 1604, 1608, and the Venice printing of 1617, it is rightfully *Libro primo*. It is so designated by Simone Molinaro in his partitura edition of 1613, in the Naples print of 1617, and throughout this book. The numerical designation is missing from the Baldini prints of the first three volumes.

II. *Madrigali a cinque voci; Libro secondo* (Ferrara: Baldini, 1594; Venice: Gardano, 1603, 1607, 1616). This volume is designated as *Libro primo* in all of the Venice printings. See above.

III. *Madrigali a cinque voci; Libro terzo* (Ferrara: Baldini, 1595; Venice: Gardano, 1603, 1611, 1619).

IV. *Madrigali a cinque voci; Libro quarto* (Ferrara: Baldini, 1596; Venice: Gardano, 1604, 1611, 1616).

V. *Madrigali a cinque voci; Libro quinto* (Gesualdo: Carlino, 1611; Venice: Gardano, 1614).

VI. *Madrigali a cinque voci; Libro sesto* (Gesualdo: Carlino, 1611; Venice: Gardano, 1616).

VII. *Partitura delli sei libri de madrigali a cinque voci* (Genoa: Pavoni, 1613).

VIII. *Madrigali a sei voci* (Naples: Magnetta, 1626).

IX. *Sacrae Cantionum quinque vocibus; Liber primus* (Naples: Vitali, 1603).

X. *Sacrae Cantionum quarum una septem vocibus, caetere sex vocibus; Liber primus* (Naples: Vitali, 1603).

XI. *Responsoria et alia ad Officium Hebdomadae Sanctae spectantia sex vocibus* (Gesualdo: Carlino, 1611).

Collections containing works by Gesualdo which do not appear elsewhere

XII. *Salmi delle Compiete de diversi Musici Neapolitani* (Naples: Beltrano, 1620).
XIII. *L'ottavo libro de madrigali a cinque voci di Pomponio Nenna* (Rome: Robletti, 1618).

Manuscripts containing works by Gesualdo which do not appear elsewhere

XIV. Conservatorio di San Pietro Maiella, Naples, MS 4.6.3. contains an instrumental gagliarde by Gesualdo.
XV. British Museum MS Add. 30491 contains a 'Canzon francese del Principe' which is probably by Gesualdo.

A modern edition of all the music which appears in the above sources is to be found in the *Complete Works of Carlo Gesualdo* edited by Wilhelm Weismann and Glenn Watkins (Hamburg, 1957–66).

ALPHABETICAL LIST OF WORKS

The following list is alphabetical in two sections, secular and sacred. The roman numeral which follows each title is keyed to the collections listed above.

SECULAR WORKS

A voi, mentre il mio core, IV
Ahi, disperata vita, III
Ahi, dispietata e cruda, III
Ahi, già mi discoloro, IV
Ahi, troppo saggia nell'errar, I
Al l'apparir di quelle luci ardenti, II
All'ombra degl'allori, XIII
Alme d'Amor rubelle, VI
Al mio gioir il ciel si fa sereno, VI
Amor, pace non chero, I
Ancide sol la morte, VI
Ancidetemi pur, grievi martiri, III
Ancor che per amarti, VI
Arde il mio cor, IV
Ardita Zanzaretta, VI

Ardo per te, mio bene, VI
Asciugate i begli occhi, V
Baci soavi e cari, I
Bella Angioletta, I
Beltà, poi che t'assenti, VI
Candida man, II
Candido e verde fiore, VI
Caro, amoroso neo, II
Che fai meco, mio cor, IV
Che sentir deve il petto mio, II
Chiaro risplender suole, VI
Come esser può ch'io viva, I
Come vivi cor mio, XIII
Cor mio benche, VIII
Cor mio, deh, non piangete, IV

Quanto ha di dolce Amore, I

Quel 'no' crudel che la mia speme ancise, VI

Questa crudele e pia, IV

Questi leggiadri odorosetti fiori, I

Resta di darmi noia, VI

Se chiudete nel core, IV

Se cosi dolce è il duolo, I

Se da si nobil mano, I

Sei disposto, VIII

Se la mia morte brami, VI

Sento che nel partire, II

Se per lieve ferita, II

Se piange, oimè, la Donna del mio core, III

Se taccio, il duol s'avanza, II

Se tu fuggi, io non resto, V

Se vi duol il mio duolo, V

Se vi miro pietosa, III

Sfogando il suo dolor', VIII

Si gioioso mi fanno i dolor miei, I

S'io non miro non moro, V

Son si belle le rose, I

Sospirava il mio core, III

Sparge la morte al mio Signor nel viso, IV

Tall'or sano desio, IV

T'amo, mia vita, V

Tirsi morir volea, I

Tu che con varii accenti, VIII

Tu m'uccidi, o crudele, V

Tu piangi, o Filli mia, VI

Tu segui, o bella Clori, VI

Veggio, si, dal mio sole, III

Videla poi vezosa, VIII

Voi volete ch'io mora, III

Volan quasi farfalle, VI

Volgi, mia luce, IV

SACRED WORKS

Adoramus te Christe, X

Ad te levavi, X

Aestimatus sum cum descentibus, XI

Amicus meus osculi, XI

Animam meam dilectam, XI

Ardens est cor meum, X

Assumpta est Maria, X

Astiterunt reges terrae, XI

Ave, dulcissima Maria, IX

Ave, Regina coelorum, IX

Ave, sanctissima Maria, X

Caligaverunt oculi mei, XI

Da pacem Domine, X

Deus refugium, IX

Dignare me, laudare te, IX

Discedite a me omnes, X

Domine, corda nostra, IX

Domine, ne despicias, IX

Ecce quomodo moritur justus, XI

Ecce vidimus, XI

Eram quasi agnus innocens, XI

Exaudi, Deus, IX

Franciscus humilis et pauper, X

Gaudeamus omnes, X

Hei mihi, Domine, IX

Illumina faciem tuam, IX

Illumina nos, X

In monte Oliveti, XI

In te Domine speravi, XII

Jerusalem, surge, et exuete, XI

Jesum tradidit impius, XI

Juda mercator pessimus, XI

Laboravi in gemitu meo, IX

Maria, mater gratiae, IX

General Index